Language and
Discrimination

APPLIED LINGUISTICS AND LANGUAGE STUDY

General Editor:
Professor Christopher N. Candlin, Macquarie University

Language and Discrimination

A Study of Communication in Multi-ethnic Workplaces

Celia Roberts, Evelyn Davies and Tom Jupp

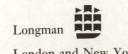

Longman

London and New York

Longman Group UK Limited,
Longman House, Burnt Mill, Harlow,
Essex CM20 2JE, England
and Associated Companies throughout the world.

Published in the United States of America
by Longman Publishing, New York

First published 1992

British Library Cataloguing in Publication Data
Roberts, Celia
    Language and discrimination : a study of communication in
    multi-ethnic workplaces. – (Applied linguistics and
    language study).
    1. Industries. Immigrant personnel. Education. Curriculum
    subjects : English language. Teaching
    I. Title II. Jupp, T. C. (Thomas Cyprian) *1939*- III.
    Davies, Evelyn *1931*- IV. Series
    428. 2407

        ISBN 0–582–55265–6

Library of Congress Cataloging-in-Publication Data
Roberts, Celia, 1947–
    Language and discrimination : a study of communication in multi-ethnic workplaces
    / Celia Roberts, Tom Jupp, and Evelyn Davies.
        p.   cm.— (Applied linguistics and language study)
    Includes bibliographical references and index.
    ISBN 0–582–55265–6
    1. Language and languages — Study and teaching — Social aspects.
2. Sociolinguistics.   3. Discrimination in employment.
4. Linguistic minorities — Education.   5. Intercultural education.
6. Intercultural communication.   I. Jupp, T. C. (Thomas Cyprian)
II. Davies, Evelyn, 1931-   . III. Title. IV. Series.
P53. 8. R64   1990

306.4'4 — dc20

Set in 10/12 pt Ehrhardt, Apple Macintosh

Produced by Longman Group (FE) Limited
Printed in Hong Kong

Contents

General Editor's Preface

One does not have to be an applied linguist to recognise that one key obstacle to the development of contemporary society is not resources or infrastructure but human interaction and communication. Such an obstacle, however, regularly looms less large and is less frequently and systematically addressed than many others, despite its centrality to the organisation and process of the workplace. In this underplaying of the importance of communication, of course, the workplace is no different from other social settings whether educational or social, for example those concerned with health and welfare provision in the community. Nor is it the case that issues of worker-worker, worker-supervisor and union-management communication are restricted either to types of industrial system or even less to geography. Although the focus of this latest contribution to the Applied Linguistics and Language Study Series is that of the UK, the research literature identifies similar concerns in the USA, in Australia, and, though less frequently so far for a variety of historical and structural reasons, in the emerging industrialised societies of Asia, Latin America and Southern Africa. In this way, Language and Discrimination extends much beyond its apparent UK domestic focus to one which is of world significance. What is more, this universal theme shares another characteristic, very much the central focus of this particular book, that of inter-ethnic and intercultural communication.

In a similar way, its audience is not restricted to professionals engaged in applied linguistics and language education, though they are central to its concern. Of course, its natural focus is language and communication, how they can be taught and acquired in the conditions of the workplace, how such communication can be most effectively described, linguistically and ethnographically, and how curricula and their supporting materials can be designed and their associated programs delivered. There are, however, other equally significant readerships. The arguments and the illustrations of the book address educators and educational administrators more generally, but also important groups beyond the education institution per se, training managers in industry and commerce, social policy makers, trade unionists and government officials, as well as that range of professionals whose work necessarily impinges on workplace communication; health and safety staff and workplace counsellors being special and significant examples. But above all, this book addresses the workplace itself, the social world from which its illustrations are largely drawn and to which its arguments are centrally directed.

Celia Roberts, Tom Jupp and Evelyn Davies together with the very many co-workers they represent, have succeeded in providing an example of applied linguistics in action. They have written a book which not only describes the communication of the workplace, but which demonstrates through the interactions they detail how the prejudices and discriminations normally attended to (if at all) in the broader context of sociological analyses of particular societies at large, are in fact constructed in the everyday practices of human interaction. Exploring with them the interaction order, in Goffman's terms, allows us to be open to explanations of how societies as a whole both reinforce their social formations and have their inherent discriminations and inequalities reinforced through the daily intercourse of their members. However, such critical awareness and concern is not enough to engender social change. Knowledge of the conditions and circumstances of the production and reception of workplace communications are a necessary prerequisite for judgement and evaluation. Hence the need to link communication to policy and to practices in the workplace itself.

One might have thought that such a connection between awareness and knowledge, could be taken as axiomatic. A glance, however, at how applied linguistics has apparently been able confidently to explore communication in specialised settings, be they in the workplace or elsewhere, without that connection to an understanding of the social order shows how such confidence can be misplaced. In a similar way, examples abound where industrial policy-makers and government bureaucracies have only a superficial grasp of what is desirable and, above all, what is feasible in terms of communications and language/literacy training in the workplace. What is needed is a methodology for translating such informed awareness into action, into curricula and working programmes. For the first time in this remarkable book we can chart how such policy and such research can be put into action. The authors have provided us with a document for educational planning, illustrated richly from workplace and classroom practice, which offers clear guidance for other educationalists to adapt to their own particular circumstances. Most importantly of all, however, for the future development of applied linguistics and by no means only addressed to the workplace, they have shown how critical awareness, social and subject-matter knowledge and practical action need to move hand in hand. This achievement of the many teachers, learners and co-workers in the production of this book is plainly evident as one reflects on the activities it chronicles. The history of Industrial Language Training as a movement and as a system in the UK would have on its own been ample justification for a volume in the Applied Linguistics and Language Study Series. From the outset of the planning of the book, however, the authors had other purposes in mind: to demonstrate in particular how communication in the workplace is characteristically connected to issues of power, serving to discriminate and to exclude, with the effect that ethnic minority workers in particular, but also many others whose communicative competence is inadequate, are prevented from achieving equity and rights. Breaking out of the cycle of deprivation whereby poor communication condemns workers to positions of inferiority and exploitation wherein they cannot expand their communicative competence is both the challenge to and the justification for the educational programs documented here. Such programs do not only entail innovation in curriculum content, whether in terms of language or subject-matter, they also imply changes to how learning in the context of the workplace might most effectively take place. Here once again we can assess the consistency of the book: joint training programs between white managers and supervisors and black workers are not left at the level of some liberal desideratum but arise as a consistent and obvious curriculum consequence of the overall social perspective of the ILT program.

An applied linguistic readership will not only see the book as relevant to issues of educational policy and curriculum innovation, however. It is equally about relevant models of linguistic description. It demonstrates conclusively how particular models ought not to be fortuitously elected in relation to the educational programs they seek to serve. Models ought to be in harmony with goals. Here we can see the detailed working out, among a large group of practitioners, of an awareness and a discovery of such relevant models. Notably, this discovery was one which did not light upon a single God's truth solution. We might now see the combination of the sociological analysis of a Cicourel, the ethnographically grounded discourse analysis of a Gumperz and the systemic functional analysis of a Halliday as being the obvious points of departure. The strength and the honesty of the account captured here is that this combined position was one which had to be collectively worked towards, and that at times when considerable forces argued to the contrary and resources for advocating the new were meagre. It is very much to the credit of the authors and their co-workers, as well as to the academic researchers with whom they were in regular communication, that such a progress was possible and so productive.

Language and Discrimination is thus a landmark in applied linguistics research and practice. It will stand, I am quite certain, as a model for collaborative action. Although the central funding for Industrial Language Training came to an end in 1989, it is already clear that what was learned by participants in the genesis of this book about workplace communication, about relevant models of description and analysis, about communication and anti-discrimination training, about ensuring equality of opportunity in practice and not merely in theory, is transferable to other contexts. In this alone, the book is not by any means only a chronicle; it is more significantly a charter.

Professor Christopher N Candlin
General Editor

Acknowledgements

The Publishers are grateful to the following for permission to use copyright material:

Derek Hooper for the London Transport Job Interview and Ford Motor Company Training Interview; Equality at Work, Blackburn College, Feilden Street, Blackburn, BB2 1LH (formerly Lancashire Industrial Language Training Unit [ILT]) for Transcript of Job Advice Centre interviews, Training material 'Interview Frames', Transcript of request for extended leave, Training material of bad interview, Survey of backwinder in cotton textile plant, Training notes on mother tongue interviewing, Case study from the Cost of Job Seeking, 1983 In Search of Employment and Training, Independent Learning Project, Training for Change, Syllabus for Communication for Employment and Training, Cistern Exercise, Problem solving exercise; David Bonamy for transcripts of the Hospital Kitchen Dialogue, Buses 104 & 107, and Discussion of holiday rules; Alan Murray for a case study based on interviews and a Language Awareness Training film; Ram Chandola for a Language Awareness Training film; Margaret H. Simonet for a Framework for Linguistic Analysis; Sian Dodderidge for the transcripts of a staff discussion in a bus company and a video role play methodology; Alison Slade for the transcripts of an interview with a personnel officer and Bad Work; Sue Hodlin for the survey in a cereals factory; Jacek Opienski for a preparatory course syllabus; Hugh Pidgeon for the chart 'Changing the Cycle of Communication'; Barbara Darling for the material 'All we Doing is Defending'; Catherine Ballard for the transcript of The House in Bangladesh; Clarice Brierley for the CRE Survey Procedure, Student Autonomy Project and Framework for Analysis; Valerie Yates for the CRE Survey Procedure; Peter Sayers for transcripts of The House in Bangladesh, Urdu on the Air, Personnel Officer, DHSS Supplementary Benefit and Extended Leave; Local Authority Apprentice Interviews Devised and Developed by Elisa Christmas in cooperation with LEA and ILTU Colleges from the London Borough of Newham; Denise Gubbay for the transcripts of the Role Play

Methodology and Plumbing Dialogue; Department of Employment Information Branch, Moorfoot, Sheffield for the extract from the report 'ESL: The Vocational Skill' © Crown Copyright; BBC Continuing Education and Training Television department for the extract from 'The Interview Game'.

We are unable to trace Razinder Singh for permission to use the Backwinder Chart and would appreciate any help to do so.

Language Awareness in the
Classroom
CARL JAMES
PETER GARRETT

Language and Discrimination
A study of communication in multi-ethnic workplaces
CELIA ROBERTS, EVELYN DAVIES
AND TOM JUPP

Transcription conventions

The following set of simple conventions is used for all data, except where a detailed technical analysis is required:

?	rising intonation indicating a question
..	pause of more than one second
( )	unintelligible or conjectured speech
< >	non-lexical phenomena, e.g. <cough>
SMALL CAPITALS	extra prominence
.	utterance completion
,	short pause
____	name omitted for reasons of confidentiality
=	latching

Prosodic notation

Prosodic notation is included in example texts only where this is essential for full understanding. The notation used here is that developed by John Gumperz (1982a):

/	minor, non-final phrase boundary marker
//	major, final phrase boundary marker
\	low fall tone (below word)
\	high fall tone (above word)
/	low rise tone (below word)
/	high rise tone (above word)
∨	fall rise tone
∧	rise fall tone
–	sustained tone
ı	low secondary stress (below word)
ı	high secondary stress (above word)
⌐	pitch register shift, upwards
∟	pitch register, lowered
[	conversational overlap
..	short pause
( )	unintelligible speech

This book is dedicated to John Gumperz, a remarkable scholar and teacher, and to the staff of the Industrial Training Service 1970–1989.

1 Discrimination and language learning: an overview

1 Introduction

This book is based on work carried out in multi-ethnic workplaces during the 1970s and 1980s by the UK Industrial Language Training Service, the aims and objectives of which are described in Appendix 1. The service started in 1970 as an initial response to the English-language needs of ethnic-minority* workers with little or no English. At this time, although local education authorities recognised the need for the provision of English as a Second Language classes, the majority of ethnic-minority workers were unable to attend adult-education classes because of the nature of their work – for example, long working hours and changing shifts. At the same time, they were effectively cut off, both inside the workplace from management and unions, with little access to the white English-speaking culture and channels of communication, and outside from access to public and community services. In this context the workplace itself was the logical place in which to provide the opportunity to acquire and use English. In the event, it proved to be a strategic site for both educational action and research, covering not only language training for workers with little experience of English but also training for supervisors, union stewards and others to improve their skills as communicators with regard to relationships in multi-ethnic settings.

The aim of this book is to describe the practice of Industrial Language Training (ILT), to relate this practice to current theories in linguistics, sociolinguistics, sociology, anthropology and social psychology which informed the practice, and to describe the ethnographic and linguistic analysis which both grew out of and fed into practice and theory. In these ways, the book is an account of the inter-

---

* The term 'ethnic minority' is used to describe any group with a different ethnic background from the white, British majority. The minority ethnic groups with which ILT worked were predominantly of South Asian origin, from the Indian subcontinent or East Africa, but in London the work was with considerably more mixed ethnic groups, including Cypriots, Turkish, Spanish, Portuguese and West Africans.

relationship of theory and practice over a period of fifteen years. During this period ILT developed in a number of ways but always as a continuing critique of its initial objectives and its developing methods.

This chapter provides an overview of issues to do with language and culture, inter-ethnic communication and language learning which are dealt with in much greater depth in subsequent parts of the book. It also provides an introduction to the context in which these issues arose: the employment of ethnic-minority workers in British industry in the 1970s, their access or lack of access to public services, and their search for new training and for employment and promotion opportunities in the 1980s.

The chapter deals with four major topics:

(i)   The expanded view of language which teachers and trainers developed in response to the workplace context and to the needs of minority and majority people working in this context.

(ii) An analysis of the structure of employment opportunities for many ethnic-minority workers, the social identity this creates for them and the role of white 'gatekeepers' in their access to wider rights and services.

(iii) An analysis of some of the issues arising for cross-cultural training and for English language learning and teaching.

(iv) The setting out of a framework for English language education which seeks to take account of the factors set out in (i), (ii) and (iii).

The chapter concludes with an outline of the approach to cross-cultural training and to English language teaching which was developed by the Industrial Language Training Service and a summary of the material contained in the chapters which make up the rest of this book. The developments described in this book were possible only because ILT was a national service, nationally coordinated. Small units, responsive to local need, were strengthened and supported by the National Centre for Industrial Language Training (see Appendix 2), which was able to draw on and disseminate good practice throughout the scheme.

This book is about multilingual and multi-ethnic workplaces, from the perspective of teaching English language and developing awareness about inter-ethnic communication in English. The ethnographic studies of workplaces, similarly, were carried out to identify the needs of workers, trade unionists and managers when communicating in English. The use of community languages other than English is a very important contextual factor, but this book is not about the use of those languages in the workplace; nor is it concerned with their maintenance and development. These are issues which fall outside the scope of this study, and ones which deserve research and analysis in their own right.

2   Facing reality

The facts of racial discrimination in employment and in access to services continue to be documented with shameful regularity. These facts, together with direct or indirect experience of racial abuse and harassment, form part of the structured experience of black* people in Britain. However, these facts are not perceived as such, or are perceived very differently, by most white people. Many ILT staff were shocked when they started collecting data in workplaces and public services. On the one hand, they found themselves in the enviable position of being able to study their future students' day-to-day language needs before designing training for them; on the other hand, they realised that the notions of language and of language teaching which they brought with them were far too limited to analyse and modify the reality they encountered. This reality is illustrated in the two examples which follow.

The first example (Data 1.1) is of audio-taped data collected in a woollen textile mill in West Yorkshire. The manager of the small factory calls in a South Asian worker and warns him that unless his work improves he will be sacked. A full transcript and analysis of this data is provided in Chapter 2.

The second example (Data 1.2) is extracted from videotaped data collected at a Jobcentre. This data is referred to later in this chapter and the full transcript is discussed in Chapter 3.

The first extract illustrates in a brutal way the reality of unequal power. While this should be absolutely clear to anyone, South Asian people and many English people are likely to interpret the way language is used in this data in rather different ways, particularly if they hear the actual recording. The second extract also raises issues of

---

* *'Black workers' in this book refers to people who define themselves as black in relation to the struggle for equality and power in a white-dominated society. In this political context, 'black' includes South Asian groups and any other members of ethnic minority groups who do not wish to be associated with the white majority. However, some individuals from ethnic minority groups resist the term 'black' since it does not reflect their ethnicity. In this book, 'ethnic minority' will be used to describe any individual or group not belonging to the white British majority . 'Black' will be used to describe Afro-Caribbean and Asian groups when issues of equality and power are in focus.*

DATA 1.1 IN THE MILL [Data collected by Alison Slade, Calderdale ILT]

Manager:	Now I'm sick of it. You're either going to do the job properly, or you're going to get out.
H:	I am sorry. Next time =
Manager:	= There won't be a next time.
H:	I ( ) I am sorry. Next time do it properly.
Manager:	Yes. Well, the next time that girl complains to me about your bad work I shall sack you. Is that clear? You're going to an English class, do you understand what I just said?
H:	Yes, I... English...
Manager:	You understand. You know what I'm going to do?
H:	Next time... Sir.
Manager:	There won't be a next time.
H:	I'm sorry =
Manager:	= because the next time that girl complains to me =
H:	= I'm sorry...
Manager:	It's no good being sorry. You keep on making bad work over and over and over again.
H:	I am sorry. I am very sorry...
Manager:	It's no use standing there like that saying you're sorry, you're sorry. You just keep on making bad work. Now I'm telling you the next time you make bad work like that , you're finished.
H:	OK, sir. I'm sorry.
Manager:	(to Language Teacher) Did he understand? Do you think he understood?

fairness and power, although in a much less explicit way, since the adviser never explains the purpose of her questions. The video from which this example is drawn was shown to groups of white and Asian professionals as part of a training course. Most white participants interpreted the adviser as being kindly but somewhat ineffectual in her attempts to go through the routine interview procedure with someone

DATA 1.2 JOBCENTRE INTERVIEW [Data collected by Roger Munns, Lancashire ILT]

E: Good morning Mr Abdul, I'm Mrs Eastwood um – now I see you've filled this form in to say that you're out of work at the moment. I'd just like a little chat with you about the sort of work you've done and then, hopefully, you know, we can find you another job um – where was your last job at? Where did you last work at?

A: Last work – I'm working Rochdale.

E: In Rochdale yeah. What was the name of the firm?

A: T_____ Rochdale.

E: T... right.

A: T____ ____ ____

E: Right. What sort of a firm were they?

A: Spinners.

E: Spinners, yeah and how long did you work there?

A: Five years.

E: Five years, yeah. And what was your job there?

A: Spinning job.

E: You were a spinner, yeah.

A: Yes, spinner.

E: Yeah, right. Can you just tell me a little bit about the job, what, were you doing?

A: Well – er spinning job – machinery job – so I controlled my machine..

E: Yeah – what did you actually do as a spinner – were you setting machines?

A: Yes, I'm setting machines. I operate machine.

E: Yeah – what sort of machine?

A: Just called spinning machines.

E: They've no particular name – they're just general spinning.

A: General spinning.

E: Yeah – how many machines did you run?

A: Well – one hundred five bis spindle drilling.

E: Mm, yeah.

A:	One side.
E:	Yeah.
A:	Five hundred five spindle.
E:	Sorry.
A:	One hundred five spindle.
E:	Right.
A:	Look after one parcel...

unfamiliar with the type of questions asked and their underlying meanings. Most Asian participants evaluated her strategies as racist.

These two examples show why ILT staff quickly recognised the need for a view of language which went well beyond an analysis of form and function, connecting language both to the social contexts of culture and power and to the assumptions and expectations which individuals project into language use. Despite widespread acceptance of notions of communicative competence and communicative language teaching, there has been little discussion about the extent to which cultural and social knowledge should be explicitly developed or the extent to which the structured experiences of the learner enter into the interpretive process and need to be explicitly acknowledged.

3   An expanded view of language

An expanded view of language must take account of the 'meaning potential' (Halliday 1978) and the socio-cultural potential that any language may have for particular individuals. 'We do not understand words by deriving meaning from them, but by bringing meaning to them' (Smith 1982). So our view of language must be contextual. By context we do not mean simply features such as setting, purpose, relationships or channel. Our contextual view of language includes an understanding of the wider context in which ethnic-minority workers live and work, an understanding of their experiences of racism and disadvantage and of the cultural knowledge which is part of their first language, and an understanding of how language in interaction creates a context which is particular to that interaction but which also reflects and helps to form social systems and institutions. So, we are concerned in this book with the relationship between this expanded notion of language, and discrimination and disadvantage in employment.

Within individual interactions, the interlocutors bring a range of assumptions, expectations and intentions which operate at three levels:

Schema: knowledge and assumptions brought to the interaction;
Frame: strategies for and interpretation of what is going on in the interaction;
Language: uses and forms.

The extent to which all these are shared between interlocutors will affect the quality and outcomes of an interaction. In the process of interaction, interlocutors may have a sense of converging or diverging at these three levels and this too will affect the interaction. An individual's sense of identity feeds into that individual's schemata, frames and uses of language and these in turn, modify the sense of identity, as something that contributes to the interactive process.

3.1 Schema

The notion of schema refers to the accumulated cultural and social knowledge and structured experiences which individuals bring to any interaction. Some of this knowledge is facts about the world, but most of it is the baggage of beliefs, values and interactional knowledge learned through growing up, living and working in particular cultures and through routine social contacts at personal and institutional levels.

Social and cultural knowledge and attitudes may surface explicitly in the meaning attached to particular uses of language. It is important to understand that the white-majority speaker, frequently in a more powerful position than the ethnic-minority speaker, will thus perceive and evaluate the ethnic-minority speaker on the basis of language use. But what is perceived as language use may reflect differences in cultural knowledge, attitude and ideology.

Our work often focuses on a lack of shared cultural and social knowledge. But it would be quite wrong to consider issues of language, discrimination and disadvantage only in terms of unfamiliar cultural and social knowledge and the need to acquire this knowledge. Ethnically determined expectations and attitudes can affect the progress and outcomes of an encounter even where there are no surface cultural differences. However, it is beyond the scope of this book to examine critically the ways in which such expectations and attitudes enter into inter-ethnic encounters where language and social and cultural knowledge are more extensively shared (as is the case for the majority of young black and white people in Britain).

3.2 Frame

From our knowledge and experiential schemata, we make certain assumptions about how an interaction is typically structured, how to behave within it and how we expect others to behave. For example, we will choose an appropriate communicative strategy if we want people in superior positions to do something for us. We may try to build up a positive image of ourselves, or reason with them on the logic of the case, or show that we rely on them to help us. Similarly, we will interpret a superior's reactions according to the particular interpretive frame we believe we are in at that time. For example, our boss may say 'I'll see what I can do'. Her intention may be to convey good will but genuine uncertainty. But it may be interpreted by us as a decision in our favour if we believe she has the power to make things happen.

3.3 Uses and forms of language

Depending on the particular frame we think we are in, we choose and use certain discourse-management techniques and language forms to display our intent and convey our understanding. It is, as we have suggested, at the level of use of language that judgements are based about behaviour, attitude and relationships. It is at this level that, in inter-ethnic communication, language, discourse management and non-verbal behaviour are frequently misunderstood, misinterpreted or reinforce the negative stereotypes arising out of ethnically determined attitudes. So language use, interpretive frames and a person's wider knowledge and experience are part of a single process, and any one can be the basis of understanding or misunderstanding. Thus an analysis of inter-ethnic communication has to take account of all three.

Within any particular interaction, people's schemata and interpretive frames are not necessarily static. Participants negotiate meaning by revising their schemata and frames in the light of the feedback they receive. But for this process of negotiation to work, there has to be a shared system of language use which can provide a means for the interlocutors to reflect the intentionality and understanding each of the other. If the schemata and interpretive frames are very different and the patterns of language use are also not shared, then neither side has the tools for repair. As people start to talk past each other, the language forms they use to repair the confusion or clarify the misinterpretation may serve only to confound the problem.

For example, the Jobcentre adviser in Data 1.2 may appear inquisitorial over-personal or ill-informed to a black client (as she may to white clients if there is a mismatch of schema, frame or language use with them also). The client continues to use narrative strategies to describe his previous jobs and the adviser persists in asking him more and more questions on the same theme. He cannot see the point of her questions. She cannot find a way of gaining the expected response, in which the client evaluates his past experience and indicates his knowledge and skills. Situations such as this are often never resolved. But since the employment adviser is in a position of relative power, it is *her* judgement of the client which will affect *his* job opportunities.

When speakers and listeners have widely different schemata and different styles of communicating, they draw further and further apart. Gregory Bateson's work with schizophrenics led him to call this phenomenon 'complementary schismogenesis' (Bateson 1972). Two people find they are uncomfortable with the way each other is talking. Perhaps one speaker is too personal, talks too loudly or too long, is too direct or indirect. A typical reaction is for the other to accentuate those features in their own style which contrast with the speaker's. So the quieter and more taciturn speaker talks even less and more softly. This leads to the original speaker becoming louder and even more talkative. And so on. In unequal encounters such differences are not simply irritating; they can lead to discrimination both perceived and real.

This brief discussion has ranged widely over the issues of language, discrimination and disadvantage in order to convey our notion of an expanded view of language. Such a view of language goes a long way beyond a structural or functional view. It includes a critical view which engages with language as creating social identity, with the role of language in creating and maintaining social structures, and so with issues of language and power. The functional view of language has often not engaged with these issues. Many 'functions', for example 'clarification', are universal, but whether and how and in what way 'clarification' will occur linguistically depends on expectations and interpretations. The pedagogic applications of functional language frameworks are often inadequate and too narrowly defined for a multi-ethnic context. The functional view of language has remained so durable because it is a teachable view. An expanded notion of language does not strait-jacket language into something teachable. It recognises that many aspects of language will be learned not taught. An expanded, communicative view of language requires a pedagogic content which is based on the realities of speaker interaction. It has to take account of the socio-political context in which language has to be learned, how learners perceive themselves in relation to that language and its speakers, and how they are perceived and received by that language culture. Language learning and the language classroom in a multi-ethnic society must address the relationship between language and discrimination.

It is easy to explain why such an expanded view of language emerged from working in real contexts with ethnic-minority workers. These workers are adults who have already been fully socialised into a pattern of schemata, interpretive frames and language use through a different culture and language. We, as teachers, were accountable to them and to sponsoring agencies for supporting them in acquiring communication skills which would be effective not in performing linguistic tests but in workplace and vocational training settings and effective in terms of access, equal opportunity and job satisfaction. These criteria of effectiveness put equal and often greater responsibility on the white-majority English-speakers in the workplace to modify their approach to communication.

The task was to change the communicative environment of a workplace and to redefine the bureaucratic processes of access so that they took account of cultural and linguistic diversity. It would clearly be unjust if those with the least communicative power in Britain were expected to bring about these changes. Training focused only on black workers would assume an assimilationist or, at best, integrationist approach. Training for white and black workers and managers was a commitment to a pluralist approach, to effecting change where power – or at least some power – lay.

4 The context: workplace settings

The workplace settings described in this book are of two kinds. First, there are the workplaces where ethnic-minority workers have, typically, been given employment. Second, there are the public services where some ethnic-minority people work but where the training issues concern the type of service encounters offered to ethnic-minority clients by white staff. Both settings are what Gumperz (1982) calls 'strategic research sites' because they exemplify the problems of inter-group communication in modern industrial society.

Most major urban areas of Britain have become multiracial, multi-ethnic and multilingual. This has happened in many industrialised parts of the world and for a series of similar reasons: the need to fill unpopular jobs; historical 'chains of migration' from less developed areas or countries to these urban areas; obligations towards refugees; the right of family members to be united. This is the pattern of factors which has operated whether we think of Panjabis or Afro-Caribbean people in London, or Greeks in Melbourne, Finns in

Stockholm, North African Arabs in Marseilles, Portuguese in Toronto, Vietnamese in Wellington or Mexicans in Houston.

World-wide, these settlers represent a very large group of adult language learners but it would be inappropriate, even for us as language teachers, to regard them primarily as language learners. Indeed, many of these people would never have entered a language classroom if they had not moved country, and, in any case, a major part of their experience and acquisition of the language of the country where they have settled takes place outside any classroom. As educators, we want to be informed about their experience and needs as they touch upon language learning. But what has already been said about inter-ethnic communication points to the limitation of any approach to language learning which is based on a definitive analysis of need by the teacher alone. We must match an understanding of experience and needs with a willingness to give autonomy to students to examine their own experience and develop their own communicative strategies. Experience and practice with regard to this need for learner autonomy is discussed in Chapter 5.

Ethnic minorities occupy a distinctive position in the major industrial cities of many countries throughout the world. Ethnic-minority workers who took up the unskilled, unsocial or poorly paid jobs were and are underpinning the better-paid, more skilled or more socially prestigious jobs of the local labour force. As a result, social class becomes quickly fixed and reinforced by the nature of the person's work, not by educational achievement or social position in the society of origin.

Studies of the pattern of employment of ethnic minorities in Britain (Department of Employment 1974; Smith 1977; Brown 1984) and analysis from field work in multi-ethnic workplaces (National Centre for Industrial Language Training 1977) showed that only a few manfacturing and service industries accounted for most of the employment of ethnic-minority workers:

(a) semi-automated industries which expanded rapidly in the 1950s and 1960s and required additional unskilled labour, but were located in areas of labour shortage in, for example, food processing, plastics manufacture and mass-production engineering;
(b) traditional industries which were deskilled, reorganised, and had an insecure market, such as textiles, clothing and foundries;
(c) service industries with labour shortage in some parts of the country, particularly Greater London, in, for example, transport, hospitals, and hotels and catering;

(d) clerical and routine administrative jobs in the Civil Service and nationalised service industries;
(e) certain low-status professional jobs in medicine and in education;
(f) among mainly South Asians, self-employment in small businesses, particularly retail businesses.

A closer examination of each of these employment categories confirms the marginal nature of the ethnic-minority workers' position in the type of lower-level labour market described. We can see that the main areas of employment were in jobs where skills are minimal: either in jobs which were semi-automated and routine, or in the lower levels of service industries. Many of the jobs in employment category (a) were within industries which have also been characterised by marked fluctuations in demand for their products and by substitution of further new technology for labour. The position of workers has been even more insecure in category (b) because these have been deskilled and dwindling industries in Britain for the last twenty years, or industries which survive only by offering very poor working conditions. In employment categories (a) and (b), the human environment is marked by close supervision, machine discipline, and often by shift work and by the concentration of ethnic minorities in particular work sections.

The jobs in category (c) are rather different and more diverse in character. They are usually marked by low pay, unsocial hours, or both. However, although the job tasks are relatively simple, the need for communication and understanding with clients may arise frequently in some of these jobs – for example, transport work or cafeteria service.

Jobs in categories (d) and (e) are different from (a), (b) and (c) in the sense that employment of this type requires recognised educational or vocational/professional qualifications. Nevertheless, the employment patterns of ethnic minorities in these categories indicate marginality and low status within the organisation or profession. Our own work in three Civil Service departments has shown that many clerical officers of South Asian origin are overqualified for their positions, and some have had work experience in East Africa at much more senior levels. Among doctors, 11 per cent of general practitioners and 21 per cent of hospital doctors first qualified in the Indian subcontinent (Smith 1982). Smith found that overseas hospital doctors were heavily concentrated in the more junior grades, and, to a lesser extent, within the less popular or 'shortage' specialities such as geriatrics, anaesthetics and psychiatry. The jobs held by South Asians in government departments, the public services, and in schools, while usually having a relatively low status within the particular organisation, often provide an important point of contact between the organisation and the general public (Jupp, Roberts and Cook-Gumperz 1982).

Category (f), self-employment, reflects both choice and necessity. For many South Asians from East Africa, setting up their own businesses meant using skills and experience gained as part of the business community in East Africa. But self-employment has also represented an alternative for many South Asians to the racism and disadvantage experienced in job-seeking and employment.

So, most ethnic-minority workers filled gaps in the labour market and were, as a result, rapidly stereotyped as having the abilities and status compatible with these low-level jobs. At the same time as social class was fixed by the nature of the work they could get, negative stereotypes of race and ethnicity embedded in the historical values experience of the majority were projected on to the new groups. Thus a negative identity in which social class and ethnicity reinforce each other began to operate with the third element of ineffective or different language use and communicative style (Figure 1.1)

The cycle creates and confirms a social identity perceived by the dominant white English-speaking group as one of incompetence and uncooperativeness. This in turn is perpetuated by constraints on the development of communicative power, particularly for the recently arrived, and continues to affect attitudes and expectations with regard

Figure 1.1   **Cycle of socially created identity**

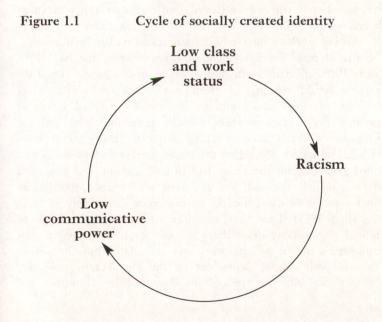

to their children and their children's employment potential. The development of communicative power among recently arrived ethnic-minority workers was one focus of the only major international study of natural second-language acquisition (Perdue 1984), and some of the approaches used in this project are discussed in Chapter 5.

It is very difficult for the great majority of white people, including most language teachers, to accept completely that this is a socially created identity, that the perception of lesser competence or uncooperativeness is a stereotype and in no sense objective. Most white British people either do not know or do not believe that ethnic-minority workers settled in Britain have, on average, about as much education as white workers. Nor do they take into account the awesome challenge of having to survive and achieve in a different culture and language.

The perspective for ethnic minorities is very different: differences of conversational inference will confirm a perception that they are not listened to, taken seriously or valued by members of the dominant group. The differences in discourse conventions referred to are not merely or even primarily, imposed by the limited linguistic means of the second-language speaker and learner. They are differences which for a long time were dismissed as non-standard language practices whereas they are now recognised as reflecting the identity, shared values and shared communicative strategies of groups. It is in a linguistic and interactional study of these differences, in a recognition that conversational style will not be shared, and that stereotypes can then come unconsciously into play as a way of bringing meaning to inter-action, that our work on inter-ethnic communication has been based.

The rise of mass unemployment in Britain during the late 1970s and early 1980s affected South Asian workers in categories (a) and (b) particularly harshly. Many of them were made redundant by a combination of closures and automation, and experienced increased competition from white workers for the remaining jobs and for service-industry jobs in category (c). Consequently, many South Asian workers can no longer depend on the labour market for low-status and unskilled jobs. Instead, they have had to seek training and jobs on a wider basis than in the past, and at a time when racism, discrimination and a cluster of disadvantages operate more damagingly on their chances (Jupp 1981). They have, therefore, had to turn increasingly to the official employment and welfare services for help in coping with unemployment and in seeking work and training. Ethnic minorities are thus becoming more dependent on the bureaucratic processes and face-to-face interview procedures described by Gumperz and

Cook-Gumperz (1982). At interviews in social security benefit offices, in careers offices, in jobcentres, and with training agencies, workers are constantly evaluated for work purposes by the officials of these agencies on the basis of how they project themselves, that is how they communicate in English. For example, research into ethnic minorities and unemployment (Smith 1981) concluded that South Asian workers with unskilled manual work experience and perceived poor communication skills were less well served by the employment services. At the same time, employers were becoming more selective and introducing more formal recruitment procedures which also depended on communicative evaluation.

This takes us on to the second type of workplace setting. This includes jobcentres, and social security offices where those out of work collect unemployment benefit. It is a bitter irony of modern society that those least powerful in dealing with bureaucracies are those thrust most frequently into contact with them. The unwaged and those on low wages are the most likely to need welfare benefits, to need state housing and to face a number of bureaucratic and communicative hurdles when applying for any type of grant.

It is this group which finds itself routinely having to face society's 'gatekeepers' (Erickson and Shultz 1982). Gatekeepers control access to scarce resources in a modern urban world where it is increasingly impractical and unacceptable to provide access through informal networks. Counselling interviews, job and welfare interviews, even court trials, are typical gatekeeping encounters. These face-to-face interactions are focused in a short time-span and significantly influence the life chances of the individual. For this reason, procedures and standards are established which are regarded as independent of the evaluator's individual preference. It is assumed, in theory, that these are uniform meritocratic standards of evaluation. In reality, neither procedures nor standards may be shared between the gatekeepers and their clients.

In addition, evaluation is often based on communicative interaction. There is no such thing as inter-ethnic conversational objectivity. Gatekeepers have to rely heavily on establishing shared experience and on shared communicative style in which indirect meaning can be clearly signalled and understood so that the clients always understand the frame in which they are participating at each stage. For the gatekeeping encounter to work, a lot depends on the clients' control of 'the rhetorical strategies of the bureaucratically accepted modes of communication' (Gumperz 1982).

5 Issues for training in inter-ethnic communication and for language learning

The difficulty involved in exposing the interactive nature of gate-keeping, rather than accepting a view based on the 'objectivity' of procedures and standards,is that it is very difficult to create awareness and understanding of the issues involved. Understanding gatekeeping is central to cross-cultural training both for the monolingual majority and for linguistic minorities. The BBC film *Crosstalk* (Gumperz, Jupp and Roberts 1979) was a first attempt to do this in Britain in the context of training 'gatekeepers' for cross-cultural encounters and has been influential in raising awareness of these issues.

A detailed discussion of the development of cross-cultural training is given in Chapter 3. The principles underlying such training are:

1. People have to become aware, by examining their own practice, of the role of expectation and perception in negotiating meaning.
2. They have to become aware of the role that the selection of language and the use of certain discourse-management techniques plays in this process.
3. When this is understood, they are more able to look at contrastive examples of their own and other people's spoken interaction, and acknowledge their own ethnocentricity.
4. Finally, they have to start to work out strategies which will be both explicit and non-face-threatening to the other person, and avoid the unconscious abuse of power.

These are conclusions we have arrived at over a very long period of time. We always recognised that people who were trying to communicate needed to understand that the other person had a very different view of the world.

For example, early training for white supervisors and managers consisted of giving cultural background information such as reasons for emigration, religious backgrounds and naming systems (Davies and Jupp 1974; Henley 1979). The information presented was to have a very real impact on staff practices, particularly in public services such as the health service (Henley 1979, 1983). But this information needed to be combined with training in communication. So, the next stage was to introduce exercises in language awareness, helping white trainees to understand the difficulties of communicating in a second language, illustrated in the BBC *Worktalk* films and manual (Khan and Pearn 1976). The third stage, cross-cultural communication skills with an anti-racist perspective, developed from *Crosstalk* and a recognition of its limitations.

The process and objectives of language acquisition by ethnic-minority workers has to be distinguished from foreign-language acquisition in your own society in tutored settings. Much more needs to be understood about the processes of second-language acquisition by adults who 'have to learn in order to communicate and have to communicate in order to learn' (Simonot and Allwood 1984) within discouraging contexts which are at the same time critical to the learners' life chances. These adults, because of their position in the new society, often have a restricted pattern of contact with, and opportunity to acquire and to use, the second language. Contact may be largely linked to employment and to securing rights and necessities for themselves and their families. Opportunity for use may be sporadic and in environments that are unfamiliar and frequently hostile, often being confined to stressful formal or informal interviews and negotiations with gatekeepers.

The term 'second-language acquisition' does not reflect the reality, for adults, of having to learn and work in an entirely new language and culture. This is a process of language socialisation as well as acquisition. By language socialisation, we mean the learning of speaking practices and language behaviours which construct and guide social interaction within specific social contexts. The question of how language is learned cannot be considered independently of the social context in which learning is available and which provides the social grounds necessary for talk.

Research in first-language acquisition has recognised that, as children learn a language, they learn and wish to be socialised into the particular culture in which they are brought up, and are welcomed into it (Halliday 1975). However, the process of adult language socialisation for ethnic minorities cannot be compared with that of first-language development, because the social contexts are so different.

The structural conditions of the workplace mean that, typically, there is little or no opportunity for the kind of unstressed peer-group interaction within which language socialisation most readily takes place. We have already described the kinds of situation in which South Asian workers have an urgent need to communicate. These are usually stressful situations involving significant status differential, with white management, supervisors, and union stewards communicating downwards to ethnic-minority operatives. The fact that there are few social contexts in which unstressed peer-group interaction can develop is well illustrated by Table 1.1 which sets out the ethnic background of a group of fifty-six women workers on an evening shift in a food-processing plant in West London. This is an example of category (a)

TABLE 1.1   Ethnic background of workers on evening packing shift, instant
coffee processing plant

India		East Africa	
Panjab (Sikh):	15	Kenya:	4
Panjab (Hindus)	3	Uganda:	3
Other:	4	Tanzania:	1
British Isles		*Elsewhere*	
Local:	3	Italy:	3
England:	4	Portugal:	2
Ireland:	3	Ukraine:	1
		Pakistan:	2
Caribbean		Singapore (Sikh)	1
Jamaica:	3	Iraq(Christian):	1
Barbados:	2	Guyana (Muslim):	1

(Source: NCILT 1977)

jobs in the previous list (p. 11)

In such workplace contexts, contact between majority and minority groups is often minimal. Frequently, an ethnic-minority worker will only communicate with an English supervisor over an important personal issue such as pay. This type of communicative task does not provide the minority-group workers with an opportunity to learn, from gradually accumulated experience, how to use language either to get things done or to maintain social relationships in their second culture. Workers with little language or education, therefore, acquire only limited and instrumental English, which reinforces white-majority stereotypes of them and serves to inhibit further any possible learning contexts. South Asian workers who have learned English before coming to Britain and have used it previously for academic or professional purposes also lack the appropriate social contexts for language socialisation with the white-majority groups and this reinforces their use of an ethnically specific style of speaking English (Jupp, Roberts and Cook-Gumperz 1982). Thus many of the factors and conditions identified as supportive of second-language acquisition do not exist for the majority of these workers.

Language-learning programmes have a significant role to play in overcoming such disadvantage. However, an increased emphasis on achievement in the second language, if treated in isolation from the social and economic context of the ethnic minorities, particularly in a context of unemployment and contracting public services, can only be perceived as further evidence of discrimination based on a deficit view on the part of the majority. This deficit-based approach can be avoided if objectives for formal language-teaching programmes for ethnic minorities are linked to people's social and cultural identities, to their experience of living in the new country, including their experience of discrimination and disadvantage, and to the dynamic of their developing and changing objectives in the new society. In this sense, language learning is a long-term process and one which should be linked to broader programmes for education, for training and employment, and for access to public services and facilities. The maintenance and development of minority-community languages and the provision of trained interpreters at critical points are part of the same context. Finally, ethnic-minority workers cannot acquire English successfully unless native English-speakers take positive steps to overcome communication difficulties in the way we have suggested in discussing cross-cultural training. It is important to stress that this applies to language teachers themselves, as well as to everyone else. Teachers may experience the same social and cross-cultural barriers to contact with their students and consequently apply the same stereotypes of ethnic minorities as many other people.

For some teachers, 'It is extremely tempting, faced with the enormity of the task, to retreat before its challenge, to lower one's sights, and to settle for something very much less. To retreat behind a linguistic or a pedagogical expertise' (Trim 1979) – in other words, to settle for some modest and isolated linguistic objectives on the grounds that 'I'm a **language** teacher'. Such a stance echoes that of the gatekeepers, who appeal to standards which in theory are above ethnic and cultural variations. Both gatekeepers and teachers can unconsciously and powerfully contribute to the perpetuation of disadvantage and discrimination.

6 A framework for language education

This book describes some of the attempts made to develop a language-teaching approach relevant to all trainees – black and ethnic-minority workers and the white personnel with whom they work. This approach is based on what we believe to be an appropriate, fair and acceptable **contract** for learning which identifies the level of accountability and share of responsibility of the providing **institutions**, the **teachers** and the **trainees**. The basis of such a contract has to be a clear understanding and acceptance of the relationship between provision designed to help people learn English and the wider issues of opportunity and discrimination and of what can be expected to be achieved.

6.1 Responsibility of the institution

The majority of trainees do not want to study English for its own sake; they want to reach self-determined goals which require English. The teaching programme, therefore, wherever provided, needs to link clearly and realistically to genuine access to wider employment, promotional, vocational or educational opportunities. For example:

Workplace courses should be linked to broader employee-development courses, the promotion ladder, and possibilities for further personal study or experience. To be effective the employer must accept the need for parallel training for key interlocutors such as supervisors, personnel and training officers, trade-union officials and fellow workers.

College courses should provide access to both vocational and academic study according to the required content, tastes and assessment requirements. First-level college courses demand not only the ability to grade students by language achievement, but the ability to offer a range of provision defined in terms of access and opportunity into which further language development can be built. As with employers, when a college sets up pre-vocational access programmes it cannot ensure access unless the people responsible for entry and selection are aware of how ethnocentric and potentially discriminatory their criteria are, and of how to assess students properly and positively. Similarly, the technical teachers who provide 'taster' or skills sections of the first-level curriculum, and the technical teachers who will teach them later, all require training for effective inter-ethnic communication. These are the college gatekeepers.

Adult and community courses have a responsibility to avoid isolation, low status, and lack of measurable outcome and progression. They should be clearly linked with other vocational and leisure classes and offer a range of provision defined in terms of access to wider opportunities and local services. The providing authority needs to give attention to the appropriate recruitment and training of the English as a Second Language (ESL) teachers.

6.2 The responsibility of the teacher

The teacher's pedagogic approach is all-important. The constituents of an interactive language-learning methodology will include an understanding of how cultural and social knowledge enter into language, of how different communicative styles can trigger frames and schemata which block communication and lead to negative and misleading conclusions, and of how language at the level of discourse can be explicitly learned. The methodology will also include an understanding of unequal encounters and their role in forming an unequal society, and an explicit acknowledgement that students will wish to choose the extent to which they retain their own communicative style in interacting with native English-speakers. We stress here **methodology** because this includes **materials**, much of which comes from the students' and teacher's own experience and it includes **syllabus**, specified in terms of teaching/learning **procedures** and **learning goals** rather than as a **content** or **language list**. The syllabus is built on student objectives, as opposed to teacher or linguistic objectives

In order to take account of the need to focus on inter-ethnic communication, to avoid a deficit view of learner need, and to preserve the trainees' right to modify their language behaviour by choice based on knowledge, four factors are needed as part of a shared agenda for teachers and students. These are:

- communication;
- awareness;
- autonomy;
- assertiveness.

The first two factors, communication and awareness, focus on the responsibility of the teachers, and the second two, autonomy and assertiveness, on the needs and responsibility of the students, which the course must meet and support.

The teacher's understanding of **communication** needs to incorporate the expanded notion of language which has been described above and not confine the syllabus to teacher-specified linguistic objectives. This expanded view of language requires a focus on language **awareness** in terms of interaction between cultures and demands a language-learning methodology in which interactions are consciously analysed. This, in turn, implies and requires that native English-speakers are involved as part of the process.

The process must also take account of the trainees' need for the other factors of **autonomy** and **assertiveness** and provide the confidence which empowers trainees to make further progress as conscious learners who are fully aware that self-direction based on knowledge equals power.

6.3 The responsibility of the trainee

Students are likely to have a clear view of the way in which they want to present themselves. They need to be aware of the culture-specific standards of self-presentation that exist in both oral and written communication but it is up to them how far they wish to assert their ethnic identity in their presentation of self. Similarly, notions of appropriacy and politeness, which in the early days of functional language training both within ILT and elsewhere were often the main goal, should not imply that the process and goals of interaction should necessarily be harmonious and accommodating so that 'learners engage in accommodation rather than negotiation' (Candlin 1984).

7   The approach of Industrial Language Training

The work of the UK Industrial Language Training Service, which is drawn upon as the context and background for these curricular ideas, was based from the outset on an educational 'contract'. (See Jupp and Hodlin, 1974; Davies and Jupp 1974; Brooks and Roberts 1985.) This contract specified:

- that trainees be given paid work-time release;
- that training consist of short courses on an industrial model;
- that courses involve native-speaking interlocutors;
- that key personnel in gatekeeping roles also be trained;
- that language learning be based on the learners' *immediate* communicative environment, tasks and intentions, culture and practice.

The starting point for ILT work in fulfilling this contract was data collection and ethnography, the provision of language training for minority ethnic groups, and awareness training for white interlocutors. A continuing critique of the contract, as we have already suggested, led to developments in all three areas, examples of which are presented and discussed in subsequent chapters of this book.

7.1 Data collection and ethnography

Early work in industry started with participant observation as described in Chapter 4. This soon led to more systematic surveys of workplace communication needs by trainers, still somewhat isolated from managers and trade unionists. Finally, an approach developed in which trainers worked closely with management and trade unions in initial surveys and then in using data collection both as an awareness-raising exercise and as a source of authentic material to be used in the training itself.

7.2 Provision of language training for ethnic-minority workers

In the early 1970s, the most pressing perceived need was for elementary language training for workers with little or no English (Jupp and Hodlin 1974). It was soon evident that many workers were held back from promotion and from participating in trade unions even though they had some experience of English. Post-elementary and, later, advanced language-training courses were established for bilingual supervisors, shop stewards and managers. An obvious development from this was mixed groups of native and non-native speakers of English on team-development and quality-assurance seminars. Language training was also linked to technical retraining programmes for redundant workers.

7.3 Awareness training for white interlocutors

Initially, training for white managers, supervisors and trade unionists took the form of background-information seminars (see Davies and Jupp 1974; Henley 1979). These focused on an understanding of reasons for emigration and gave descriptive information about, for example, naming systems, religious backgrounds, previous work experiences and patterns and the particular needs of ethnic minorities in, say, the health service. The aim of the seminars was to provide information so that the white majority group could learn to make sense of what appeared to them as strange or difficult behaviour. (See Chapter 4 for examples of typical attitudes to ethnic-minority workers.)

This type of training was, at the time, a unique and pioneering attempt to reach white people in the workplace and to discuss issues which had so far been either ignored or dealt with only in racist gossip. However, the provision of such information, usually by white trainers, was sometimes counter-productive, and perceived by black and increasingly by white people as itself racist. Background cultural information was no response to the level of racism and the effects of unconscious discrimination in the workplace, and did little to change behaviour and attitudes. The information was often accommodated into existing negative stereotypes and could even be used against ethnic-minority workers.

In response to these concerns, training developed which aimed to change communicative relationships (Wilson 1981). The focus became the nature and quality of inter-ethnic communication, and training included language-awareness exercises (Yates, Christmas and Wilson 1982). Out of this work developed an approach in which mixed groups worked together, relating issues of communication to wider issues of attitudes, discrimination and racism. This training used naturally-occurring videotaped data of typical gatekeeping interactions. This approach is further described and discussed in Chapter 3.

7.4 Materials and methodology

Early language-learning materials were based on authentic data and structured by a functional syllabus. Having started with functions, the ILT trainers began to redefine the communicative syllabus in terms of first- and second-language speakers' interaction. Increasingly, role-play and simulation were used to re-enact the typical and often stressful and unpredictable encounters that workers faced. From this developed strategies for basing lessons around trainees' language and using contrastive techniques to raise their awareness of native-speaker varieties of language use. This, in turn, led to a focus on student autonomy and greater interactive awareness, as will be described in Chapter 5.

8 Conclusion

From this chapter, it will be clear that from an early stage socio-political realities obliged the teachers involved to recognise the limitations of looking only at language and obliged them to recognise the need to understand language and communication within a detailed analysis of social and cultural contexts. This awareness was to affect the evolution of the work in terms of **perspective**, **context** and **methodology**. (Brooks and Roberts 1985.)

8.1 Perspective

There was a shift from the job-specific language of the workplace and the perceived functional needs of workers and management to a wider focus on inter-ethnic communication and the detailed analysis of naturally-occurring data. Analysing such data required both theoretical hypotheses and analytic tools which language teachers did not possess and therefore had to seek out and evolve. There was also a gradual shift in perspective from multiculturalism to anti-racism. This changed perspective led to a sharper capacity on the part of teachers to distinguish between communication or language issues and matters of racism or equal opportunities. The role of language and communications within the wider perspective of discrimination and disadvantage was reassessed. Syllabuses were restructured so that trainees' perspectives became central to workplace learning.

8.2 Context

There was an extension of context to include not only shopfloor workers and their supervisors in manufacturing industries but also black and white professionals in the public sector. In particular, issues of access, by black clients, to public services such as housing, further education and training, employment advice and the health services, led to training for personnel to improve ethnic relations and inter-ethnic communication. The employment context itself also changed. As the recession of the late 1970s and early 1980s closed down factories, leading to the collapse of working life for workers in engineering, textiles, labour-intensive industries and the heavy industries such as steel, training for re-employment and increased opportunities became a priority.

8.3 Methodology

Finally, there was a shift in methodology. Methods for increasing student autonomy were developed. There was a greater focus on the use of trainees' first language and developing strategies for communicating and learning which would take trainees beyond the limits of a short workplace course. Significantly, there was an increased emphasis on using trainees' awareness as bilinguals, and white monolinguals' lack of awareness, to involve them together in the analysis of inter-ethnic communication.

The rest of this book looks at the development of these areas in more detail.

Chapter 2 attempts to draw a map of existing and developing theories of interaction. These have informed our own theories which have grown out of practice. This was not a map that we started with, and like many early cartographic attempts the map has changed, and will continue to change, over the years. It is a map for practitioners and aims to show how theory and practice blend together. It is time practitioners stopped being bashful about theories. As Halliday says,

'One has to come out loud and clear and say that there has to be a place for theoretical work. It's just that you have to see theoretical work as not divorced from practice, but rather as a set of ways of organising experience so that you do things more effectively' (Baynham 1986).

Chapter 3 relates this map to cross-cultural training for white management, trade unionists and gatekeepers. The reason for putting this chapter before the chapter on language learning and teaching was to establish the centrality of training white native English-speakers if issues of language, discrimination and disadvantage are to be tackled.

Chapter 4 looks at the research, both ethnographic studies of the workplace and detailed discourse analysis of inter-ethnic communication. Again, this research grew out of immediate practical concerns about the nature and scope of language and communicative training. It grew out of a recognition of our ignorance about language in the workplace, about the perceptions and experiences of ethnic-minority workers in industry and about adult language acquisition and socialisation in an often hostile environment. It grew out of a concern that we needed to find a way of relating the fine-grained detail of interactional processes to the larger interactional outcomes which were affecting the quality of people's lives at work and their employment and promotion opportunities.

Chapter 5 describes the evolution in language-learning approaches from the mid-1970s onwards. The evolutionary process is deliberately highlighted for a number of reasons. First, we thought it would be useful to chart how notions of language learning respond to particular and changing contexts. Second, we wanted to show the need for a continuing critique of current approaches. Third, for readers relatively new to work-related language training, we thought it useful to bring to the surface some of the limitations of the earlier work.

Chapter 6 draws together the themes of the book, relates the work described both to the employment and training climate of the late 1980s and to current theory and practice in language training, and highlights further issues where there is a need for theory and practice to interact and inform one another.

Further reading

This is an introductory chapter, and readers who wish to take further the concepts and references given here on issues of language and interaction should read Chapter 2 and the suggested reading that follows it. The other references in this chapter are to the major social surveys of ethnic minorities and to specific materials and articles produced by ILT practitioners.

For an overview of the social and economic position of ethnic minorities in Britain, readers are referred to a series of surveys carried out by the Policy Studies Institute (formerly the Political and Economic Planning Unit). These include the PEP survey *Racial Disadvantage in Britain* (Smith 1977), the survey of *Unemployment and Racial Minorities* (Smith 1981), and a major report, *Black and White Britain*, updating the 1977 survey (Brown 1984). These are relatively large-scale studies of the total impact of racial disadvantage on the black population of Britain.

Early ILT work was based on *Industrial English* (Jupp and Hodlin 1974). This describes the theory developed out of the practice of the first few years of in-company language training and presents materials used on typical elementary language courses. The materials used in early cross-cultural training are well illustrated in *The Background and Employment of Asian Immigrants* (Davies and Jupp 1974) and in Henley's work for the health and social services (1979, 1983a, 1983b, 1983c). A more recent training manual which combines background information with advice on tackling racism is *Health Care in Multiracial Britain* (Mayers, Henley and Baxter 1985). Materials for cross-cultural communication were brought together in a manual of *Cross Cultural Training* (Yates, Christmas and Wilson 1982). A short overview of ILT work from the perspective of the mid-1980s is the article by Brooks and Roberts, 'No five fingers are all alike' (1985).

2 Mapping interaction: practice and theory

1 Introduction

Industrial Language Training developed from the early 1970s onwards. From the late 1960s, the social, cultural and philosophical issues of how language is used in communication were developing into one of the most rapidly expanding areas of work in the social and linguistic sciences. We have already explained how the social context and the lack of communication which ILT trainers observed in multi-ethnic workplaces caused us to seek new concepts of language and of language learning. It was, therefore, natural that we should both turn to and seek to contribute to theories of interaction and inter-ethnic communication.

In this chapter, we first briefly explore the potential value of theory and of systematic analysis based in theoretical concepts for anyone involved either in helping to develop communicative competence or in developing awareness of how language can enter into the processes of discrimination. We then go on to present four examples of naturally-occurring language data collected by ILT trainers, to analyse the complexities of the data and the issues it raises. These examples illustrate the difficult analytic tasks and issues we encountered and our consequent need to examine the research and academic work which was being published during the fifteen years of ILT work from 1970 to 1985 for analytic tools. The third, and most substantial, part of the chapter examines briefly the theories of interaction which we found most relevant to our developing concerns and deepening understanding of the relationships between language and discrimination. We also seek to interrelate these theories and to discuss their relevance to ILT and their limitations from the perspective of ILT.

1.1 The relationship between practice and theory in ILT

Early ILT trainers may have started out with the simple idea that, if people could talk to each other, they could communicate better in the interests of both efficiency and social harmony. Yet very early we recognised that negative attitudes were both generated and reinforced by contact and that some of the white individuals who held these attitudes seemed to base some of them on, or at least justify some of them by, differences in language and communicative style (Jupp and Hodlin 1974). It also became increasingly clear that disadvantage and inequality were not limited to those who spoke little or no English. So it was necessary to learn much more about the processes of interaction between white and black workers, or the language trainers would be wasting their trainees' time. The position of ethnic-minority workers was not fundamentally changed by offering language training to those with little or no English. Workers with communicative ability in English were still clustered in the lowest-paid and most unpleasant jobs, and there was little humanisation of their relations with employers. Contact and communication seemed more often to drive people apart than to raise their understanding and tolerance. The challenge was to work out what role communication had, and what it could do to combat disadvantage and discrimination. The connection between communication differences and discrimination in the workplace was not a clear one. It is important to stress that when ILT work was first developing, notions of structural racism and of indirect discrimination were only just emerging. This became an increasingly important aspect of understanding discrimination, and we were to come to recognise that language could play a significant, and usually invisible, role in indirect discrimination.

Over the fifteen years of Industrial Language Training, there were significant shifts in our understanding of inter-ethnic communication, and we deepened very substantially our notion of interaction. These changes came about through a combination of increased experience and observation, through discussion between white and black trainees and workers, through the discipline of seeking to understand theoretical work in these fields, and through the illuminations of working alongside some of the outstanding scholars. We valued our collaboration with these scholars for the insights and intuition they brought to us by radical examination and analysis of data, and for the confidence they gave us in trying fully to understand the tasks we had set ourselves. They valued contact with us as practitioners because they could experience the direct relevance of their research to pressing social and education needs. We successfully informed each other's work.

By these means, we came to recognise that language is never neutral or trivial. It is an extremely powerful tool for looking at, and creating, reality in different ways. What we communicate always embodies a particular way of seeing things. But its use is much more than an individual means of expressing how we see the world. It constantly reflects and helps to create the social structures and systems which control us. We came to recognise the relationship between language and power.

Theories of interaction can have three major functions for practitioners:

to describe: they provide *descriptive* accounts of what is involved in interaction and thus they can also help us to develop a *critical awareness and analysis* of interaction;

to interpret: they provide *analytical tools* for understanding how people make sense when they talk to each other;

to explain: allied to interpretation, they can help us to relate the specific and local in interaction to the social institutions through which things get done and which determine our social and economic well-being.

1.2 Description

As practitioners we are often caught between two conflicting approaches. We have a duty to our learners to start from their perceptions and, certainly in the case of second-language learners, to help provide the communicative power which gives access to opportunity. This often means taking an uncritical and somewhat normative view of language. In other words, we teach people to be socially appropriate or, for example, to learn how to be better interviewees, without questioning the extent to which we may be perpetuating existing inequalities and disregarding their cultural and social identities. On the other hand, working in the field of language and communication in a multi-ethnic society requires us to be questioning and critical about ways of doing things. We are constantly made aware that the discourse we hear around us and use ourselves is not normal, natural and neutral in any absolute sense, but reflects and helps to reproduce particular ways of thinking and doing which are determined by our social position and our social relationships. By teaching students how to make polite requests or to apologise, we are teaching them to act out a particular social identity. And yet we cannot refuse to teach people to be more effective in particular social interactions.

It is a tension we have to live with. But it means we must look to work in critical sociology and to the work of linguists concerned with describing language as a social process, as well as to the more obvious theories of discourse analysis and ethnography.

1.3 Interpretation

Communication is about making meaning. But there is a great deal more to meaning than grammar or the literal sense of words. There is everything else which makes up the processes by which we convey our intent and make inferences. There is also the fact that the grammar and semantics of textbooks and dictionaries do not bestow any absolute meaning on language. What people mean to each other in particular interactions is the reality of communication.

If we are to help learners towards communicative competence, we need to account for all the factors involved in communication, and theories of interaction have been essential in helping us to do that over the last ten years. We need to look at how interactions are collaboratively constructed and managed. In other words, when people ask questions, pass remarks or contradict, how do those particular exchanges provide the context for the next thing that happens? We also need to understand what people bring to interactions. This means not only knowledge of the world but also assumptions about the way things get done in interaction. For example, on what occasions do you need to hedge or justify a request that you have made? How do you give bad news? How confrontational is it appropriate to be at meetings?

Theories of interaction can provide us with new ways of looking at data. The more we understand about interaction, the more we are able to find in the data. So these theories have been essential to our capacity to analyse data so that it can provide a more effective base for teaching and learning. A useful way of illustrating the concerns of this chapter is to ask why certain utterances whose surface meaning is easy to understand – that is, whose grammar and vocabulary seem uncomplicated – are so often problematic in interaction. For example, the typical interview question 'What does your job involve?' is often perceived as a difficult one to answer by second-language speakers. (See Chapter 1, Data 1.2.)

1.4 Explanation

By examining how individuals communicate together, we can establish whether specific groups interact in specific ways. Different speech communities have different communicative conventions. In teaching language and communications, we need to understand these differences, understand what can happen when groups with different communicative conventions are in contact, and understand how individual judgements about speakers feed into a general categorisation of these speakers as part of a group. We also need to take account of factors traditionally within the domain of sociology, such as class, region, ethnicity and gender, and situational features. In other words, we are interested in how ethnic differences and inequality are reflected and reproduced in interaction and in institutions.

So, we need to understand the language of institutional settings and how such language is likely to be particularly opaque or inaccessible to ethnic-minority groups. The largely subtle and hidden ways in which institutions control access to the resources and opportunities that they offer need to be disclosed to their gatekeepers and demystified for ethnic minorities.

1.5 Theory and experience interacting

Theories have helped us to understand more about language, have taught us how to analyse, and have helped to develop our teaching /training approaches.

Theory influences practice in many and not necessarily logical ways. Often, what practitioners get from theories is very different from what theoretical workers intend to convey. To the practitioner, theories are elastic. The ideas get pulled in the direction of current practice and current concerns. The meaning of a theory depends on what practitioners bring to it.

Practitioners are also influenced and constrained by many other factors. Notably, in this field, our perceptions of race relations and our own ethnocentricity and racism affect our judgements. Perhaps one of the reasons why theories about interaction have had an impact on practitioners is that some linguists were willing to address practical and political issues. For example, in the late 1960s and early 1970s William Labov and his colleagues directly confronted the issue of a deficit model of black English.*

The map of theories of interaction that we attempt to draw in the third part of this chapter is a map of understanding for the late 1980s. It includes many theories which we now read quite differently from the way we did when we first had access to them ten or fifteen years ago. Theories which provided us with an unquestioning view of reality then, we may now perceive as only metaphors of a time gone by. The

---

* *The most famous case in which Labov was involved was the Ann Arbor schools case in Michigan. Black parents took the Education Authority to the courts because they claimed the schools were failing to provide adequate education for their children. Labov acted as an expert witness. The parents finally won their case and the schools were required to change their practices.*

map identifies the influences on our training work over the years. It is
a map which still has a great deal of uncharted territory. But it was
these theories that were most clearly helpful in devising language-
learning and cross-cultural training programmes. A formative synthesis
of these theories goes like this: interaction is so complex at so many
different levels that training must go beyond any functional patterning
of normative dialogues or simple notions of cultural background knowledge; it must take account of how people's meaning systems have
developed through small-group interaction, of our assumption that
others interpret experience and organise and convey meaning as we
do, and of the dynamic and so variable nature of any interaction.

Language is fundamental to communication, interaction and understanding. In tackling the role of language in inequality of opportunity
and race relations, ILT trainers had three problems to resolve:

1. how to relate cross-cultural and social issues to language technicalities;
2. how to ensure that language difference is not seen as language
   deficit;
3. how to develop non-racist training strategies which require
   language accommodation from both sides in inter-ethnic communication.

It was trainers' experience in the workplace, and the kind of authentic
data they collected, which determined the theoretical background
needed to illuminate these tasks. The data gave us access to an
understanding of what goes on in actual inter-ethnic interaction, and
we then had to turn to theorists to look for analytical tools for further
description, interpretation and explanation.

For this reason, examples of inter-ethnic data form the second part
of this chapter and provide a backdrop for the theories of interaction
discussed in the third part.

2 What is happening?
An analysis of some naturally-occurring data

2.1 Data of inter-ethnic communication

Most of the data of inter-ethnic communication that was collected in
natural settings by ILT trainers illuminated the disadvantaged position
of ethnic-minority workers. The data was not collected specifically to
illustrate the inequality that minority ethnic groups faced, but it did
so with harsh regularity.

The possession of such data led trainers to search for theories of interaction which might validate and assist their intuitions and interpretations, provide further insights into the 'texts', and furnish tools for the description, analysis, interpretation and explanation of these unequal encounters so that the findings could be used effectively in language training.

Such data was principally collected in:

(i)   the workplace, in on-the-job encounters between supervisor and worker, or meetings at work;
(ii)   contact with the public services: for example, in interviews with housing officers, the social services or advice agencies; and
(iii) selection and appraisal interviews for jobs and training.

Four examples are discussed here to provide a context for the subsequent description of the theories of interaction which were found most helpful in analysing such texts.

These four pieces of data are typical in that:

(i)   The *unequal relationships* between black and white people are captured in the interaction. [Data 2.1 In the Mill]
(ii)   *Cultural assumptions* enter the interaction and affect its outcome. [Data 2.2 In the Personnel Office]
(iii) The situation is one of *protracted negotiation*, both in terms of the task, and linguistically and communicatively, in the attempt to find a shared schema and meaning. [Data 2.3 Job Interview]
(iv)   The *presentation of self* through the speaker's way of structuring information and discourse, even in what might be considered a task-oriented activity, is crucial to the evaluation and decision made by the white person in power. [Data 2.4 Staff Discussion at the Bus Company]

DATA 2.1 IN THE MILL (see page 36)
[Data collected by Alison Slade, Calderdale ILT; an extract from this data has already been presented in Chapter 1]

DATA 2.1 CONTEXT
This is a real encounter which took place between a manager and an Asian worker in a textile mill in 1976. The mid-1970s was a time when the great majority of ethnic-minority workers in the textile industry were in the most unskilled jobs, often on the night shift and either in non-unionised companies or members of a relatively weak trade union. They had few rights and fewer expectations in an alien environment where they were seen as no more than a pair of hands.

This kind of data was collected as part of the language trainers' early process of needs analysis. They would visit trainees' workplaces with tape recorders in order to establish the typical activities and encounters that workers with little or no English had to face. Such needs analysis provided content for the language-teaching syllabus, and evidence of the kind of language strategies that trainees already had or could realistically aim for. Shockingly, on one such visit, this encounter took place in the presence of the trainer, to whom the manager appeals for support at the end of the transcript.

DATA 2.1 AGENDA

The transcript demonstrates:

(a) How workers with limited English may have no power even to negotiate the right to speak.
(b) How ethnic-minority workers with limited English present themselves to, and are reduced as people by, dominant white management, although they may be forceful, fluent and confident personalities within their own language culture.
(c) How language difficulties, even when they are very obvious, are not the only factors to cause communication breakdowns: native speakers' assumption that they have the right to dominate and control, and the way that this is reinforced by the worker's lack of ability to negotiate the right to be heard, affect the detailed processes of routine interactions and their outcomes.

DATA 2.1 ISSUES

Faced with data like this and the type of descriptive models of discourse that were being developed at the time by theorists, the needs of such workers seemed obvious. It seemed clear that basic language skills were required so that workers could 'speak for themselves'. This was, at heart, a deficit model. But it depended on exciting new concepts related to the notion of communicative competence which went far beyond notions of grammatical competence, and raised issues of how people negotiate discourse in such a way that they are listened to.

The type of topic domination and denial of speaker rights illustrated here oppressed the worker and denied him the chance to communicate and so learn. It also created a bullying management style which would not have been acceptable to white workers. This raised issues concerning the need for cross-cultural training through which to confront white people in power with the knowledge that such negative and frustrating interactions were jointly constructed and that they had a responsibility to make changes in their own language behaviour.

DATA 2.1 IN THE MILL – TRANSCRIPT

Manager: What's this? Off here last night... What did you do? You had a break up here, and you ran it through, straight on the bobbin, never pulled it off, did you? ... You know what you've done, don't you?

H: S( ) ( ) s( )

Manager: You did that, didn't you?

H: No, no...

Manager: Yes, you did. That's how you made that. So that there are two ends there. That's how you made that ... EVERY day. EVERY day the girl on that machine complains about bad work that you make. Every day. Now I'm sick of it. You're either going to do the job properly, or you're going to get out.

H: I am sorry. Next time =

Manager: = There won't be a next time.

H: I ( )

I am sorry. Next time do it properly.

Manager: Yes. Well, the next time that girl complains to me about your bad work I shall sack you. Is that clear? You're going to an English class, do you understand what I just said?

H: Yes, I ... English ...

Manager: You understand. You know what I'm going to do?

H: Next time... Sir.

Manager: There won't be a next time.

H: I'm sorry =

Manager: = because the next time that girl complains to me =

H: = I'm sorry ...

Manager: It's no good being sorry. You keep on making bad work over and over and over again.

H: I am sorry. I am very sorry...

Manager: It's no use standing there like that saying you're sorry, you're sorry. You just keep on making bad work. Now I'm telling you the next time you make bad work like that, you're finished.

H: OK, sir. I'm sorry.

Manager: (to language teacher) Did he understand? Do you think he understood?

DATA 2.1 COMMENTARY

It is an understatement to say that the manager controls the interview through-out. He uses a number of devices to muzzle H. The most obvious strategy he uses is to interrupt and talk down to him. But he uses several others. First, he questions H, not to seek an explanation or a justification but to check H's understanding and simultaneously imply a threat:

You know what you've done, don't you?	(line 4)
do you understand what I just said?	(line 20)
You know what I'm going to do?	(line 23)

So, H. has no opportunity to present his side of things. Second, and related to this, whenever H. can take a turn, it is either only to have his understanding checked, or after a statement about his bad work and the threat to sack him. And these threats are recycled in a different and cumulatively stronger form each time:

You're going to get out.	(line 13)
I shall sack you.	(line 19)
You're finished.	(line 36)

After an early attempt at denial (line 7) H. responds to these threats by apologising:

'I am sorry'	(line 14)
'I'm sorry'	(line 26)
'I am very sorry'	(line 32)

and reassuring the manager:

'Next time'	(line 14)
'Next time do it properly'	(line 17)
'OK, Sir'	(line 37)

Faced with such categorical statements from the manager, this response seems H's only course of action if he is not to lose his job on the spot.

However, the manager uses H's response against him in two ways. First, he does not accept H's repeated apologies and reassurances as an adequate reaction to the predicament he is in, although for H, this may well be an acceptable and the only way to respond to such public disciplining. Second, the manager twists H's meaning of 'next time', meaning in the future, in a confusing way against him. He chooses to interpret 'next time' as 'next time I do bad work', and so

DATA 2.1 COMMENTARY *continued*

simultaneously denies H's apology and reassurance about 'next time', while maintaining the threatening possibility that there will be a 'next time' to sack him but not a 'next time' as an opportunity for H to do good work.

The powerlessness and humiliation of the worker in this disciplinary interview speak for themselves. The manager's suspension of all notions of decent human contact reflects widely-held and unchallenged racist assumptions about Asian workers and how they can be treated.

DATA 2.2 IN THE PERSONNEL OFFICE (see page 39)
[Data collected by Alison Slade, Calderdale ILT]

DATA 2.2 CONTEXT
In this encounter an Asian night-shift worker (IA) in a textile mill tries to negotiate a job for his son with the personnel officer (Mrs B). (Mrs S is the language trainer present to collect data.) Informal recruitment into unskilled jobs was common at the time (1976) and often encouraged by companies. 'Chain recruitment' was a means of bringing into the factory the friends and relatives of good workers without the expense and bother of formal recruitment. Of course, such informal recruitment methods had always been commonplace among white workers. But it was held against black workers, who were criticised for having a 'a herding instinct', 'always sticking together', 'looking after their own kind'.

DATA 2.2 AGENDA
The transcript demonstrates:

(a) How learners can sometimes develop a sophisticated communicative competence in inter-ethnic communication even where their grammatical competence is quite limited.
(b) How cultural assumptions enter into language interactions and may affect their outcome.
(c) How interpersonal skills can be more significant than the accuracy with which meaning is conveyed at any point in a conversation.

DATA 2.2 ISSUES
Unlike the mill worker in Data 2.1, IA was able to negotiate inter-ethnic communication so that he was listened to. Such data indicates a need to perceive and to judge 'communicative competence' in terms of conversational strategies rather than language accuracy or fluency. For ILT

DATA 2.2 IN THE PERSONNEL OFFICE – TRANSCRIPT

IA:	You find a job for my son... Say you know, this last month and my fast. Boy say I not working on the fast.
Mrs B:	Not working on the first?
IA:	On the fast Ramadan you know. What you thinks I bringing in the next Monday?
Mrs B:	Have I seen your son before?
IA:	No. This one my big son.
Mrs B:	Well, you better send him in and let me have a look at him... eleven o'clock on Monday.
IA:	Yes. I coming eleven o'clock.
Mrs B:	Not early, because I'm here.
IA:	No, not early because I sleeping. I often sleep on the ten o'clock.
Mrs S:	You wake up, you mean, at ten o'clock.
IA:	OK. I coming in.
Mrs B:	How old is your son?
IA:	16 year 2 months.
Mrs B:	Can't help him.
IA:	This one learning first day, not night.
Mrs B:	Can't help him.
IA:	What for?
Mrs B:	All the men in this mill are on 55 hours.
IA:	55 hours?
Mrs B:	All the men.
IA:	Old men?
Mrs B:	All men.
IA:	Young men and just 8 hours every day.
Mrs S:	But Mrs B says – not the OLD men. ALL the men – everybody – must work 55 hours.
Mrs B:	Ladies work 40 hours.
IA:	This is young boy, the same like lady ⟨laughter⟩.
	They are too young. If not wanted then too long time...just 40 hours per week.
Mrs B:	(sighs) I don't know where? Don't know where because all =
IA:	= I work over there 8 year, why not you help to me?

Line numbers in right margin: 5, 10, 15, 20, 25, 30, 35

DATA 2.2 IN THE PERSONNEL OFFICE – TRANSCRIPT
continued

Mrs B:	But I can't change a rule Mr A. The rule is, the men work the 55-hour shifts and the women work 40-hour shifts. It's a rule. I can't change a company rule.
IA:	Him not doing the 55 hour... boys?
Mrs B:	No. Not under 18.
IA:	Too young?
Mrs B:	He's got to be 18. Sorry, I can't help.
IA:	You can't help. Where him going? I not =
Mrs B:	= Has he been to an English school?
IA:	Yes, 4 years.
Mrs B:	I'll talk to Mr M. about him, but just now I can't see any place for him.
IA:	Overlooker tell me tomorrow night?
Mrs B:	I'll see Mr M. and tell your overlooker.

(line numbers in right margin: 40, 45, 50)

DATA 2.2 COMMENTARY

What is striking about this interview, is that IA manages to make it a conversation but at the same time to reach his objectives despite several difficulties in his way. On two occasions, the language trainer intervenes to clarify two potential sources of misunderstanding. But IA gives the strong impression that he can handle misunderstandings and any challenges to his purpose in an effective way.

Mrs S:	You wake up, you mean, at ten o'clock.	
IA:	Okay. I coming in.	(line 15)

Here he dismisses the potential red herring and confirms the earlier agreement to his objective in line 9.

Communicative Competence
Throughout this interaction, IA's communicative ability overrides any weakness in his grammatical competence and helps to make him successful. For example:

1. *He is sensitive to context*

DATA 2.2 COMMENTARY *continued*

He uses an appropriate discourse convention to set the scene so that his objective is stated, and his request – to bring in his son to see Mrs B the next Monday – will be granted:

You find a job for my son...	(line 1)
What you thinks I bringing in the next Monday?	(line 4)

2. *He is able to keep crucial topics on stage*
He uses confirmation:

Yes. I coming eleven o'clock.	(line 10)
Okay. I coming in.	(line 15)
Overlooker tell me tomorrow night?	(line 50)

3. *He can compensate for and repair communication difficulties*
For example, when there is a confusion over 'first' and 'fast', he reformulates as 'Ramadan':

IA:	Boy say I not working on the fast.	
Mrs B:	Not working on the first?	
IA:	On the fast Ramadan you know.	(lines 2–4)

Cultural Assumptions

IA's overall assumption is that Mrs B is a person with perceived power who can therefore help him if she wants to. When she is in danger of slipping into a gatekeeper role:

Can't help him.	(line 20)
It's a rule. I can't change a company rule.	(line 39)

he negotiates in two ways – by suggesting ways round the rule.

IA:	55 hours?	
Mrs B:	All the men.	
IA:	Old men?	
Mrs B:	All men.	
IA:	Young men and just 8 hours every day.	(lines 23–27)

They are too young. If not wanted then too long time...just 40 hours per week.	(lines 32–33)

DATA 2.2 COMMENTARY   *continued*

and by personalising the request:

> I work over there eight year, why not you help to me?
> You can't help. Where him going? I not   =   (line 36)

Interpersonal Skills
Of particular interest in this transcript are IA's 'anaphoric' strategies where he mirrors and so comments humorously on Mrs B's utterances:

> Mrs B: Not early, because I'm here.
> IA: No, not early because I sleeping.   (lines 11–12)
>
> Mrs B: Ladies work 40 hours.
> IA: This is young boy, the same like lady.   (lines 30–31)

and his assertive ability in pegging an uncertain promise to a particular time.

> Mrs B: I'll talk to Mr M about him, but just now I can't see any
>   place for him.
> IA: Overlooker tell me tomorrow night?   (lines 48–50)

trainers mounting short courses, this put a premium on identifying the interpersonal skills required in stressful and often unpredictable situations where the conversation was judged on its outcome and not on the accuracy with which meaning was conveyed at any point.

The data also illustrates how assumptions about the organisation and culture of a British workplace enter into the language and negotiating strategies in the interaction. The issue here was the fixed nature of company 'rules' and whether these were in practice negotiable according to different circumstances. IA seems to assume they are negotiable if he puts his own personal case strongly enough. In the context of institutional racism this issue is a breeding ground for much real and perceived discrimination.

DATA 2.3 JOB INTERVIEW (see page 44)
[Data collected by Derek Hooper, London ILT]

DATA 2.3 CONTEXT

In this interaction, an applicant, B, is interviewed by N for the job of driver/conductor with the regional transport service. B is a bilingual

Asian with near native-speaker competence in English. [Extracts from this interview appear in Programme 1 of the BBC series *The Interview Game*.]

DATA 2.3 AGENDA
The transcript demonstrates:

(a) How ethnic-minority candidates may communicate fluently in English but not share with majority English-speakers the same assumptions about the purpose of the interaction or have the same views on what is a socially appropriate way of fulfilling that purpose. In other words, they do not share the same schemata or interpretive frames.

(b) How formalised situations such as job interviews tend to highlight lack of shared assumptions because they are highly conventionalised and culture-specific. They work in hidden ways. Candidates are only judged positively if they are able to interpret the hidden meaning behind the interviewer's questions. This type of encounter shows the link between individual interactions and institutional decision-making and discrimination.

(c) How different expectations about the objectives of an interaction affect communication. The evidence in this data suggests that the interviewer does not get the expected answers. This is partly because the candidate appears to see the interview more as a test than as an opportunity to display his knowledge or sell himself, and partly because of different assumptions about self-presentation.

DATA 2.3 ISSUES
In looking at such data and interpreting what was happening, it was important that we did not make speculative assumptions about what the interactants meant or how they felt about each other. When participants were asked about such interactions, what was clear was that they saw the same interaction in different ways; that expectations on each side were often not met; and that frequently neither side felt satisfied with either the process or the outcome.

The issue here is how judgements are made in inter-ethnic communication which can reinforce disadvantage and discrimination even where differences are 'hidden' and usually not perceived. This is particularly so in activities such as an interview, and it is still regrettably rare for ethnic-minority candidates to be interviewed by someone who shares their cultural experiences. Their responses are therefore interpreted through a different value system, and their behaviour, ability and motivation judged accordingly.

DATA 2.3 JOB INTERVIEW – TRANSCRIPT

N: Right Mr B before we actually start can I just say you've actually taken an arithmetic and English test.

B: Yeah.

N: Which you've passed so you don't have to worry about that any more OK.   5

B: Yeah.

N: So all I want you to do is just relax a bit and I'll ask you some questions about your previous experience and background OK and about why you wish to join L ____ Buses and then give you the opportunity of asking me anything you wish to ask me...   10 about the job, anything you're uncertain about ... OK ... once we've finished that I'll explain to you about the preliminary driving test you've got to take and I'll also explain to you about the medical all right?

B: All right.   15

N: So just relax, just take it nice and easy OK ... at the moment you are working for ...

B: R ____ Laboratories.

N: As a process operator.

B: Yeah.   20

N: Yes, and you've been there for how long?

B: Four years.

N: Four years ... Why do you actually want to leave? It's a nice steady job.

B: Well the thing is um you know it's better to change the jobs and   25 get other jobs. I was very interested in working for L ____ Transport (PHONE RINGS IN BACKGROUND) You know, right at the beginning so.. Because I couldn't get the job I had to take the R ____.

N: Uh huh. So did you actually apply to us before for a job?   30

B: I applied once very l... once when I came here you know a long time ago.

N: And what happened then... at that stage?

B: Well um I failed the test. (Chuckles)

N: You failed the test (laughs). All right, what job was that for?   35

B: That was for train guard.

N: For a guard and you failed the test at that stage, OK.
      And since then you've worked as a process operator. What do you think L ____ Buses is going to offer you that R ____ don't offer you?
      40

DATA 2.3 JOB INTERVIEW – TRANSCRIPT   *continued*

B: Well, quite a lot of things, for example like um ... Christmas bonus.

N: Uh huh.

B: So many things, holidays and all that. Well, we get holidays in R ____ but you er ... get here more holidays than you get in R ____ (laughs).   45

N: All right. O.K.... Before you actually went to R ____ four years ago you were in Africa.

B: Yes.

N: And that was where, Kenya?   50

B: No, Malawi.

N: Malawi, and you were doing what there?

B: We had our own business there. I was working in a shop, it's a grocery shop.

N: What made you decide to sell up and come to England?   55

B: Well um you know it's just like what happened in Uganda (PHONE) could happen there, come to this country you know and settle myself.

N: Did you find it easy to settle here?

B: Not quite, I was alone here, I had no relations and nobody ...   60

N: You came over totally cold, nowhere to go ...

B: Yes.

N: Nowhere to live.

B: I was looked after by the government. I'm alright now.

N: OK. You've been driving for two and half years.   65

B: Yes.

N: You obviously don't drive in the job you're doing. What sort of driving experience have you had?

B: In this country?

N: Um hum.   70

B: I've got um light goods vehicle driving licence and I've... I don't think done nothing wrong.

N: What sort of vehicles have you driven?

B: Well, Cortinas.

N: Basically car experience rather than vans or anything larger...   75

B: Yes.

DATA 2.3 COMMENTARY

The first significant question asked by the interviewer is a typical one about the candidate's current employment:

> N: Why do you actually want to leave? It's a nice steady job.
>
> B: Well the thing is um you know it's better to change the jobs and get other jobs. I was very interested in working for L ____. You know, right at the beginning so... Because I couldn't get the job I had to take the R ____.   (lines 23–29)

The applicant gives two clear reasons for leaving: that it is a good idea to change jobs and that he is interested in working for L ____ transport services. The candidate's comments after the interview indicate that he was very concerned to show his keenness... 'The strongest point was when I came here for an interview when I passed my interview I should show myself that I am really after the job you see... that was my strongest, to show them I'm really after the work.'

However, the interviewer's response gives no evidence that he judged this reply as a good reply which shows the candidate's motivation. In fact, the interviewer ignores B's response to his question and probes instead into B's previous unsuccessful job application.

The candidate's reply is initially rather impersonal and then, although he says he is very interested, he does not say why. It is quite common for candidates to give what is perceived as an impersonal response and to say they are interested, keen, committed, without adding more or showing their interest through example. The conventions of the traditional British interview, however, demand that candidates 'sell' themselves personally. These conventions also demand that candidates not only say they are keen, or would be good at the job, but give an example from their past experience to prove it. The candidate's honesty combined with rather different assumptions about how personal to be or how to present one's commitment and worth, set the interview off on the wrong footing.

The interviewer's next 'open' question is also indirect:

> N: For a guard and you failed the test at that stage, OK.
>   And since then you've worked as a process operator.
>   What do you think L ____ is going to offer you that R ____ don't offer you?
>
> B: Well, quite a lot of things, for example like um... Christmas bonus.
>
> N: Uh huh.
>
> B: So many things, holidays and all that. Well we get holidays in R ____ but you er... get here more holidays than you get in R ____.
>
> N: All right. O.K.   (lines 37–47)

The hidden message of this question is 'What does the job mean to you and what do you bring to it?' Quite understandably the candidate answers the

---

DATA 2.3 COMMENTARY *continued*

---

question literally and talks about the good aspects of the transport job such as bonuses and holidays. The interviewer's response 'All right' with a low falling tone, again indicates that this was not an expected or preferred answer from the candidate. Again, the convention of the traditional British interview is to pick up on the hidden meaning and answer by talking about how one's experience and abilities are relevant to the job or how the job will offer a challenge.

Later, when asked a factual question about his driving experience, the candidate gives what may well be interpreted as a defensive answer:

> N: You obviously don't drive in the job you're doing. What sort of driving experience have you had?
>
> B: In this country?
>
> N: Um hum.
>
> B: I've got um light goods vehicle driving licence and I've... I don't think done nothing wrong. (lines 67–72)

It is common in many countries for an interview to be a test in which the interviewers try to catch you out. It is not, therefore, surprising that B interprets this question as an attempt to probe his weaknesses, and fails to follow the British interview convention of integrating facts with some evaluative comment. The interviewer responds by reformulating the question about driving experience:

> N: What sort of vehicles have you driven?
>
> B: Well, Cortinas.
>
> N: Basically car experience rather than vans or anything larger...
> (lines 73–75)

thereby reinforcing the negative tone of the interview which the candidate fails to retrieve.

In job interviews a set of schemata are activated by the structural properties of the interaction, so that particular inferences are triggered by the wording and ordering of speakers' turns. In order to fulfil the expectations of the interviewer, the candidate, who had no difficulty in choosing appropriate language, had to choose 'appropriate' behaviour, and his ability to do so rested on knowledge of the *purpose* of the interviewer's questions rather than their surface meaning. Even with this knowledge, applicants can experience difficulty in acting according to the 'rules of the game'. For example, in this particular interaction the candidate was asked for experience he had had no opportunity to acquire, or which had been gained in a different context abroad and which he did not expect the white interviewer to value.

More crucially, the rules of the game were inappropriate for him, and he would not necessarily feel culturally comfortable with the expected ways of being personal and selling himself. The issue here is the extent to which people can or should be trained or expected to change their culture-specific behaviour. Since the outcomes from job interviewing are routinely discriminatory the onus lay with the job interviewers to change their practice.

This indicates not only a need to train interviewers in the communication aspects of equal-opportunities interviewing, but also a wider need to challenge traditions of interviewing which are not designed for cross-cultural situations and which are therefore bound to discomfort and disadvantage ethnic minorities.

DATA 2.4 STAFF DISCUSSION AT A BUS COMPANY (see page 50)
[Data collected and analysed by Sian Dodderidge, Kirklees ILT]

DATA 2.4 CONTEXT
This is a transcript of part of a meeting between a white trainer/conductor and a group of ethnic-minority conductors who were not happy with the arrangements made for their release ('cover') and payment ('make up') for language training.

The white conductor/trainer, K, had been told of these grievances, but was not happy himself with his role as management apologist. Throughout the meeting there was a relationship of mutual goodwill and willingness to talk through the problem. Assumptions about the goals of the meeting were shared, the jargon of the company was familiar to everyone, and all the participants respected the status and interests of the others even though K had, in fact, more authority.

In this extract, only K and one of the bus conductors, A, are talking. A has a North Indian background.

DATA 2.4 AGENDA
The transcript demonstrates:

(a) How, where there are shared assumptions, quite marked differences in conveying meaning and managing the interaction do not lead to communication breakdown. Conversely, without those shared assumptions, these differences could easily lead to misunderstanding and loss of information.

(b) How some of the features of the communicative styles used by native English-speakers and North Indian speakers of English affect the extent to which turn-taking is not smoothly achieved, despite the obvious good will, and can lead to information loss.

(c) How the differences between the white interactant's style and the style of the Indian interactant is just that – difference and not deficit.

(d) How these differences are reflected in how arguments are tied together, and ways of showing connection and emphasis. For example:
   1. different notions about how far features of discourse need to be marked explicitly by using grammar and lexis, e.g. in standard English, topic-switching is usually explicitly marked by comments such as 'OK, now let's turn to', or 'by the way', 'another thing', etc.;
   2. different assumptions about how far speakers need to use grammar and lexis to make their talk seem cohesive, e.g. using pronoun references, or how much speakers can rely on shared knowledge of context;
   3. different ways of signalling speaker involvement or perspective, e.g. whether a speaker is taking the blame or blaming someone else;
   4. different uses to which intonation and stress are put to convey meaning i.e. the way in which intonation and stress and syntax work together, e.g. to show emphasis or to show what is new information.
   5. how contrasts are made, e.g. main and subsidiary, or *this* as opposed to *that*;
   6. how self-corrections are handled.

DATA 2.4 ISSUES

This kind of data indicated that it is not simply grammar or different cultural assumptions that lead to information loss in inter-ethnic communication. Bilingual speakers regularly find that they have not been understood because of subtle differences in prosodic features, and in ways of showing emphasis and of making connections between different parts of discourse.

It was clear from this kind of analysis that unconsciously used aspects of language – particularly prosodic features – can cause severe difficulties in understanding on both sides. Bilingual speakers, such as the bus conductors, could be frustrated and irritated by native English-speakers' inability to respond to them. Native English-speakers could underestimate bilingual speakers' competence in English or attribute difficulties in understanding to lack of intelligence, motivation or will to negotiate.

DATA 2.4 STAFF DISCUSSION AT A BUS COMPANY – TRANSCRIPT

A: ... change your duty you know.

K: Ya.

A: If you early turns we'll make up, er, you do first bit and second bit we will cover that.

K: Ya.   5

A: And if you middle turn, no if you late turn we make up you know middle turn.

K: Ya.

A: So, why they have change change mind?

K: Ya, Well if we did =   10

A: = And er second second... second suggestion, just a minute, second suggestion, you give us second suggestion you knows. Anyway if you come, with late turn I give you time and a half, anyway you know, spread over any time. Two days, Thursday and Tuesday we will pay you two and a half hours   15 overtime. Now second time again broken that agreement you know. We will never pay you. (Murmurs of agreement) We can't spend time over here you know. All time, all time spend over here you know, because, ... spose ... we ... we have done first bit up till five to ten, five till ten, and spend half, two and a half   20 hour here ... Last, I give you example for last week you know two and a half hour I left spend here, and went to town for shopping. I've spare only fifty minutes left, at home, I have ... lot of headaches, lot of nervous every thing you knows.

K: Ya, ya.   25

A: Well I am not satisfied on this.

K: No. (Murmer) To answer your questions on that one. First of all, we did discuss at great length with management, as my two friends here will probably back me up on that. And management did say at that particular time, now we had a lot of conductors,   30 did say, that yes they would cover your jobs for yer, where possible, and you would get paid the two and a half hours. That I can assure you, was said at the very very beginning.

A: Management just don't know what they fixing, what they can do in future you know..   35

K: I... In the...

A: Every time, they can change their mind (murmurs of agreement) every time.

K: In the second =

A: = Any time .   40

K: In the second instance where that two and a half hours, I was fully aware, well unaware, put it this way, I was unaware that

DATA 2.4 TRANSCRIPT *continued*

you was not going to get paid for it, because when you came in,
someone came in last Thursday, and said they'd not got paid, I
immediately went into wages office, and asked them why you'd   45
not got paid. And they said that the management had said, that
if you're on a spread-over then you wouldn't get paid the two
and a half hours. Well I argued for some time about this, and
the wages department said yes, OK, we will pay them the two
and a half hours, when they're on a spread-over, that they did   50
tell me.

DATA 2.4 COMMENTARY

There are two quite different and equally valid systems at work here to show
emphasis and correctness. K, the native English speaker, uses a combination
of stress patterns and syntax to show contrast and develop his line of argument:

K: To answer your questions on that one // First of all / we did
discuss at great length / with management // as my two friends here
will probably back me up on that // And management did say / at
that particular time //
now we had a lot of conductors // did say / that yes / they would
cover your jobs for yer, / where possible, / and you would get paid
the two and a half hours. That I can assure you / was said at the
very very beginning //   (lines 27–33)

K, uses an emphatic 'did' throughout, reinforced by accenting the auxilliary,
prosodically. He also lowers his pitch register to indicate additional contextual
information and conditions. His key points – that these matters were discussed
with management and that management confirmed there would be cover and
extra pay – are linked together by the emphatic 'Did' so that main points and
background or subsidiary information are clearly marked syntactically and
prosodically. A, on the other hand, relies on the juxtaposition of lexical items
and parallelism of structure to make his argument coherent.

A: If you early turns we'll make up, er, you do first bit and
second bit we will cover that.

K: Ya.

A: And if you middle turn, no if you late turn we make up you
know middle turn.

K: Ya.

A: So, why they have change change mind?   (lines 3–9)

DATA 2.4 COMMENTARY   *continued*

Parallelism
A, produces what is, in his terms, a cohesive argument through a series of structural parallels. At lines 7 and 11, and later at line 18, the beginning of each parallel section is marked with an 'if clause' and 'you' as if the management were speaking to the conductors. Another example of parallelism repeated is the juxtaposition of 'you' with 'turn'. This repeated construction signals that there are two parallel cases and so helps to hold the argument together.

Lexical Juxtaposition
The lexical juxtaposition of 'you' and 'turn' makes any verb superfluous. Another example occurs earlier in line 8, 'we will cover that'. Here, 'that' refers to the 'second bit'. The reference would be made clear in the standard variety of English by stressing 'second bit' and 'that'.

However, here, (and this is typical of the communicative style of speakers like A), it is the lexical juxtaposition alone that unambiguously refers 'that' to 'second bit'. In its own terms, A's discourse is cohesive.

If we now analyse one of his turns in depth, we can see how his system of making meaning relies on *context* and *word order*, whereas the standard variety of English relies on a combination of *stress* and *syntax* to mark the main points of emphasis.

A: If you / early turns ˈwe'll ˈmake ˈup // er
      ˈyou ˈdo first bit and ˈsecond ˈbit / ˈwe will cover that // (lines 3–4)

A, dramatises the context and speaks as if management were addressing them. So there is no need to put the main stress on the pronouns to show the contrast between management and conductors. The pronouns speak for themselves. By juxtaposing 'second bit' and 'we will' A is showing that management – 'we' – will cover for the second turn.

However, for the standard variety speaker, this may be confusing. First, the connective seems to join 'second bit' back to 'first bit', and second, the last utterance 'we will cover that' is marked off slightly with a pause after 'bit' which makes the final word 'that' ambiguous. In the standard variety, speakers would expect this reported conversation to be in reported speech, and the contrast between what management would do and what the conductors would do to be emphasised through stress. Someone speaking closer to the standard variety would make changes in both the prosody, and syntax and lexis, to produce an utterance something like this :

Management told me / that if we / were on early turn // if we did / the first bit // they would cover / the second bit //

The standard-variety speaker would rely on making their point by using contrastive *stress* on 'we' and 'they' and on 'first' and 'second', and by marking off the explanatory utterance 'if we did the first bit' through *intonation* to show that it is in parenthesis.

Because the context and the facts are so well known to both participants in this interaction these marked differences and ambiguities do not affect the communication of meaning. Without this they would be a source of confusion and frustration.

Since many of the features of bilingual speakers' English are the product of deeply ingrained language uses and strategies characteristic of their first language (for example, how to show emphasis and contrast), it would have been presumptuous to focus training for bilingual speakers on attempting to develop all the language habits of a native English-speaker. Instead, a process of awareness-raising and suggestions for compensating on both sides for these habitual differences have been tried out both for bilingual speakers and for native English-speakers in supervisory, management and union positions.

This issue of prosodic features and related discourse strategies also highlighted the need for very specialised knowledge and skills in the analysis of interactive discourse, and a crucial role for ILT trainers who shared the trainees' language and culture.

In working with native English-speakers who had power or responsibility over bilingual speakers, it was important to find ways of explaining and demonstrating the link between the issues of communication, in management and race-relations, and the technicalities of language use, so that supervisors could adopt different and non-threatening ways of conveying and clarifying information which did not rely on, for example, the use of reported speech, stress intonation, or other culture-specific ways of expressing meaning which might not be readily understood by bilingual speakers of English.

2.2 The implications of such data

These four examples of data collected in multi-ethnic workplaces demonstrate that the communicative environment of the workplace is both complex and rigid. The disadvantaged position of ethnic-minority workers, clustered in the lowest-status jobs, is reinforced by the negative ethnic stereotyping of white staff and workers. Different assumptions about the goals of an interaction and different ways of speaking are seen as broad cultural differences relating to behaviour and attitude. In other words, the perceived behaviour of people with cultural and linguistic conventions which are different from those of the white minority group tends to be interpreted by that group in terms of their own conventions.

Analysis of inter-ethnic communication and discussion with interactants showed that listeners were constantly drawing inferences which were quite at odds with the speakers' intent and which were based on the listeners' experience of how to make sense of the world about them. In other words, their accumulated experiences of interaction, their culture, was entering into their interpretation of the message they were receiving. The failure to make sound judgements about people's competence, intentions and behaviour meant that the disadvantaged position of ethnic-minority workers was constantly reproduced and reinforced.

Any training had to focus, therefore, on attempting to change communicative relationships in the workplace. Many ethnic-minority workers who acquired some English could cope with routine instrumental interactions at work but not with situations requiring protracted negotiations on the terms of those with power. In addition, they were largely isolated from the informal networks of the workplace, particularly those networks which operated between workers and first-line managers, technical staff and shop stewards. They were, therefore, cut off from learning about the custom and practice of the workplace and from the discussions which help to make sense of the rules and procedures of a workplace.

The experience of working in a multi-ethnic workplace left most workers feeling either cautious and isolated or suspicious and uncertain. They felt able to cope with routine situations at work, and either lacked the confidence to want to learn to communicate in a variety of situations or felt that the difficulties they faced stemmed from uncaring and negative attitudes on the part of the company and not from language difficulties, and that there was little or no connection between attitude and language.

If workers were to consider language training worthwhile, and if they were to benefit from it, the training needed to be responsive to them in a number of ways. First, the training had to help them be effective in a range of situations. Second, trainees needed to be reassured that their efforts to improve communicative relationships would be matched by positive attempts to understand and adapt by the white majority. Finally, the training needed a methodology which constructed 'texts' from the trainees' own experience and included comparative analysis and discussion.

The response to the kind of situation described must come from practitioners but it needs to be informed by theories of interaction. The complexity of the situation requires theories to guide the practitioner which are as comprehensive as possible, and relate clearly to the realities of disadvantage and discrimination.

3 Theories of interaction

From the mass of literature available on the social, cultural and philosophical issues of how language is used as communication, three major concepts informed the work of ILT. These were: the concept of cultural and linguistic relativity, the concept of language as a socially constituted phenomenon, and the concept of the linguistic dimension of discrimination. These three concepts are illustrated, from many different perspectives, in the work discussed below. This section, therefore, examines briefly the theories of interaction which include these concepts, discusses their relevance for ILT and, where appropriate, considers the limitations of the work for ILT. At the end of the section, we return to the three key concepts and summarise our understanding of them in the light of the theories we have outlined.

3.1 *The ethnography of speaking*

Issues

The term 'ethnography of speaking' was developed by Hymes (1962) to account for the language behaviour of a particular society. The notion has been further extended by Gumperz and Hymes and their associates (1972) and by Bauman and Sherzer (1974). Ethnography, the detailed study of a society or a group in its own terms, had used language as *evidence* of patterns of behaviour. But before Hymes, language had not been seen as *creating* activities in its own right. Hymes called such language-created activities 'speech events' and isolated seven features which would need to be specified in order to describe a speech event: topic, setting, role, status, channel, medium, and message.

Hymes was concerned to identify features which would account for the different ways in which speech events are organised in different cultural communities. He argued that speaking, like the linguistic code, is patterned and functions as part of our cultural system: 'People who enact different cultures do to some extent experience distinct communicative systems, not merely the same natural communicative condition with different customs affixed' (Hymes 1966). In other words, there are rules of use which any member of a community needs to know and use if they are to be communicatively competent. Hymes developed the notion of communicative competence in order to identify what speakers need to have in addition to grammatical competence if they are to be recognised as members of a speech community.

The rules of use are specific to a particular culture, and so all language behaviour is culturally relative. This notion of cultural relativity is central to our understanding of social appropriacy, of the conventions and patterns of typical encounters within a given speech community.

Hymes's idea of conversational rules needs some further explanation. He uses the term 'rule' to mean 'social norm' or convention and not in the sense of a grammatical rule which describes an invariant, well-formed structure that all native speakers would find acceptable, such as the agreement between subject and verb. Hymes's rules are well illustrated in, for example, 'co-occurrence rules' (Ervin-Tripp 1972), which regulate message type according to speaker status and role and range from acceptable collocation to appropriate register. The flouting of a co-occurrence rule is obvious in this utterance: 'I'm greatly honoured to be invited to bring my missis.'

Relevance to ILT

The ethnography of speaking provided an explicit statement about the social and cultural aspects of speaking. It showed practitioners that language was 'undivorceable from its social context' (Hymes 1974) and so could be meaningfully taught only within a social context.

The notion of communicative competence has, as is widely recognised, transformed language teaching. Given that ILT was training in the workplace, communicative competence was specifically developed in relation to the identified speech events of the workplace setting. For example, typically:

Role	Status	Setting	Topic	Medium/ Channel	Message
Super-visor Worker	Relatively high Low	Super-visor's office	Making a com-plaint	Face-to-face oral commu-nication	'I've come to find out why I've not been given any overtime for a month ...'

(NCILT 1976)

The sociolinguistic variables identified by Hymes helped ILT to develop 'sociolinguistic competence' (Canale and Swain 1980) in learners so that they could be effective in any aspect of negotiations at work.

Hymes's focus on the cultural and linguistic relativity of language use encouraged ILT to compare and contrast interactions between two (or more) native speakers and between native and non-native speakers to attempt to isolate what rules of use learners might be bringing with them from their first language. This analytical approach to the development of awareness in second-language learners is discussed in detail in Chapter 5.

Limitations for ILT

The ethnography of speaking, as developed by Hymes, left several questions unanswered. First, he and other ethnographers (e.g. Frake 1972; Keenan 1975) tended to describe the more formal and public speech events such as sermons, public meetings and other ritual activities. Or they chose everyday events, such as asking for a drink (Frake 1972), but in a culture perceived as unfamiliar and exotic. However, these strange or ritual happenings seemed to have little relevance in the workplace. We needed to know more about ordinary, everyday encounters such as taking instructions, making conversation or explaining a personal problem.

Second, Hymes's approach was essentially correlational. He correlated the social and cultural features of a particular event with the linguistic features of participants' talk. In other words, given a certain setting, role and topic – for example, a group of supervisors discussing quality with the departmental manager – we can anticipate what the socially appropriate language behaviour will be in terms of who talks when about what. But this does not help us to understand in detail what happens in the interaction. In particular, it does not help us to understand how speakers make sense of each other moment by moment, by drawing on their linguistic, cultural and social knowledge, or how the whole event is interpreted by different speakers.

Third, the notion of 'competence' in communicative competence has become somewhat confused. Both Hymes and other writers have often conflated the notion of competence as the knowledge of how to do something with the ability actually to do it. So both performance and competence are often implied in the notion of communicative competence. Language pedagogy has tended to maintain this confusion. Most language teaching, including most ILT work, has focused on communicative performance rather than communicative competence in the sense of knowledge about communicative use. However, ILT also attempted to develop communicative competence through awareness exercises and analysis of contrastive interations. We could not assume that language learners had this competence or would make connections between performance and competence without these connections being made explicit. Some linguists, such as Halliday (1978), would not support the distinction; but in pedagogic terms, alerting learners to competence and performance as separate notions helped, indirectly, to raise the question of choice. If learners acquired the cultural and social knowledge for a particular event, and the skills required to perform in that event, they could, to some extent, choose how far they wished to adjust their language to the socially defined expectations for participating in that event.

3.2 Pragmatics

Issues

Pragmatics, unlike the ethnography of speaking, is not concerned with the interactive norms of particular communities. It is concerned, at a more general and philosophical level, with trying to understand and explain how people 'mean' to each other. Meaning here is used in an active sense, as Halliday uses it in his study of child language development (1975). In learning how to talk, children learn how to mean; it is these ways of meaning, rather than ways of speaking, which are significant.

Pragmatics is concerned with speaker meaning and not utterance meaning, and as such adds a crucial dimension to the traditional studies of language in terms of syntax, phonology and semantics. There has been considerable discussion as to the extent to which pragmatics and semantics can be seen as different since they are both descriptions of meaning. A useful position to take is that of Levinson (1983), who suggests that if semantics is defined in terms of truth propositions then pragmatics is clearly not simply an extended semantics.

Pragmatics goes beyond this definition of semantics in two important ways. First, it is concerned with meaning in context; second, it is about speaker/listener intentions. So pragmatics is concerned not with syntax and the literal meaning of words but with meaning intended by the speaker and interpreted by the listener.

Since pragmatics is centrally concerned with meaning in context, the notion of context must be briefly discussed. For linguists, 'context' consists of those aspects of a situation which determine the form and meaning of utterances. Some linguists make a distinction between linguistic context and social context. The linguistic context is constructed from the linguistic elements of an utterance. So the choice of a particular linguistic form is determined by the linguistic environment in which it occurs. For example, speakers are more likely to use 's' than 'is' if the preceding word ends in a vowel, as in 'He's a doctor' (Labov 1969). The social context has been defined in terms of domains such as the home, the school and the press, and in terms of the situational variables discussed by Hymes. However, defining context in this way ignores many of the complexities of context in real interaction. Linguistic and social context, defined as a set of variable features, do not simply determine a speaker's choice. Levinson (1983), in a review of the literature on context, concludes that we have no very clear idea of what it is except that it is 'whatever (excluding semantics) produces inferences. The great difficulty, as Levinson suggests, is analysing what produces inferences for particular individuals in a particular interaction.

So any understanding of meaning in context needs to take account of the unique way in which an interaction is built up turn by turn, and to relate this to the processes of inferencing that are based on general maxims, principles or assumptions. We now return to a discussion of speaker intention.

The notion of speaker intention is at the heart of speech-act theory, first developed by Austin (1962) and extended in considerably more detail by Searle (1969, 1975). Their central argument is that language performs social acts. When we say 'I warn you' or 'I promise you' or 'I apologise, those words themselves are the warning, the promise or the apology. Words don't just say things; they do things. And often what words do is not what is contained in the surface message but is in the conventional meaning associated with the words, as in all the typical polite-request forms like 'Can you shut the window?', where the surface message is a question but the intended meaning is a request. Utterances, Austin proposed, can perform three kinds of act:

locutionary   that is, the sense of sounds that indicate that something is being said;

illocutionary   that is, the social act performed by the speaker or what the speaker intended to do, such as accept, request, deny etc.;

perlocutionary   that is, the effect the utterance has on the speaker, for example to outrage, persuade or gain agreement.

Since language performs social acts, speaker intention and how it is interpreted by the hearer depends upon social context. For example, where a speaker has a much higher status and more powerful role than the listener a request such as 'Can we close down the packing line for an hour?' may well be justifiably interpreted as an instruction. Speaker intention also depends upon what Searle called 'felicity conditions'. He illustrates how these conditions work with the act of promising (Searle 1969). For instance, 'I promise I'll never forget' is a promise if the hearer hopes the speaker will not forget but it becomes a threat if the hearer has committed some unforgivable crime. In the first case the felicity conditions for making a promise have been fulfilled, but in the second they have not. In addition, Searle's notion of indirect speech acts has helped to identify the extent to which ordinary interaction is indirect. Searle made a distinction between direct speech acts, e.g. 'Pass me the paper' or 'I name this ship *Invincible*', and indirect acts, where the intention of the speaker is not comprehensively encoded in the words of the utterance, e.g. 'Could you pass me the paper?' In fact, as Levinson and others have shown, most speech acts are indirect and that is what produces so many pragmatic problems for learners.

More recent work on pragmatics has been concerned with discovering how speakers make sense to each other. In an interaction, listeners and speakers make sense or try to make sense of what is going on not simply by decoding the meaning of the words and their functions but by integrating what they hear with what they assume the interaction is all about. So they have to bring what Gumperz has described as sociocultural knowledge into their interpretation. The study of pragmatics is useful in helping to explain how the particular and the individual works with the general and the systematic. Meaning can be interpreted only in a particular context, but it is possible to get the meaning only because the processes of inferencing that are required are based on general maxims or principles.

In *Pragmatics* (1983) Levinson sees these inferential processes as systematic. For example, listeners can identify a speakers' intention to request or refuse from the language itself and from the placing of the utterance in a particular context. Similarly, there are certain presuppositions about the way speakers communicate which people will generally rely on.

The clearest statement of the assumptions people make in order to get on with a conversation are Grice's maxims of cooperation (1975). Grice's maxims are derived from his notion that conversations are cooperative events and are organised around a cooperative principle. These maxims are:

Quantity: say as much as but no more than is necessary;
Quality: do not say what is false, be truthful;
Relation: be relevant;
Manner: be clear, unambiguous, brief and orderly.

Grice suggests that people can communicate together because they follow these maxims. If the hearer believes one of these maxims has been violated, they will search for a reason. This process of going beyond the speaker's apparent intention Grice calls 'implicature' (1981). For example, if an employer receives a reference for a job applicant which states only that the applicant has worked for a certain number of years and has always been punctual, the employer might well consider that the maxim of quantity has been flouted since the reference is clearly not informative. The employer is likely to implicate that the writer has been less than satisfied with the applicant's work.

The concepts of cooperation, flouting and implicature have made an important contribution to our understanding of interpretive processes, based as they are on the everyday reasoning abilities of human beings. But, as Leech (1983) and Brown and Levinson (1986) point out, people, when they interact, are motivated by politeness as well as rational efficiency. So, for example, we frequently flout the maxims of quality, quantity and manner in order to be polite, as in Leech's example 'Cold in here, isn't it?', where the maxim of quantity is flouted.

Brown and Levinson are concerned with the universal phenomenon of politeness in interaction (1978). Any act of communication is an imposition on the other. So, they maintain, there is the same strategic orientation to preserve 'face' across all cultures. In other words, in every act of communication, people are trying to have an effect on the other person, make contact, emphasise what they have in common, but also simultaneously to protect themselves, not to give too much away, to be autonomous. Building on the work of the linguist Robin Lakoff and the sociologist Erving Goffman, Brown and Levinson describe these two basic and in some ways conflicting orientations as 'positive and negative face'. In order to accommodate everyone's positive face, there are a range of positive politeness strategies which emphasise what the speaker and hearer have in common, minimise the social distance between them and take a lot for granted about the other person (see Data 2.2 above). These strategies will include being informal and joking, exaggerating your interest and sympathy and approval of the other, and assuming you know a lot about the other person. Likewise, there are a range of negative politeness strategies which both protect the speaker and show respect for the listener. These strategies do not make any assumptions and tend to soften or 'hedge' statements and requests so that they appear less direct and imposing. Typical strategies are to be pessimistic ('I don't suppose you could ...'), to be more impersonal, or to use softening or hedging markers such as 'I think', 'sort of', 'in a sense'.

Positive politeness strategies are more likely to be direct and negative politeness strategies to be indirect. When a speaker is concerned only with the goals of the interaction and not with face-saving, what they say will be absolutely direct – or 'bald-on-record'. When a speaker shouts a warning or an instruction, for example, that will be bald-on-record. At the other extreme, the speaker may be so concerned about face-saving that they go 'off record' and do not say what they have to say at all, or say it only very ambiguously. They may hint, not complete what they have to say, be vague, ironic or metaphorical.

Brown and Levinson propose, therefore, that all speakers operate along a continuum from bald-on-record, through positive politeness, to negative politeness and off-record strategies. By comparing the use of politeness strategies in three different languages they have argued very convincingly that many of these strategies are universal and that even the linguistic forms used are often similar. For example, both English and Tamil use the same type of request form to instruct politely and indirectly, as in 'Can you shut the door?'

It is important to stress the universality of these strategies, what Goffman calls 'face-work' (Goffman, 1967, 1981), because they can provide a common set of understandings for those learning English and those on cross-cultural training courses. It is equally important to appreciate that different groups and societies may use quite different means for achieving these strategies. Brown and Levinson propose three factors which may affect how face-threatening an interaction is. These are, first, social distance, that is how well you know someone; second, relative power and status; and third, how a particular imposition is ranked in a specific culture, for example borrowing money from a member of your family. In different societies, there are different assumptions about how to behave towards people you know or who are more powerful than you, and there are different assumptions about what is reasonable and unreasonable behaviour in, for example, making requests, asking for favours or talking about yourself.

So, although the use of deference is a universal strategy, *when* to be deferential and *how* deferential to be will often be culture-specific. Once again, the notion of linguistic and cultural relativity is explored but, in this case, in the context of universal strategies.

Brown and Levinson's work shows a major development in pragmatics in that the philosophical work on speaker/hearer intention /interpretation is allied to a sociological and anthropological concern with how interaction relates to social structures. Another important break from the earlier philosophical tradition is their use of data from three quite unrelated languages, two of them, Tamil and Tzeltal, non-European.

Relevance to ILT

Speech-act theory had an early direct influence on ILT work and on language teaching generally through the Council of Europe's *Threshold Level* (van Ek 1975) and Wilkins's functional taxonomy in *Notional Syllabuses* (1976) and the work-related language materials for doctor–patient communication (Candlin, Leather and Bruton 1974). It was not surprising that speech-act theory was so readily taken up by teachers since it accorded with their intuitions about language use and provided a rationale for developing an approach based on speakers' intention rather than speakers' grammar. Labels such as 'greet', 'request', 'report' are part of our everyday repertoire, and teachers did not feel the need to study speech-act theory in detail once the notion of performing functional acts had been accepted.

So, linked to Halliday's more general notion of language performing basic functions, speech-act theory encouraged teachers to use a functional analysis of interactions as the means of making language meaningful to learners. This still remains a generally useful way of looking at more routine interactions. For example, it is possible to teach interaction by teaching typical sequences such as: CRITICISE, APOLOGISE, INSTRUCT, REASSURE. Speech-act theory helped to make this kind of simple pattern of interaction accessible to the more elementary learner, and helped the learner to look behind the words at speaker intention.

It was also useful to introduce these functional categories in cross-cultural training for white staff. They were helped to see that there is no one-to-one correspondence between form and function and that many of our speech acts are indirect. This was an important tool in challenging the negative ethnic stereotypes based on workers' behaviour. For example, 'You're late, you know' said by a supervisor to a worker was routinely interpreted as a criticism by white staff but they could be helped to see that the utterance was in the form of a propositional statement and that it was the social context that triggered their interpretation of it. Language learners could interpret this indirectly conveyed criticism as a literal statement that they were late and not perceive it as a request for an apology.

The centrality of context in the field of pragmatics has had a more recent influence on ILT, particularly in cross-cultural training. We recognised that context was not something fixed which determined or influenced the interaction, but something created in the interaction turn by turn as speaker and listener interpreted and responded to each other. In other words, context did not simply embed meaning and explain 'what X meant by X' but was part of 'how Y came to be produced' (Haberland and May 1977).

Pragmatics was useful in helping us to understand what interactants can and cannot do if they are to communicate meaningfully together. In other words, there may be systematic pragmatic constraints which are as binding as syntactic or phonological constraints. Levinson describes some of these. He shows that people from the same cultural background will tend to make the same inferences about a particular conversation, for example about the other's status, about the time and space in which the interaction and the topics discussed take place and about the amount of shared knowledge speakers have of a subject. All these inferences can be traced to what was actually said and, in turn, these inferences are derived from general principles such as Grice's cooperative principle.

If this is the case, then pragmatics offers the language teacher and learner conversational principles which do not rely on general notions of appropriacy to explain why certain utterances are or are not acceptable. Instead, learners and teachers can look at the systematic pragmatic constraints on speaker performance in specific contexts. In other words, we can systematically trace how speakers give evidence of understanding each other by looking in detail at how speakers make inferences from the facts that trigger them. For example, an initial 'Well' can trigger an inference in the listener that what is going to be said is relevant to the previous speaker's utterance even if there is nothing in the form of the utterance to indicate this, and that 'well' has a pragmatic meaning implying that the speaker may not be in agreement with the previous speaker.

Grice and, more recently, Brown and Levinson have linked the general, philosophical issues of meaning and interpretation to social issues and the interpretive processes of people in interaction. So teachers could explicitly address these issues in learner performance. For example, an analysis of the Jobcentre interview given at the beginning of Chapter 1 (Data 1.2) would show that the job-seeker flouted the maxims of relevance and quantity because the adviser did not make explicit the purpose of her questions.

Politeness was a major preoccupation in early ILT work, so Brown and Levinson's work found a ready response. Their work on politeness strategies contributed to our understanding of inter-ethnic communication in two ways. First, in its emphasis on universals in politeness, it was an important reminder that many discourse strategies are universal and need to be made visible so that learners can rely on this shared knowledge when communicating in a second language. Second, it illustrated the cultural differences in when and how these strategies were used and so introduced into pragmatics issues of cultural and linguistic relativity.

In inter-ethnic communication, when politeness strategies are used differently, they can affect the whole way the interaction goes and the judgements that both sides make of each other. This is particularly true in critical events such as job interviews. Here, a white interviewer may use positive politeness strategies such as first names, jokes and an informal style in the expectation that the ethnic-minority candidate will do the same. However, ethnic-minority candidates may well have quite different expectations about what strategies to use towards someone in a powerful position. They may wish to use negative politeness strategies in which they say little, do not assume they know what the interviewer wants and do not attempt to 'sell themselves'.

Brown and Levinson make the point that many exchanges are simply not comprehensible without understanding the concepts of face and face-threatening acts. This is an even more important issue in inter-ethnic communication, where lack of familiarity or distrust of each other's strategies and how they are differently used can lead to subtle and unconscious forms of discrimination. For example, the closing sequence of a workplace interaction in which a request or complaint has been made will frequently include a statement from the supervisor or person in authority designed to reassure and to close the interaction, such as 'I'll see what I can do' or I'll talk to X about this'. Such a statement is designed to appeal to the positive face of the requester and save the face of the supervisor in so far as it defends his or her position as someone with at least a degree of power and responsibility. However, it is often perceived by ethnic-minority workers as an assurance that something will be done, and if there is no favourable outcome they feel let down and often discriminated against. So an utterance which functions primarily as a face strategy can be perceived, where there are cultural differences, as an explicit undertaking to make something happen.

Limitations for ILT

Recently, there have been many criticisms of speech-act theory (see Levinson 1983; Stubbs 1983) and, as language teachers, we have become increasingly aware of its weaknesses in complex interactions. The most telling criticisms are, first, that we can only assign a speech act to an utterance in an arbitrary way and, since what the speaker intended depends on that particular context, there can be an endless proliferation of speech acts. For example, the utterance 'But I needed to get the key', in different contexts, might be an act to defend, vindicate, apologise, exonerate, excuse, or plead. Second, since speech acts have been dealt with at the level of single utterances, assigning a speech act tells us little about how the conversation actually proceeds. Third, since language is multifunctional, a particular utterance may perform several speech acts simultaneously. Finally, speech-act theory has been criticised for assuming that speech acts are universal. In other words, Searle seems to assume that there is such a thing as a 'warning' with which we would all agree. However, shared notions of what language in context constitutes a warning depend upon the shared knowledge that communities develop in interaction.

Despite the influence of Grice's work on our understanding of conversation, there are limitations to his work. First, in the concept that the cooperative principle and the maxims derived from it are universal. There is now some evidence that these maxims do not account for the ways people achieve conversational goals in all cultures. Communicators within a mono-cultural group are likely to share a perception of what is relevant or how explicit it is necessary to be in conveying a particular message. In inter-ethnic communication the two sides cannot assume that they share the same ways of judging relevance or the same assumptions about what needs to be said and what can be left unsaid. If notions of being conversationally cooperative differ between different cultures, then wrong inferences can easily be drawn. Second, as Taylor and Cameron (1987) point out, Gricean maxims are presented as imperatives – for example, 'Be relevant' – and these sound like prescriptive norms. There is a danger for teachers that they might be taken as such and be imposed on learners when, in reality, first-language speakers of English do not themselves always follow them.

Brown and Levinson's explorations of politeness and face remain very influential but, as they concede in a reissue of the 1978 article as a book (Brown and Levinson 1987), some of their assertions need modification. Their main criticism of the 1978 work is that the politeness strategies are presented as too categorical. In other words, they now consider that the complexity of the reasoning process which individuals use to interpret speaker intent was underestimated. For example, a negative politeness strategy such as 'Be pessimistic about the success of a face-threatening act' is not always polite: 'an utterance like "You don't want to pass the salt" should be polite; that it is not, of course, is due to the fact that it attributes impolite desires to the addressee' (Brown and Levinson 1987). As such, it contrasts with such negative politeness strategies as 'I wonder if you could possibly ...', which fits the definition of being pessimistic about the face-threatening act.

While the basic theoretical framework remains a powerful tool for understanding social interaction, some caution is needed in interpreting the politeness strategies. The Brown and Levinson framework is also somewhat limited by using examples at the level of individual speech acts rather than at the level of discourse, and because relatively little attention is given to cross-cultural differences as compared with universals in politeness strategies.

3.3 Social semiotics

Issues

We have already seen how two traditions, anthropology and philosophy, have engaged with the issue of language as a social process. But neither ethnography nor early studies in pragmatics developed a detailed theory of how language structure relates to social meanings. In four key books in the 1970s (1973, 1975, 1976, 1978) and in the more recent functional grammar (1985), Halliday has developed a theory of language as a system of meanings. Halliday's central theme is that language must be looked at as meaning rather than structure. If language is seen as a system of meanings, then its social role can be understood. Language not only reflects and transmits the values and relationships of a society; it actively creates and maintains them. So all the time we are getting things done with language; we are creating a piece of reality and sanity for ourselves. We are constructing social reality (Berger and Luckmann 1967), in the sense that we are making relationships and establishing roles and identities in the choices of language that we make and our oritentation to the world consists, in part, in our language behaviour. We are also acting out the social systems and structures which help us, as a society, to order the world and make sense of it, even if, as with many power structures, we do not benefit from them.

So, Halliday argues, it is our habits of meaning rather than our habits of talking which matter, and this has a profound effect on our understanding of second-language acquisition (SLA) among adults. In adult SLA, 'it's not simply a case of saying – all I've got to do is to map a new set of semantic structures onto the same semiotic model of the situation ... an assumption a lot of people make in practice, saying in effect: I will assume that we all have the same meanings and I'll simply have to reword' (Baynham 1986).

These habits of meaning have been built up through contact with those we regularly associate with: 'our habits of meaning are those of the people we regularly identify ourselves with, the primary reference groups that define our semiotic environment' (Halliday 1978). Meaning, therefore, is relative to the particular cultural group we are in. And the greater the differences between cultural groups, the greater the differences in ways of meaning. It is for this reason, Halliday argues, that there are much stronger reactions to different ethnic styles of speaking than to different regional styles of speaking, despite the fact that a regional style may be a lot less like the standard variety in terms of grammar, lexis or phonology than the ethnic style.

Different ethnic styles reflect different ways of meaning, and that is threatening.

Halliday's ideas on linguistic/cultural relativity are based on the work of Benjamin Lee Whorf, particularly Whorf's work on culturally relative grammars, Whorf suggested the notion of areal affinitiy – that is, that there are cultural areas which produce ways of meaning. So, for example, we can talk of Standard Average European. In other words, the European languages as a group are used by speakers of these languages to convey meaning in largely similar ways. For example, the relationship between such features as word order, the use of reference to create cohesion and establish context, and the use of intonation and stress and other aspects of prosody to show emphasis and contrast will be broadly similar in these languages. Halliday quotes research which shows that non-Swahili speakers whose language was not related to Swahili but came from the same cultural area found Swahili easier than English.

Halliday's study of child language development has shown how fundamental to early ways of meaning is the use of prosody. For Halliday, and others working on speech in interaction, prosody includes intonation, pausing, pitch, loudness and rhythm, and stress as a perceptual category. Children learn to control certain intonation patterns and pitch and volume long before they have even the first words of the adult language. This shows how deeply embedded in the subconscious are these early rhythms and tunes and so how difficult they are to change when learning a second language. Since they are so deeply 'owned', asking people to learn and use the prosodic systems of the second language may well challenge their sense of self.

In his study of how children learn to mean, Halliday developed further his work on the functions of language. He showed that children learn a functional system of communicating long before they can use the linguistic code of an adult language. As children, we learn to do things with a system which eventually becomes language; at the same time, and crucially, we are learning how adults use language to transmit, maintain and, at an individual level, create social values. So the process of language development and socialisation go hand in hand. For adults learning a second language there is no such simple process of language socialisation.

Halliday identified three basic functions: the *ideational* – that is, the conveying of experiences and ideas; the *interpersonal*; and the *textual* – that is, those aspects of language which make it hold together as chunks of discourse or text (see the section on discourse cohesion and coherence below p. 75). These three functions operate together in any situation and it is by specifying what the context, role-relationship and mode of communicating are that we can predict what language will be used. So, like Hymes, Halliday is concerned with how language is determined by and determines situations. He suggests that many transactions are patterned and predictable:

> Much speech does take place in fairly restricted contexts where the options are limited and the meaning potential rather closely specifiable ... Many of the routines of the working day represent situation types in which the language is by no means restricted as a whole, the transactional meanings are not closed, but nevertheless there are certain definable patterns, certain options which typically come into play.
>
> (Halliday 1973)

Halliday's work on language and social meaning coincided with considerable interest among sociologists in the ways in which social structures and systems are created and maintained, at a micro level, through interaction. Some of this work is described in sections 3.4 and 3.5 of this chapter.

Relevance to ILT

Halliday's emphasis on meaning rather than structure and on the functional nature of language use was very persuasive. First, Halliday's notion of language actively creating and affirming values and relationships was a most valuable pointer to the relationship between language and power,which was a major concern of ILT. Second, this approach accorded with our intuitions that language development could not be isolated from the process of socialisation if adult workers were to gain some measure of communicative power in the workplace. Halliday's theory, that meaning is culturally and linguistically relative (developed from Whorf's work), gave insights into the difficulties both sides perceive in inter-ethnic communication. In particular, this work was relevant to our understanding of why miscommunication appeared to be more frequent with South Asian bilingual speakers than with bilingual speakers with a European background. Halliday suggests that at the fundamental processing level of segmenting utterances into units of information and tying language to context, European languages will be broadly similar whereas other groups of languages are likely to do this basic processing in a variety of quite different ways.

Halliday's work on early child language development was influential in helping us to understand the issues of teaching prosody to adult second-language learners. Since aspects of the prosodic system are learned in the early months and prosodic knowledge remains, at an unconscious level, an essential part of how people mean to each other, it was important that we understood how different prosodic systems could create miscommunication. It was equally important to hold off from attempting to teach English prosody to adult learners but to take an alternative approach which focused on raising awareness of different systems and on teaching compensating strategies, such as lexicalising information otherwise conveyed prosodically, when English prosody proved difficult to notice and use.

Halliday's three basic functions of language and his notion of patterns of interaction were helpful in the development of elementary and post-elementary language materials. This notion helped the language teacher to identify key situations, meaningful to the learners, and to show the regularities that were likely to occur. The three basic functions influenced the design of post-elementary materials (see Chapter 6) in the division of the materials into discourse, transactional and information units.

Limitations for ILT
Halliday's influence on ILT was in helping to organise ideas about the social nature of language. His detailed data-based work on intonation and child language socialisation needed to be mediated and reinterpreted through the theories and data-driven work of those studying adult language socialisation and inter-ethnic communication, notably Gumperz (see section 3.6 below). In other words, Halliday's functional approach to language could not, by itself, explain the difficulties faced in adult SLA or in inter-ethnic communication but it contributed powerfully to our appreciation of the issues and influenced the work in discourse analysis which was to have a significant impact on ILT work.

3.4 Discourse analysis

Over the last twenty years, discourse has been defined in a number of ways depending upon discipline background and specific orientation:

(i)   Linguistic units above the level of sentence (Sinclair; Coulthard; van Dijk; Stubbs).
(ii) Language in its social context (Brown and Yule; van Dijk).
(iii) Strategies for interpreting interactive signs and conventions (Gumperz).
(iv) Cohesion and coherence (Halliday and Hasan; Tannen).
(v)   Language as the means for organising social, political and economic values (Foucault).
(vi) Language as reflecting and maintaining power relations (Fowler, Hodge, Kress and Trew; Fairclough).

In this section we will examine three different approaches to discourse analysis. First, we will examine Sinclair and Coulthard's focus on structure and rules, on the idea that there is a 'grammar' to discourse. Second, we will consider a socially-oriented speaker perspective on discourse analysis and consider how notions such as 'schema', 'topic' and 'cohesion' provide descriptive tools for understanding how people make sense to each other in interaction. Third, we will examine critical discourse analysis, which aims to go beyond description to explanation.

Discourse structure and discourse rules

Sinclair and Coulthard's analysis of classroom discourse (1975) was the first discourse analysis to be widely read by applied linguists and teachers. This work and the studies by Brazil, Coulthard and Johns (1980) and Coulthard and Montgomery (1981) were attempting to establish a grammatical model for discourse. Influenced by Halliday's systemic/functional grammar, they established a ranking system for classroom discourse with the **lesson** as the highest rank and the **act** as the lowest rank. Through a continuous process of classification, they showed how each level of the hierarchy fitted into the one above or below to form a discourse structure. One of the most useful levels in the system is the **exchange** – the minimum unit of interaction. At the level of exchange, classroom discourse appears highly predictable: the teacher *initiates*, the pupil *responds*, the teacher gives *feedback*.

Sinclair and Coulthard, then, aimed to show that discourse has a predictable structure. At the lowest level of the hierarchy, within this structure, the **move** and the **act** are defined by their function in the discourse. This theory differed from speech-act theory in that the acts and moves were not based on intention, which as has been suggested could lead to an endless proliferation of speech acts, but were fixed by their position in the discourse, for example to *respond* or *mark a boundary*. In this way they hoped to produce only a small number of categories to generate a large number of structures.

Closely allied to the notion that discourse has predictable structures is the notion of 'well-formedness' in discourse (Stubbs 1981, 1983). A well-formed discourse, Stubbs argues, is governed by rules which determine what people consider allowable in discourse. Stubbs concedes that these rules are not similar to grammatical rules because they can be used strategically; he also recognises that in discourse there will always be considerable indirectness which allows for ambiguity and imprecision – in fact, 'without such imprecision life in the social world would be impossible' (Stubbs 1983).

Nevertheless, he maintains that by looking at repairs in conversation it is possible to uncover people's concept of rule-governed, well-formed discourse.

Socially-orientated discourse analysis

Schema and frame

Central to a more socially-orientated approach to discourse analysis is the study of how people make sense to each other as they communicate. This type of analysis is concerned not with attempting to establish rules for a well-formed discourse but with the processes of self-presentation, interpretation and inference which people use to maintain discourse and make it understandable and relevant. Two key concepts, 'schema' and 'frame', have been borrowed by discourse analysis from other disciplines. The term schema originated in cognitive psychology (Bartlett 1932) and has recently been widely used by those working in artificial intelligence. It is used to describe the set of expectations based on prior experience about events, objects and settings which people bring to an interaction. For example, in a white British counselling interview, the client's schema about the encounter will usually lead them to expect that they will do a lot of the talking to present and evaluate their case and that they will receive some general advice and encouragement or reassurance as well as specific help. The focus in 'schema' has been on knowledge structures. These structures form the background knowledge that we bring to an event and which has generally been described in terms of fixed knowledge or 'scripts', in the sense that we know what a restaurant script would be like. For example, van Dijk (1977) describes the pattern of communicative exchanges in a restaurant which starts with being shown a table and ends with paying the bill and, possibly, being ushered out.

However, a socially relevant discourse analysis has needed to extend this notion of the schema beyond something fixed and cognitive. First, the notion needs to include attitudes, values and orientation to the world, both cultural and individual. Second, the original concept of the schema was of a set of knowledge structures brought to a text or interaction, which did not account for schemata changing or being modified in interaction.

The notion of 'frame' is useful here, both to extend our understanding of 'schema' and to help account for the processes of adjustment that occur as people try to make sense of each other. In much of the literature the notions of schema and frame are used interchangeably. However, two interpretations of the term 'frame' originate in very different traditions from that of cognitive psychology.

The first is the idea of an 'interpretive frame'. This was developed by the anthropologist Bateson. He came upon this idea while watching monkeys at the zoo. How did they know, when they were fooling around, hitting each other, that this was a game? He suggests that they use interpretive frames to evaluate what is going on or at least to help them understand the messages conveyed. He suggests that people also use interpretive frames to delimit a set of messages or meaningful actions. So, at any point in an interaction, we are identifying whether it is, for example, an interrogation frame, a justification frame, an advice frame. The frame alerts the listener to what is going on at each stage of the interaction.

Bateson (1972) suggests here that all communication has a dual nature: that it both conveys a message and conveys a message about the message – a metamessage. Communication and the learning that is done through communication always have this double aspect. This is why when we overhear a fragment of conversation we can so often infer the context from it, and, conversely, when we are given a context we can normally agree on the kind of interaction to take place.

The dual nature of language is, of course, central to speech–act theory as well. Bateson extends the concept of the metacommunicative nature of language beyond the level of utterance to show how a sequence within discourse is framed or given a metamessage which both contains and integrates the exchange. The 'interpretive frame' notion helps to expand the notion of schema to include interactional knowledge, and it also helps to connect the sets of expectations people bring to an interaction with the inferential processes activated from moment to moment to make sense of the interaction.

The second notion of frame is that developed by the sociologist Goffman in his study of face-to-face interaction as a domain in its own right, a domain which he called 'the interaction order' (Goffman 1983; Drew and Wootton 1988). While not underestimating the importance of the schemata that people bring to interaction, Goffman's main interest was in the detailed ways in which we present ourselves to others.

Goffman's writing on the presentation of self was not confined to the mechanisms of interaction, such as who gets to speak when. He viewed interaction as a moral activity in which participants are concerned with such matters as how showing involvement conveys politeness, or how we monitor effectiveness or lack of it, sincerity or fraud, as the interaction progresses. Like Bateson's, Goffman's 'frame' defines a particular moment of social reality. So, for example, the staging of a public lecture constitutes a frame, but lecturers can break that frame themselves by introducing another: for example, 'I haven't got time to do all of this so I'll just give you the conclusions'. This frame then sets up a slightly different situation from the previous one. Frames are not derived from what people have in their heads but are created by the situation as it unfolds. They both create the situation and constrain it.

The notions of schema and frame together provide an analytic tool which combines cognitive, interpretive and moral processes to account for how people can bring shared meaning to an encounter. The notion of frame as developed by Bateson and by Goffman also helps to describe the interaction between what is brought to an encounter and how people orientate themselves towards and so make sense of each other in it. A good example of schema mismatch and consequent wrong interpretation of frame occurs in the Jobcentre interview briefly analysed in Chapter 1 (Data 1.2).

Topic
In addition to the presentational and interpretive work that speakers must do to interact together socially, they will also be exchanging information and so talking on a topic. It has been notoriously difficult to define where a topic begins and ends, particularly in informal conversation. This section will not attempt to discuss the issues of definition but will concentrate on two issues: topical relevance and involvement, and topical control.

Everyone has had the sensation of wondering why something is being talked about or reintroduced. Once a particular topic has been initiated, both sides expect what is said next to be relevant in the sense that speakers expect each other to be cooperative and so make connections with what has just been said (see section 3.2 above). Listeners and speakers tend actively to contribute to making the topic relevant by using a number of devices. One of these is topic collaboration, which involves speakers picking up and extending a topic either by explicitly referring to some aspect of it or by indicating in some more indirect way that the listener should interpret their utterances as relevant. A specific aspect of topic collaboration is topic incorporation. Here the speaker responds collaboratively by speaking on the topic and then incorporates this topic into what they wish to talk about.

Topic incorporation is an important way of gaining topic control. A skilful use of topic incorporation means that the speaker can 'hold the floor' and can dominate the conversation both by talking more and by talking about the topic of their choice. The piece of data 'In the Mill', analysed at the beginning of this chapter (Data 2.1), is a telling example of this. The manager deliberately incorporates the Asian worker's topic, which is an attempt to reassure the manager about 'next time', into his own topic, which is a threat to sack the worker. It is important to remember that where there is inequality of power, in terms of both status and communicative power, devices such as topic incorporation often signal the opposite of a cooperative, other-orientated speaker.

Cohesion and coherence

We have looked briefly at two ways in which speakers orientate themselves towards others through the use of topic. The linguistic means for doing this and for developing the topic in longer turns of talk or in written texts have been analysed in studies of cohesion in discourse. Halliday and Hasan's study (1976) examines in detail how topic development or thematic progression is achieved through grammatical means. 'Cohesion occurs where the interpretation of some element in the discourse is dependent on that of another.' The main factors which indicate cohesion are implied semantic relationships, lexical equivalence and choice, some syntactic devices including time/place relations, logical connectors, substitution, discourse reference markers, comparison, ellipsis, structural parallelism and, finally, prosodic features.

The data from a discussion in a bus company, analysed earlier in this chapter (Data 2.4), illustrates well two different systems of cohesion used by the English conductor/trainer, K, and the bus driver, A. In lines 27–35, K uses a number of cohesive devices. He ties in his opening statement cohesively by using the deictic phrase 'that one' as

K: To answer your questions on that one. First of all, we did discuss at great length with management, as my two friends here will probably back me up on that. And management did say at that particular time, now we had a lot of conductors, did say, that yes they would cover your jobs for yer, where possible, and you would get paid the two and a half hours. That I can assure you, was said at the very very beginning.

A: Management just don't know what they fixing, what they can do in future you know.

(Data 2.4: lines 27–35)

a substitute for the noun phrase 'that point' or 'that matter' which would sum up A's previous long turn. He uses discourse markers such as 'first of all' to frame his points, and the logical connector 'and'. When he introduces the fact that discussions were held with management there is an implied semantic relationship between 'we did discuss ... with management' and the topic A has raised. The cohesion lies in the fact that K's listeners are likely to assume that the discussion was about cover and pay and not about some unrelated topic. K rounds off his turn with a further deictic pronoun, 'that', drawing the key points of the discussion with management together. K's argument is also made cohesive by the prosodic features he uses, as we have shown. A uses a mix of structural parallels and lexical juxtaposition. At lines 3, 6 and later 13, he connects his argument together with the structure 'if ... you ... turn'. However, he does not show this connection prosodically as a speaker with English as their first or dominant language would. Similarly, although A's use of lexical juxtaposition is perfectly cohesive in his system, it does not

A:	If you early turns we'll make up, er, you do first bit and second bit we will cover that.
K:	Ya.
A:	And if you middle turn, no if you late turn we make up you know middle turn.
K:	Ya.
A:	So, why they have change change mind?

(Data 2.4: lines 3–9)

have the syntactic or prosodic markers which would make it obviously cohesive to an English speaker.

Halliday and Hasan's work is primarily concerned with how grammar and lexis mark or imply cohesion. However, a piece of discourse can hang together when there are no cohesive ties provided that interactants share sufficient background knowledge and agree to make the connection. Widdowson (1978) calls this *coherence* and contrasts it with cohesion, where identifiable elements in the text relate to each other. Widdowson's now famous 'bath' example makes the point clearly:

A: That's the telephone
B: I'm in the bath
A: OK

Here, the two sides share enough knowledge to know that B is unlikely to want to get out of the bath and talk on the phone, dripping wet. So B's answer is coherent in that it acknowledges A's statement and gives an explanation as to why B is not willing to act on it. In the following example, the situation is more complicated:

A: There's a rushed job on, can you get this photocopied by two?
B: The only time I could do it is in my lunch hour
A: That's fine

B's response to A is both cohesive and coherent. However, B may find A's response only partially coherent. A replies as if B has given an unproblematic response but B is probably giving a conditional acceptance and thereby opening negotiations with A on the basis that lunch hours have certain socio-cultural assumptions attached to them. By failing to interpret B's response appropriately, A has not given B an acceptably coherent response.

So coherence is not simply a linguistic construct, but a social and cultural one. General criticisms of speakers' incoherence usually conflate features of incohesion and incoherence. The relationship between a speaker's utterances may not be marked syntactically, lexically or semantically, and so the discourse appears to lack cohesion and/or the speaker's meaning appears to have no pragmatic connection with previous utterances by the speaker or other participants in the interaction and so to lack coherence. In both cases, judgements about speakers' competence depend upon inferential processes which are themselves based on culture-specific schemata.

Critical discourse analysis

The discourse analysis discussed so far is, in the tradition of most linguistics, essentially descriptive. However, there is a group of linguists, in Britain and Australia, who have developed a 'critical linguistics'. Influenced by work in critical sociology, by the French historian Foucault (1970) and by the philosophers and sociologists Bourdieu (1977) and Habermas (1979), this group has developed critical discourse analysis which aims to go beyond description of discourse to interpretation and explanation of why discourses are produced.

Critical discourse analysis is a socially and politically committed analysis in which language is understood and explained in terms of its key role in maintaining power relations. Language is described and explained as 'an instrument of control as well as communication' (Kress and Hodge 1979). Language is never neutral but always embodies ideologies which are themselves the fabric of power relations and social struggle: 'Language is both a site of and a stake in class struggle and those who exercise power through language must constantly be involved in struggle with others to defend (or lose) their position' (Fairclough 1989).

A critical approach to discourse analysis, in contrast with much other discourse and conversation analysis, is not based on informal conversations but concentrates on data where the discourse types embody the ideologies which legitimise power relations. These include news reporting, political interviews, counselling, job and police interviews, and advertising. These are examples of 'unequal encounters' in terms of power relations, or as in news reporting and advertising, of discourse manipulating while apparently informing in a natural and neutral way.

This type of data is particularly revealing, critical linguists argue, because it shows how discourse controls by consent. Readers and listeners are usually not aware that they are receiving an ideologically-based message when, for example, they read about a 'riot' rather than an 'uprising' or when the passive is used to describe how students were killed in the street so that the agent of this killing is never mentioned. Similarly, in unequal encounters, the less powerful speaker rarely questions the other's right to ask questions and define the answer in their own terms. Critical discourse analysis takes account of the linguistic code (grammar, vocabulary and prosody), of discourse processes such as cohesion, coherence and topicalisation, and of schema and discourse types. The most significant aspect of this work is the detailed description of linguistic structures and vocabulary in order to explain how discourse manipulates people and maintains the social status quo.

For example, in a comparison of reports of the Notting Hill Carnival in *The Sun* (a right-wing tabloid newspaper) and *The Morning Star* (a left-wing newspaper), Trew (in Fowler *et al.* 1979) shows how *The Sun* focuses on black people and the police acting out events whereas *The Morning Star* describes the events in terms of underlying processes, the difference being reflected in both grammar and vocabulary: for example, 'hooligans' in The Sun versus 'hooliganism' in *The Morning Star*. So the contrasting uses of the linguistic code convey two different messages: *The Sun* portrays black people as deliberate troublemakers; *The Morning Star* portrays the events as arising out of fundamental social divisions. Readers are manipulated by the language to take up a particular position on the causes of the Carnival troubles.

Similarly, in a detailed analysis of the grammar and vocabulary used by Margaret Thatcher in a radio interview, Fairclough (1989) describes and explains how she manages to combine authority with listener solidarity in contributing to the building of a new right-wing consensus in which the capitalist and worker are united in a share-owning democracy. Thatcherism is a blend of law-and-order, the free market and an appeal to ordinary people. The 'discourse of Thatcherism', Fairclough argues, helps to create this 'authoritarian populism'. Thatcher creates a discourse which draws the listeners into her world through, among other devices, a series of modal expressions and the use of 'we' (as in 'we must' or 'we have got to') and a set of assertions about people expressed in the language of ordinary people, often in clichés. The purpose of the interview is to construct listeners who are persuaded by *her* vision because she has made it *their* vision.

The kind of detailed linguistic unpacking undertaken by critical linguistics challenges what appears normal, natural and neutral, whether it is the news or job interviews. It adds an important dimension to the unitary notion of background knowledge and serves to show 'the strong and pervasive connections between linguistic structure and social structure' (Fowler *et al.* 1979).

Relevance to ILT

The discourse-analysis approach developed by Sinclair and Coulthard had an important influence on ILT in the early years. The concept of structure at the level of discourse led to the use of naturally-occurring data and its analysis in terms of patterns of sequences. We also started to look at monologues, or longer chunks of speaker utterances, in the same way (see Chapter 5, p.269).

It was clear to us, however, that we could not teach discourse as a rule-governed activity in any prescriptive sense. We attempted, at first, to teach sequences of interaction as if they were well-formed by discourse rules. But the analysis and teaching of sequences of exchanges soon became less important than discussion and joint interpretation of encounters, distinguishing between the real constraints on language choice and inference, and the possibilities available given the amount of ambiguity that exists.

The joint interpretation of encounters led us on to the notions of schema and frame. These notions have considerable explanatory power, particularly in relation to inter-ethnic communication. Understanding speakers' schemata is crucial to understanding why an interaction was effective or not and, equally important, why an interaction was *perceived* as effective and fair or not.

In inter-ethnic communication, the structured experiences of the two sides are likely to be different, and so they may bring different schemata to the encounter and consequently find themselves in different interpretive frames. Analysing differences in interpretive frames, as in the job interview data (Data 2.3), and eliciting schema differences from participants is an essential part of both cross-cultural training and language training.

One important aspect of schemata is knowing what topics are appropriate and relevant; and interlocutors, to be sharing the same interpretive frame, need to be talking topically together. Work on topic and topic control has been particularly relevant to ILT, where data for training materials focuses on the lack of equality in conversational control. Topic incorporation is an important way in which listeners can introduce a new topic and so gain topical control or 'hold the floor'. If speakers are unable to do this they may find that the conversation remains dominated by the other speaker.

This unequal distribution of talk is, of course, typical of many encounters where there are differences in power and status and in communicative power. How talk is distributed relies heavily also on the turn-taking strategies discussed in the section on conversation analysis below (3.5). In analysing inter-ethnic communication it is important to look at the relationship between topic and turn-taking if we are to understand why speakers so often feel frustrated, either because they were or felt unable to say what they wanted to say, or because the lack of collaborative sequences made them uncertain about what had been understood or agreed on. The piece of data entitled 'In the Mill', analysed above (Data 2.1) is a telling example of this.

In analysis of an inter-ethnic training appraisal review interview in a Skillcentre, Thorp (1983) showed how topic and turn-taking worked together to create an unequal and largely unsatisfactory encounter. She showed that the instructor had much longer turns at talk, introduced all his topics in his first major turn without indicating clearly when he was shifting topic, and spent the rest of the 14-minute interview recycling them. She also showed that these were not strategies the instructor used in his interviews with white native speakers. In addition, she showed that the trainee's responses and back-channel signals were not interpreted as satisfactory by the instructor. This prevented both of them from talking collaboratively, caused the instructor to use 'hyper-explanation' in which his turns became longer and longer and the content more simple, and so prevented the trainee from discussing what most concerned him. (See section 3.6, p.99, for further discussion of hyper-explanation.)

As well as giving the trainee few chances to speak, this kind of encounter will also affect how the instructor judges the trainee. Judgements about both communicative competence and more general competence will also be made on the basis of speakers' coherence and cohesion in discourse. It was important, therefore, to build into the development of discourse skills an approach which combined raising awareness of the overall structure of discourse with considerable work on the cohesive ties that hold oral discourse together.

In this way, ILT drew on a number of features of what might broadly be called descriptive discourse analysis. The influence of critical discourse analysis was less direct because much of the work in critical linguistics became familiar to the authors only in the mid-1980s. However, ILT shares with those working in critical discourse analysis a view of language and power which requires the analyst and the trainer to go beyond description to an explanation which accounts for how interaction serves to maintain existing power structures and to discriminate against the powerless.

Critical discourse analysis is significant for those working in ESL and in cross-cultural training because it confronts the teacher, the learner and the trainee with the need to become aware, and so critical, of how language functions as a social and political force. Learners and trainees can be helped to see how language embodies a specific view of reality, how language variation reflects and expresses social differences and so is inseparable from social and political factors, and how language serves to reinforce existing inequalities.

In the ESL classroom, this means that learners are not simply encouraged to learn socially appropriate language but are also encouraged to challenge the notion of appropriacy. Learners can be helped not just to extract information from a text, such as a newspaper article, but to become more critically aware of how that information is manipulated.

In cross-cultural training, particularly in relation to interviewing procedures, trainees are made aware of the fact that such procedures are not objective, and so intrinsically fair, but are based on power and specifically class-based ways of seeing the world. Not surprisingly, this approach can lead to resistance, but it appeals to professionalism and can be effective in helping trainees to be critical about their own discourse. Most professionals would consider that interviews should provide interviewees with an opportunity to present themselves and so can be encouraged to reconsider their own discourse strategies with a view to 'equalising interpretive opportunity' (Candlin 1981).

Limitations for ILT

The 'discourse rules' model of discourse analysis, although important in its focus on structure above the level of sentence, has limitations which were significant for ILT. The type of exchange structure devised by Sinclair and Coulthard did not transfer well to other types of activity or to analysing sustained discourse by a single speaker. The teacher-dominated classroom on which their analysis was based gives a much more overtly structured discourse than many other contexts and is more susceptible to this type of discourse analysis because the objectives and power relationships are well understood and mutually accepted.

It is also increasingly evident now, even in the most highly routinised activities, that the rules of discourse are not as clear or as binding as they appeared in Sinclair and Coulthard's pioneering work. That is to say, a sequence of utterances does not determine what comes next in the way that a singular subject determines a singular verb. So, it was not possible to teach a grammar of discourse in the way that it is possible to teach grammar.

The 'rules' approach to discourse and the concept of 'well-formed' discourse were too rigid and too normative to be acceptable in the language classroom. A more useful approach was to help students reason out the meaning of discourse in context, using some of the tools developed by conversation analysts (see section 3.5 below).

The other features of discourse analysis discussed above, such as schema, frame and topic, have generally been described with reference to white speakers with English as their first language. The limitation, therefore, of much discourse analysis lies in its presentation and illustration of the issues. Discourse is largely presented as being about white, usually middle-class, speakers and writers. However, beneath the surface concern lie concepts which are readily transferable to the analysis of inter-ethnic communication.

Similarly, critical discourse analysis, with some notable exceptions, although centrally concerned with language and power, has not addressed inter-ethnic issues. And it has tended to focus on how the grammar and vocabulary of speakers and writers reflect underlying ideologies rather than look at other discourse features which control communication or lead to miscommunication.

3.5 Ethnomethodology and conversation analysis

Issues

If a broad definition of discourse is taken, such as 'how humans use language to communicate' or 'all texts above the level of a sentence', then conversation analysis (CA) can be seen as part of discourse analysis. However, CA has its roots in a very different tradition from the discourse analysis of, for example, Sinclair, Coulthard and Stubbs described above.

The roots of CA, and its fundamental strengths, lie in ethno-methodology. This is an area of sociology developed by Garfinkel as a reaction to prevailing orthodoxies in sociological theory and methodology. Ethnomethodology is the study of how ordinary people use their common-sense knowledge to make sense of and respond to the activities they are involved in. The term itself combines two ideas: first 'methodology', the idea that people have a methodology to study their knowledge of ordinary affairs (although this methodology usually remains implicit), and second, 'ethno', the idea that it is the participants' own interpretation of social interaction which is significant.

Central to the theory of ethnomethodology is the assumption that people use practical reasoning to produce orderly behaviour together and that the orderly structures of social interaction are part of the wider social order. So interaction is studied as a social rather than a linguistic process. Conversation analysis developed as a specific research interest from this assumption about the competences people use to interact in an effective way, and focused on the fine-grained detail of conversation to analyse the mechanisms by which people accomplish interaction in an orderly way. The focus of CA is on the structure of conversation and how it is linked with wider social structures.

There are several basic concepts which underpin CA. First, the notion of 'accountability' among speakers. Behaviour, it is argued, is always designed to take account of how it will be interpreted and analysed. This is in contrast to much discourse analysis and sociology outside the ethnomethodological tradition which considers that behaviour is determined by rules. As Sacks (1971), one of the founders of CA, commented, listeners are constantly asking 'Why that now to me?' and speakers intuitively take account of this.

Following from the notion of accountability is the focus on 'sequential organisation' of conversation. Each contribution creates a new context which the next speaker has to take account of. So meaning is not inherent in the utterance but depends upon how it is responded to by the speaker. For example:

A: Hey, get out, there's a fire!
B: Oh yes very funny

B treats A's warning shout as a joke and so changes its meaning. Now A either has to admit that his joke did not come off or has to restate his warning in such a way as to convince B that there really is a fire.

In both 'In the Mill' (Data 2.1) and 'Job Interview' (Data 2.3), analysed earlier in this chapter, there are examples of the more powerful speaker choosing to interpret the other's meaning in a way which disadvantages the ethnic-minority worker.

Finally, and related to the two concepts just discussed, there are the concepts of 'intersubjectivity' and 'interactional accomplishment'. Intersubjectivity is the means by which individuals come to a shared interpretation of what is going on and the rules behind this activity, so that each conversation, interview, lesson, court hearing, and so on, is accomplished through interaction. The emphasis is, therefore, on conversation as a joint construction in which both sides play a part in the conversational outcomes.

The methodology used in CA has become its hallmark and has influenced other types of discourse analysis and work on pragmatics. Conversation analysts always use naturally-occurring oral data (audio-taped and, increasingly frequently, videotaped), which is transcribed in such a way that the analytic focus is on the timing and sequencing of each contributor's utterances. The analysis of the data is based solely on the evidence in the data. In other words, it is only what the speakers display to each other in linguistic, paralinguistic and non-verbal features which is available for analysis.

This is a key issue in CA. It is argued that analysts cannot be directly concerned with people's inferential processes but that it is possible to track these processes from the way in which they respond. So, each speaker's turn is evidence, out in the open so to speak, of their private reasoning processes. Nothing in the interaction can be ignored as meaningless or insignificant. Everything counts, unless it can be proved otherwise, as part of a systematic and orderly way of managing the talk and making it meaningful to participants.

Several basic concepts have developed out of this methodology which can be neatly illustrated in the following example:

T1	C.	So I was wondering would you be in your office on Monday by any chance?
T2	(2.0)	[two seconds' pause]
T3	C.	Probably not.
T4	R.	Hmm yes. =
T5	C.	= you would?
T6	R.	Ya.
T7	C.	So if we came by could you give us ten minutes of your time?

(Levinson 1983)

Here, the 2-second pause after C's initial request is followed by a further turn by C. There is evidence in this small and relatively trivial piece of data of the systematic organisation of conversation. First, interlocutors need to know when they can speak, or take a turn. Sacks, Schegloff and Jefferson (1974) have shown how turn-taking in conversation is highly organised to coordinate and maintain speaker and listener involvement. In this example, speaker C expects R to take a turn at T2 in response to her request. This type of linked response – request/acceptance or rejection, greet/greet, self-deprecation/ disagreement, and so on – is described by Schegloff and Sacks as 'the adjacency pair' and it is one of the frequent means by which speakers know that they are being offered a turn at talk.

However, R does not take up the turn and C's follow-up, 'Probably not', is an example of a third basic concept in CA, 'preference organisation'. Listeners are regularly confronted with offers, invitations or, as in this case, requests to which they have to respond. Conversations are organised, conversation analysts argue, so that the preferred response is unmarked. In other words, if the listener can accept the offer or invitation or agree to the request then they will do so as a routine response to the first part of an adjacency pair. If, on the other hand, they cannot comply, there are certain strategies that are systematically used to withhold, avoid or delay the 'dispreferred' response. Such strategies are hesitation, fillers such as 'well', and apologies.

R's silence after C's request is interpreted by C as a marker of a dispreferred response and she softens the blow of R's refusal by suggesting it herself. This is an illustration of the practical-reasoning work that goes on behind the scenes and shows that the shared interpretation arrived at is largely done in indirect ways.

Relevance to ILT

Conversation analysts have contributed in several important ways to our understanding of inter-ethnic communication. First, they have given us new insights into how conversation is systematically managed as a cooperative activity in monocultural communication so that speakers can, generally, understand each other and avoid conflict. Second, they have helped us to see how interactions are jointly constructed. This joint construction makes training for both first- and second-language speakers of English essential. In any interaction, each question, answer or statement helps to shape the subsequent response. In unequal encounters, especially in gatekeeping interviews, judgements are made about ethnic-minority clients and applicants based on gatekeeper-constructed responses. Third, they have helped to provide a link between individual interaction and the systems and structures of our society which affect our daily lives. As the French historian Foucault has said, institutions are held together by language. The conversation analysts have begun to document what that means.

In addition, the analytical tools used in CA on naturally-occurring data have been influential in ILT pedagogy both in cross-cultural training and language learning. Recent CA work has focused on talk in institutional settings. This research has examined how interaction in institutions compares with ordinary conversation. It is a particularly fruitful line of investigation for language and cross-cultural trainers. It has started to reveal what interactional knowledge is required for participants to be effective in such domains as the classroom, the courtroom, and doctor–patient and other service–client relationships.

It is clear from recent CA work that the kind of knowledge required to be successful in these settings cannot be separated off from the interaction itself. In other words, health status or the identity of a student as a 'good' student in the classroom depends on how knowledge is interactionally displayed or accomplished. For example, attention-getting in the classroom is critically related to learning opportunities and evaluation of students, and conversation analysis of doctor–patient interviews has shown how verbal and non-verbal strategies work together to give either patient or doctor control at particular points in the interaction. As patients, we want doctors to take our complaint as seriously as we do. They will do this only if we can present ourselves convincingly as a patient with a serious problem and do not find ourselves being controlled and prevented from displaying our perception of the problem.

Both language learners and cross-cultural training participants can be made aware of how judgements about people depend upon what they display in interaction. These judgements are much more than fleeting impressions, especially in gatekeeping situations. Evidence from interactions rapidly becomes fixed as sets of descriptive categories about people when it is written down on school-report forms, medical case notes or job-interview forms. For example, a patient who asks a number of questions may be documented in medical notes as 'neurotic' and a young person interrogated about behaviour which does not conform to adult society's norms may be written up as 'delinquent' in social work case notes.

Finally, the methodology of CA provides an approach for the language classroom. Learners can be helped to discover the practical reasoning that lies behind the interaction and to see that they can become analysts of interaction in English just as they are analysts, implicitly, of conversation in their first language just by being competent members of a community. They can be helped to perceive the routine of the language of institutional settings and can develop the conversational resources needed to control topics, take the floor or set the scene for gaining agreement or acceptance.

Limitations for ILT

Some of the theoretical and methodological limitations of CA, which have been generally identified, are also limitations for ILT. CA has always attempted to avoid criticisms levelled at other types of discourse analysis that they depend upon the intuitions and interpretations of the analyst. CA, it is argued, is concerned with formal structures and mechanisms inherent in the data and available to the analyst without further interpretive analysis. (To this extent, it has after all much in common with the discourse-rules approach of Sinclair and Coulthard and the Birmingham School.) CA also strives to be autonomous in ignoring any psychological characteristics that underlie intention, as in the concept of preference organisation. Preference organisation is described in terms of conversational structure, not personal preference.

However, a closer look at CA suggests that it is not as autonomous an approach as its practitioners say. Because the data analysed is mostly of white middle-class interaction, the evidence in the data largely accords with the analysts' (usually themselves white and middle-class) intuitive understanding of how people make sense of each other in conversation. For example, the two-second pause in the short interaction given above can be interpreted as a dispreferred response only if we can be sure that C was not expecting to get a negative reply anyway. If C was expecting R to say no, then R's non-take-up of a turn may not be significant and C's reaction cannot be explained solely by the turn-taking system. In other words, analysts have identified devices in the data, such as turn-taking and adjacency pairs, and then interpreted the data on the assumption that the speakers are orientated towards these devices.

CA, therefore, is limited because it takes little account of the cultural context of interactions, has no way of accounting for interethnic communication and lets in intuitive understanding and assumptions, through the back door, so to speak, by taking for granted that the practical-reasoning processes of the analyst are the same as those used by the speakers. CA has also been criticised for its lack of rigour in linguistic analysis, particularly in phonology and paralinguistics.

So, for ILT purposes, it was important to borrow many of the strengths of CA and combine them with ethnography. CA's insistence on naturally-occurring data, on the fine-grained detail of interaction and on its sequential organisation were significant influences on the analysis of inter-ethnic communication carried out by ILT. But they were tools to be used in a wider analysis which also took account of the socially-orientated and critical discourse analysis described above and was fundamentally directed by the ethnographic and linguistic work of Gumperz in his analysis of inter-ethnic communication.

3.6 Inter-ethnic communication

Issues

Studies of inter-ethnic communication have drawn on two main disciplines, anthropology and linguistics. More specifically, inter-ethnic communication has been informed by ethnography and socio-linguistics, which, in combination, have led to the development of an approach variously described as micro-ethnography (Erickson and Shultz 1982), constitutive ethnography (Mehan 1979) or, with a more sociolinguistic orientation, as interactional sociolinguistics (Gumperz 1982a, 1982b).

This section will focus on the work of Gumperz but will also discuss the work of a number of American ethnographers and socio-linguists who, like Gumperz, have worked comparatively with different language and ethnic groups in order to understand the relationship between general and universal ways in which people interact, and those ways which are culture-specific.

Language and disadvantage

Gumperz's fundamental arguments are:

(i)   There is a linguistic dimension to discrimination which is rarely perceived as such.

(ii)   Different groups may differ systematically in the way they convey meaning and attitude in talk and this can reinforce and even create negative stereotyping.

(iii) By looking at communication breakdowns, it is possible to analyse what these differences are and help both sides to learn to look out for and repair these breakdowns and to understand the cumulative consequences of not taking action.

Gumperz draws on the work of linguists, ethnographers and sociologists in examining the relationship between cultural conventions of communicating, specific linguistic features and how interaction is organised systematically as a joint production by speakers. He is primarily interested in exploring the processes of interpretation and inferencing by speakers that lead to either good or less than completely successful communication. He is interested in describing these processes and relating them to the cultural norms and assumptions

that individuals have developed by virtue of growing up and interacting in a particular speech community. He has also studied the
social outcomes of communication as they affect the life chances of
individuals.

The research sites from which data are collected are situations of
public negotiation such as interviews, meetings, encounters at work,
where the interactions are likely to be stressful and protracted and
where the outcomes are critical in people's lives. These are the strategic research sites mentioned in Chapter 1. These interactions are unequal encounters in terms of the task, the roles of the speakers, and in
the fact that in a multi-ethnic society the decision-maker, the instructor or the boss is frequently white and the other is black.

Gumperz's methodology, like that of the ethnographers and the
ethnomethodologists, is to collect data of naturally-occurring situations. These data are then interpreted by both sides. The joint interpretation is used as the basis for analysis and for identifying
interesting and awkward moments. Elicited data are used to test out
hypotheses from this analysis at the level of utterance.

Gumperz's studies of inter-ethnic communication have extended
Hymes's comparative work on the rules of speaking by examining
what happens when the speaking conventions of individuals from
different ethnic groups are misinterpreted. Gumperz argues (1984)
that inter-ethnic communication should not be analysed in terms of
rules that speakers must use but in terms of the extent to which
conditions are created that make possible shared interpretation.

One of the great contributions of ethnic minority groups has been
to make the majority aware of how culture-specific are the schemata
and ways of interacting which are taken for granted as normal.
Communication breakdowns or unexpected responses serve to amplify
the subtle and usually taken-for-granted processes which make interaction smooth and successful.

Gumperz has shown that at every level, from general notions about
how to get things done, or about what is relevant and significant,
down to the most specific linguistic features of stress and intonation in
talk, different ethnic groups may operate differently. He has also
shown how these communicative differences feed into the processes of
evaluating individuals and stereotyping them. In other words, he has
shown the interconnection between momentary and apparently insignificant misunderstandings and larger social consequences.

Ethnographers of speaking and those working in pragmatics have
helped us to understand how language use is systematically tied to a
particular context. Ethnomethodologists have shown how speakers col-
laborate together in a systematic way to produce conversation jointly.

Gumperz draws on the former's understanding of inferences and the latter's understanding of the management of conversation in his notion of 'contextualisation cues'. These are the signals in talk which trigger expectations about what the activity is. We make on-the-spot judgements all the time about what is going on, and contextualisation cues are essential to this. And we are also constantly modifying our judgements, again as a result of contextualisation. These cues help to channel the interpretations the listeners may have in a particular way and they help the interactants to see how what is being said ties in with preceding and following utterances.

Contextualisation cues can be any linguistic features, but Gumperz has demonstrated how prosodic cues – intonation, rhythm, pitch and pausing – and such paralinguistic cues as voice quality are both particularly significant and unconsciously processed. Where an overall style of communicating is shared, these conventions help speakers to agree on what is going on between them and to track the conversation as it shifts, for example in terms of specific goals or attitudes – in other words, to help them feel they are on the same wavelength. Where communication styles are not shared these cues can affect the whole interaction. Because they are misinterpreted both sides can have a sense of 'wrong-footing' which makes them question what has gone before and what will happen next.

Contextualisation cues are one example of the way in which elements in the linguistic code can trigger wrong inferences. Gumperz and his associates have examined other ways in which differences in syntax and prosody can lead to miscommunication.

There are both individual features of syntax and prosody and ways of using syntax and prosody together which are systematically different among different speakers of English. Bilingual speakers, both those who use English grammar and vocabulary in a near-native way and those whose control of these features is more limited, may use syntax and prosody to signal discourse cohesion and coherence in culture-specific ways.

Prosody plays a vital role in creating expectations and signalling connections in spoken interaction. For example, as we have said, prosodic signals are important contextualisation cues for deciding what kind of an activity we are in: is this a chat or an advice-giving session or both? Prosody also helps us to chunk the stream of speech into utterances, to distinguish between the main argument or theme and subsidiary points and to give us clues about the speaker's attitude or orientation. For example, in the Anglo* variety of English, speakers

---

* *'Anglo' is used here to describe the variety of English used by most white native English-speakers and by those who use this variety even if it was not the first language or variety of English that they acquired.*

process information by chunking it into information units, usually consisting of a noun phrase and a verb phrase. The information unit is conveyed prosodically by a single tone-group unit, with the stress on the most prominent syllable. Listeners will perceive these tone groups and will chunk the stream of speech accordingly as a normal piece of information flow (Halliday 1967). In the Anglo variety of English the proposition // I can't come tomorrow // would normally be uttered in the unmarked form with the stress on the second syllable of 'tomorrow' and with a falling tune. With this intonation the proposition would usually be interpreted as a statement of fact with no markedness as to speaker orientation.

On the other hand, if listeners hear unexpected stress on syllables, they will note it as a marked form and search for the reason why: for example, // ꞌI can't come tomorrow //, with the stress on 'I', suggests to the listener contrastive stress; that is, 'I can't come but someone else will'.

So unexpected stress is likely to be either because the speaker wanted to make a contrast between ꞌthis and ꞌthat or because they wanted to convey a particular attitude which normal information flow would not convey. For example, in the proposition // Joe likes his job //, with a low fall on the stressed syllable or tonic, 'job', information is conveyed in the expected or unmarked way. By contrast, // ꞌJoe likes his job // would usually be interpreted as '**Joe** likes his job but **other** people do not like theirs'.

Speakers of non-Anglo varieties of English will not necessarily use prosody in this way. So in inter-ethnic communication the listener may perceive something as marked when the speaker did not intend it to be so. Conversely, listeners may try to make sense of the others' talk but find no prosodic clues which would help them to decide, for example, what is the new information and what has already been given or what is the key word which carries the speaker's message. The transcript 'Staff Discussion at a Bus Company' (Data 2.4), discussed earlier in this chapter, is a good example of potential information loss because of systematic differences in conveying meaning through prosody.

The result of these ambiguities may be frustrated comments such as: 'I wasn't really sure what his point was'; 'She seemed to say one thing and then contradict herself'; 'I can't understand why English people get so emotional when they're talking'. In other words, different uses of prosody are interpreted as lack of competence or wrong attitude. In more equal encounters these differences are often discounted but in the unequal situations that routinely occur between black and white in Britain they serve to reinforce negative ethnic stereotypes.

In order to give a more detailed account of how prosody and syntax may operate in systematically different ways in ethnically different styles of communicating, we shall focus on inter-ethnic communication between white-majority English-speakers and speakers with their origins in the Indian subcontinent, since these form the largest ethnic minority group in Britain and are the group with whom Gumperz has done his most detailed work. We are aware of the range of speaking styles even within an ethnic group, but it seems possible to identify some general differences between Anglo English-speakers and those whose English is influenced by a North Indian language.

In North Indian languages much of what has been called normal information flow is signalled in the syntax where English would use prosody. For example, the topic or important point in an utterance is usually conveyed in English prosodically, through stress and, to a lesser extent, through word order: for example, // The trial's on Thùrsday //, where a high-fall tune is used to convey emphasis, or // ˈThursday's the day of the trial //, where 'Thursday' is stressed by putting it up front and making it the theme of the utterance, and also by stressing it intonationally. In North Indian languages, word order, which is much freer than in English, has much greater salience in highlighting the topic. Similarly, speakers of North Indian languages will use the syntactic resources available to them to convey attitude where an English speaker would use tone of voice, such as the raised, accusatory tone of voice in: // ⌐The door's opèn// The implication of responsibility would be conveyed in North Indian languages through verb inflection. In particular, these languages rely on a system of verb auxiliaries or grammatical particles to express perspective on and attitudes towards actions, such as 'hi' and 'to' in Hindi. For example (the emphatic particle is italicised in each instance):

a.   ye *hi* tin ləRke...
     (these particular three boys...)
b.   ye tin *hi* ləRke...
     (only three of these boys)
c.   ye tin ləRke *hi*...
     (only these three boys, and no one else...)

(Gumperz, Aulakh and Kaltman 1982)

In the standard variety of English the message in (a) would be conveyed by stressing 'these', in (b) by stressing 'three' and in (c) by adding a lexical item such as 'only' and stressing 'these' and 'three' as well.

In inter-ethnic communication different uses of prosodic signals and different ways of using syntax and prosody together can, therefore, lead to information loss and misinterpretation of attitude. Information loss occurs because the listener cannot work out, for example, what the topic is, what is given information and what is new, what the relationship is between the previous utterance and the one being spoken and whether the speaker has finished speaking or not. Attitudes are often misinterpreted by both sides because, for example, certain uses of intonation have a culture-specific meaning, as Bhardwaj (1982) has shown for 'Panjabi English'. The equivalent of the low-fall or 'normal' pitch in English indicating a statement or new information will convey, in Panjabi, attitudes such as boredom, rudeness or lack of respect. In Panjabi, stating or giving new information in a polite or respectful way is usually done with a low-rise intonation which might suggest uncertainty or monotony to a native English-speaker. Examples of attitude misinterpretation were elicited by using a video of a simulated job interview where the applicant was a Panjabi speaker, which was shown to a group of Asian and white professionals as part of an academic course (see Data 3.1, p. 124). The Asian professionals commented that the applicant's prosody suggested someone who was sincere. The white professionals considered the applicant over-confident and, on further analysis, related this to the way in which he chunked his information into small units with frequent shifts in register, up and down.

A further complication is that a prosodic signal in one language may be present to convey information – for example, a rising tone in English is used to show the connection between sentences – but may be used in the other language to convey an attitude such as politeness and respect, as we have just suggested. For example: // I can't come today //, with a low-rise tune, suggests to the English-speaking listener that a further utterance will follow, either giving an explanation or offering an alternative. However, the same intonation used by a Hindi or Panjabi speaker of English might only convey politeness. So the English-speaker's expectations about further information will not be met. Similarly, the Hindi- or Panjabi-speaker may be frustrated or offended by the English-speaker. For example, the English high fall, which is used so frequently to show contrast or emphasis, can easily be interpreted by Panjabi-speakers as over-emotional and even convey-ing irritation and implications that the listener is stupid.

Much of the work of Gumperz and his associates has focused on the use of prosody in inferential processes and the way in which grammar, lexis and prosody are used as contextualisation cues and miscues in inter-ethnic communication. As we have suggested, differences in the use of these features can lead to both information loss and misinterpretation of attitude. Indian speakers of English may consider white English-speakers unnecessarily emphatic, too indirect or too emotional. The latter often judge the English discourse of speakers from North India as lacking cohesion, loose, illogical or slow, or consider them too deferential or impolite.

In the following example, from an interview to collect data for a training course, M intends to be polite but appears to the white speaker to be rude. M (the interviewee) is explaining to W (the interviewer) about his work as a clerk in a civil-service department, in particular that his job involves 'costing of expenses':

> M: Now if this is not a special type of furniture, general furniture, used by all the departments in routine with the ( ) desks and the chairs like that...
> W: Yes
> M: then it goes into general folio. Now, end of the year...
> W: That's something special is it?
> M: That's right, something special work, costing is special work. Now at the end of the year you see I take the total of the furniture, money spent by the department...

(Gumperz, Aulakh and Kaltman 1982)

The authors argue that M misinterprets W's deictic use of 'that', which is intended to refer to what happens at the end of the year. In the Anglo variety of English, deictic references usually refer back to an item which has just been mentioned. M assumes that 'that' refers to the general topic of costing, because in North Indian languages deictic references are considerably looser than in English and rely on shared assumptions about speakers' knowledge rather than on explicit textual referents. So 'that' will refer to the general topic of costing since both sides agree that 'costing' is the topic they are talking about.

To M, W's interrupting question is not relevant to the information he is giving her now; but he acknowledges her by repeating her words, which in his style of English is a sign of politeness. He then returns to where he left off, which is what she was referring to anyway. The impression given to W is that M has not answered her question, and to her he sounds rather patronising in the way he repeats her words.

A further problem in this interaction is, why does W interrupt M in the first place? The likely explanation is that W has lost her way in M's discourse. The information in the long explanation that precedes this extract is chunked quite differently from the way information units are presented in the standard variety of English. It appears that W is not clear what is new and what given information, what are the connections between utterances and what is the speaker's perspective. As an interviewer she is in a position of power, and uses this to interrupt M in order to establish the significant elements of his job around which she can organise her thoughts about his work.

The importance of Gumperz's work is to show how these cues both trigger and feed into the attitudes of speakers and listeners so that power differences and negative ethnic stereotypes are perpetuated and reinforced. And these cues are not specific features of speakers' linguistic codes which they can learn to change but are part of their ethnically specific style of communicating – a style which may not be consciously controlled by speakers and which is a part of their ethnic identity.

Culture, style and inequality

There is a strong tradition in the USA of combining ethnography and sociolinguistics in detailed case studies of specific ethnic groups. The scholars whose work is discussed briefly in this section have made a major contribution to our understanding of cultural relativity and its role in creating disadvantage and discrimination in a white, 'Anglo'-dominated society.

Their work, like that of Gumperz, has been concerned with five major aspects of communication in inter-ethnic settings:

(i)   amount and distribution of talk;
(ii) topic and topic control;
(iii) aspects of the discourse system such as topicalisation and thematisation (the way ideas are put forward and certain) items selected for emphasis), relativisation (the way ideas are connected together) and speaker perspective (the particular mood or orientation that speakers give their utterances);
(iv) schema and interpretive frame;
(v)   politeness and self-presentation.

Working together, these different elements constitute speakers' style of communicating. In multi-ethnic societies, ethnically specific styles of communicating are both expressions of identity, and, frequently, a cause of communication breakdown and real or perceived discrimination.

A number of these elements have already been discussed. Here, we will illustrate how ethnically specific styles of communicating can lead to inequality for particular groups in particular settings. Tannen's work on inter-ethnic communication has been particularly concerned with cultural differences in the amount and distribution of talk and she has also been influential in popularising the notions of schema and frame in inter-ethnic settings.

Tannen has examined ordinary conversation, story-telling and medical interviews to discover how different cultural groups bring different
assumptions and different styles to the act of communicating. In
writing about New York Jewish conversational style (1981), she says:
'"Style" is not something extra, added on like frosting on a cake. It is
the stuff of which the linguistic cake is made ... style refers to all the
ways speakers encode meaning in language and convey how they
intend their talk to be understood.' Style is learned in the course of
interactive experience; and to the extent to which that experience has
been within a particular ethnic group, style is ethnically determined.
Tannen is interested in the way a distinct ethnic style is perceived by
members of different ethnic groups. She uses her own experience to
illustrate how conversational overlaps among New York Jewish
speakers are interpreted as rude interruptions by others. She also
shows how in Greek- American interaction indirectness or the assumption that your partner is being indirect can cause misunderstandings.

Differences in communicative style between interlocutors can cause
information loss and the kind of obvious negative attitudes that
Tannen describes. These differences can also affect the entire
progress and overall quality of the interaction. Bateson (whose work
on interpretive frames has already been mentioned) showed how,
even in intra-ethnic communication, differences in style could pull
people, quite unconsciously, further and further apart. He coined the
term 'complementary schismogenesis' for one of the unconscious
ways in which two people react to each other. Tannen has helped to
popularise this notion and show its relevance to inter-ethnic
communication.

Complementary schismogenesis is the process whereby an interaction becomes increasingly imbalanced, as was mentioned in Chapter 1.
If one speaker talks for a long time, loudly and aggressively, the other
speaker tends to talk less, more quietly and less forcibly. This, in
turn, makes the first speaker even more dominating. And so on. This
is another example of how the message behind the explicit message,
the metamessage, can easily go unnoticed or be misinterpreted. If one
speaker is uncomfortably silent, then by talking more the other
speaker tries to convey that silences are embarrassing; but this is only
indirectly conveyed, through the metamessage.

Several scholars have studied the communicative style of native
American Indians and their interaction with white Anglo-speakers.
The work of Phillips, Erickson and Scollon and Scollon has been
particularly influential.

The Scollons have looked, in particular, at the contrastive discourse
systems and notions of politeness and face between Athabaskans and

white Anglos. They have shown how Athabaskan- and Anglo-speakers tend to use different systems for showing what information is in the foreground and what is background information. In English, foreground information tends to come first, whereas in Athabaskan languages foreground information tends to come in the last clause of a sentence and is marked by a pause. When Athabaskans speak English, it is common for their important points to be overlooked and for their pausing to be interpreted as hesitation or uncertainty, whereas in fact it is an emphatic device (Scollon and Scollon 1983).

The Scollons also observe quite different ways of self-presentation between Athabaskans and white Anglos. The latter use talk to find out about people, and expect children and those in lower-status positions to display their knowledge by talking about it. Athabaskans have a high degree of respect for the other as an individual and believe in guarding their own individuality by talking very little with people they do not know well. They also tend to use negative politeness strategies, such as being pessimistic about themselves and the future. For example, they might refrain from talking about the future altogether or talking about themselves in a positive way. These differences in communicative style have contributed to the discrimination that Athabaskans have experienced, for example, in the differential judicial-sentencing patterns between Anglos and Athabaskans. Athabaskans were, on average, likely to be given longer prison sentences than Anglos.

Phillips has also looked at differential sentencing patterns between Anglos and American Indians, and has examined how children on the Warm Springs reservation are socialised into ways of learning and behaviours for learning different from those expected in the American school system controlled by the white majority (Phillips 1983).

Comparative studies of native American Indian and Anglo styles of communicating and learning show persistent differences in the way talk is managed and individuals present themselves in such settings as meetings, interviews and the classroom. Erickson and his associates have described these settings as 'gatekeeping' encounters.

This concept, introduced in Chapter 1, has become a powerful metaphor in understanding institutional discrimination. It highlights the fact that the great majority of bureaucratic encounters are nego-tiations in which the applicant's worth is being judged, even though in most cases no such goal is made explicit. The interviewer, teacher or manager has the power of a gatekeeper to either give or deny access to the scarce resources and opportunities which are on offer.

Erickson and Shultz (1982), in their study of college counselling interviews, showed how the counsellor acted as gatekeeper in terms of the advice on opportunities given to students. They showed that awkward and uncomfortable moments in the interviews correlated with the kind of advice given. Where a positive atmosphere was established, students were given positive advice on the next steps in their academic career. In more uncomfortable interviews, more time was spent on checking up on students' grades and less encouragement given to pursue more advanced courses.

Three factors accounted for whether atmosphere and outcomes were positive: the social identity of the students in terms of their background; the culturally-defined style of communicating used by counsellor and students; and the 'performed social identity' of the student, that is the particular attributes of the student revealed during the interview. A key aspect of performed social identity is 'co-membership'. Interlocutors establish co-membership when they find they have something in common. Obvious attributes such as ethnicity, gender or social class will often form the basis of co-membership, but it may be established when speakers find they went to the same school, have the same sporting interests in common or even have mutual friends. The Erickson and Shultz study showed that although shared ethnicity and shared cultural styles of communicating often predicted more helpful interviews and more favourable outcomes for students, other types of co-membership were even more salient.

Erickson and Shultz showed how the three factors of background, style of communicating and performed social identity worked together in gate-keeping encounters to determine how far students, from a range of different ethnic backgrounds, should have access to the educational opportunities on offer. Erickson has also shown how ethnically specific styles of communicating among black Americans lead to awkward moments and persistent 'talking down' to black people by their white interlocutors.

Turn-taking and topic control work smoothly and comfortably when interlocutors share the same style of speaking or are flexible in adjusting to the other's style. Erickson calls the comfortable, rhythmic coordination of speaker and listener 'conversational synchrony'. A key means of identifying whether an interaction is progressing smoothly is to establish the extent of asynchronous moments in it. For example, there may be unexpected interruptions, pauses awkward to one of the participants or shifts in body posture which break the rhythm.

The coordination of verbal and non-verbal means in producing synchrony and allowing each side the chance to speak is often ethnically specific. Erickson has shown how white-Anglo and black Americans have different ways of showing they are listening and different ways of offering their conversational partner the turn at talk. These differences routinely lead to interactions where the white speaker takes increasingly long turns because they perceive a lack of response from the black speaker. This apparent reluctance to respond causes the white speaker to explain and re-explain themselves at increasingly lower levels of abstraction. This is a manifestation of the 'hyper-explanation' mentioned earlier (p.80).

Relevance to ILT

Gumperz, in the comprehensiveness of his approach, in his choice of research areas and in his methodology, has made an immense contribution to our understanding of inter-ethnic communication and the role of communication in discrimination and disadvantage. The key concept for ILT work is that there is a linguistic dimension to discrimination which is rarely perceived or accounted for. By examining the detailed processes of interpretation and how speakers come to share meaning, and relating these to systematic differences in discourse systems, particularly at the prosodic level, Gumperz made the essential link between varieties of language use and the evaluation of speaker intent to show how language works as a hidden force in discrimination.

These insights were turned into practical training activities, an example of which is given in Chapter 3 (section 4.1). An important aspect of Gumperz's methodology was readily transferable to language and cross-cultural training. This was the recording and then joint interpretation by both sides of what had happened in the encounter. This ethnographic approach to linguistic analysis was used by ILT workers both as analysts, in deepening our understanding of inter-ethnic communication, and as trainers, in teaching both language learners and the white majority group about differences in communicative style and how judgements of behaviour and personality are based on these differences.

Gumperz and his associates' detailed case studies of North Indian speakers of English led us to a greater focus on comparative work between North Indian languages and English and raised awareness of the need to study the variety of spoken English used by speakers of these languages much more systematically. In particular, Gumperz's analysis of prosody in discourse cohesion and the conveying of speaker attitude was translated by us, working closely with him, into practical training materials – such as *Crosstalk* – for white gatekeepers.

The other work on inter-ethnic communication described in this section had obvious relevance to ILT because it drew together the different aspects of communicative style and related them specifically to communication between different ethnic groups. The framework for analysis described in Chapter 4 was directly based on the concepts of discourse and style in inter-ethnic communication developed by

Gumperz, Tannen, Scollon and Scollon, Phillips, and Erickson. This was used initially to train ILT staff, who then developed their own analytic tools and training approaches as illustrated in Chapter 3 (section 4.2).

The concept of gatekeeping developed by Erickson and Shultz was a powerful one for ILT. It became a key organising concept in setting up programmes to tackle the issue of professional behaviour and institutional discrimination. It was persuasive because it helped to focus on the individual's responsibilities as representative of an institution and because it forced an analysis of the often unconscious and invisible ways in which interactional processes lead to 'closed-gate' outcomes for black clients and applicants. The gatekeepers, through a process of analysis and awareness-raising described in Chapter 3, came to see that the atmosphere, progress and outcomes of an interview depended absolutely on the communicative style of both sides. Clashes of style operated as an invisible gate, denying access to resources and opportunities.

Clashes of style can lead to complementary schismogenesis. For example, in a council housing department a white housing officer becomes increasingly stiff, bureaucratic and cold and his black client talks more and more forcefully (Gumperz and Roberts 1991). The interview reaches a complete impasse when the client asks 'What do you expect me to do – put all my family in one room – will that get me a house?', and the officer's response is silence. Once speakers are in this mutually reinforcing imbalance, they can climb out of it only by drastically changing their own contribution.

Presentation and analysis of such mutually-reinforcing negative spirals can raise awareness among white gatekeepers of the need to be explicit about communication difficulties when things start to go wrong and the need to be flexible in their own styles of communicating.

Finally, like ethnomethodology, studying inter-ethnic communication has helped reveal what is going on behind the familiar and routine in everyday interaction. The awkward or unexpected moments which often occur in interviews reveal how highly conventionalised – and, on inspection, absurd and hypocritical – are many of the routine formalised activities such as questions like 'Why do you want this job?' and the kind of response expected. In other words, minority ethnic groups have become the ethnomethodologists of our multi-ethnic society. By bringing schemata to inter-ethnic encounters which often differ widely from the schemata of the white gatekeepers, ethnic minority groups challenge the gatekeepers' taken-for-granted uses of language and the assumptions behind them. Their unexpected or angry and frustrated responses, either during or after such an interaction, and their elicited interpretations of the white speakers' utterances have challenged people to reassess their familiar patterns of communication, just as Garfinkel did when he required students to carry out a series of exercises at home to show how the routine and familiar could be made strange when the usual interactive assumptions were suspended (Garfinkel 1967).

Limitations for ILT

Any limitations for ILT of studies in inter-ethnic communication lie not in the studies described above but in the lack of any follow-up work in Britain which might take it further. Apart from Gumperz's case studies of North Indian speakers and to a lesser extent of Afro-Caribbean speakers, no systematic studies combining sociolinguistics and ethnography have been undertaken of inter-ethnic communication in the British setting.

One possible reason for this is the resistance among some trainers in race relations and equal opportunities to accept this approach. Much of the work of the American scholars discussed here is complex and difficult and not widely understood outside their field, and has therefore been dismissed by some trainers and teachers. As we have suggested above, examining the detailed linguistic processes that feed into speakers' judgements of each other has been criticised as a 'cover-up' for dealing with racism directly. Another reason, suggested by Thomas in her work on 'Cross-cultural pragmatic failure' (1983), is that both teachers and learners may be reluctant to accept that learning a language means learning to use the cultural schemata and styles which are part of it. In other words, students are expected to use new behaviours and so take on a new social identity when communicating in the second language. ILT workers, in their approach and materials in both language teaching and cross-cultural training, have had to tread carefully in the field of ethnically determined communication styles. If inter-ethnic studies are used as an excuse for not tackling racism or as a justification for cultural imperialism in the ESL classroom, then they are being damagingly misinterpreted and misused.

3.7 Language and social psychology

Issues

Work in language and social psychology has been primarily concerned with the dynamics of attitudes and motivation, as they affect language acquisition and use, and with the role of language in maintaining group and, specifically, ethnic identity. As such, it has relevance for both language learning and inter-ethnic communication.

The studies on attitude and motivation in relation to language learning by Gardner and Lambert in Canada (1972) and by Schumann in the USA (1978) have been the most influential. These studies have shown that motivation, supported by positive attitudes, is crucial to successful learning. They have also suggested that motivation is not a unitary notion but that learners are on a continuum between integrative and instrumental motivation: in other words, they may be more willing to identify with the culture of the target-language group or they may be learning the language for specific instrumental purposes such as getting a job or passing an exam. Gardner and Lambert found that instrumental motivation is more likely to be effective in a second-language learning situation whereas integrative motivation is more helpful in the foreign-language classroom. Gardner has also suggested that in second-language contexts individual differences, such as aptitude, are less important than in monolingual contexts and so, by implication, that social factors are more important in second-language contexts.

Gardner and Lambert's work encompassed both foreign-language learning and bilingual contexts. Schumann, working with adults in a second-language learning context, related attitudes and motivation to the social and psychological distance between the learner and the target-language group. Where there is little social and psychological distance, he argues, learners will 'acculturate' and so acquire the second language. Social distance, defined in terms such as degree of social contact, perceived social equality between second-language group and target-language group and how culturally close they are, is seen as more salient than psychological differences such as language shock and culture shock. Schumann argued that where social distance was great, then contact between second-language and target groups would be minimal. Little inter-group contact would mean few opportunities for target-language input and so adult learners' language would 'fossilise'. Schumann called this process 'pidginization', analogous to the process of acquiring pidgin.

In Britain, the prime movers in developing work on language and social psychology have been Giles and his associates. Giles's studies of language and inter-group behaviour are concerned with establishing the critical role of language in maintaining and developing social identity and in the social evaluation of speakers. His work attempts to answer two questions: why do people speak the way they do in different contexts, and why are speech variables important in evaluating others?

In answering these questions, Giles has focused on ethnic groups and on ethnicity markers in speech (Giles 1977, 1979; Giles and Powesland 1975). He has shown that phonological, prosodic, grammatical and lexical markers are used by speakers to reinforce their ethnic identity and are a critical means of impression formation for listeners, who inevitably evaluate speakers' styles of communicating. Giles's studies of speaker evaluation consistently replicate the finding of Lambert's original work, using the 'matched guise' technique, on attitudes to different speech styles: that speakers are rated more highly, the nearer they conform to the high-status language or language variety.

Giles and his associates have developed a model of speech diversity termed 'interpersonal accommodation theory'. This model provides an explanation as to why speakers vary their style of speech in interaction. It attempts to explain some of the complexities of motivation, attitudes and intention which underlie speaker variation according to topic, roles, relationships, etc. (see p. 56, above, on Hymes's sociolinguistic variables.)

Accommodation theory is relevant both to inter-ethnic communication and to second-language learning. It takes further Lambert's work showing positive attitudes to high-status varieties by looking at attitude and language behaviour in interaction. Giles argues that people are likely to converge towards each other in their speech style if they desire social approval of each other. So, for example, in a job interview applicants are more likely to adapt their way of speaking to interviewers than vice versa.

Similarly, if people want to identify themselves strongly with their own group and create a distance between themselves and any speakers from the out-group, then they will tend to use and possibly exaggerate markers of ethnic identity in their speech. In inter-ethnic communication, therefore, the degree of difference in speech style and the extent to which the two sides converge or diverge will have a significant impact on how either side judges the other.

Giles's work on second-language acquisition is a development from his accommodation theory. Learners' motivation to gain social approval or to distance themselves from others in interaction depends on how they define themselves in ethnic terms. Giles argues that learners are likely to have a high level of motivation and so acquire a high level of proficiency if, for example: identification with their own ethnic group is weak; they consider that their group has low status; they do not consider their group very distinct or distant from the out-group (the majority group in the case of most multi-ethnic societies). So accommodation theory has some explanatory power in understanding impression formation in inter-ethnic communication, in suggesting ways in which motivation to learn a second language is related to ethnic identity and in accounting for style-shifting in second-language acquisition (Beebe and Zvengler 1983; Beebe and Giles 1984).

Relevance to ILT

Despite the extensive literature on language and social psychology from Canada and the USA, and more recently from Britain, the impact of such studies on ILT work has been very limited. Some of the reasons for this are outlined in the section on limitations below.

Gardner and Lambert's studies on the critical role of motivation in language learning, and in particular of instrumental motivation, reinforced intuitons and observations about adult second-language learning. Lambert's work and that of Giles and his associates also clearly shows that there is an important dimension of negative stereotyping which is triggered by accent and other markers of speech. These studies are useful in establishing the regularity with which individuals will make rapid judgements about personality and competence on the basis of language. The results of this research can be cited in cross-cultural training to show the prejudices that are in all of us and which have to be accounted for. For example, several studies have shown the effect of non-standard accents on attitudes and judgements in simulated job interviews. An exercise which takes a similar approach but takes into account much more than accent is outlined in Chapter 3 (section 4.2).

However, miscommunication and negative judgements may not be the result only of unconscious use and evaluation of different styles. Differences in style may be specifically maintained or highlighted. Giles's concept of speech divergence is useful here. Participants in cross-cultural training need to be made aware of the role of language in establishing ethnic identity and that members of ethnic minority groups may wish to assert their ethnicity by using and perhaps exaggerating ethnically specific styles of speaking.

In this way, ethnicity is maintained by the speakers identifying themselves, through speech, as different from speakers of other ethnic minority groups:

> Ethnicity refers generally to the perception of group difference and so to social boundaries between sections of a population. In this sense ethnic difference is the recognition of a contrast between 'us' and 'them' ...
> Ethnicity is not, therefore, the same as culture or 'race'. It is not simply difference: it is the *sense* of difference which can occur where members of a particular cultural or 'racial' group interact with non-members'. Racist

exclusion ... is a version of ethnic boundary-keeping which constitutes a fixed liability to the racial minority designated 'out', whatever the advantages expected or gained by those designated 'in'.

(Wallman 1979)

Limitations for ILT

There are two main reasons why work in language and social psychology has had little impact on ILT. The first relates to the theoretical field of social psychology and the second to its methodology.

Social psychology is concerned with the attitudes, intentions and identities of individuals and how they position themselves within a group. These studies, and in particular the studies of ethnic identity and motivation towards language learning, attempt to correlate certain broad social factors, such as the status of a group and its language and the degree of contact between ethnic groups, with individual attitudes and intentions. As a result, some general explanations about inter-group behaviour and language acquisition and maintenance are provided. However, the results of these studies do not go beyond these general correlations to give any explanation of how individuals negotiate their ethnic identity or how they create or avoid opportunities for learning a second language. In other words, these studies are not concerned with processes in interaction, nor with explanation.

As practitioners, it is useful to know about research which establishes the primacy of motivation, the role of convergence in speech style or the concept of social distance, but this does not take us very far. In order to design training programmes, it is essential to know how these constructs are realised in interaction and to see their relationship to the wider socio-economic position of ethnic minorities. Work in language and social psychology has not as yet provided these insights, and indeed has not been designed to do so.

The theoretical limitations of this work are reflected also in the methodology. The methods used are primarily experimental, in the tradition of most studies in psychology. More recently these studies have been complemented by case studies and by observation of naturally-occurring events, such as in the courtroom or classroom. But such observation still tends to be a preliminary to the central methodology of controlled experiments and attitude questionnaires. This means that studies in language and social psychology rarely give accounts of what is actually going on in naturally-occurring interactions. Instead, the practitioner is faced with abstract cognitive models, over-simple correlations of attitude and social factors, or highly detailed statistical evidence from attitude-measurement instruments.

Many of the concerns of social psychologists are also the concerns of sociolinguists and ethnographers: issues of ethnic identity, judgements of motivation and content, theories about similarity and attraction which are related to the concept of co-membership and the wide field of schema theory. Yet the scope and methodology of sociolinguistics and ethnography have made these issues relevant and accessible in a way that social psychology has not. Some recent work by, among others, Giles, Powesland and their associates suggests that the different disciplines may be drawing close together. These studies discuss the negotiation of shared meaning and the processes of discrimination arising from ethnically specific speech cues. So it is possible that ILT workers and similar practitioners, in the future, will be able to draw a more detailed map of interaction which links language and social psychology with linguistics, sociolinguistics and ethnography.

3.8 Implications for practitioners

The map of interactions described here is, obviously, a very selective charting of the intellectual territory. To continue the map metaphor, it is only one of many possible projections. But it was these theories that were most clearly helpful in devising language-learning and cross-cultural training programmes.

At the beginning of this part of the chapter, we identified three major themes which draw together the theories which have had most influence on ILT. These were: the basically social nature of human language – language as *socially* constituted; cultural and linguistic relativity; and language as a dimension in racial discrimination. These major themes have surfaced repeatedly in our map of interaction and we will now summarise the main theories which, for ILT purposes, cluster together under these three themes, and show the key connections between them (see Figure 2.1).

Inevitably, this chart boxes and separates concepts without being able to show the persistent leakage that occurs from one to another. It is also not possible to show all the connections and influences between different theories. For example, conversation-analysis theories form part of a general theory about language as a social phenomenon, so conversation is placed under box 1; but it clearly connects with discourse style in box 2, in terms of topic and turn-taking in discourse, and with box 3 in relation to institutional discrimination. What this chart aims to do is show that we drew on the disciplines of linguistics, anthropology and sociology to develop our understanding

Figure 2.1

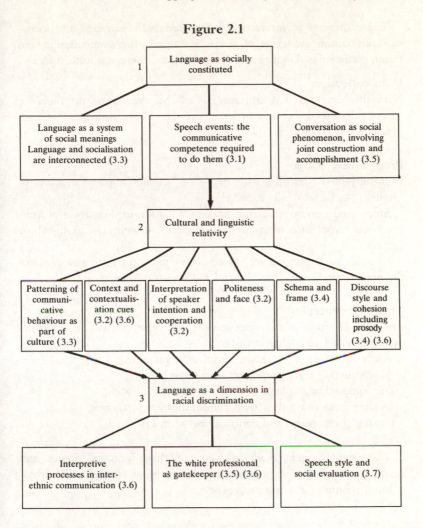

(Numbers in figure 2.1 refer to the sections in this chapter)

of the essentially social nature of language (box 1) and that we related this understanding to more specific issues to do with the nature of culture and language in interaction (box 2). These issues, drawn from linguistic philosophy, ethnography and discourse studies, helped to develop specific tools of analysis for studying inter-ethnic communication. In turn this analysis drew on the work of sociolinguists and ethnographers, and in a very limited way on that of social psychologists, to develop an approach for both language learners and participants in cross-cultural training which had as its central theme the concept of language as a dimension in racial discrimination (box 3).

These theories of interaction influenced both language and cross-cultural training in terms of data collection, programme design and training strategies. Under each of these heads, there was a need for:

Data collection

Naturally-occurring data and analysis of that data using the tools for analysis described above in order to provide a firm data base for both practical and theoretical development.

Programme design

Ethnically-mixed training with first- and second-language speakers of English, black and white, together.

Structured opportunities for learners to make explicit their perceptions and experience of communicating and learning in multi-ethnic Britain.

Cross-cultural training for white professionals to raise awareness of the need to understand, accept and modify *their* behaviour.

Training strategies

Analysis of inter-ethnic gatekeeping encounters and experiential exercises based on such encounters.

Student autonomy in the learning process, including:
– reconstructing texts from their own experiences;
– becoming ethnographers of their own communication;
– tackling tasks using their own communication strategies;
– making comparisons and contrasts between L1 and L2.

The next chapter takes up some of these practical issues and describes the design of programmes and training strategies for cross-cultural training for white gatekeepers.

Further reading

A good introduction to the ethnography of speaking is *The Ethnography of Communication* by Saville-Troike (1982). The collection by Gumperz and Hymes, *Directions in Sociolinguistics* (1972, new edition 1986), remains a standard text and the basis for later developments in conversation analysis and pragmatics. Frake's 'How to ask for a drink in Subanun' (1964) is a classic early example of the ethnography of speaking.

The most comprehensive study of *Pragmatics* is Levinson's book (1983) with that title. Leech's *Principles of Pragmatics* (1983) is a detailed study of pragmatics in relation to Grice's principles. Brown and Levinson's work on politeness (1978; reissued 1987). *Politeness: Some Universals in Language Usage*, links detailed linguistic analysis to social structuring and is important both for pragmatics and for inter-ethnic communication.

The key reading on social semiotics for language teachers is Halliday's *Language as Social Semiotic* (1978). His two earlier books, *Explorations in the Function of Language* (1973) and *Learning How to Mean* (1975), relate his functional approach to language development. Halliday's work on cultural relativity is based on Whorf's idea of culturally relative grammars. Selections from Whorf's work have been edited by Carroll in *Language, Thought and Reality* (1957).

Wide-ranging discussions of discourse analysis, not associated with a particular 'school' or approach, are to be found in Brown and Yule's *Discourse Analysis* (1983) and the *Handbook of Discourse Analysis* edited by van Dijk (1985), particularly Volume 4. The series *Discourse Processes*, edited by Freedle, Chafe, Tannen and others, represents extensive studies by linguists, sociolinguists, and cognitive anthropologists in the field of discourse. Sinclair and Coulthard's approach is well illustrated in *Towards an Analysis of Discourse* (1975) and *Studies in Discourse Analysis* (1991), edited by Coulthard and Montgomery.

The notion of schema has been developed by those working in artificial intelligence: *Scripts, Plans, Goals and Understanding* by Schank and Ableson (1977), and Winograd's *Understanding Natural Language* (1972).

Bateson's work on frames and on 'complementary schismogenesis' is described in his collection of essays *Steps to an Ecology of Mind*. Goffman's work has not only influenced sociolinguistics in the development of 'frame', as in his *Frame Analysis* (1974), but his 'face-work' ideas were reworked by Brown and Levinson in their theories of politeness. Goffman's work on roles and participation, in particular *The Presentation of Self in Everyday Life* (1959) and *Forms of Talk* (1981), influenced Hymes and Gumperz; and in a recent book edited by Drew and Wootton, *Erving Goffman: Exploring the Interaction Order* (1988), sociologists and linguists pay tribute to his wide-ranging influence in mapping interaction.

Halliday and Hasan's work on *Cohesion in English* (1976) and the notions of schema and frame are given a relevant context for the language teacher in Widdowson's *Teaching Language as Communication* (1978) and his *Learning Purpose and Language Use* (1983).

Critical discourse analysis is well illustrated in *Language and Control*, by Fowler, Hodge, Kress and Trew (1979), and in Fairclough's *Language and Power* (1989). The influences on critical discourse analysis are best approached in Foucault's 'The order of discourse' (1984) and Habermas's *Communication and the Evolution of Society* (1979).

A good introduction to conversation analysis is Atkinson and Heritage's *Structures of Social Action: Studies in Conversation Analysis* (1984). A number of the founders of CA, including Schegloff and Sacks, are represented in this collection. Garfinkel's *Studies in Ethnomethodology* (1967) formed the basis for work in conversation analysis. The classic study of turn-taking is *A Simplest Systematics for the Organization of Turn-Taking for Conversation* (1974), by Sacks, Schegloff and Jefferson. Several conversation analysts have focused on talk in institutional settings: Mehan, in *Learning Lessons* (1979), and McDermott, in *'Kids make sense'* (1976) have looked at educational settings, Heath at medical settings in *Body Movement and Speech in Medical Interaction* (1986). Cicourel's work in medical settings and with young offenders (1981, 1983) illustrates how people become fixed as bureaucratic categories.

Gumperz's theories of interactional sociolinguistics are best described in *Discourse Strategies* (1982a) and in his work on inter-ethnic communication illustrated in *Language and Social Identity* (1982b), edited by him. Other particularly relevant publications by Gumperz are *Language and Social Groups* (1971), edited by Gumperz; 'Sociocultural knowledge in conversational inference' (1977); 'The conversational analysis of inter-ethnic communication' (1978); 'Individual and social differences in language use', with Tannen (1979); and 'Interactional sociolinguistics in the study of schooling' (1986). A useful collection of papers on the language of institutions is *Discourse Analysis and Public Life* (1986), edited by Ensink, van Essen and van der Geest.

Style and culture-specific styles of talking are the subject of Tannen's *Conversational Style* (1984). Scollon and Scollon have written about inter-ethnic communication in Alaska in *Narrative, Literacy and Face in Inter-Ethnic Communication* (1981). Phillips has also studied Anglo and native American Indian communication in *The Invisible Culture* (1983). Erickson and his associates, in their studies of educational ethnography, have also looked at Anglo–Indian communication for example Erickson and Mohatt's 'Cultural organisation of participation structures in two classrooms of Indian students' (1982). In *The Counselor as Gatekeeper* (1982), Erickson and Shultz developed the notion of gatekeeping in inter-ethnic communication with a number of different ethnic groups.

In the field of social psychology, Gardner and Lambert's *Attitudes and Motivation in Second Language Learning* (1972) is a classic text. Schumann's work is best illustrated in *The Pidginization Process: A Model for Second Language Acquisition* (1978). Giles's influence on second-language acquisition is well illustrated in Beebe and Zvengler's article 'Accommodation theory: an explanation for style shifting in second language dialects' (1983). In Britain, the work of Giles and his associates is well represented in *Language and Social Psychology*, edited by Giles and St Clair (1979); *Social Markers in Speech*, edited by Scherer and Giles (1979); *Speech Style and Social Evaluation*, by Giles and Powesland (1975) and *Recent Advances in Language, Communication and Social Psychology*, also edited by Giles and St Clair (1985).

3 Cross-cultural training

1 Introduction

This chapter describes the short training courses provided for people in positions of power and responsibility in relation to bilingual speakers of English. These people are mainly white and native speakers of English. The training which was developed in ILT focussed on two major groups of such people:

(i) People in supervisory positions in workplaces, for example managers, supervisors and shop stewards.

(ii) Gatekeepers (see Chapter 1, p.15 and Chapter 2, pp.98–9) who control access to, for example, employment opportunities, advice on social services entitlements, public housing and education. They usually exercise this control through a relatively highly structured interview process which is considered to be 'objective'. Because gatekeeping is largely exercised through the process of verbal interaction, it became a major focus for this type of training.

The need for cross-cultural training for these groups of people was briefly discussed in Chapter 1. We argued that if real changes are to take place which challenge the disadvantages black and bilingual speakers face, then limited language training for the latter group is a quite inadequate response. Training targeted solely at ethnic minority workers would not only be unjust but would imply deficits solely on their side and a focus on assimilation.

Styles of communication across cultures are a part of the interactive process which can reinforce racism, and an understanding of them can inform language teaching. We do not claim that understanding interaction cures racism – the issue is not located in culture and cultural differences as such. But an understanding of the processes of interaction between people from different cultural and linguistic backgrounds does assist in heightening the perception of those who do not wish to discriminate – and people usually believe they are not discriminating. This book is about one aspect of human behaviour which feeds into the abuse of unequal power – the linguistic dimension of discrimination that feeds the attitudes, actions and outcomes which create and maintain racism.

The short courses for supervisors and gatekeepers described in this chapter typically lasted for two-and-a-half to four days (up to about twenty-five hours in total). They were usually provided at people's workplaces; they were directly related to the participants' workplace responsibilities, and were held during work time as in-service training. This is why the courses are described as 'training', and it is for the same reason that the term 'language training' is also used throughout this book. The use of the term training does not imply a limited skills-based learning or instrumental approach as opposed to the longer-term and broader approach of 'education'. The type of course we describe in this chapter cuts across this dichotomy which is often predicated between training and education.

Training	Education
short-term	long-term
specific work-based skills	overall understanding in context
personal development (related to one aspect of personality or particular behaviour)	general empowering and growth
related to society's identified needs	related to the cognitive growth of individuals and therefore to the pool of knowledge in society

Because the courses deal with raising awareness and developing understanding they aim to provide participants with tools of analysis and a questioning frame of mind. It is hoped that these will have long-term and empowering implications for participants and will contribute both to their own growth and to workplace change. If this is to claim too much for such courses, it should at least prevent them from being merely a set of recipes and tips, for example, on how to interview better.

The aim of this chapter is to demonstrate how observation and analysis of inter-ethnic communication by ILT staff, and their understanding of and collaboration with relevant research and theoretical work in areas of linguistics and of communicative interaction (as described in Chapter 2), were directly applied to cross-cultural training. The chapter first examines what is meant by cross-cultural training and its aims. We then describe the content and learning techniques which were developed for such training courses. The fourth part shows the development over time of this type of training and illustrates the range of learning covered in it. The emphasis in these examples upon gatekeeping interviews reflects our increasing conviction of the critical role such interviews have come to play in the life chances of ethnic minorities in Britain (see Chapter 1) and our increasing understanding of how such interactions work and can be discriminatory in their outcomes.

2   The nature and aims of cross-cultural training

The term 'cross-cultural' has proved problematic. It is used here because it was the term adopted at a time when the ideological objections to which it could give rise were not fully perceived and understood. With experience and hindsight it is an awkward term to define or defend. The focus on culture and difference can be, and has been, criticised by those who, while recognising the subtleties of its role in discrimination, see its emphasis as misleading because it can detract attention from the main issue of racism. Such people prefer a basic challenge to procedures, emphasising that new procedures can be non-racist. We have retained the term because this training is about subtleties and complexities of communication and language use which cannot easily be simplified or eradicated by the objectivity of procedures, and because, in order to expose and examine these subtle processes, it deliberately focuses on contrastive factors in inter-ethnic communication.

It is useful here to take the broadest possible definition of culture as that which defines the group part of an individual's identity in terms of learned and shared behaviour. This may become significant only when misunderstandings or other conflicts occur in interactions among members of different communities – 'what is interesting as "cultural" in linguistic analyses of intercultural communications are those properties of the shared knowledge of a social group which, because of their distinctiveness, cause or may cause trouble in interaction with members of another group' (Knapp, Enninger and Knapp-Potthoff 1987). Defining culture as shared systems of meaning entails all groups in the process of examining their own culture. It also assumes a dynamic view of culture in which individuals' culture is structured and changed by context and experience.

Inter-cultural communication, in the quotation above, describes the ongoing interaction between members of different cultures. We use the term cross-cultural for training programmes in order to focus on the contrast between different communicative styles, as in 'cross-linguistic', and to analyse these differences. However, the training that developed in ILT is not simply concerned with helping groups acknowledge and understand difference. It recognises the social and political reality that most differences are part of a person's identity and, for ethnic minorities, are stigmatised when compared with the overwhelmingly white, class-based, English-speaking norms of those with power. The training aims, therefore, to help people not only to understand and accept difference, but to take positive action to ensure that the services they represent are diverse and flexible enough to accommodate difference and to combat discrimination. These broad definitions of 'culture' and 'cross-cultural' include class, race, gender and regional differences. Our work, however, has focused on inter-ethnic communication and on the bald facts of racial discrimination. The issue of the double disadvantage related to race and gender cannot be ignored; but over the last ten years, it has been the over-arching issue of discrimination against minority ethnic groups which seemed a priority to ILT. Given this priority, it could be argued that the training should be called 'race' or 'inter-ethnic' training. After all, the training is concerned with an important aspect of racism in a particular contact situation, and, crucially, with the 'felt boundary between "us" and "them"', as Wallmann (1979) defines ethnicity.

The retention of 'cultural' in the title of this chapter is for several reasons. First, the training is concerned with communications and aims to improve communicative flexibility in any inter-ethnic contacts. It is not about 'how to talk with the Indians, how to talk to the Chinese, how to talk with the English'. 'Cross-cultural training' suggests a more wide-ranging approach in which participants learn to acknowledge and then question their own culture-specific way of communication. Second, the training is concerned with overcoming difficulties in inter-ethnic relationships which arise from linguistic/cultural differences which cannot meaningfully be separated. It is this aspect of ethnicity, rather than any other boundary-drawing, which is important here. Finally, as we have suggested above, our approach is set in the wider context of cultural/language differences and inequality that are related to gender, class and other socially defined differences.

The type of cross-cultural training described in this section is different both from cultural-information seminars and from the type of anti-racist training called race-awareness training. There are severe limitations to providing only cultural information, as we suggested in Chapter 1. Such information is often fitted into an existing set of beliefs or is 'learned' without any real transference to relationships with individuals outside the classroom. So no change in behavioural outcomes takes place.

Race-awareness training programmes also have limitations. They are usually based on a psychological model concerned with individuals' personal attitudes (Katz 1978). This approach has been criticised on three counts. First, there is some scepticism about the extent to which such a personal, individual approach can change institutions at the level of systems and practices. 'By reducing social problems to individual solutions such training passes off personal satisfaction for political liberation and then wraps it up in a Madison Avenue sales package promising instant cure for hereditary disease' (Sivanandan 1985). Second, critics are not convinced that the kind of 'guilt-tripping' that such training often encourages is useful. It can produce paralysis not action. Third, it tackles the oppression of racism without acknowledging the oppression and alienation felt by the white working class. Although there are some elements of cultural- and race-awareness Training in cross-cultural training as defined here, its focus – communications – and its methods are very different.

2.1 The aims of cross-cultural training

The aim of cross-cultural training is to enhance awareness and skills so that participants can carry out their jobs in a fairer and more effective way. Although the focus of any course is the development of skills, training is always set in the wider context of institutional change and sets the scene for more long-term, fundamental changes in perceptions, attitudes and practice. No short course of training in any aspect of racism is likely to have much impact unless it is part of the implementation of an equal-opportunities policy and has real commitment from the institution which employs the participants.

Training white supervisors, personnel officers and trade unionists was always an integral part of ILT. (See Davies and Jupp 1974, and Yates, Christmas and Wilson 1982.) Changing the communicative environment or communicative relationships in the workplace meant tackling change with the group which had most frequent contact with ethnic-minority workers on the shop-floor.

During the 1970s and early 1980s, it became increasingly clear that there were identifiable groups of people whose jobs gave them a decision-making role which could crucially affect the life chances of ethnic-minority workers. The recession had a disproportionately negative impact on such workers (Lancashire ILT Unit 1983). At the same time, public services such as housing and health became more and more bureaucratised. The impact of both the industrial collapse in some parts of Britain and increasing bureaucratisation was to put increasing emphasis on formal face-to-face interaction. There are now few situations where employment, advice or services are offered without some sort of interview. People have to talk their way through to getting help, to getting things done, to getting access to scarce resources. Their success depends, often to a large extent, on how they are judged by the interviewers.

These interviewers are the gatekeepers described in Chapters 1 and 2. They may be civil servants, local-authority officials in housing, social services and environmental health, personnel officers, Youth Training Scheme supervisors, doctors, health visitors, teachers, advice workers, careers officers and many others. Of course, training gatekeepers cannot, alone, achieve equal opportunities. Policies and systems must be introduced or changed. However, it is at the point of face-to-face interaction that many decisions are made, and it is at the point of interaction that policies and systems are actually implemented.

The fact that the great majority of this target group were still white in the late 1980s is an indicator of how much discrimination still exists. Obviously, one of the aims of any anti-racist training is to alert organisations to the ways in which they are being unconsciously discriminatory. Most trainees on any anti-racism programme in companies, education, local authorities and elsewhere will belong to this white group which, as a group, is likely to be relatively unaware of the issues of communication and its relation to discrimination. This is because the great majority of them are monolingual, with little or no experience of working in a different culture and no direct experience of racial discrimination.

There are advantages and disadvantages in training all-black or all-white groups, just as there are advantages and disadvantages in training ethnically-mixed groups. However, when training is concerned with the way in which discourse processes depend upon background assumptions and power relationships and how different cultural groups may signal and interpret intent, the value of mixed groups is very great, as will be seen in Training Material 3.1 (p. 130). The fact that so much of our experience with cross-cultural training has been with all-white groups reflects social and political realities and not any underlying pedagogic principle or preference.

To summarise, the aims of the training must:

(i)   be linked to the development and management of equal-opportunities policies;

(ii) be directly geared to the work context and focus on participants as professionals;

(iii) tackle behaviour, attitudes and practice together;

(iv) reflect and provide direct access to the perceptions and experience of people from minority groups;

(v) be linked to institutional targets which can be monitored – for
     example, in a company, the number of people from minority
     ethnic groups in senior company posts or, in a public-housing
     department, the number offered attractive rehousing.

2.2 Key issues in cross-cultural training

Professional training courses, to be successful, must focus on the
participants' day-to-day professional skills and behaviour. However, a
purely behavioural model is not adequate for tackling issues of racism
and discrimination. Some people may not feel they need to change at
all. Motivation to challenge their existing practices and to unlearn
many 'natural' assumptions needs to be developed before skills
training can begin. Also, a simple change model which assumes that a
change in behaviour will pull along a change in attitude is not
sufficient. Different attitudes are expressed at different times as part
of people's ways of presenting themselves and managing situations.
People's attitudes do not simply change or remain unchanged. So
training needs to develop good practice by helping participants to be
more flexible, sensitive and questioning in dealing with all individuals,
and to help them understand why they need to make changes in
policy and practice.

The approach of cross-cultural training is to build on existing
professionalism in interviewing and communicating generally, to
disturb without threatening and to show how inter-ethnic skills and
sensitivities can be developed. The majority of participants on courses
are people with good will who acknowledge the facts of discrimination. However, encouraging people to examine the *processes* by which
discrimination takes place through interaction is much more difficult.
Discourse processes depend upon background assumptions and power
relationships. Styles of communication across cultures are part of an
unconscious interactive process which can reinforce racism. Examining
this process means asking people to examine their own behaviour and
motivation, and this can be very threatening. Discrimination based on
language is one of the least visible and measurable aspects of racism –
an invisible gate. But gates, by definition, can be opened. They can be
opened by gatekeepers, or pushed open by those able to assert their
right to enter.

As we have suggested, many decisions are based on face-to-face
interaction. Both sides can feel frustrated, irritated and demotivated
when things go wrong. Neither side may feel it has enough control
over the encounter to bring it to a satisfactory conclusion, even
though the gatekeeper has some institutional power.

Clients and applicants in gatekeeping encounters often comment that they were unable to say what they wanted, or felt they gave the 'wrong' answer, but were not sure why. They often feel discriminated against, and perceived discrimination is as damaging as real discrimination. Interviewers often give sweeping impressionistic judgements – 'He didn't come across', 'She wouldn't fit in', 'I wasn't sure about his story' – but are unable to say why. Or they feel vaguely dissatisfied with the processes and outcomes of the interview. In job interviews, it is quite common for black applicants to feel they came across well but for interviewers to be dismissive or critical of them.

Whether interviewers and gatekeepers are over-certain or uncertain about their judgements of black people in interviews and service encounters, they are usually unwilling or unable to locate their judgements of individuals in specific evidence from the interaction. Or, if they do have a particular reason for a negative judgement, it is usually where the black person's *behaviour* has been judged according to white norms. In order to help participants on training courses to develop analytical skills so that they can monitor themselves in the future and check that they are not judging the evidence of an interaction in an ethnocentric way, the use of naturally-occurring videotaped interviews is central to cross–cultural training.

3 The content and methodology of cross–cultural training

3.1 The use of video- and audio-taped data

Examining the ways in which participants may discriminate in their interactions with bilingual people need not be threatening. The majority of participants on training courses always believe they are not discriminating and reject the suggestion if it is simply asserted. However, people respond more positively to evidence than to exhortation. The use of taped material from real interactions is therefore crucial to engaging people in a real examination of their own practice rather than protecting themselves behind an emotional reaction. Particularly with videotaped material, participants recognise their own experience and cannot easily reject reality.

The advantages of using video- and audio-taped material are threefold:

(i)   It helps people to develop an objective and analytical way of look-ing first at others' and then their own behaviour.

(ii) It gives them a new metalanguage with which to talk about the process of discrimination and misunderstanding which is not generalised or emotionally charged.

(iii) It helps them to relate the bald facts of discrimination to the reality of day-to-day interactions and the decisions based upon them.

Videotaped naturally-occurring interviews, such as the examples discussed in Chapter 2 (Data 2.1–2.4), provide the core-content material for training courses. Video provides the real context of talk and captures the subtle and momentary reaction of which talk and its outcomes are constituted. It provides a document of what happens in real time; but once this reality has been captured, it can be slowed down, frozen or speeded up to give a new perspective. Conversation analysts (see Chapter 2, section 3.5), particularly those working on the integration of verbal and non-verbal communication, have shown how detailed is the organisation of interactions by doing analyses, frame by frame, on videotaped talk.

Industrial language trainers in the process of collecting ethnographic data for the setting up of language-teaching programmes were well placed to acquire taped material. However, there are often understandable difficulties, ethically and qualitatively, in using this material for training purposes. Much early videotaped training material is therefore scripted or based on role-play. In later cross-cultural training materials (Gumperz and Roberts 1980; Gumperz, Jupp and Roberts 1979), a technique was introduced whereby the original participants re-created, through unscripted role-play, their previous real encounters. This type of material has been useful in giving an understanding of how syntax and prosody are used in culture-specific ways and how judgements are formed of people by their use of syntax and prosody as well as by their accent. However, increasing attention has been given to how the whole interaction is managed and to the assumptions about ways of interpreting a particular encounter. These issues can be properly addressed only by using naturally-occurring material, as in the more recent BBC series *The Interview Game* (Roberts 1985). This is because, inevitably, role-play creates its own perspective so that there is always an ambiguity about the interactants' motivation and sincerity.

Interview data, as opposed to other kinds of naturally-occurring data, is now the focus of the training for a number of reasons quite apart from the obvious practical one that it is relatively easy to set it up, to control quality, and to obtain permissions in advance. Interviews are absolutely critical in creating or denying equal opportunities. And, as Fairclough (1985) and Candlin (1981) have shown, interviewers act out and so legitimise the ideologies of the institutions they represent. Interviews capture the culture of the institution and so provide a magnifying glass for looking at cross-cultural communication in its broadest sense. And because they provide such a distilled form of institutional white culture, they are particularly opaque and frustrating events to many ethnic-minority people. Some elements of the interview may even be offensive or quite meaningless. Given that meaning develops out of shared experience in interaction, the wider the differences of interactive experience, the more difficult it is to share meaning and styles of speaking. The job interview, for example, is one of the most culture-specific events that people regularly face, and its conventions coincide precisely with the white middle-class style of speaking.

Naturally-occurring video data is, then, essential to cross-cultural training. However, it would be extremely counter-productive if only inter-ethnic interviews were used. Participants are quick to point out what the black client is 'doing wrong'; and interviewees are then seen as the 'the problem'. Participants need, first, to examine examples of white/white interviewing to see how what appears as normal to them is, in fact, culture-specific. They also need to be exposed to encounters between individuals from the same minority group to observe how interactions work successfully for them.

This type of training is highly sensitive, and trust has to be built up at the same time as trainees' attitudes and perceptions are disturbed and broadened. For this reason, videos of situations other than those familiar to trainees are often used. For example, Jobcentre staff might be shown a housing advice interview, doctors might be shown a job interview, etc. With such material, constructive analysis is possible without defensiveness or deflection on the lines, 'We don't do it like that here'. There may also be many elements transferable from this type of 'gatekeeping' interview to the ones that participants regularly take part in.

3.2 The analysis of data

Any analysis of naturally-occurring video material is done in the context of the practical concerns of training, and can represent only a partial reflection of the relevant theories of interaction described in section 3 of Chapter 2. Material is not categorised along theoretical lines, but with the needs of course participants in mind, particularly their need to 'see' elements which otherwise would remain invisible.

We are concerned with what makes the interaction work – or not – and with bringing to the surface patterns of cooperation and mis-communication which can be related to generalised stereotypes and the facts of discriminatory outcomes. This is essentially a 'speaker-perspective' global analysis of the interaction which owes more to the conversation-analysis approach described in Chapter 2 (3.5) than to the spotting of trivial surface 'mistakes' in language use which is more familiar to language teachers.

However, as we have already indicated, the analysis goes beyond what conversation analysts address. The way participants interpret each other as evidenced in the data is related to the wider social and political issues of the structured experiences of discrimination felt by black people and to the issues of the representation and ideology of their white interlocutors. In this way the data can be used as an effective pedagogic tool in a variety of language-awareness or language-teaching situation.

Framework for analysis

Drawing upon some of the theoretical work discussed in Chapter 2, we can use a framework for analysis for training purposes, viz:

Framework for Analysis (from Roberts 1983)

Dimension 1.	*Schema*: knowledge and assumptions brought to the interaction		TOP ↑
Dimension 2.	*Frame:* strategies for and interpretation of what is going on in the interaction		
Dimension 3.	*Discourse management and style*:	⎱ uses and forms of language	
Dimension 4.	*Syntax, lexis and prosody:*	⎰	↓ BOTTOM

This framework was briefly presented in Chapter 1 (3.1–3.3) and the theoretical concepts underlying it have been examined in Chapter 2. In analysis, there is a constant process of moving from the top dimension downwards and from the bottom dimension upwards, i.e. 'top-downing' and 'bottom-upping'. In these ways, the material can be systematically 'mined' from different angles once it has become familiar. A discussion of the particular relevance of each dimension in the overall analytic framework follows, together with examples from relevant video data.

Dimension 1. Schema

Schemata, as outlined in Chapter 1 and Chapter 2 (section 3.4), are the sets of experience and knowledge that participants bring to an encounter. They are the presuppositions that we have about how to get things done, our notions of roles, responsibilities and relationships and what seems relevant, typical and significant in our world. For example, a doctor and patient may have very different assumptions about what 'healthy' means (Tannen and Wallett 1983), or a worker from an ethnic minority may have different notions from her white supervisor about what is a reasonable request for a day off. Many people from ethnic minorities, as a result of difficult experiences of immigration officials and at passport offices, may have a schema which makes any interview with a white official into an interrogation. One of the most important schema differences is likely to be in notions of how direct or indirect to be, and this will affect both ways of interacting and the content of talk.

Schema differences in one training interview led to a technically good candidate being rejected (Furnborough, Jupp, Munns and Roberts 1982). The candidate, who was Asian and had already passed his maths test, was interviewed for a government-funded training place on an engineering course. He felt he had done everything and yet he was still rejected. He failed the interview because his maths and engineering were considered by the white interview panel to be below standard. But in a debriefing after the interview, they were found to be quite adequate. He was rejected because he did not meet the interviewers' assumptions about the importance of *displaying* knowledge of these subjects in an appropriate way. But the candidate did not see the point of their questions and did not know what were the social rules of the tasks he was set – was he allowed to work out the maths question on paper or not?

Dimension 2. Frame

The interactive frame (see Chapter 2, section 3.4) describes the speaker's intention and the listener's way of interpreting it at any moment in the interaction. For example, a housing officer may be in the frame *eliciting information from the client*. But when the client starts making 'unreasonable demands' in terms of the housing he expects to get, the housing officer switches frame to *defending the system* (Roberts 1983). Schema and frame operate together continually. If people do not share the same schema or do not agree on what frame they are in, the lack of understanding in one can easily make the other go wrong. This is exemplified in Data 3.1.

DATA 3.1. CROSS-CULTURAL INTERVIEWING TRAINING AT A MOTOR COMPANY (see page 124)

[Data analysed by Derek Hooper, London ILT, and Celia Roberts]

DATA 3.1 Context

This material was collected as part of the process of a training course for management in a large motor-vehicle company. T and S are manager participants on the course and IS a South Asian worker seeking promotion to a supervisory grade. The interaction uses the

DATA 3.1 INTERVIEW TRAINING AT A MOTOR COMPANY – TRANSCRIPT

T: How do you get on with the supervision, with the foreman in the plant, I ____ S ____ ?

IS: Er...well...till I was working as I started there was no problem. As soon as I started to apply, looking for staff job after some time all of a sudden – I don't know what happened. I got from 5 S...not from all, from all members of the staff, a little, a different treatment or behaviour or attitude towards me.

S: You say different, I ____ S ____, do you mean different for the worse or for the better?

IS: Er...well as they were quite fair with me before, couple of 10 gentlemen but later on I saw some different...er...impression on their mind about me.

T: Interesting. I wonder why...er...why you I ____ S ____ think that was when you first joined you say that things were all right and then you noticed you'd been applying for staff positions 15 er...you since noticed a difference in the attitude...what...of people who before you got on with quite well. I was wondering why, why you thought there was a change which I understand from what you're saying was not for the better?

IS: Er...well...there could be some human factor on their mind you 20 know all five fingers are not alike.

T: Uh.

IS: As I said, not all, only couple gentlemen they...shown such sort of attitude you know. Faces and in depths of mind they...you can read me, I can read you. Maybe wrong, my wrong 25 judgement but...er...I can say it could be a little jealousy that, immigrant and looking for such a staff job perhaps, those people would not like to work with me on some other things. There may be possibility I can't say with confidence there may be possibility. 30

T: Were these, were these, were some of these people who were not staff colleagues of yours who might object.

IS: Yes.

T: Not necessarily people you were working for but other people who were working with you as a Grade B or Grade C operative 35 ... who were resenting the ... er ... maybe a bit jealous ... what that ... um ... er ... you said ... thought that possibly ... could be ... er ... envious, that the difficulty perhaps, working for you, this is the ... er ... perhaps was it, putting words into your mouth, a possibility thought that, that you were looking for 40

DATA 3.1 TRANSCRIPT *continued*

something above yourself, or looking for something above what you should be going for...you've not...come to this country...er...I don't want to put words in your mouth, this is the impression I'm getting tell me if I've got this wrong.

IS: Er yes it's very interesting question, as I was a member out of 45 the immigrant community as a F ____ worker, it was but natural if they put me as a foreman, there could be some surprises, through some some men working, my colleagues, I did notice little different views on some of my fellow members which they are, I can say as soon as they come to know my 50 qualifications that I am the right person who has applied for this job...er...they felt reasonably but mostly as I was working with F ____ Company and I had good friends and good working relation... mostly...them my friends, fellow workers, colleagues, they did not show any sort of ill feeling about my...   55

DATA 3.1 Commentary

T and S's schema, which underwrites their questioning, seems to be: candidates should display a balanced and analytical view of working relationships which gives evidence of their understanding of human psychology. IS's schema, by contrast, seems to be: candidates should be cautious and polite and not say anything which might be used against them. If this assumption is correct, it is in line with the advice given in handbooks on interviewing published in India (for example, Vohra and Vasudeva n.d.). These handbooks use the terms 'interview', 'test' and 'examination' interchangeably, suggesting that interviews are as much a 'test' as an opportunity to present yourself effectively. Great stress is placed on courtesy and 'sweetness of demeanour'. The great majority of questions are knowledge-based (rather than questions about past experience or skills that might be appropriate for the job in question, which are typical of British job interviews). For example: 'What is the significance of the words "cold war"?'; or 'What are the characteristics of the Modern Age?' (op.cit).

It is clear from his answers that the candidate, IS wants to indicate that some supervisors reacted negatively to him once he started to apply for promotion. But his skilful attempts to *suggest*, in a somewhat gnomic fashion, rather than be categorical, do not satisfy the interviewers. The interviewer, T, switches frame from *elicit information* to *elicit agreement*. As IS responses become more suggestive and shorter, T's turns become longer and more directive.

simulated role-play technique described above (p.120). This section of the taped data is used to illustrate a mismatch of schemata and the way in which this leads to frame-switching.

Dimension 3. Discourse management and style
Part of the speaker's style is their discourse system – the way information is structured and information and attitudes conveyed. The link between discourse and the linguistic code at or below the level of the sentence is the discourse system. This third dimension of our analytic framework is concerned with topic control and initiating turn-taking, the amount of talk and the style of questions and responses. It is a kind of stripping down to the component parts of the interaction to see how they fit together. Take the interview in Data 3.1. The way this interview is managed shows:

(i)   very few collaborative sequences between interviewers and candidate;

(ii) different ways of structuring information in explanations and descriptions: for example, in some of his answers, IS sets the context first with illustrative examples and concludes with his main point;

(iii) a significant amount of hyper-explanation by interviewers;

(iv) a number of interruptions.

These features are further identified in Data 3.2 (p.134).

Dimension 4. Syntax, lexis and prosody
This is the analysis done at or below the level of sentence. This is the most discrete level of analysis and gives us cues for checking our hypotheses about the other three dimensions.

As we have shown, the contextualisation mechanisms used by bilingual speakers may be quite different from those used by speakers of standard-variety English. In addition, different uses of syntax, lexis and prosody can affect attitudes and cause information loss. For example, where a white candidate might choose to use the system of modality in English to express indirectness (for example, 'I think it might be possible that'), a bilingual speaker might use metaphors or proverbs translated from their first language. For example, in Data 3.1 the message the candidate wishes to convey would be something on the lines of 'You know what I mean, it shows what is in their hearts. But I am being indirect because I don't want to imply criticism of you'; and he uses a common Panjabi metaphor, 'No five fingers are all alike', to illustrate the differences that exist between people.

> IS: Er...well...there could be some human factor on their mind you know all five fingers are not alike.
>
> T: Uh.
>
> IS: As I said, not all, only couple gentlemen they...shown such sort of attitude you know. Faces and in depths of mind they...you can read me, I can read you. Maybe wrong, my wrong judgement but...er...I can say it could be a little jealousy that, immigrant and looking for such a staff job perhaps, those people would not like to work with me on some other things. There may be possibility I can't say with confidence there may be possibility.
>
> (from Data 3.1)

IS's first language was Panjabi, and his English was judged in training sessions quite differently by Panjabi and English viewers. Punjabi listeners thought he came across as heartfelt and tentative. The English listeners judged him as pedantic and over-confident.

The features leading to this kind of misjudgement are not apparent from printed tapescripts, which is why the use of actual video recordings is so important in training sessions. The example from Data 3.1 may assist the reader to appreciate the point being made here about prosodic features. The Panjabi viewers' interpretation was based on

> IS: Er...well / there 'could be some human fàctor/on their mi̇nd //
> you know / ⌐all five fingers are not al̄īke //
>
> T: ...Uh
>
> IS: As I sàid / ⌐not àll only / coùple / gèntlemen / thèy / ⌐ shown / such sort of attitu̲de // you know / faces and in depths of mīnd // they ... you can read m̄e / I can read yōu //
>
> (from Data 3.1)

the candidate's use of low-rising intonation, or lack of falling intonation, to convey respect and politeness, and may also have been based on the chunking of information into small units to indicate emphasis or concern. The English viewers' interpretation was also based on the way the candidate chunked his information into small units with frequent and major shifts in pitch register. The effect of this on the English viewers was to give emphasis to almost every point so that the candidate was judged as too confident and too concerned with detail, even pedantic.

In protracted negotiations and interview situations, all four of our analytic dimensions interact with each other. For example, awkward moments that arise from long pauses or interruptions (Dimension 3) can reinforce assumptions brought to the interview (Dimension 1). Or different notions about how a job or advice interview should be conducted (Dimension 1) are never made explicit because of difficulties experienced in interpreting the other (Dimension 2) or because of information loss (Dimension 4).

3.3 Uses of data for training

Technique 1

Some analysis of data will not be part of the training, but will be used to give preliminary information to participants about:

- typical patterns of interaction in white encounters;
- typical patterns of interaction in ethnic-minority encounters which are related to particular ethnic groups;
- the hidden and indirect ways in which interviews are organised by interviewers;
- general comparisons and contrasts about culture-specific notions of how interviews should be conducted and what constitutes a satisfactory interview.

Example. John Gumperz has analysed a series of counselling interviews in an Asian Resources Centre and a housing advice centre (Gumperz and Roberts, in press). The encounters between Asian counsellors and clients were qualitatively different from those between white counsellors and clients. In the **Asian** encounters, the clients routinely gave very little information; the counsellor asked questions, and inferred from factual responses what the difficulty was. In the **white** encounters, the clients regularly explained their position with a mix of fact and evaluative comment. In **cross-cultural** encounters, where the counsellor was Asian or White, the differences in interactive style led, at times, to more protracted negotiation, feelings of discomfort as evidenced at the surface level, and less clear outcomes.

Technique 2

The framework for analysis (p.122) is not necessarily given to participants, but is used by the trainers either to analyse in-depth with participants a short stretch of video or to extract salient moments from a number of encounters.

Example. Extracts from an interview for a training course were given to participants. They were asked to guess the intention of the interviewer and how the interviewee interpreted the interviewer. This could then be related to the different levels at which communication works and the different ways in which it can go wrong.

TRAINING MATERIAL 3.1 EXTRACTS FROM SKILLS TRAINING APPLICATION INTERVIEWS (pp.130–3)
[Material devised by Ann Simpson, Lancashire ILT]

TRAINING MATERIAL 3.1 Context
The trainer videotaped a series of real interviews held at a Skills Training Centre. Candidates were seeking admission to courses after being made redundant. From the video material the trainer assembled a number of short exchanges for use in two training exercises (see Training Material 3.1). In the first exercise, the cause of the miscommunication is given and participants are asked to suggest the intention of the interviewer and the interpretation of the interviewee. (The relevant columns in the example are therefore blank when given to trainees.) In the second exercise, after a training input on the analysis of interaction, participants are given the interviewee's interpretation and asked to locate the communication breakdown in the dimensions of the analytic framework described above (section 3.2). (This column is again left blank for trainees.) In this material, A is always the interviewer and B the candidate.

Technique 3
A segment of a videotaped interview is shown to participants. This illustrates specific features of both the English speaker's and the ethnic-minority candidate's discourse management and style, and how these do not work well together. Given the unequal positions of the interlocutors, this creates an unfavourable overall impression on the part of the interviewer. After these features have been identified, discussion is focused on what the interviewer could have done to avoid disadvantaging candidates and to perceive their strengths. The techniques is exemplified in Data 3.2.

DATA 3.2 EXTENDED LEAVE (see page 134)

This is a further extract from the interviews quoted in Data 3.1 on p.124. (For a more detailed analysis of this series of interviews, see Roberts and Sayers 1987.)

TRAINING MATERIAL 3.1 INTERVIEW FRAMES Exercise A [Ann Simpson Lancashire ILT]

CROSS-CULTURAL INTERVIEWS

Exercise A:

	Actual Dialogue	What do they mean?		What do they think?	
		Intention of Interviewer	Interpretation of interviewee	Cause of Misinterpretation	
A:	You have to consider your domestic circumstances should you be accepted.	Unconscious echoing of regulations as expressed in bureaucratic documents	Not recognisably about family etc.	Formal language.	
A:	There'll be an initial assessment period of three weeks.	Acquainting interviewee with rules.	Unable to understand language though idea not a problem if expressed differently.	Jargon	
A:	If you had known that you wouldn't get a job when you came back from Pakistan would you still have gone?	Warning that employers may find this unacceptable.	A straightforward request for information about intention to visit Pakistan.	Indirectness	
B:	Yes.				
A:	If you get a job will you leave it to go back to Pakistan?				
B.	Yes, in two years.				

A. B.	Do you drive a car? Yes, I passed test first time.	To find out about mobility.	A 'test' question to find out about skills.	Hidden purpose of question.
A. B.	Do you smoke? (Sikh) No thank you.	Friendliness.	Offended.	Unaware of cultural differences.
A. B.	What we'll do now, we'll keep you on our register for two months. If you haven't got fixed up with a job and you still want to be on the register, I've put the date on here, if you can pop in a couple of weeks before and just let me know we'll still keep you on. Do you understand? Yes. You mean you can find a job for me in two weeks?	Gives information.	Understands familiar words and constructs a sensible meaning from them – but the wrong one...	Long speaking turns.
A: B:	About how long did you work at C ____ ? I left in January 1981, and I started on 14th May 1968.	To get a general idea of length of time.	Relates this to previous interview experience, e.g. with immigration or DHSS officials where failure to supply exact detail is penalised	Role of interviewer not explicit.
A: B:	What have you been doing since you were made redundant? Nothing.	Probing to assess motivation.	Must tell the truth.	Different view of the function of an interview.

TRAINING MATERIAL 3.1 INTERVIEW FRAMES Exercise B [Ann Simpson Lancashire ILT]

CROSS-CULTURAL INTERVIEWS

Exercise B: Locate the cause of this misinterpretation

Actual Dialogue	Interpretation of interviewee	Dimension	
A: Come in and sit down Mr Mohammed.		D1:	The interviewer does not appreciate the significance of alternative naming systems.
B: It's Mohammed Inger.	Insulted.	D4:	The interviewer's actual use of language offends.
A: Have you any CSEs or O Levels?	Has not been asked about overseas qualifications therefore assumes they are irrelevant.	D1:	The significance and value of different qualifica–tions is not appreciated. The interviewer's assump–tions about his role in the interview does not allow him to 'sell' his qualifications.
B: No.			
A: I always service my own car.	Expression of doubt.	D3, 4:	'Really' is a phatic utterance to maintain conversational cooperation, but neither the function nor the intonation used are interpreted correctly.
B: Really?			

TRAINING MATERIAL 3.1 INTERVIEW FRAMES Exercise B *continued*

A: What did your job as a spinner involve?	Question about process in general because stressed word not obvious perceptually.	D2: Minority-group interviewees may not share a frame for interpreting 'What does your job involve?'
B: Well first it was unloaded and sorted then it was washed then it came to spinning, then the weaving shed.		D4: The word 'spinner' is not perceived as the important word.
A. Ok. I've said enough now you fire away.	Words have no relationship to 'It's your turn to speak'.	D4: The particular choice of language is inappropriate.
A. Have you done anything in your own time to improve your knowledge of electricity?	Unsure about relevance and appropriateness.	D1, 2: Again, a mismatch of schema and frame.
B. Yes, I rewired my own home.		D3: The lack of appropriate feedback prevents the interviewee from selling his skills.
A. Did you do anything else?		

See page 122 for guide to dimensions

DATA 3.2 EXTENDED LEAVE – TRANSCRIPT

Int: What are your feelings, Mr S ____, because we do have some
       complaints from time to time about the extended leave system...
       um... and certainly some of the white workers do feel that this is
       abused sometimes by black workers, particularly Indian and
       Pakistani workers. What are your feelings about somebody who   5
       perhaps chronically overstays on extended leave?

S: Er ...

Int: You said you've done it once with, if you like, forward
       permission, you warned the superiors and you haven't got a bad
       record for punctuality on returning. But what are your feelings   10
       about the worker who perhaps every time he goes on extended
       leave, comes back late with no form of warning to the staff.

S: Well, during my stay most of the immigrants, particularly Indian
       and Pakistanis, they started after me and we are quite friendly
       with each other, we know about each other. Well so far as I'm   15
       concerned I've got no problem whenever I wanted to go, there is
       no doubt about that. So I know the other ... my friends, but
       there are some isolated cases where there is a possibility that
       those gentlemen might have abused this system or this facility.
       There is a possibility, but as I know some cases they are   20
       genuinely in difficulty as their families are living there ... they
       have to go after a year or two and they are in problem. I have
       got one case, now from the last year that gentleman is with
       Company for the last twelve, thirteen years. He lived in
       England, he got citizenship, everything, now he has got a   25
       problem with the immigration authorities, well this is not your
       ultimate family some children are not yours, we don't issue an
       entry certificate. So, such ... that gentleman has to go at least
       year or after two years, and as some gentlemen abuse the system
       it reflects on such cases gives wrong impression to the   30
       management and due to poor communications I believe there
       may be some misunderstanding between the employers and the
       management.

Int: I think that particular problem wouldn't be a great difficulty in
       the post that you're applying for at ____. I think you might have 35
       noticed from the job description that at the plant where this
       vacancy is that the workforce is 98 per cent white. I think, in
       fact, you'd find that was far less of a problem than in ____ plant.
       However it does lead on to another problem which one has to
       face when you're applying for this type of job. You'd be dealing   40
       with people's queries about wages, obviously, from the job
       details and you were an hourly paid worker yourself, so you
       know how annoyed people get when there's something not right
       with their pay packet.

S: Oh yes.   45

DATA 3.2 COMMENTARY

This extract illustrates four important features of Dimension 3 – discourse management and style:

- lack of collaborative sequences;
- ways of structuring information;
- hyper-explanation;
- interruption.

The interviewer's first question is very ambiguous. It is not clear whether she is asking a question in the interview frame '*an invitation to display a balanced view*' or a personal probing to assess whether Mr S will fit into a largely white Management. The candidate's interpretive frame would seem to be '*I must justify myself and the group I represent*' – this is forced on him by her rapid interruption with hyper-explanation of his first attempt to respond, embedded in which is criticism of his ethnic group.

The candidate's lengthy response to the question compounds the frame mismatch. Mr S's answer is 'Due to poor communications I believe there may be some misunderstanding between the employees and the management on this issue' – a very good answer. A native speaker of English would have structured their answer by putting this summary first and supporting it with information and examples. But Mr S's excellent English is influenced by his native Panjabi where the way of structuring information is to lead up to the key response with justifications and examples which include rhetorical devices such as the unmarked quotation of other people's views, summarising the general point at the end.

In the interviewer's last input, which again contains hyper-explanation, it is difficult to identify a question which relates to the probable frame '*an invitation to display understanding of people*', and Mr S is unable to make any response other than minimal agreement.

The usual initial reaction of interviewers to this tape is that 'Mr S has some problems with communication and is not able to explain things clearly'. Some participants confess that because they could not follow his lengthy explanation they had 'switched off' and failed to hear the sentence at the end. (Ethnic-minority participants are well aware of the 'switching off' of white English people in conversation with them. In their own training sessions, they have described this metaphorically as 'the double-glazing effect'.) The trainer will give brief information on Panjabi discourse style, then quickly re-focus participants on the discourse style of the *interviewer* and its appropriateness for, and effect upon, the Panjabi speaker. This type of data can be used to help participants question their interview practice, to see the damaging effects of current practice, to help them see a candidate like Mr S in a positive light and to learn to be more flexible in the way they interpret varieties of communicative style.

Analysis of other taped extracts can then be used to show specific contrasts and to develop specific skills. For example, preliminary analysis by the trainers might show that white interviewers gave bad news unclearly and indirectly. Other segments of indirect information-giving can then be used for trainees to practise giving information and explanations clearly and directly. Or, for example, participants can work on different styles of turn-taking so that clients do not feel they are constantly interrupted or talked down to. Or, again, participants can be encouraged to see how their interactive role helps to construct their evaluation of the candidate or client.

Technique 4
Other pieces of taped data can be used to highlight not a skills need, but the need to check one's own cultural and institutional schema.

Example.   On a course for Department of Health and Social Security staff, an unemployed Bangladeshi worker, who had been invited in for a simulated interview, was concerned that his savings might disbar him from Supplementary Benefit. But the DHSS officer's schema – that unemployed workers must be presenting themselves to check up on their benefit entitlements – was so fixed that he failed to pick up on the man's real query. It was only after repeated viewings of the video that participants were able to isolate the point at which the client expressed his real practical concern:

    MA: Been three year here
         No money, you know
    Int: Not got enough money
    MA: Yeah
         I saving next time any money ten pound
         Five pound I keeping in bank and building society
    Int: Yeah
         What sort of money do you have coming in at the moment
         Are you unemployed and signing on?
                                              (Roberts and Sayers 1987)

Here MA gives crucial background information about how he has saved, but uses the *-ing* form, probably to give dramatic emphasis to the fact that he has saved (Bhardwaj 1988), so the interviewers do not pick up on the fact that he already has savings. The last words of his turn, 'bank and building society', are given with a low fall which suggests to the English listener that he has finished making his point. In many North Indian languages both completion and intention to continue are conveyed with low falls, but there is a subtle difference in the tone which an English-speaker would fail to pick up. MA may also be following the schema outlined in Technique 1, in which the Asian client gives little information and waits for the interviewer to infer his point. The interviewer fails to recognise the relevance of MA's information and simply takes up his turn at talk with the set routine of questions. The crucial factor here was that the Bangladeshi's syntax and prosody, at this particular point, were quite far removed from the standard variety of English. This is another example of difficulties in Dimensions 1 and 4 reinforcing each other and leading to a misinterpretation of intent.

Technique 5

Some trainers have used a sequence of short extracts of the same interviewer, in interviews with clients from a variety of different ethnic groups. These clips are particularly useful where the interviewer follows a highly structured plan, for example in Jobcentre employment-advice interviews. In these cases, comparisons can be made across interviews as to the relative success of this style of interviewing on different clients. Data 3.3 is an example.

DATA 3.3 JOBCENTRE INTERVIEWS (see pages 138–41)

[Data collected by Roger Munns, Lancashire ILT]

DATA 3.3 Context

In these two extracts the employment adviser, E, is a white woman. In the first extract the client, M, is a white man in his fifties. In the second extract the client, A, is also in his fifties and is from Bangladesh. Part of his interview was discussed briefly in Chapter 1. [Note: It is important for the reader to compare the two transcripts.]

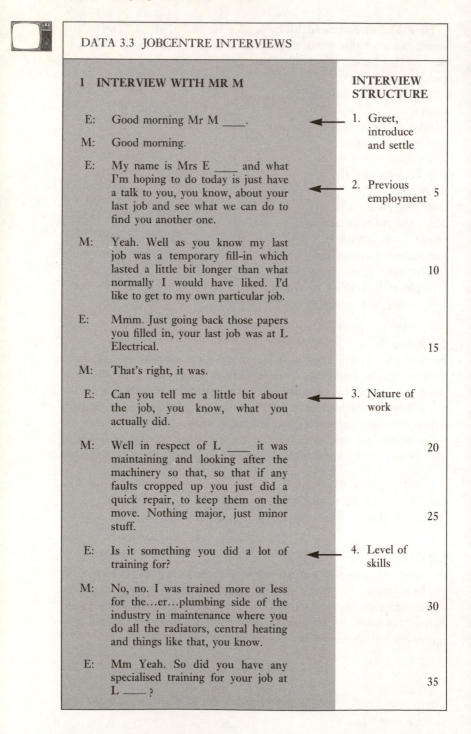

DATA 3.3 JOBCENTRE INTERVIEWS

1 INTERVIEW WITH MR M	INTERVIEW STRUCTURE

E: Good morning Mr M ___.

— 1. Greet, introduce and settle

M: Good morning.

E: My name is Mrs E ___ and what I'm hoping to do today is just have a talk to you, you know, about your last job and see what we can do to find you another one.

— 2. Previous employment 5

M: Yeah. Well as you know my last job was a temporary fill-in which lasted a little bit longer than what normally I would have liked. I'd like to get to my own particular job.

10

E: Mmm. Just going back those papers you filled in, your last job was at L Electrical.

15

M: That's right, it was.

E: Can you tell me a little bit about the job, you know, what you actually did.

— 3. Nature of work

M: Well in respect of L ___ it was maintaining and looking after the machinery so that, so that if any faults cropped up you just did a quick repair, to keep them on the move. Nothing major, just minor stuff.

20

25

E: Is it something you did a lot of training for?

— 4. Level of skills

M: No, no. I was trained more or less for the...er...plumbing side of the industry in maintenance where you do all the radiators, central heating and things like that, you know.

30

E: Mm Yeah. So did you have any specialised training for your job at L ___ ?

35

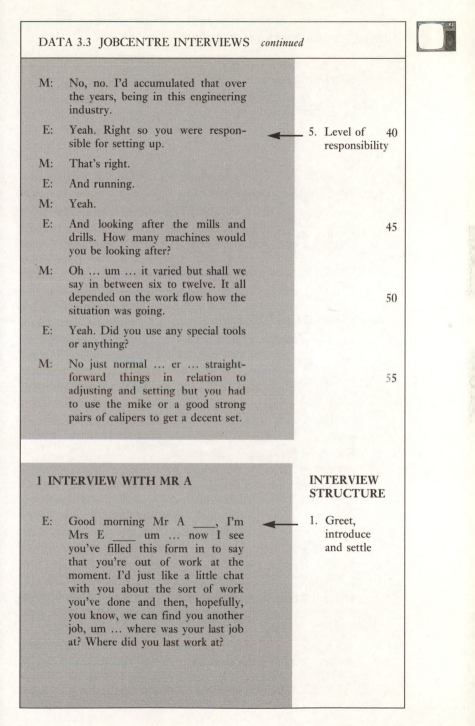

DATA 3.3 JOBCENTRE INTERVIEWS *continued*

M: No, no. I'd accumulated that over the years, being in this engineering industry.

E: Yeah. Right so you were responsible for setting up.   ⟵   5. Level of   40
                                                       responsibility

M: That's right.

E: And running.

M: Yeah.

E: And looking after the mills and drills. How many machines would you be looking after?   45

M: Oh ... um ... it varied but shall we say in between six to twelve. It all depended on the work flow how the situation was going.   50

E: Yeah. Did you use any special tools or anything?

M: No just normal ... er ... straight-forward things in relation to adjusting and setting but you had to use the mike or a good strong pairs of calipers to get a decent set.   55

1 INTERVIEW WITH MR A

INTERVIEW STRUCTURE

E: Good morning Mr A ___, I'm Mrs E ___ um ... now I see you've filled this form in to say that you're out of work at the moment. I'd just like a little chat with you about the sort of work you've done and then, hopefully, you know, we can find you another job, um ... where was your last job at? Where did you last work at?   ⟵   1. Greet, introduce and settle

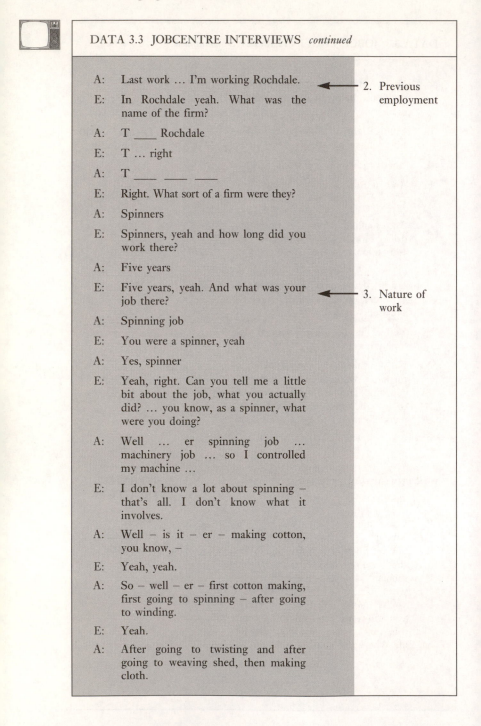

DATA 3.3 JOBCENTRE INTERVIEWS *continued*

A: Last work ... I'm working Rochdale.

                      ←——— 2. Previous
                                    employment

E: In Rochdale yeah. What was the name of the firm?

A: T ____ Rochdale

E: T ... right

A: T ____ ____ ____

E: Right. What sort of a firm were they?

A: Spinners

E: Spinners, yeah and how long did you work there?

A: Five years

E: Five years, yeah. And what was your
    job there?   ←——— 3. Nature of
                                    work

A: Spinning job

E: You were a spinner, yeah

A: Yes, spinner

E: Yeah, right. Can you tell me a little bit about the job, what you actually did? ... you know, as a spinner, what were you doing?

A: Well ... er spinning job ... machinery job ... so I controlled my machine ...

E: I don't know a lot about spinning – that's all. I don't know what it involves.

A: Well – is it – er – making cotton, you know, –

E: Yeah, yeah.

A: So – well – er – first cotton making, first going to spinning – after going to winding.

E: Yeah.

A: After going to twisting and after going to weaving shed, then making cloth.

DATA 3.3 JOBCENTRE INTERVIEWS *continued*

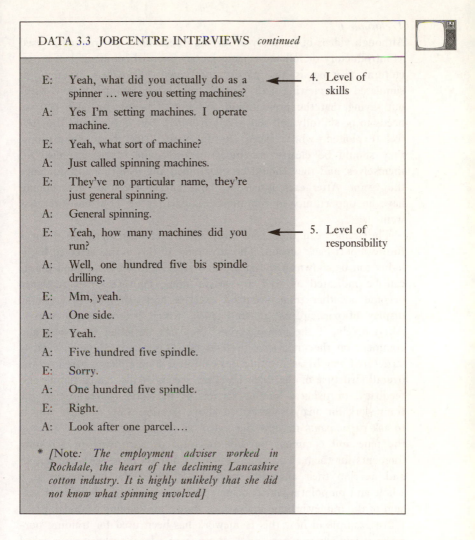

E: Yeah, what did you actually do as a spinner ... were you setting machines? ← 4. Level of skills

A: Yes I'm setting machines. I operate machine.

E: Yeah, what sort of machine?

A: Just called spinning machines.

E: They've no particular name, they're just general spinning.

A: General spinning.

E: Yeah, how many machines did you run? ← 5. Level of responsibility

A: Well, one hundred five bis spindle drilling.

E: Mm, yeah.

A: One side.

E: Yeah.

A: Five hundred five spindle.

E: Sorry.

A: One hundred five spindle.

E: Right.

A: Look after one parcel....

*   [Note: *The employment adviser worked in Rochdale, the heart of the declining Lancashire cotton industry. It is highly unlikely that she did not know what spinning involved*]

To guide discussion after viewing these interviews, participants are asked to focus on:

1. How comfortable the client was. [Note: Ethnic-minority participants usually see the interviewer as 'patronising', 'bullying' and 'ill-informed'. Some white participants see her as 'patient', 'friendly'.]
2. Whether the interviewer makes adjustments in communicative style.
3. How effective these are.

Technique 6

Although videos of naturally-occurring interactions are frequently used as introductory or follow-up material, an essential component of cross-cultural training is the participants' own videotaped attempts at simulated interviewing with 'clients' from ethnic groups. It goes without saying that the presentation and use of people on such courses needs to be skilfully and sensitively handled. Not only should they not feel exploited when asked to take part in these simulations; they should be clearly convinced of the value of the exercise for themselves, and they should be guaranteed any feedback and guidance they want. After each interview, both interviewer and client should have an opportunity to comment immediately on how the interview went.

The trainer can then take away the material and analyse it for a future report-back session. The advantage of this is that selected highlights can be shown to the group in a structured way and good points can be indicated as well as weaker ones. However, this tends to become a rather trainer-centred exercise and can lead to a public display of participants' incompetence, which is counter-productive. Alternatively, if the group agrees, they can be asked to review and comment on the interviews themselves. This can be done in a fairly structured way by asking them to complete simple charts based on the overall structure of the interviews, on specific skills, e.g. listening and feedback, or using a simple version of the four dimensions in the framework for analysis described above (section 3.2). Another way is to ask participants to view the video on several occasions and to stop the tape and comment on any awkward or surprising or arresting moments for them. The group can then discuss these with the trainer and develop their analytical skills by charting the interaction as a whole and pinpointing areas of potential or actual breakdown on a version of the framework for analysis, as shown in Training Material 3.2.

An example of how this framework has been used for training purposes is one where a personnel officer from a local authority was asked to re-create the kind of initial or screening interview which he would regularly undertake with applicants for a wide range of posts. It was agreed that this material could be used for future training purposes. A black 'applicant' who was currently unemployed and hoped to seek employment in the authority agreed to take part in the simulation.

TRAINING MATERIAL 3.2 MODIFIED FRAMEWORK FOR
COMMUNICATION ANALYSIS
[Devised by Clarice Brierley, Birmingham ILT]

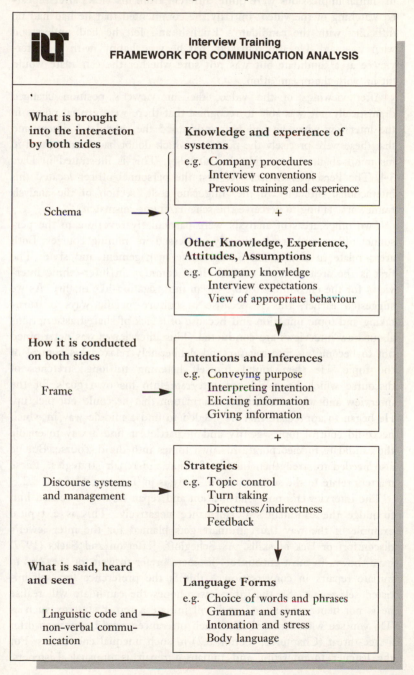

ILT

Interview Training
FRAMEWORK FOR COMMUNICATION ANALYSIS

**What is brought
into the interaction
by both sides**

**Knowledge and experience of
systems**

e.g. Company procedures
      Interview conventions
      Previous training and experience

Schema

+

**Other Knowledge, Experience,
Attitudes, Assumptions**

e.g. Company knowledge
      Interview expectations
      View of appropriate behaviour

**How it is conducted
on both sides**

Intentions and Inferences

e.g. Conveying purpose
      Interpreting intention
      Eliciting information
      Giving information

Frame

+

Strategies

e.g. Topic control
      Turn taking
      Directness/indirectness
      Feedback

Discourse systems
and management

**What is said, heard
and seen**

Language Forms

e.g. Choice of words and phrases
      Grammar and syntax
      Intonation and stress
      Body language

Linguistic code and
non-verbal commu-
nication

Immediately after the interview the personnel officer was asked to give his impressions of the encounter and the applicant. Interestingly, his initial impressions were quite different from his views after repeated watching of the video. Initially, he commented that he had had no difficulty with the candidate's English and felt he had understood what was said. He also remaked that he was 'happy' with the interviewee as a candidate but was not sure whether the candidate would 'fit in' with the organisation.

After viewings of the video, the interviewer's position changed dramatically. He was able to recognise that there were crucial points in the interview when he had not understood the candidate's intent and that these were precisely the points at which doubt had been created in his mind about the candidate's suitability. This is illustrated in Data 3.4. The Personnel Officer. At first the personnel officer located this interactional difficulty in the 'linguistic code' section of the analysis framework, failing to perceive the schema/frame mismatch.

Two other areas of analysis were particularly revealing to the personnel officer and are frequently addressed in training courses. Both areas relate to Dimension 3: discourse management and style. The first is the area of topic control. It is common in inter-ethnic interviews for the encounter to take on an interrogation-like quality. As we suggested earlier, this is because of culture-specific ways of turn-taking and topic initiation and because of a lack of shared assumptions about how interviews are conducted. This interviewer was determined not to become an interrogator and deliberately relaxed his control of the topic. He then found himself listening to long stretches of discourse which he could not integrate into his own goals for the interview and which contained information that he could not pick up. He began to appreciate that he needed to find a middle way in which he could control topics gently and in particular find a way to enable the candidate to incorporate his own topics into the discourse. But he also needed to strengthen his clarification and repair strategies. These matters relate to the second area of analysis in Training Material 3.2.

The interviewer's poor clarification and repair strategies caused him to judge the candidate's performance negatively. This is a typical example of the way the candidate gets blamed for the interviewer's discomfort or lack of skills. As Schegloff, Jefferson and Sacks (1977) have shown, in most encounters listeners prefer to wait for speakers to initiate repairs in conversation – this is the preference for 'self-initiated self-repair'. So the interviewer hopes the candidate will realise he is not being understood and will initiate a repair strategy such as 'Do you see what I mean?' But such utterances would appear to offer a face-threat (Chapter 2, section 3.2) in such unequal encounters. For the listener to interrupt and initiate a repair is unusual. Listeners,

DATA 3.4 THE PERSONNEL OFFICER – TRANSCRIPT
[Data collected and analysed by Peter Sayers, Bradford ILT]

Interviewer: I mean, how did you find out how to do it, did somebody show you ?

Candidate: Well, er, I saw somebody when they're working you know, that's why I know.

Interviewer: So you found out from them ?

Candidate: Yeah, everything is no hard the people try, because the people when's done nothing don't know anything, but when after learn and see they use the brain, you know, if the somebody can do it, why I can't, I can easy you know if I try, so that's why I know.

DATA 3.4 COMMENTARY

In this short extract there is a schema/frame mismatch. The interviewer's frame is *elicit how skills are acquired*, derived from the schema that a candidate needs to show trainability qualities and that these are best deduced by asking the candidate to give specific examples of how new skills were acquired. The candidate's frame, however, could be described as *explain my general philosophy of life*, derived from a set of schemata about job interviews which assume that candidates should show their negative face and should not be too personal or push themselves forward.

The schema/frame mismatch is further complicated by the surface structure of the candidate's English. There are other places in the interview where the candidate's syntax and prosody are different from the standard variety but do not pose comprehension difficulties. It is the schema/frame mismatch and different surface features *in combination* which lead to the negative judgement of the candidate's suitability.

even in positions of power, prefer not to tell the speakers directly that they have not understood them.

As a result of viewing the video and analysing it with the trainer, the personnel officer was made aware of a number of issues which he could immediately translate into practical action. First, he recognised that he had ignored the fact that the applicant was a bilingual speaker and that there were language differences for which the interviewer had to develop specific strategies. Second, he acknowledged that he had made sweeping judgements about the candidate which were not located in the actual evidence of the interaction. Third, he realised that by attempting good practice – relaxing topic control – he had constructed with the applicant an interactive environment which did little to support the candidate and, because of lack of shared assumptions, encouraged contributions from the candidate which the interviewer would then evaluate negatively as irrelevant or inappropriate.

The personnel officer learnt from his analysis that he needed to initiate repairs even though this was unusual and went against the grain. He realised that by not doing so, he was assessing the candidate on responses which he had rated as confused or even meaningless. He recognised the need to be much more explicit about lack of shared understanding than the normal conventions of politeness would allow. In this respect, the Scollons' suggestion that interviewers should present only a negative or deferential face (Scollon and Scollon 1983; and see Chapter 2, section 3.6) needs to be modified so that the interlocutors can go on record with their difficulties and resolve them.

Technique 7
We have described how detailed analysis of data from several viewpoints is one crucial focus of this training. However, it is absolutely essential that this is balanced for participants by devising other training materials which ensure that learning is experiential. Therefore, to conclude this section on techniques for using data and to lead into the next section on course planning, we include here an example (Training Material 3.3) of an experiential learning exercise which is not dependent on taped data.

TRAINING MATERIAL 3.3 OSCILLOGRAPHIC EVIDENCE
[Part of an input by John Gumperz on the course Developing Awareness Skills for Inter-Ethnic Communication (see section 4.1 below), Brent ILT and NCILT]

TRAINING MATERIAL 3.3 CONTEXT
The course was for the management of a company aware of the need for good communications, concerned about whether they were communicating well with staff from different cultural backgrounds, and committed to an advanced language-training programme as part of an effort to promote more of their staff from overseas to higher grades.

After some of the areas described in Techniques 1–6 had been exemplified and discussed on the course, the managers were told that

---

TRAINING MATERIAL 3.3 OSCILLOGRAPHIC EVIDENCE – TRANSCRIPT

G:	Oscillographic evidence indicates <laughter> that tone grouping is the major determinant in speech planning. A tone is made of three ingredients. First there is pausing, then there is nucleus placement, the nucleus is usually placed at the point of highest pitch obtrusion, thirdly, there is the tune.
Manager:	Wait wait. Can you... can you stop there. I've got the part about pausing. Nucleus? What's that?
G:	Nucleus placement.
Manager:	Yes, how do you describe nucleus, in what way? What do you mean?
G:	A nucleus usually consists of two features, loudness or amplitude and pitch obtrusion, shift in pitch. The nucleus is usually placed within a particular word, on a particular lexical item, within a tone group. Now there are some theories that hold that tone groups are syntactically constrained. The relationship of syntax to tone grouping however is a matter for further investigation. <Group laughter – lecture stops>
2nd Manager:	You are going on the assumption that we all understand what you are saying. And your assumptions are wrong.

(Gumperz and Roberts 1980)

---

a professor of linguistics was going to give them a technical lecture on language and that they were to interrupt when they did not understand. The example given is a transcription of the end of this session, in which the lecturer deliberately included terminology which would be unfamiliar to his listeners. The lecture was stopped at the point where the transcript ends, and the question then asked by the trainer was 'Why didn't you interrupt sooner?'

The focus here was on interrupting strategies, but this exercise was intended also to convey something of the position of some of the company's Indian workers in conversation with an English person. In other words, the white managers began to experience what it is like to only partially understand a speaker and to sense that the speaker is making no attempt to take account of the listener's different expectations and skills.

TRAINING MATERIAL 3.3 COMMENTARY

Four main points arose in discussion:

1. The students had their 'lecture schema' active. That is, they expected that Gumperz would tie his talk together and make a clear point, and waited for the point to emerge before interrupting.
2. Gumperz used inflections that signalled that he had a point to make.
3. Although they didn't understand any of the words, their knowledge of the style and inflection, as in 1 and 2, enabled the students to fill in from context.
4. The managers complained that they weren't sure of the appropriate strategy for interrupting. They had been given no specific instructions – 'You didn't indicate... whether you wanted us to bang on the table, or what.'

The effects of 1, 2 and 3 were summarised in one student's answer to the question of why they didn't interrupt. He said: 'Because quite often, when someone's talking, although you don't understand what it is he's talking about initially, the longer he talks, it may become clear.'

---

4 Examples of cross-cultural training courses

4.1 Developing awareness skills for inter-ethnic communication

This example is based on the work carried out by Gumperz and Roberts in 1977 (Gumperz and Roberts 1980). This training course was the first of its kind and many of the insights gained from it were used in making the BBC film *Crosstalk* and the accompanying booklet (Gumperz, Jupp and Roberts 1979). The training approach concentrated only on what we have called Dimensions 3 and 4 of the framework for analysis – discourse management and style; and syntax, lexis and prosody – although some broader issues of inter-ethnic communication were to be touched upon.

The underlying aim and approach of this early attempt at cross-cultural training is characterised by principles based on:

(i)   The need to recognise and talk explicitly about communication difficulties and the kind of negative stereotyping that they lead to.
(ii) The need for black and white participants to do this analysis and awareness-raising together, using concrete examples.
(iii) The assumption that participants cannot be **taught** to communicate more effectively in inter-ethnic settings. They have to **learn**

to be communicatively flexible in their own way. This is because every interaction is locally produced – that is, it depends on the responses interactants elicit from each other.

Context

The training took place in north-west London, at a major computing firm. This firm was concerned with the storage and issue of spare parts. The workforce was white and Asian, with the latter originating mainly from East Africa. Some Asians were engineers and accountants but the majority were stock and tally clerks. The training was aimed at this group and their immediate supervisors, who were all white. The company was keenly aware of the need for efficient communication, all the more so since they considered they had an open style of management which included considerable negotiation with individual employees on the subject of their careers and annual appraisals. The course was very short, consisting of nine hours for each group. The white supervisors and the Asian workers each had two seminars separately and then combined for a final joint seminar.

In pre-course interviews and discussions, it was clear that the Asian employees and the white supervisors had a number of negative perceptions of each other which were rarely attributed to any difficulties in communication. The Asian staff felt that managers were not very approachable, that they made arbitrary decisions and did not listen to their Asian employees. They felt rather insecure about their positions and tended to give up quickly if they got a 'no' response from management. Managers and supervisors felt that many of the Asians did not come to them with their problems, that they did not know how the unwritten rules of the company worked – what was fixed and what negotiable – and, specifically, that 'they did not know how far to go with a person'. The comments of the two groups together built up a picture of difficulties in sorting out problems and a lack of shared assumptions about appropriate ways of negotiating together.

From the research by Gumperz on inter-ethnic communication (see section 3.6 in Chapter 2), it was clear that many of these perceptions stemmed from differences in systems of communicating. For example, bilingual speakers from the Indian subcontinent are frequently confused and irritated by what are seen as over-apologetic or over-polite refusals by white English-speakers, where the definiteness of the refusal is in doubt. Similarly, bilinguals frequently attest to the English-speaker 'glazing over' or 'switching off' when they are giving explanations or narrating a past event. Native English-speakers, on the other hand, are confused or irritated by the apparent lack of cohesive features in the discourse of bilingual speakers; and differences in prosodic features can make bilingual speakers sound boring or pedantic or over-emotional to native speakers, while native speakers themselves seem aggressive or over-personal to bilinguals. It was the aim of the course to help both sides to understand the linguistic and communicative base of many of their negative perceptions of each other.

Content
Each three-hour seminar was in four stages:

(i) Introduction to an area of language analysis (from Dimension 3 or 4);
(ii) Contrastive tape-analysis exercise;
(iii) Joint analysis and discussion of prepared and naturally-occurring audio-taped material;
(iv) Participant role-play and analysis.

The first seminar started at the most discrete level by examining the different ways in which stress and pitch are used in different varieties of English. Through a series of short exercises and prepared contrastive role-plays, participants were helped to see how information is lost and attitudes misinterpreted when stress is not placed to show either normal information flow or contrast or emphasis. Data 3.5 Time Sheets is an example. Here, A is a North Indian speaker of English, and B and C are native English-speakers. (The full prosodic notation is not used here because the data was also used as training material; the transcripts employ a simple system of marking to show emphasis (underline) and strong emphasis (double underline) which could be readily understood by trainees.)

The next seminar focused on the use of prosodic features in longer stretches of discourse. In particular, participants were shown how intonation is used by Anglo English-speakers to signal shifts in focus, topic, attitude or relative importance. The use of different signals by bilingual speakers often causes Anglo English-speakers to switch off or to assume that the bilingual speaker is not being rational or coherent. Allied to this theme, there was also analysis and discussion of contrastive tapes showing the use of back-references to tie the various parts of a story-line together.

Both the management and the bilingual group were introduced to a number of metacommunicative notions such as signalling, inference, implication and tone of voice. The purpose was to create a common language for analysing communication, and one which was relatively neutral and free from the evaluative undertones and personal feelings

DATA 3.5   TIME SHEETS – TRANSCRIPT
[Role-plays acted out by Pathway ILT, West London and Jaswinder Sidhu, NCILT]

Instructions to role-play participants

You want to get back some timesheets from a colleague.
You ask him for 'the sheets.' He says he put them back on your desk. You deny this. He says he's sure he did and identified them in the process. But they are not the sheets you wanted. You were looking for some other sheets.

Role-play 1: Anglo English/Anglo English

C: Dave / you got those <u>sheets</u> for me please //

B: I put them on your desk <u>yesterday</u> Pete //

C: You <u>sure</u> / I haven't <u>seen</u> em //

B: Yeah sure / it said on the top of them <u>check</u>list for April / isn't it //

C: No no / they're not the <u>ones</u> / no I want the <u>time</u> sheets //

B: Oh sorry / I thought you meant the <u>check</u>lists //

C: No / that's alright //

Role-play 2: Indian English/Anglo English

A: Excuse me David //

B: Yeah

A: Could I have those sheets <u>back</u> please //

B: Those <u>sheets</u>? / I put them on your desk <u>yesterday</u> //

A: Haven't seen on my ⌐<u>desk</u> //

B: Ah / I'm <u>sure</u> I did / I'm <u>sure</u> I did

Commentary

Much of the emphasis conveyed through prosody in the standard variety of English would be conveyed syntactically in North Indian languages. Similarly, the raised pitch that Anglo English-speakers might use to show emphasis or contrast would be used by speakers of North Indian languages only to display familiarity or emotion.

When A. asks:

// Could I have those sheets back please //, putting stress on 'back', he sounds as if he is accusing B. Later, A tries to sort out the misunderstanding:

// No / No not checklists / I want the timesheets //

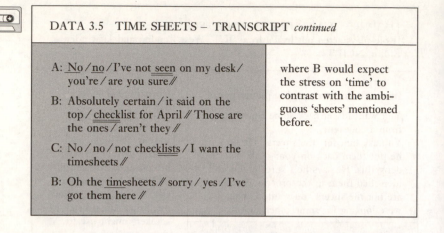

DATA 3.5   TIME SHEETS – TRANSCRIPT *continued*

A: No / no / I've not seen on my desk /
you're / are you sure //

B: Absolutely certain / it said on the
top / checklist for April // Those are
the ones / aren't they //

C: No / no / not checklists / I want the
timesheets //

B: Oh the timesheets // sorry / yes / I've
got them here //

where B would expect
the stress on 'time' to
contrast with the ambi-
guous 'sheets' mentioned
before.

which so often are the terms on which these topics are discussed. Both
groups found this new language easy to handle and were soon developing their own terms, such as 'the double-glazing effect' (created by one
of the Asian participants) and 'they're on two parallel tracks'.

The final joint management/Asian-staff seminar provided an opportunity to discuss together, using the shared metalanguage, many of the
issues raised by both groups in earlier sessions. Some of the same
material was used again, but this time the focus was less on how
different groups may produce different varieties of English than on
how these groups may interpret the same piece of interaction differently. For example, in the sample tape conversation between a white
supervisor and an Asian clerk in Data 3.5, the white supervisor's
remark // Those sheets? // was interpreted by several Asian participants
as angry or a little aggressive and by English participants as inquiring.

To give a flavour of the actual sessions, and the level of the participants' interest in and enthusiasm for language issues, Training
Material 3.4 is a transcript of extracts from a lengthy discussion of
'Timesheets' by the white group. The group has listened to the two
contrastive versions; A is the trainer.

Several other contrastive role-play tapes were used in different
seminars and those raised a number of wider issues. These concerned
the relationship between communicative style and the differing norms
and assumptions about work relationships. The discussion was sparked
off by a tape in which a white supervisor used a mild form of
invective, 'Why the devil'. Differences in group norms centred on the
contrast between the expected informality in an English setting and
the more hierarchical and formal workplace relationships more typical

TRAINING MATERIAL 3.4 TRANSCRIPT OF CLASSROOM ANALYSIS OF TIMESHEETS [NCILT]

A: Okay, what's the general impression of the difference between the two?

B: More friendly rapport.

A: Yeah, I think that that sort of sums it up, doesn't it? That it just seems to be more friendly rapport. Can you explain why they seem to be more friendly?

C: Yes indeed, now you've got that same problem again where the Indian guy raises his voice level, when he says, you know when the guy says almost chummily, 'Ah no no' (   ) and the Indian guy gets what sounds (   ) irate (   ) up 'No, no'.

A: Yeah, it goes right up, doesn't it? Let's listen to it again. <listen to tape to line 3> Mm hm. Any comments there?

C: It's, it's a build-up. That guy, the Indian guy, says 'Can I have those sheets back?' He's being slightly offensive because he's emphasizing 'back' rather than 'sheets'.

M: No, he should have said, 'I haven't seen them on my desk.'

J: That's right. You see 'on my desk,' my reaction would be to say, 'well, maybe you've seen them someplace else' (general laughter).

C: That thing shifts the emphasis from, from 'you' to 'me'. Because I'm ... if I say, 'I haven't <u>seen</u> them on my desk.' that means, maybe I'm at fault.

J: That's right.

C: You can't say, 'I haven't <u>seen</u> them on my desk.' You know that's putting the emphasis on you to put 'em on my desk.

A: That's right.

C: And you're shifting the, the =

A: = The blame

C: The battle is going, you know.

J: Yeah.

C: It's a very ... confrontation, he's going backwards and forwards like that.

TRAINING MATERIAL 3.4 TRANSCRIPT OF CLASSROOM ANALYSIS OF TIMESHEETS [NCILT]   *continued*

J: That's right, exactly.

N: In that particular case when we were saying that we felt a little bit of, uh, urgency coming out of the Englishman, or a little bit of irateness, is that going to be interpreted, by the Asian, as an irateness? Or is it gonna be interpreted as, how he would have normally spoken under the circumstances?

J: Well...

N: Are you with me?

A: Hm. But I'm sure... yes, that the Asian person, listening would, would interpret that, would infer from that, 'This man is really, much too excited, and therefore, rude.' I mean, often I think exci... that kind of excitement in the voice as interpreted as rudeness...

C: Yes...

A: Should we just... there's another little point I think it's worth making after this one. <Plays tape lines 5–7.> The supervisor goes 'I'm sure I did, I'm sure I did.'

C: He doubled his 'I'm sure I did, I'm sure I did.' and the guy came back with, 'No, no!'

J: <laughs>

C: He obviously feels that, uh, to do it twice over.

A: Yeah, and what about the pitch of his voice there?

J: Goes up.

      <Several: Sure, yeah>

P: Sheets.

A: Yeah, he stresses 'sheets'. And what would we stress?

P: Time.

A: Right.

P: That's what (   ), we identify it.

A: Right. He doesn't identify what he wants. He could say, 'My god,' you know, 'what a silly guy. He doesn't really say what he wants.' Because it takes just a bit of time, we have to struggle a bit, to realise that he's contrasting the checklist sheets with the time sheets. But he doesn't make that contrast at all, does he?

of South Asian cultures. These differences affect how personal a perspective to adopt, how far one can use joking or casual invective, and how personal to be when either making or granting or refusing requests. When, for example, the participants tried a role-play based on one of the tapes concerning a problem with a payslip, the English supervisor expressed a personal sense of responsibility while the Asian supervisor implied that the responsibility belonged primarily with others.

The contrastive role-play tapes divided into three categories to illustrate communication difficulties which lead to misunderstanding:

(i)   'Sorting out'   –   when a mistake has been made which has to be sorted out;
(ii) 'Countering'   –   negotiating over a problem;
(iii) 'Explaining'   –   extended description and reporting.

In the last joint session participants enacted their own role-plays, which used situations of particular concern such as communicating with engineers over the telephone. The annual appraisal interview was also identified as a key encounter for all staff. Since many of the individuals might have recently been involved in just such an interview, it was agreed to role-play a job interview as an example of an analogous evaluative process.

The sessions ended with a summary of the main points participants felt they had learned about inter-ethnic communication:

(i)   Communication is a two-way process. Communication can break down, and it can break down on either side.
(ii) Just as negative stereotypes can be built up by communication, they can be broken down by successful communication.
(iii) The standard variety of English and the English influenced by South Asian languages are both language systems. Their speakers have automatic and systematic ways of perceiving things and reacting. For each group, compensation for those aspects of the system difficult for the other group, and explicitness, are the key to better communication.
(iv) These differences are not ethnic differences *per se*. Communication at work is often stressful, so both sides need to appreciate what they can do to make communication more effective. For speakers it is important to know how much to say, whether the context has been clearly set, whether the information has been presented so that the implied connections are clear and any intended action stated explicitly. As listeners, it is important to

know when to express how much has been understood, how to express lack of understanding and seek clarification and how to interpret the message, particularly how personally to take it.

The general evaluation of the course was encouraging. Although the focus was on language and communication, the informal and good-humoured atmosphere of the sessions allowed management and Asian staff to get to know each other better and to discuss some of their specific problems together. In the last session, participants started putting forward possible strategies for combating future communication problems. They left the course with a new analytic metalanguage with which to discuss any future problems. They had proved to themselves that they could analyse even subtle and complex communication breakdowns and that they could use this analysis to challenge some of the assumptions about the behaviour and attitudes of the other ethnic group.

4.2 Anti-racism interviewing course for government training and employment advisory officers

Context
The training was set up and run by three ILT units, Birmingham, Bradford and Lancashire, between 1982 and 1984. This was a series of courses for any key personnel in public training and employment advisory services. The rationale for the training was that three recent surveys had shown that bilingual and black speakers were less likely to benefit from these public services than their white counterparts (Smith 1981).

Aim
To enhance the skills and awareness of advisory staff, within the context of an equal-opportunities policy, so that a fairer and more effective service was offered to black clients.

Objectives
To help participants to:

- identify ways in which selection, screening and interviewing can be discriminatory;
- identify ways of adjusting or changing procedures which had a discriminatory outcome so that black clients could get equal benefits from the services;

– identify specific skills in cross-cultural interviewing;
– put these skills into practice when interviewing bilingual speakers;
– demonstrate an understanding of the difficulties faced by black clients in using the services offered.

Content

The precise form of training varied from course to course, but all courses included:

– an analysis of how judgements are made in interviews;
– an analysis of application forms and how they are used to make judgements;
– awareness-raising exercises on how easy it is to discriminate indirectly;
– experiential exercises to help monolingual English-speakers to appreciate the difficulties of communicating in a second language;
– exercises on the need to be aware of cultural differences and to help participants develop sensitivities towards such differences for themselves;
– video analysis of naturally-occurring interviews highlighting what can go wrong and how to effect change;
– simulation and analysis of interviews between participants and black clients.

Organisation

The courses consisted of four modules to be run over four days, with a gap of several weeks between the third and the fourth module. Modules 1 and 3 were designed around a few major activities. Module 2 consisted of more specific exercises held together by a conceptual framework. Module 4 allowed for follow-up or reinforcement in issues of discrimination, the development of specific skills or extension to different types of interview.

Only the first two modules are described here, because Module 3 consisted entirely of naturally-occurring and simulated video interviews of the type discussed in some detail in section 3.1 of this chapter.

Module 4 was an extension of the other modules and also contained suggestions for more general activities on institutional racism related to the then current practice of training and advisory officers. These are outside the scope of this discussion.

Module	Activity
1. Making Fair Decisions	Raising awareness and developing sensitivity
2. Communication and Change	Experience of and identification of specific skills
3. Practising and Developing Skills	Participation in simulated interviews
4. Taking Things Further	Discussion of implications and further practice of specific skills

Module 1: Making fair decisions

The central exercise referred to in the Module 1 Handout (Training Material 3.5) was an exercise in which participants were invited to view a series of selection interviews and to rank the five candidates in

TRAINING MATERIAL 3.5 PRE-COURSE INFORMATION

ilt

Interview course: Module 1
Making Fair Decisions
RAISING AWARENESS AND DEVELOPING SENSITIVITY

Aims: To gain acceptance of the statement that if everyone is to be treated equally, then it is necessary to treat individuals differently.

To raise awareness of the issues involved in inter-ethnic interviewing.

Methods: This is done by focussing first on the fact that inter-ethnic interviews may be different and then by concentrating on what it is about intra-ethnic interviews which make them such culture-specific events. This will be done through experiential exercises using your existing forms and standard procedures. The central exercise in this module is the analysis of the selection interviews for a local authority apprenticeship. Again, this exercise will be experiential and not just analytical.

The course methodology requires participants to make their own judgements and then to query them in the light of additional information and insights.

There will be an opportunity, at the end of this module, to draw together insights into culture-specific aspects of conventional interviews.

order of preference. The aim of this exercise is to show how inter-viewers make highly subjective judgements of candidates and to analyse the process whereby the interviewer's stereotyped judgements 'shape' the candidate. In the particular example used on these courses, the video was of five candidates – four black and one white – applying for an apprenticeship in electrical engineering with a local authority. Participants were asked to concentrate on the interviewees and assess them. After viewing the video, the participants ranked the candidates. The rankings were noted and compared with the preferences of the interview panel, which are shown in Training Material 3.6. (See pp. 160–1.)

The great majority of participants agreed with the interview panel on making their first and second choices – either the single white candidate or the black candidate who wore a suit and glasses. Their lowest choice was almost invariably the fifth candidate. The main reason given was that the top two candidates made them feel comfortable. The black candidate looked and sounded 'right'. They felt sympathy for the white candidate and could relate to his background.

After seeing the video, ranking the candidates, and comparing their ranking to that of the local authority's interview panel, the trainees were invited to view the post-interview discussion with the candidates, which was also on video. This informal discussion was much more revealing of the candidates. It was clear that candidate 1 was really not interested in the job at all. Candidates 3 and 5, by contrast, came across as very capable of expressing their views on the interview process in an analytical, sensitive and honest way. For example, the last candidate discussed the fact that he was very frank in the interview about his shortcomings because he believed the panel should assess him 'for what he is'. This is a far cry from the usual assumptions about 'selling yourself' at job interviews.

After viewing the post-interview discussion, participants were asked to re-rank the candidates. The great majority changed their minds quite radically, moving candidates 2, 3 and 5 up the ranking and downgrading 1 and 4. Many participants felt uncomfortable and dis-turbed after this part of the exercise. In the initial process of ranking the candidates, there were usually lengthy discussions and comments in which the participants together constructed firm views about what the five were like. After the post-interview discussion had been shown, their apparently 'sound' judgement had to be rapidly dismantled. And no one likes their judgements exposed as unsound.

In order that the trainees might not find the exercise so threatening that they, in effect, withdrew from participating, the next stage was to

TRAINING MATERIAL 3.6   SUMMARY OF INTERVIEW PANEL'S IMPRESSIONS
[Exercise devised and prepared by Eliza Christmas, Newham ILT, and adapted by Jenny Ferris, Calderdale ILT]

Interviewing Course : Module 1
LOCAL AUTHORITY APPRENTICESHIP INTERVIEWS

	Panel's Interview Notes	Trainer's Interview Notes
Candidate 1	"A good candidate." "Seems to be on the ball." "Looks right and sounds sensible." "Smartly turned out – looks bright." "– has made an effort."	He is seen as a good interviewee. The overall impression is good but vague.
Candidate 2	"Introverted?" "... bit of a communication problem – hard to understand." "Chewing gum" "Not a very good track record academically." "Is he up to the Course?"	He is not chewing gum.

TRAINING MATERIAL 3.6 SUMMARY OF INTERVIEW PANEL'S IMPRESSIONS *continued*

Candidate 3	"Attitude problem – bit aggressive." "Obviously thinks we are straight white and boring." "Can imagine him hanging roung snooker halls." "Main interest sports ..." ... has he got the motivation?"	They feel he is mocking the interviewer. [In fact in the post-interview discussion this candidate said he felt very nervous and was trying to make himself feel more confident.]
Candidate 4	"Promising candidate." "Seems to be very nervous." "Shy and diffident – seems to have had a raw deal conscientious steady sort of lad." "Pretty sound school report." "Should fit in well."	He is the only white candidate. The impressions are positive. The panel readily identified and sympathised with the candidate's nervousness – there were a lot of encouraging noises. The panel find him very easy to relate to and a whole fiction is built up around him as a 'poor boy' with a widowed mother – [None of this is true].
Candidate 5	"Not really interested." "English weak." "Irritating head and eye movements doesn't seem all there." "Not much to say for himself." "Main interest Art – got his head in the clouds."	The over-riding impression is negative. The pauses before he answers make the panel impatient, and he is often cut off early. Longer and longer questions and hyper-explanation, with the candidate answering only 'yes' and 'no'.

examine together, more analytically, the way in which the interviewers' questions 'shaped' each candidate in turn. Before the start of the interviews, the chair of the interview panel commented that 'there was not much to choose between them on paper'. However, the range of questions, the way they were asked and the panel's response to them differed systematically between candidates (see Training Material 3.7).

As a result of this exercise, most participants were ready to accept that many judgements of candidates in interviews are influenced by the interviewers' own expectations and behaviour, and to talk about the following issues which had been pinpointed through discussion of the five interviews together with the candidates' comments afterwards:

1. The applicant is judged by how comfortable the interviewers feel.
2. Strong impressions are made in the first minutes of the interview largely based on appearance and non-verbal behaviour. These impressions cannot be backed up by actual evidence from the interview.
3. There is a global undifferentiated view of 'the interview', as an activity. A suit and tie are considered the right dress whatever the interview is for. Participants have to be encouraged to question their assumptions about dress. Candidate 1 is suitably dressed for a bank job but there is no reason why a suit and tie should be worn at an interview for an electrical-installations apprenticeship.
4. The types of questions asked 'shape' the candidate. That is, they push her/him into a standard mould for the interviewer so that stereotypes or impressions are reinforced and the candidate cannot show what sort of person they really are. For example:
   - Candidate 1 is asked more practical questions about academic ability.
   - Candidate 5 is asked a lot of long, closed questions to which the answer is only 'yes' or 'no'.
   - Only candidate 2's *failures* in exams are raised.
   - Candidate 3 gets a lot of questions about sport.
   - Many questions to candidates 2, 3 and 5 are couched in negative terms, e.g. 'Nothing more advanced than that?'
5. There is a strong case for most of the questions, particularly the technical ones, being *exactly* the same for each candidate. However, it is also important that interviewers help to create a positive dynamic in which questions and follow-ups are responsive to the applicants' way of presenting themselves.

TRAINING MATERIAL 3.7 DIFFERENT QUESTIONS

iLT

Interviewing course: Module 1
QUESTIONS: GENERAL EDUCATION AND ABILITY TO COPE
WITH COLLEGE COURSE

Candidate 1 – Obviously with your exam results you won't know yet what grades you'll get but you will have had an assessment from you teacher; are you confident that you'll get fairly good grades?

Candidate 2 – Now you didn't take many exams when you were at school... erm ... this is a point which obviously may worry us to the extent that if you were selected the course you would be going on would involve some fairly rigorous work; it's quite a hard course, do you feel you'd be able to cope with a lot more study than perhaps is indicated at the level that is on your form?

    – Did you not take any more exams or is that the only ones that you passed?

    – So how many others had you taken that you failed?

    – Three more, what sort of grades were they? Do you recall?

    – Mmm I see, what subjects?

    – I see, not very good ... never mind.

Candidate 3 – So ... you left school not so long ago ... enjoying your freedom?

    – Now, the sort of course you go on, if we sent you to college if you were successful, is very rigorous. Not obviously every person would be able to cope with it, do you think you would be able to manage with lots of study and that sort of thing?

    – It wouldn't interfere with your sports would it? I seem to see that you like to do a lot of sports?

    – So you'd be able to fit in some college work in-between?

Candidate 4 – Now you took a nice lot of exams at school. Obviously you got fairly good grades as well. You find studying quite easy?

TRAINING MATERIAL 3.7   DIFFERENT QUESTIONS
continued

Candidate 4 – Oh really, but you think you'd be able to cope with work plans and everything else because it's quite a rigorous course?

– My, you do sound conscientious! Very good.

Candidate 5 – Now I see you haven't got the grades for your exams yet, you've just taken them. How do you think you're going to do?

– Oh dear. I notice spelling isn't perhaps one of your best points, obviously you'd need to have a good command of the English language to be able to cope with the course if you were successful and obviously it's quite a strenuous course at college, do you really feel that you'd be up to it?

– You do? Although as you say, you don't think you're going to do particularly well.

– Why is that, are you just not very good at exams or in all honesty have you not really tried, done much revision?

– Oh dear! I see. Fine (Returns to subject later.)

– Of the exams that you've taken which do you think might give you the best grade?

– Art, I see. Do you want to go into art college or something like that, something a little less strenuous perhaps?

– Apprenticeship's a second choice really. I see. That's all. Thank you.

---

6. There are strong conventions about the 'interview game':
   – You must show you are keen even if you are not – the 'stylised honesty' of the interview.
   – The response 'yes' or 'no' is not enough (even if it appears to be an adequate answer).
   – There are 'right' questions for the applicant to ask at the end.
   – There must be just the right level of deference/confidence to make the interviewers feel comfortable.

Many candidates from ethnic minorities are surprised by such conventions and, not having internalised them, react to them as a complicated exercise in mutual hypocrisy.

7. Except with candidate 4, the interviewers fail to build up any personal rapport and so fail to see the 'real' person behind the candidate. The kind of positive feedback given to him, e.g. 'My, you do sound conscientious!', is almost totally lacking for the other candidates.
8. There are clear cultural differences in the way the candidates present themselves and show their anxieties, which tend to be interpreted according to English cultural norms.
9. The whole rhythm and management of the interview depends crucially on the initial good or bad impression. With 2, 3 and 5, there is very little evidence of conversational cooperation – of the interview approximating to a conversation. The tendency is for the interviewers to taked complete control, as longer and longer closed questions get shorter answers so that the balance between panel and applicant is skewed and the interviewers talk more and more and at increasingly low levels of abstraction. The candidate becomes monosyllabic as the more powerful speakers pump up their style of speaking in an attempt to change the style of the candidate.

Module 2: Communication and change (Training Material 3.8)

As can be seen from the transcript of classroom analysis in Training Material 3.4 (p.154), managers and counsellors with key gatekeeping roles may analyse communication on a fairly primitive level. It is necessary, therefore, to establish a common and professional framework and metalanguage for analysis which can be shared by the trainers and the course participants.

The framework given to trainees in Module 2 was the one which has been illustrated in Training Material 3.2 (p.143), covering; schema, frame, discourse management and style, and linguistic code. Each category of the framework was discussed in some detail, and illustrated through practical exercises.

Exercise 1   *Schema: knowledge and assumptions about employment-advice interviews*

Aim: To illustrate how the apparent efficiency and objectivity of highly structured advice interviews can fail to provide an adequate service to bilingual speakers.

Content: Data 3.3, on the contrastive Jobcentre interviews (p.138), was used. [This is an example of how the same piece of prepared data can be used for a multiplicity of language-teaching and language-awareness-raising purposes.]

Discussion of the data was steered to establish that:

1. The interviews are run on the assumption that clients understand the hidden purpose of the adviser's questions, that they know how

TRAINING MATERIAL 3.8   PRE-COURSE INFORMATION

iLT

Interviewing course: Module 2
COMMUNICATION AND CHANGE

Aims: By focussing on behaviour in interviews to show trainees they can change and that they have the resources within them to change.

To show that interviews are constructed out of language, so trainees must understand the nature of communication.

To establish a framework for communication which explains that:
We are operating at different levels all the time – we need to make changes at *all* these levels but *any* change at *any* of these levels can help.

To show trainees that the way they operate is not, inevitably, the right or only way.

To extend the interview model, i.e. a highly concentrated piece of interaction in which life chances depend upon personal evaluation, to counselling and advice interviews.

Methods: In Module 1, the issue of being *fair* was raised (particularly in the Selection Interview tapes). This module identifies skills and shows change can take place in order for trainees to be *effective* as interviewers. This is done not by giving a lot of information or checklists of do's and don'ts but by developing sensitivities and resources that lie in everyone if only they are attended to. Changes are manifested in behaviour. And it is on behaviour that this module focuses. However, trainees need to explore the knowledge, assumptions and expectations which generate behaviour.

This module offers a series of exercises on different aspects of communication. To ensure that these aspects are not seen in isolation, trainees are first introduced to an overall framework for communication. Any exercises chosen fit into this overall framework.

to categorise their activities to fit the Jobcentre bureaucratic categories and that they know how detailed to be.
2. Clients who have strategies for controlling the interview have even more chance of gaining quality advice and being judged as worthy of the possible jobs on offer.

3. The bilingual speaker, who was a teacher in his country of origin but has had to work at largely unskilled manual jobs in Britain, is a highly cooperative interviewee and provides a great deal of information. However, the white adviser is never able to establish collaboratively the smooth and rapid exchange of information which her set questions are meant to produce. She is unable to participate or then repair the difficulties that arise over such questions as 'What does your job involve?'

Exercise 2   *Frame: interpretation of question strategies*
Aim: To examine the ways in which questions can be misinterpreted and change the direction of the interview when there is a mismatch of schema and frame.
Content: The same contrastive advice interviews (Data 3.3) were used, and the participants were asked to complete a chart (see Training Material 3.9) where the Interpretation column was left blank.

Discussion was steered to establish:

1. Although the responses are not very different in the amount of detail they give, the employment adviser responds to job-seeker 1

TRAINING MATERIAL 3.9   JOBCENTRE INTERVIEWS

ilt	**Interviewing Course: Module 2** **JOBCENTRE INTERVIEWS**	
Employment Advisor **Question**	**Job seeker 1** **Response**	**Job-seeker 2** **Response**
Can you tell me a little bit about the job, what you actually did?	Well, in respect of L ___ it was maintaining and looking after the machinery so that, if any faults cropped up you just did a quick repair, to keep them on the move.	Well ... er, spinning job, machinery job ... so I controlled my machine.
	Interpretation She wants to know in a general way about my experience and skills.	**Interpretation** She wants a brief literal description of the spinning process.

with a number of explicit questions about training and the level of skilled work done on the machine.

2. By contrast, she responds very indirectly to job-seeker 2, the bilingual speaker. She expresses her apparent ignorance of the spinning process in order to encourage him to be more specific about the type of machines he worked with. But the request is so indirect that he interprets it at face value.

3. She then compounds the problem by trying to exploit his narration of the spinning process to find out whether he could set machinery as well as operate it. He, however, interprets this as a request to continue with his description. She wants him to be analytical about his skills and experience but prompts him with questions which encourage more discursive narration.

Exercise 3 Discourse management
One of the most common forms of professionally produced training films are those that rely on humour to get their point across. Even in the sensitive area of race relations, it is quite possible to use humour

TRAINING MATERIAL 3.10
HOW TO MAKE SURE A CANDIDATE FAILS YOUR INTERVIEW

ilt   **Interviewing Course**
                    HOW TO MAKE SURE CANDIDATES FAIL

Conduct your interview using the strategies in this list:

1. Misuse or mispronounce the candidate's name.
2. Be jokey and informal.
3. Ask inappropriate, personal and irrelevant questions.
4. Correct the applicant's grammar or pronunciation.
5. Ask open questions beginning 'Tell me ...'
6. Ignore previous work/educational experience and status.
7. Do not explain the reasons behind lines of questioning.
8. Interrupt a lot.
9. Ignore what the candidate says and change the topic.
10. Talk down to the candidate and over – explain things in general abstract terms.
11. Convey questions through intonation only.
12. Use a lot of modal verbs – 'should you be accepted you could start ...'
13. Take long speaking turns with complex multiple embedding.
14. Use a lot of technical vocabulary.
15. If the candidate says something positive, give no feedback.
16. If the candidate acknowledges a weakness, do not respond.
17. To show your humour/cynicism/solidarity say the opposite of what you mean.

effectively. One way of doing this is to construct a deliberately bad interview, and then to contrast it with a successful one. Another is to construct an ironic list of do's and don'ts (Training Material 3.10).

Exercise 4 Linguistic code

Aims: To teach participants a simple set of metacommunicative terms such as tone of voice, level of voice, stress, signal, imply, to help them to describe and address details of language forms.

To raise awareness of language and non-verbal behaviour as factors in evaluating and making judgements about clients.

Content: A range of short exercises were used, drawn from *Cross-Cultural Training*, a handbook of language-awareness exercises for industry developed by ILT trainers Valerie Yates, Elisa Christmas and Peter Wilson (1982).

These were prefaced by an experiential exercise to help participants understand some of the difficulties faced by bilingual students when having to listen to and process the stream of talk they hear. [See Training Material 3.11.]

Conclusion

After Modules 1 and 2 had raised awareness and given some guidance and experiential exercises on specific points in an interview, the third and most crucial day of the training provided the opportunity for participants to simulate a cross-cultural interview. The ways in which these video simulations can be analysed have already been discussed.

TRAINING MATERIAL 3.11 URDU ON THE AIR
[Developed by Sarah Greenwood and Peter Sayers Bradford ILT]

Urdu on the air

Aim: To raise awareness of how difficult accurate listening is in a second language.

Aids: Audio tape of part of an Urdu radio programme or any other programme in minority language made for local radio.

Methods: Play tape of a number of advertisements from the Urdu radio programme. Trainees are asked to listen carefully and see if they can make sense of the adverts, using those words given in English as clues. Play each advertisement two or three times if necessary.

Then ask: What strategies are you using/relying on to work out the meaning?
How reliable are these?
Which adverts were most difficult to listen to and why?
What depth of concentration was required?

Then draw parallels with the daily situation of ESL speakers.

Most participants still perceived a significant gap between their ability to analyse what goes wrong and their ability to run a good cross-cultural interview.

Most participants left the course much more aware of the complexity of communication in an interview and with a more open attitude towards how impressions are formed and judgements are made. However, as with any training concerned with interaction, some participants remain unwilling to change the way they are with people because this represents too great a threat to their individual and social identity and security. They are too anxious about their own positions and sense of judgement to question their perceptions of reality. The effects of such inertia on the life chances of ethnic-minority workers are explored further in the next chapter.

Further reading

Two useful and practical books on equal opportunities policies are Wainwright's *Learning from Uncle Sam* (1980) and the Commission for Racial Equality's *Implementing Equal Opportunities Policies* (1983). A useful and wide-ranging discussion on equal opportunity issues in the workplace can be found in *Racism and Equal Opportunity Policies in the 1980s*, edited by Jenkins and Solomos (1986). On racial discrimination in the recruitment processes, Jenkins's *Racism and Recruitment* (1986) describes research based on in-depth interviewing of employers in the Birmingham area of Britain.

On public-sector bureaucracy in multi-ethnic societies, see Young and Connelly in *Policy and Practice in the Multi-Racial City* (1981), and *Ethnic Pluralism and Public Policy*, edited by Glazer and Young (1983).

The orientation to 'culture' in this book can be broadly defined as cognitive and is best illustrated by the anthropologist Goodenough in *Explorations in Cultural Anthropology* (1964) and *Culture, Language and Society* (1971). An important addition to the anthropologically-based concepts of culture is the perspective provided by the Centre for Contemporary Cultural Studies, particularly in *The Empire Strikes Back: Race and Racism in 70s Britain* (1982), and by Willis's *Learning to Labour* (1977). This perspective is that of a dynamic view of culture structured by gender, class and race, which is the reality of people's lived experiences. On 'ethnicity', the most relevant and accessible study is the collection edited by Wallman, *Ethnicity at Work* (1979).

The most influential book on race-awareness training is Katz's *White Awareness* (1978). Criticisms of this approach are Gurnah's *The Politics of Racism Awareness Training* (1983) and Sivanadan's 'RAT and the degradation of the black struggle' (1985). An overview of race relations training is given in Peppard's 'Race relations training: the state of the art' (1983).

4 Ethnographic and linguistic analysis in the workplace

1 Introduction

A major feature of ILT work was the collection and analysis of data in factories and public-service workplaces before training courses were established. There were three reasons for this initial survey work. First, employers, trade unions and the workers themselves were usually extremely sceptical that language training or cross-cultural training could be of any value and, in addition, such workplaces usually had no tradition or precedent for training at operative level or even for broader training for supervisory staff. It was necessary, therefore, to produce evidence for all parties that communication was relevant to improving shop-floor relations and that this in turn would make for a more effective and fairer workplace. Second, we often faced the most blatant expressions of racial prejudice and of hostility to black workers when we first started survey work, and we briefly describe this in section 2 of this chapter. So observation and its discussion and analysis with white people had to be a first step in changing attitudes and providing people with new strategies for perception and behaviour. This work was written up as a survey report for the employer and formally presented. This initial data collection and analysis was in itself a form of training and education. It was also necessary in order to establish with all parties the aims and objectives of the more formal training which it was hoped would follow. Third, the data and its analysis provided material for the training itself. However, data for this purpose did not all have to be collected at the 'initial survey' stage. Obviously, we could collect further data at any time in a variety of ways including from the participants themselves.

ILT surveys had three major aspects:

(i) Extensive factual material was collected about the workplace. For example, personnel records were used to establish facts about: shift systems, recruitment and training procedures, labour turnover, absenteeism and accident rates, trade-union membership, safety record. Personnel records, however, rarely give details of the company's ethnic-minority workforce, and data collection needs to establish such factors as country of origin, age, education, languages spoken, and opportunities to use or acquire English.

(ii) Observation was undertaken in the workplace to record the nature of work, patterns of social and work contact and examples of interaction (often recorded on audiotape). It is this observational work, interviews and data collection which form the main content of this chapter. We describe the methods used in the second and fourth parts of the chapter and we describe the analytic frameworks we developed for analysing such data.

(iii) A third area of work – which is not described here – was the extensive language-assessment interviewing with ethnic-minority workers for whom English was a second language.

Section 2 of this chapter sets out the overall context of multi-ethnic workplaces more clearly than earlier chapters have done. We highlight the structural nature of racial discrimination in such settings, the experience of and reaction to discrimination of black workers, and finally we touch on some of the wider issues which make such workplaces alienating and difficult for all the workers in them – white as well as black. Section 3 describes and illustrates the ethnographic (and often common-sense) methods used for data collection and how the emphasis and methodology of such survey work developed as our understanding expanded. Most ILT trainers were initially quite ignorant of industry and working conditions, and the position of black workers and the physical and attitudinal framework in which they operated came as a shock to them. The collection of data through participant observation of work routines, through ethnographic surveys, and through the language classes, led to understanding and articulation of ethnic minority groups' experience and perceptions. As a result, looking at the language of the workplace alone was soon seen as much too incomplete an approach, and it became necessary to widen the scope and method of data collection and its analysis. The ethnographic work described in section 3 of this chapter has documented some of the reality of life on the shopfloor and the day-to-day experiences of black workers.

The fourth section presents and demonstrates a framework for linguistic analysis of workplace interaction. The background to this framework has already been described in Chapter 2. The linguistic analysis we present has provided insights into how this reality and these experiences are enacted routinely in everyday interaction.

The two complementary strands of ethnography and linguistic analysis are then drawn together in the fifth section in an illustrative case study which returns to the opening theme of the chapter – the positioning of black and ethnic-minority workers – and demonstrates an analytical approach used to help a specific company change its practices and procedures.

2 The employment experience of black workers

2.1 The economic position of black workers

In Chapter 1 (section 4) we briefly described the types of work and the jobs undertaken by many black workers in Britain. We also outlined the way in which the social identity of such workers, despite the skills and experiences they brought to Britain, was constructed by the white majority.

The Policy Studies Institute report on unemployment and racial minorities (Smith 1981) showed that unemployment was increasing the gap between ethnic minorities and whites. The rate of unemployment was higher among minorities, and Afro-Caribbean and Asian men were at risk of being unemployed whether they had qualifications or not, whereas among whites it was the unqualified who were particularly at risk. Minorities were also more likely to accept jobs which were less satisfactory than their previous ones. Asians with little experience of English benefitted less from government training schemes and the employment service was less successful in helping them to find work.

The most recent PSI report on race and discrimination (Brown 1984) continued to show a bleak picture. Afro-Caribbean and Asian workers were more likely to be unemployed than whites and tended to continue to have jobs with lower pay and status:

> On balance, we conclude from our comparison of the 1974 and 1982 surveys and our analysis of individual jobs and job movements that the British job market has changed little in its hostility to black workers, except that it now excludes more of them from work altogether. The few changes for the better have been largely the result of a consolidation of the original immigrant position within the labour force (for example, in the health service and in transport services) or have been the result of the development of black businesses. Furthermore, the factors that perpetuate the pattern of disadvantage are strengthened by the pattern itself; the impact of racial discrimination is therefore increased by this circle of causes and effects, and we are left with a rigid pattern that not only has survived through the 1970s, but also shows no sign of breaking down in the near future.
>
> (Brown 1984)

Other important factors in this pattern of discrimination were reported to be the different educational backgrounds of many black workers, the lack of English-language fluency among many South

Asian workers, and the fact that the ethnic-minority labour market is, in some respects, different from the market open for white workers. Black workers were in effect excluded from many jobs which had become the preserve of white workers.

This last point fits well with the broader theory of a two-tier labour market (Doeringer and Piore 1971). According to this theory, it is normal in industrial society for two distinct labour markets to develop. Rex and Tomlinson (1979) have suggested that immigrants in post-war Britain provided an especially important and alienated element in the lower labour market. They characterise one labour market as open to candidates who have contacts (indeed it may not strictly speaking be a market at all, but simply a system of internal promotion within an organisation) and who, when appointed, have long tenure, a great measure of trade-union protection, welfare benefits, high wages, and also some degree of humanisation of their relations with their employers. In the other labour market, all the opposite conditions hold. There is frequent rotation of employees, much short-term and part-time employment, little in the way of welfare benefits, poor trade-union protection, and a tendency for work to be regarded purely as a means of earning money to be used in more significant life contexts. In addition to these common burdens, black workers have had to face inequality in wages, ghettoisation on night shifts and in the most unpleasant and unsafe and physically demanding jobs, and overt racism.

2.2 The physical and social environment

An understanding of the facts of discrimination and its structure in the labour market is very important, but does not convey a sense of the working conditions experienced by such workers (and by their white co-workers) or the atmosphere of racial hostility and isolation which has often been experienced by black workers in these settings. We shall briefly describe some examples of this reality. (See also the data and analysis in Chapter 2, section 2.1.)

In an engineering factory drawing metal tubes, bunches of tubes swing above the heads of the workers, to land in acid baths whose fumes spread down the shop. In a foundry, workers cover their eyes with their arms as sparks shoot from the furnace. As women workers sweat in the Turkish bath of a steam laundry, down the road other women workers shiver as they gut and truss chickens in near-refrigerator conditions. In a pet-food processing factory, long vertebrae of tins shoot down the line, putting a stop to any communication as they shunt together. Underfoot, the frozen blocks of chicken gizzards which form the 'meat' component of the dog food are already melting by 10 a.m. and the process workers skid through bloodied slime to have their tea break.

The crudity of and the distress caused by racist behaviour is clearly conveyed in the following translation of a South Asian woman talking:

> A few months back I had a bad experience at work. I had been allocated to a new machine; you see we are moved round every two or three weeks and one morning I was allocated to a new machine. The machines are quite big with a large conveyer belt, one person has to sit in the centre, the idea is to check the cleanliness of the sugar. That day I had to sit in the middle. But soon after I went in, another woman on the machine – quite an elderly woman – started saying 'Smelly! Smelly! Smelly!' I couldn't hear her properly because the machine was very loud like a railway engine in India or Pakistan, so I went up to her to ask what the matter was. Then she began to push and poke at me; as you know, I am a very shy person so I just went back to my place quietly. After a few minutes she started shouting again 'Smelly! Smelly! Smelly!' I know that an English girl would have taken a packet of sugar and thrown it at her in answer to her taunts but I became paralysed. Then she went and got a spray of an air freshener and started spraying it at me. All the other women on the machine – about eight of them – joined her in following me and mocking me. I don't know what happened to my brain, I felt completely stunned and shattered as though I was going mad. I couldn't move or think. Not all women are alike; for me this bullying was utterly shattering. By 11.30 I was so upset that I thought I would tell the forelady. I went upstairs to find her but she wasn't in. So I had to come down again and face it till 12.30. During lunch one of the ladies from another machine came up to me she said 'What is the matter with you Mrs X are you sick? You don't look well.' I told her what had happened and she urged me to tell the forelady. That is what I did, our forelady is good, she said she would sort it out. But after the whole thing I felt so bad, I had to go to the doctor. I was off work for three days. When I went back the forelady come and told me that she had given the old racist woman a good telling-off and she had cried. Since then I have never been allocated with these women and the forelady had asked me a few times whether things are OK.

> (Wilson 1978)

Even where such overt racism has not been experienced, black workers have often faced more hidden discrimination and have experienced the isolation and suspicion which develops when communications and relationships with fellow workers, supervisors and trade unionists is limited, instrumental and often based on misinformation, misunderstanding and perceived discrimination.

An interview with another South Asian worker illustrates how the workers perceive their low social power and reinforce their marginal position by their ways of interacting or avoidance of interaction with the supervisor:

> We never mix up English ladies and Asian ladies. We didn't bother to each other ... we are going in the factory, we are working, we're getting our

money and come back. Our supervisor, she don't want to talk to us. She prefer English lady to us – we thought she don't like us ... we are not like friend with her. We respect her like in our country we respect our boss and we have to listen them ... if they talk to us we are happy, if they don't bother we don't bother ... If we want anything from G [the supervisor] we didn't say, because we are frightened that if we say she will refuse ... we thought G, she upset very quick – we feel it – we never look on her face.

(Gubbay, Pathway ILT, 1978)

The way in which this sense of isolation and suspicion can affect everyone involved in workplace interaction and can lead to misjudgements, stereotyped comments and discrimination is illustrated by these extracts from other tape-recorded interviews in a wide spectrum of work settings:

"I tell her things and she laughs and doesn't look at me."

(Female packing department Supervisor)

"You don't know how far you can go with a person. They don't understand facial expressions."   (Male Supervisor)

"They make arbitrary decisions. They don't listen to us."

(group of male asian workers)

"They are afraid to ask if they don't understand."   (male Supervisor)

"They don't come to see us, they go to their Guru (another asian employee) with their problems."   (Trade Union representative)

"If you say no they go on pushing. They ask for the man at the top."

(Female Personnel Officer)

"They have confidence in me I'm prepared to listen. Others haven't got time. We must spend time to explain why. Otherwise they think we're just saying no."   (Male Manager)

The introduction of new technologies can create environments which are even more isolating for individual workers than more traditional workplace environments. In a survey conducted in a plastics factory to examine the effects on communication of the introduction of the new technologies, the following situation was recorded:

At the end of the day shift, an entire batch had to be scrapped because the South Asian worker had not been using a disk which ensures that an accurate hole can be drilled through the plastic product. It was established that the man knew the correct procedure and so was disciplined. What was not established was whether the worker understood why the use of the disk was necessary, whether the complexity and fiddly nature of the job had been explained and why the only explanation the worker was able to give was that the machine was too fast. All these matters could easily have been covered as part of the routine social exchanges between supervisor and operator if opportunities for interaction had been created and pursued on both sides and had resulted in shared knowledge and experience. The consequence, however, was the penalisation of an individual and the reinforcement of a stereotype about 'the lackadaisical attitude of these people'.

(Walsall ILT 1980)

2.3 Multi-dimensional change

The introduction of new technologies is only one aspect of what Ford calls 'multi-dimensional change' (Ford *et al.* 1976). The changing role of the supervisor is another dimension. Over the last twenty years there has been a general erosion, across industry, of supervisors' power as hirers and firers. Increasingly, they have found themselves squeezed between the decisions of a more bureaucratised management and the demands of the shop-floor, and their reactions to shop-floor workers, and to black workers in particular, must be seen in this context: 'There can be no real improvement in industrial relations while the power structure of organisations persists in withdrawing authority from supervisors, while calling on them to provide a bulwark against the demands and desires of wages personnel. No amount of psychological skills, improved wages or fringe benefits can compensate a man for living in the contradictory world of a foreman' (Ford *et al.* 1976).

This 'contradictory world' was made yet more complex by the need for supervisors to adapt their skills to meet the new situation of a multi-ethnic workforce. And since promotion opportunities have been limited or selection procedures have tended to exclude black workers from promotion (see section 5 of this chapter), it was still usual to find black workers being supervised by white men and women.

At the same time, changes also took place in the nature of workers' jobs. During the 1960s and 1970s there was considerable deskilling of craft and semi-skilled jobs, which meant few opportunities of promotion for the large numbers of unskilled black workers and a general increase in machine-paced routine jobs on automated lines. The introduction of new technologies, which, as we have said, can create even more isolation, did not lead to a fundamental improvement in the prospects and working conditions of those unskilled and semi-skilled workers not made redundant by increasing automation.

So the change to a multi-ethnic workforce was only part of this 'multi-dimensional change' which took place. Ford includes technological, organisational, economic, demographic, ideological and educational change in his description. One response to these changes has been the attempt to humanise working relationships and increase worker involvement in decision-making. This process has been almost entirely restricted to the upper tier of the labour market, to large, sophisticated companies with a strong track-record in personnel and training. Attempts to introduce organisational development, quality circles or employee-involvement schemes have helped to challenge traditional assumptions about communication systems and inter-personal communication in such companies. In turn, this has provided opportunities to improve communication through training, awareness-raising and changed systems which have been of benefit to black and white workers. However, such developments have bypassed the majority of black workers in companies where industrial democracy has never been on the agenda.

As we explained in Chapter 1, the social position and work status of black workers (the results of discrimination) were then used to evaluate them as a group with little skills potential. Such a negative evaluation is reflected in the fact that promotion, skilled work, opportunities for training, and full-time trade-union posts have not been achieved by black workers on a scale that is anything like proportionate to their numbers (Smith 1977; Brown 1984). A further factor, discussed by Rex and Tomlinson (1979), is that work relationships are much less likely to be the pivotal point around which other relationships, norms and ideas adhere for ethnic minority workers than for white workers. Again, this reinforced their marginalisation and the hostility towards them.

When ILT staff went into workplaces they had to find ways to challenge these deeply negative perceptions. To do this, it was necessary for us to study the detail of how multi-ethnic workplaces were run. In particular, it was important to establish the nature and amount of social and communicative interaction and how judgements and perceptions were created out of this experience of interaction.

Our basic assumption was that workplaces are held together by communication even if little talk is needed to perform routine duties on the shop-floor. Communication remains of great importance in such situations because decision-making, implementing change, new information all depend on it, as do the ways in which individuals and groups of workers and managers evaluate each other. So our concern was not only with the communication skills of individuals but with the whole complex human environment of the workplace. Observation, data collection and analysis were thus an essential strand of ILT work if inter-ethnic communication was to be understood in the wider social and economic context of a black-and-white Britain, and the methods developed to learn about the workplace were essentially in the tradition of ethnography.

3 Ethnography of the workplace

3.1 Ethnography

The methods developed to learn about the workplace could broadly be described as ethnographic. But in the early stages of data collection and analysis ILT practice was not based on a theory of ethnography. It was, rather, based on systematic common sense. Later, as our understanding of the issues involved in seeking to improve inter-ethnic communication became broader, more complex and more controversial, we turned to specialists in ethnography, workplace organisation and discourse analysis to deepen our understanding. Ethnography has been the most fundamental of these in helping to understand the experience of black workers and to record and analyse workplace talk. Before giving examples of workplace settings analysed in this way, it will be useful to discuss what ethnography is and how it influenced ILT.

Ethnography has been called the most basic form of social research. Its aim is to discover what is going on in the lives of a particular group of people or a particular kind of institution. 'The ethnographer participates, overtly or covertly, in people's daily lives for an extended period of time, watching what happens, listening to what is said, asking questions; in fact collecting whatever data are available to throw light on the issues with which he or she is concerned' (Hammersley and Atkinson 1983). Despite a spate of ethnographic literature over the last twenty years, particularly in the USA, few ethnographic studies have been undertaken of British multi-ethnic workplaces. (But see Wallman 1979 and Westwood and Bhachu 1988.)

Ethnographic research is a detailed investigation of the cultural and social patterns of interaction and the values, beliefs and assumptions that account for such interaction. Ethnography developed as a reaction against positivism and the influence of positivistic research on the social sciences. In particular, it was a reaction against a scientific method which assumes there are universal laws which can be un-covered through experimental and standardised procedures and described in neutral, objective terms. Ethnography, on the other hand, holds that people cannot be studied in terms of universal laws and clear-cut causal relationships. This is because people act on the basis of intentions, attitudes and beliefs all of which are continually being interpreted and reinterpreted. As a result, some ethnographers take the position that this form of social research can only be a description and no explanations or generalisations can be drawn. They believe that, since ethnography is concerned with discovering the culture of a particular group or society in its own terms, any attempt to interpret or explain is imposing an outside view.

However, as Hammersley and Atkinson point out, ethnographers cannot help but bring their own views to the process of data collection and description. By studying a group, they become in some way a part of it and, just like everyone else in the group, have to make sense of it as best they can. Within this tradition of ethnography, researchers have both developed theories about how particular groups act and interact, and have tested out the theories of other social scientists who have worked with a more positivistic perspective. It is this tradition of ethnography, beyond description to explanation, that has most informed ILT work.

Ethnography was very attractive to ILT because its rationale and methods involve:

(i)   a respect for those studied based on trying to understand people's world as they see it;

(ii)   a focus on the common-sense, the ordinary and the everyday;

(iii)   the use of common-sense methods of investigation to capture how people make sense of the world in a routine way;

(iv)   a belief that people's behaviour can be studied only in context;

(v)   flexibility: a resistance to preconceived ideas about what will be discovered and a methodology which starts with observation in the field rather than designing a range of fixed methods before the fieldwork begins;

(vi)   a focus on the *detail* of people's everyday lives and an acknowledgement of the complexity of social interaction;

(vii)   an attempt to see the strange in the ordinary so that no aspect of the routine and detail of everyday lives is overlooked;

(viii) the use of a range of elicitation techniques and analysis:

   − observing/listening;
   − audio- and video-recording;
   − interviewing;
   − documenting the physical environment;
   − documenting patterns of movement and interaction.

This rationale and these methods were fundamental to ILT surveys in multi-ethnic workplaces even before the term ethnography was known and understood by the teachers doing it. The recognition of a need to observe, collect data and analyse it was a common-sense reaction to a new and unfamiliar situation for language teachers.

The term 'participant observation' was used in the early days of ILT to describe the practice of a teacher, prior to setting up a training programme, spending a period of time working in a factory. From the mid-1970s, these methods were improved partly from the accumulated experience of ILT staff and partly from a greater understanding of ethnographic approaches. However, ILT studies of multi-ethnic workplaces must be contrasted with full ethnographic research in three respects:

1. ILT studies have never been conceived of as research projects as such and therefore can only be called partial ethnographies in their range and comprehensiveness.
2. They have focused much more than many ethnographies on audio and video recordings of talk and on a close linguistic and discourse analysis of this talk.
3. Unlike the great majority of ethnographies, ILT surveys have always been undertaken with training in mind and from a clear ideological perspective, committed to equal opportunities and to challenging racism and discrimination.

3.2 Supervisor, union and black-worker attitudes and perceptions

The most significant data collected from ILT surveys, both solicited and unsolicited, concerns the attitudes of individuals at all levels. It was clear from the start that issues of working together and of equality in multi-ethnic workplaces were not limited to language difference. The data elicited from white supervisory staff and black workers has built up a picture in which misunderstanding, misinformation and real and perceived discrimination are everyday experiences. During the 1970s this picture was interpreted largely in terms of a need to improve individual relationships and communication skills. In the 1980s wider issues of power and access and changes in the systems of communication, information and progression with the whole organisation became of increasing concern.

In a review of fifty communication-survey reports written by ILT units, covering seven different manufacturing industries between 1975 and 1980, certain recurrent themes emerge from the interview data:

Among black workers
(i) Difficulties in dealing with personal problems and with discipline and grievance procedures. In particular, workers frequently mentioned difficulties concerned with sick-leave, with extended leave to visit their country of origin, and with pay.
(ii) A general feeling that management did not give them information and did not care about them:
   - 'We would like management to tell us more, we are often not told why. Why do management not take more interest in us? We have to go to the unions to learn anything.'
   - 'When people start here they are just told how to work a machine. They should be told about the company too.'
(iii) Lack of confidence in dealing with management and stress arising from having to explain themselves in English:

- 'It's difficult for me to know how to pronounce words and so I hesitate to speak up at union meetings.' (Shop steward)
(iv) Black workers in white-collar industries and in public services such as transport (see Chapter 2, Data 2.4) and the Civil Service frequently mentioned the following as characteristics of English workers' styles of communication (when asked about inter-ethnic relations and communications):
    - say 'yes' when they mean 'no';
    - are either over-polite or rude;
    - have a superior attitude towards us;
    - lack sincerity – they are not direct;
    - interrupt us;
    - don't accept our accents and way of speaking;
    - mumble, use slang, and abuse English.

Among white supervisors and trade unionists

(i) General negative stereotyping of black workers related to personality, motivation and ability:
    - 'They're not forceful enough. They are overawed by management. They seem more servile than us.' (Shop steward)
    - 'When they're given an order, they can't discuss it so they shout ... they argue a lot and say "it's not my job".' (Foreman)
    - 'Many a time I've told these fellows and I think they're taking the mickey because they just LOOK at me you know.' (Supervisor)
    - 'Asian supervisors don't seem to come over as well.' (Supervisor)
    - 'They're like children. They can't think for themselves.' (Supervisor)
    - 'They don't take pride in their work. They are stubborn and inflexible ... they're sly, deep ... Teaching him a language doesn't alter a man's personality.' (Supervisor)
    - 'You have to swear at them – they've all got chips on their shoulders.' (Supervisor)
    - 'Swearing is the only language they understand.' (Supervisor)
    - 'I wish they had flipping labels on! I recognise their faces but there are some who've worked here eight or nine years and I sometimes don't know what their names are.' (Supervisor)
(ii) Attitudes towards working relations on the shop-floor: expressed in terms of anxiety, uncertainty or 'coping', or an awareness of the importance of good relationships and communication:
    - 'I don't want you to think I'm prejudiced – that would be

quite wrong – but I talk more to my own kind. I can make jokes. I know what clicks with them.' (Engineering supervisor)
- 'Where people understand English you can spend a few minutes with them. You can get to know them and this is another important part of being in charge rather than just discipline.' (Supervisor)
- 'I mean if they can talk English – people can see they're human beings like us, can't they?' (Supervisor)
- 'I think in work, relationships are the most important thing. If you've got a good relationship, everything else takes care of itself. If you've got a bad one, it's terrible. If you can't speak to people, you can't have a good relationship however much you try.' (Supervisor)
- 'A very good timekeeper was five minutes late one day. When he had the corresponding amount knocked off his wages, he broke down and cried. The trouble is you can't say "Come on you silly bugger" – he'd take offence.' (Manager)
- 'It's just a general frustration and one we've learnt to live with. We perhaps accept a lot more than we should do if we stop and think but well after twenty years of dealing with them, I suppose I accept a lot more than I should.' (Supervisor)
- 'They have common problems. We don't help them. We don't tell them enough.' (Manager)

(iii) Uncertainty and expressed difficulty in making themselves understood, and anxiety that black workers could not understand or explain about quality, faults, breakdowns, safety, and matters related to personal problems:
- 'We were losing hundreds of pounds every time the breakdown occurred. They knew what was happening but they couldn't explain it.' (Production manager)
- 'We're never sure if they have understood – we just have to shout at them.' (Supervisor)
- 'A man came in a week or two back and I ended up shouting at him because he wouldn't listen. He just would not listen at all. He thought we'd taxed him twice and that was it.' (Personnel)

(iv) Criticism of black workers' attitudes towards, or lack of understanding of, company practice and procedures:
- 'They go straight to the steward if they have a grievance and expect an answer straight away. They don't realise it takes time to go through different stages of the procedure.' (Manager)
- 'They just use the union without contributing – they expect to be defended automatically and they bring all their personal problems to me.' (Shop steward)

- 'Management were reluctant to discuss changes in organisation or jobs on shift because they were frightened that
  Asian stewards would not appreciate the necessity for taking
  that decision, they would not appreciate the ramifications.'
  (Union convenor)
- 'You don't get much feedback from them, and because of this
  the complaints are probably less as well. But when they do
  come up, they might be more serious because they've been
  brewing for a while.' (Shop steward)

Collecting this type of data presented many difficulties. On the one
hand, ILT researchers needed to document the perceptions of white
management and trade-unionists. On the other hand, they felt
compromised if these attitudes were not challenged and they appeared
to be colluding with the views expressed. The dilemma could never
be easily resolved. ILT staff would tend to question racist statements
when they occurred, but not in a confrontational way, and would then
take up the issues again in more formal training sessions.

3.3 Methods of data collection

ILT staff aimed to collect data over as wide a field as possible. In
addition, they had to guard against privileging one set of data over
another. Here, the ethnographic technique of 'triangulation' is helpful
(Denzin 1970; Cicourel 1974). This technique requires the researcher
to compare and contrast different data sources together, for example
the records on absenteeism with the perceptions of the absentee rate
given by supervisors, or the views of different groups of workers on
how and why decisions are made which affect their working practice.
This technique encourages a reflexive process in which data is constantly reconsidered in the light of other data.

Data-elicitation techniques ranged from participant observation, an
'insider' approach, to survey work, an 'outsider' approach. During the
early and mid-70s it was possible to be taken on as a temporary
worker to carry out participant observation. However, as competition
for jobs became tougher, this was less easy to negotiate. So teachers
developed other methods for participating in the life of the workplace.
The techniques used at different times were:

- Participant observation;
- Audio- and video-recording of interactions;
- Observation of setting and of patterns of interaction;
- Ethnographic interviewing;

– Collection of written notices and documents;
– Role-play simulations.

Technique 1 Participant observation

The trainer is taken on as another worker and is expected to do a regular day's work. Any recording of experiences is done covertly, often in the toilet, or at home. Data 4.1 is an example.

DATA 4.1-4.2 THE GROCERIES FACTORY
[Susan Hodlin, Pathway ILT, 1970]

CONTEXT

Hodlin undertook participant observation as preparation for one of the first ILT courses in a factory which manufactured cake mixes and breakfast cereals. Although her purpose was known to the senior supervisor, she was introduced and regarded by other workers and line-minders as a student, working temporarily in the factory. As far as she could tell she was treated as other workers. She worked for a week in the packing department. The report which is quoted from in Data 4.1 and 4.2 was written up from tape-recorded accounts of her experience and observations which she made every evening after work.

Hodlin's participant observation revealed both the kind of work language required for the job, and the considerable scope there was in some sections of the department for social language. It also revealed the explicit racism and virulent hostility of some workers and the range of attitudes among supervision, from a very controlling and assimilationist point of view to a highly cooperative and tolerant attitude. She wrote up the different jobs she did, using the standard format for job descriptions, and compared and contrasted the three sections where she worked in terms of working atmosphere. Examples from her report are given in Data 4.2. Hodlin also drew some character vignettes (Data 4.3).

DATA 4:1 THE GROCERIES FACTORY: JOB DESCRIPTION

Job title	(a) Packing
	(b) Filling glue machine.
Place of work	Ready Mix. Groceries.
To whom responsible	Line-minder/supervisor.
No. of operators on job	4 or 5 (room for 8).
Equipment and materials	Printed, flat Ready-Mix packets.

DATA 4.1　THE GROCERIES FACTORY: JOB DESCRIPTION
continued

Duties	(a) The inner filled packets are put into the outer packets which the operator has made up. The packet is put back on the conveyor belt to be sealed. (b) The automatic outer-packet sealing machine has two boxes at the side of the machine which have to be kept filled with glue in the form of small round 'beads'.
Description	(a) As the inner filled packets pass through the heat-sealing machine they are lifted off the belt by this operator. The operator takes a printed outer packet from a shelf above the conveyor, makes it up into a 'box' shape, slots the inner packet in upside down and replaces the packet in a slot on the conveyor belt where it then passes to be sealed. The packet is made up by turning the marked flaps in, holding these in place with the hand. (b) When the beads of glue in the box have melted the operator takes a handful from a large plastic sack and drops this into the box.
Time taken	(a) Packets passing through approx. one per second. (b) Irregular, as necessary.
Skills	None.
Language	'Squash out the air.' 'Put it like that (upside down) on the belt.' 'Leave those flaps out so it can be sealed.' 'Watch the glue.' 'How many have you packed?' 'Keep a note of the number you packed because I'll ask you.'

DATA 4.2 GROCERIES FACTORY: PARTICIPANT OBSERVATION

There are three sections in the factory: The Mixes, Instant oats and The Variant Room. This data refers largely to Mixes.

1. **Physical lay out and numbers of workers**

   There are three Ready Mix lines, each employing about twelve people. The lines are each about 150 yards long. The workers are all fulltime on the Mixes. And they are all from ethnic minorities except for two or three English people.

2. **Atmosphere**

   Very noisy. Under great pressure and the atmosphere is very tense. The line seems faster perhaps because the packets are smaller than on Instant Oats. The machines are running as soon as one is on the floor. All the workers are full-timers and they never get a break. Lighting adequate, but paint very dark.

3. **Supervision**

   Two line-minders and a supervisor. They are poor because they are very flustered and interfere a great deal. They rush round all the time looking very anxious. Workers are switched to different jobs every day (rather against their will).
   The line doesn't feel a complete unit perhaps because of size and layout, and because it is ethnic minority labour and so it's not possible to chat to anyone. The supervisors' attitude may reflect a lack of feeling of control on their part. They give an impression of being inefficient.
   The supervisors think they are understood, but it appeared that they were not understood. They often repeat something more loudly.
   If there is pressure, they snatch and interfere because they fear they won't be understood by an ethnic minority worker. They don't usually shout. There is hanging around in the morning while one waits to be told which job one is to do that particular morning.

4. **Communication between workers**

   There is very little talking. Susan Hodlin only spoke to a Trinidadian woman and a West Indian. It is very difficult to talk to someone unless one is opposite them.
   Only about four English-speaking workers. The rest are Asians. The Asians did not talk much except for the groups (four women) sitting filling from the machine. They look across the conveyor and can talk.
   Some of the jobs are individual. In general the workers are rather separated and not in a position to talk much, quite apart from the pace of work and the noise.

DATA 4.2 GROCERIES FACTORY: PARTICIPANT
OBSERVATION *continued*

5. **Race relations**
    Not a lot to say about this because effectively ethnic minorities are
    on Mixes and the Variant Room, and English people are on the
    Instant Oats. So the position is nearly one of segregation. The
    supervisor said this segregation had arisen because the English
    women had been there longest and had all worked on the first
    automated line, Instant Oats.
    However, individuals are mixing a little. The Welsh woman in the
    Variant Room, for example, thoroughly enjoys working there and
    successfully carries on quite extended conversations.
    On the Instant Oats line the three or four ethnic minority people
    had no real opportunity to talk to English people. There was a
    very antagonistic atmosphere towards ethnic minorities. The
    English workers resent them coming on to their Instant Oats line
    which they regard as 'English' property. They would rather have
    English people brought in from other factories when they have a
    rush. Probably there would be a lot of resentment if ethnic
    minorities were put to work on this line permanently.

DATA 4:3 PERSONAL STUDIES IN THE GROCERY FACTORY

Ida. A supervisor
Ida looks as if she thinks disaster is about to strike. A worried frown,
sleeves rolled up, humps her back as she walks. 'I've been here 22
years. Oh yes, they understand more than they let on ( ) halfpenny
short in their pay packet and they'll notice.'

Ida usually caused a flurry when she came up to a worker. Results:
spilled packets, fumbling, and a mute and resentful silence when 'the
immigrants' were reprimanded. She spoke normally to them initially,
but if this met with little or no response, Ida would either speak in
exaggeratedly simple and disjointed English or begin to irately raise
her voice. She invoked no 'corporate' feeling in her line, and had
obviously decided that a tight rein was the best policy when dealing
with 'these people'. She dismissed the ethnic minority workers with a
rather contemptuous shrug as slow workers whom one could never
make any faster.

Ida was very concerned with her own position at the factory. She did
not feel trusted by her supervisors, still retained a strange 'respect' or
fear for them and found it difficult to behave normally with them. She
resented the fact that she had to be paid monthly and consequently did
not get what she felt was her rightful share of overtime and so now
was not prepared to put in all the hours she had previously when paid
on a weekly basis. Her general 'aura' of discontent and tenseness was
reflected in the handling of her workers.

Technique 2 Recording of interactions (based on participant
          observation)
This involves audio/video-recording and taking notes of all interactions
that take place in the following settings: shop-floor, canteen, supervisor's and personnel office and, where recording service encounters, in
a range of centres and offices. These interactions may be one-to-one,
formal and informal meetings, on the telephone or tannoy.

Example. David Bonamy [Pathway ILT, 1975] worked as a kitchen
porter in a hospital in Surrey for a week. He was one of a team of five
porters. The other four were Spanish or Portuguese with very limited
English, and he worked with the cooks under a kitchen superintendent. Although much of the work was routine and required little
or no interaction, there were often crises, for example if a cook was
away sick or an official visit was being made by a health official. These
'crises', together with the daily deadlines to get the meals out to the
wards and staff canteen, made interaction crucial at key points in the
day. The main types of interaction consisted of:

(i)   Language to carry out cleaning jobs:
      – Instructions on what and how to clean: places such as the
        pastry room, fixtures like the steam ovens, and utensils such
        as the fish kettle or the 'spider'.
      – Questions about the quality of cleaning or about sequencing
        and timing and about the progress of his work.
      – Negative instructions often related to hygiene or safety:
        'Don't for Christ's sake put Ajax in there!'
(ii) Language to help cooks in various tasks:
      – Questions on loading, stacking and filling food containers, and
        identifying the different meals.
      – Interacting with nurses on the wards when the ward trolley is
        taken up.
         As a new porter, Bonamy plugged in the trolley to keep it hot
      but forgot to take the milk and bread off the top …

> Sister: Take that bread and milk off the top or they'll cook.
>   You'll be in trouble. You'll get your cards
> Porter: OK. Do you want the milk in the fridge?
> Sister: Yes. If there's any butter put it in the fridge too

      – Instructions on preparing food (draining, slicing, whisking)
        and on quality.
(iii) Coping with a complete process: e.g. preparing potatoes and
      cooking chips.

In addition to this data collected as part of participant observation, recordings were made of key situations in which a high level of communicative competence appeared necessary. In Data 4.4 the Spanish assistant head cook (AHC) is talking to the catering officer (CO) about complaints from the wards. (SHC is the second head cook.) Other interactions concern personal problems. In Data 4.5 a Spanish dining-room maid (Mrs C) is trying to sort out her overtime pay with the assistant catering officer (Mr T).

DATA 4.4 COMPLAINTS [David Bonamy, Pathway ILT, 1975]

Transcript

AHC: Now this the worst one, ward 4. You see, when we do the board, even if Philip yesterday done it for me, what we look is the total numbers, and if you look at here you will find only 17 soups and one portion of B, whatever B was, it's only one. But if you look up here you see one C, another B, another C, another B, another B, another C, another C ... So this is the main one, and I argued ... well I didn't argue, just told her ... because of that, well, you know, if you're going to check menu by menu all those letters, you're going to spend more time in there than you will spend in the whole kitchen.

CO: Ward 4 make their own out, yes.

AHC: Here, there's supposed to be one C, and if there wasn't they claim it. And they claimed five oranges, which hasn't been sent and I couldn't find oranges to send to this thing here, I write it here myself. They say to have, to need five, they only have four ... there's another thing, they claim C, which I didn't know they needed, they claim four ... I don't remember what this one

Commentary

The cook is referring to the patients' diet returns. Ward receptionist is supposed to add up the columns (main course, sweet, etc.) and write totals at the bottom.

The cook is saying that the total (e.g. one B) does not tally with the number of B's opposite each individual patient's name. But it's not his job to check that these tally.

The one C and the five oranges were not in the total at the bottom of the sheet.

DATA 4.4 COMPLAINTS *continued*

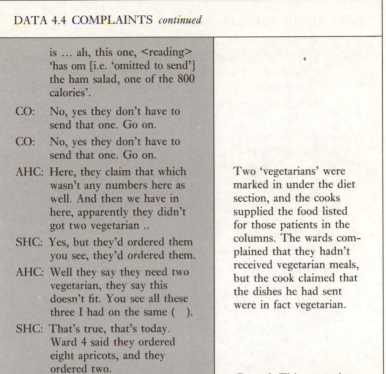

is ... ah, this one, <reading> 'has om [i.e. 'omitted to send'] the ham salad, one of the 800 calories'.

CO: No, yes they don't have to send that one. Go on.

CO: No, yes they don't have to send that one. Go on.

AHC: Here, they claim that which wasn't any numbers here as well. And then we have in here, apparently they didn't got two vegetarian ..

SHC: Yes, but they'd ordered them you see, they'd ordered them.

AHC: Well they say they need two vegetarian, they say this doesn't fit. You see all these three I had on the same ( ).

SHC: That's true, that's today. Ward 4 said they ordered eight apricots, and they ordered two.

CO: OK, I'll go down and see about that one.

AHC: You see, and they say 'I haven't done ...[etc.]'.

CO: OK, I'll chase that up. Good.

Two 'vegetarians' were marked in under the diet section, and the cooks supplied the food listed for those patients in the columns. The wards complained that they hadn't received vegetarian meals, but the cook claimed that the dishes he had sent were in fact vegetarian.

General. This transcript indicates the need for a high level o f linguistic competence in a non-routine situation.

DATA 4.5 THE PAY SLIP [David Bonamy, Pathway ILT, 1975]

Transcript

Mr T: What's your problem?

Mrs C: Is my rest day, no pay.

Mr T: For when? Overtime 21 <looking at her payslip>.

Mrs C: Sunday all day .. off.

Mr T: You weren't off? Or you were? You worked seven days?

Commentary

The situation was that the girl's payslip showed £21.00 in her section marked 'overtimes'. This would in fact be the pay for working her day off at $\frac{1}{2}$ x time and her rest day at 2 x time. What she was trying to say was that she had worked a *long* day on Sunday, i.e. from 7 a.m. to 8.30 p.m., which would mean an extra $5\frac{1}{2}$ hours'

DATA 4.5 THE PAY SLIP *continued*

Mrs C: Yes. Seven days. And off, and my rest day. Sixteen hours.

Mr T: Sixteen hours for the rest day.

Mrs C: You remember? Tuesday.. ( ) (si) ( ).

Mr T: Oh you were sick? You were sick one day?

Mrs C: Yes.

Mr T: OK then.

Mrs C: No sick!

Mr T: What? I thought you said .. I'll go and check with the card after.

overtime. So in addition to her £21.00 she should have received payment for those $5\frac{1}{2}$ hours.

The information she was trying to convey then, was roughly:

She worked seven days, entitling her to five days' pay at 1 x time, one day at $1\frac{1}{2}$ x time, and one day at 2 x time. In addition to this normal situation, she worked a long day on one of the days (probably the Sunday), so that she should have received payment for an extra $5\frac{1}{2}$ hours' overtime. Her payslip only showed payment for the one day at $1\frac{1}{2}$ x time and the one day at 2 x time.

It turned out later that she had in fact worked a long day but her clock-card entry had been very faint.

So the intended dialogue should have gone something like this:

Mr T: What's your problem?

Mrs C: My payslip hasn't got enough overtime pay on it.

Mr T: Well how many hours did you work?

Mrs C: I worked my rest day. That's sixteen hours. And my day off. That's twelve hours.

Mr T: That's right. That's twenty-eight hours. So you should get £21.00.

Mrs C: Yes but I worked a long day on Sunday, – don't you remember? I came in early on Sunday.

Mr T: OK. Give me your payslip and I'll check it with the clock card.

Mrs C: Thank you very much.

Technique 3 Observation of setting and of patterns of interaction

Any survey starts with observing and understanding the overall manufacturing process. It is also necessary to observe patterns of language use and social context, and whether the language used to talk about the process (in the following example, uptwisting, downtwisting, reeling, relaxing and backwinding) is a necessary part of shop-floor interaction.

Example. Rajinder Singh's report of a survey in a cotton textile plant [Lancashire ILT, 1976] documents the reality that in multi-ethnic workplaces there are few social contexts in which adult second-language learners can develop their English in unstressed peer-group interaction. The range of languages and varieties of English spoken and the types of interaction which are most frequent on the job allow few opportunities for language development. A close study was made of a Pakistani backwinder who interacted with his Scottish supervisor and with Polish-, Panjabi- and Urdu-speaking co-workers. The languages and varieties of English heard in the factory were: Scottish English, Welsh English, Irish English, Barnoldswick (Lancashire) English, Polish English, Panjabi, and Urdu. Observation and recording of the backwinder over one hour revealed the communication pattern shown in Data 4.6 (p. 196–7).

Technique 4 Ethnographic interviewing

This involves open-ended, largely unstructured interviewing in which the interviewer attempts to capture the reality of the informant's life and their values and assumptions in *their own way of speaking*. Either, these interviews are tape-recorded or full notes are taken. Topic areas covered include descriptions of the work process, the informant's particular job, changes that have taken or will take place, and their perceptions and assumptions about the people they work with. This technique is discussed later in this chapter, where an example of the code of conduct governing such interviewing is given in Training Material 4:3 (p. 277).

Technique 5 Collection of written documents

Useful documents include company handbooks, policy documents, safety manuals and notices, personnel records, written systems and procedures, for example of recruitment, discipline and grievances.

Some may be needed for specific purposes, for example to determine the level of literacy skills required for promotion to a higher grade, or to establish whether company language use or requirements disadvantage bilingual employees. This technique is exemplified in the case study which concludes this chapter.

Technique 6 Role-play simulations

When interactional data is insufficient, or impossible to collect because of noise or for reasons of confidentiality, role-plays are set up either with the trainers or, more usually, with staff and workers themselves enacting typical situations. What constitutes a 'typical' situation is decided on the basis of the findings of the other techniques which have been described. This technique is exemplified in Data 4.7 (p. 203) and in Chapter 5.

3.4 Use of ethnographic data

Combinations of the discrete techniques listed above are used to provide a framework for training, but also, and more importantly, to present an analysis of workplace communications to the employer which will ensure real commitment, shared objectives and a purposeful atmosphere for the training programme. Such commitment is essential if real benefits for both workers and management are to be achieved.

The data examples given in Section 3.2 above illustrate the kind of communicative environment which is typical of multi-ethnic workplaces. They are not good learning environments and, in fact, routinely provide the conditions under which negative attitudes are both created and reinforced. The examples show that language differences and difficulties mean that communication between, on the one hand, white-majority management, trade unionists and workers and, on the other hand, black workers is largely limited to the functional requirement of the job. There are low expectations of communication and contact on both sides. In particular, the fact that workers are bilingual and often multilingual is rarely recognised as a resource. Instead, communication takes place in a narrow band, made narrower by limits of ability in English, limits of opportunity for communication, and interpretation based on perceived behaviour rather than an understanding of attitude and motive. Unperceived are the attitudes, personalities, aspirations and expectations of both sides. These are largely left to surmise and can be very negative: 'All they care about is the money'; 'The managers don't care as long as we keep working'. In such a limited communication environment a company is losing the benefit of its employees' opinions, ideas and experience. Management may be aware that relationships are limited and would like to know their workers better and manage more effectively. The workers, often educationally overqualified for the work they are doing, feel undervalued and that the company is not interested in giving them training opportunities or promotion.

Developing the skills of individual workers does not necessarily affect this pattern of limited communications. Improved language skills may help in some of the informal shop-floor contacts. But if the prevailing culture of a workplace is non-participative, on the one hand there is little incentive to develop skills, and on the other hand, improved skills will lead to more frustration as workers feel ignored or imposed upon. They may also feel that language difference is being used to cloak a deeper need for equal opportunities policy and practice.

Survey reports to management, therefore, are of great importance in setting the scene for language training. For example, in the presentation of such a report to a particular company, the trainer argued that in addition to individual communication skills, four factors had to be considered by the management:

- the context of relationships in which communication took place;
- the procedures and practices (including specific schemes and systems) set up to promote good communication;
- the levels of knowledge and information which workers and management brought to interactions;
- the motivation to communicate.

A chart of the company's communicative environment was presented by the ILT staff involved: this is shown in Training Material 4.1 on p. 198. Within this framework, ineffective working practices, which include a failure to tackle language difficulties, are put centre-stage. Once an atmosphere of poor industrial relations and loss of respect for management exists, then minor issues can become confrontation. Language/cultural differences compound these problems, and the situation is frustrating and demotivating both for ethnic-minority workers and for supervision and union representatives.

A way out of this negative cycle is to establish a climate in which initiatives are encouraged and more effective communication is established at all levels. This can be done by restructuring work practices, providing opportunities for communication, and introducing

DATA 4:6 THE BACKWINDER [Rajinder Singh, Lancashire ILT, 1976]

Communication pattern of No. 2528 Moh'd Ayub, backwinder between 12 noon and 1 p.m on Saturday, 17 January 1976

Time/Contact	Purpose	Language spoken	
12.02 Friend (Asian)	To enquire what was happening	Urdu	1*
12.10 Friend (mixed)	General chat: 'What's happening?'	Panjabi	2
12.11 Workmate (Polish)	Asked him to do a favour: 'Can you pick up my clip?'	English	3
12.12 Friends (mixed)	General chat	Panjabi	2
12.15 Supervisor (Scot)	'Am I changing yarn before 2 p.m.?' 'No'	English	.5
12.20 Friend (Asian)	'What's happening?'	Panjabi	1
12.34 Workmate (Polish) (hankstretcher)	'Have you more yarn?' 'Yes, I have one and a half boxes'	English	4
12.40 He spoke to me (R. Singh)	'What is all this about?'	Urdu	1
12.42 Workmate (hankstretcher)	'Here you are! You dropped your knotting machine.'	English	3
12.44 Friend (Asian)	'Can you make a ticket for me?'	Panjabi	3
12.47 Workmate (Polish)	'All right, love?' (casual greeting in passing)	English	1
12.48 Workmate (Asian)	'Can you make a ticket for me?'	Panjabi	3
12.50 Supervisor	'Keep the machine full at 2 o'clock.'	English	6
12.51 Friend (Polish)	'How is everything?'	English	2
12.55 Supervisor	'I'll be changing yarn for different production.'	English	6
12.56 Workmate (Polish) (hankstretcher)	'Coming another yarn in No. 04'	English	4

DATA 4:6 THE BACKWINDER *continued*

12.59 Workmate (Polish) (hankstretcher)	'Bad yarn' He reported to the supervisor	English	4
12.59 Supervisor	'This is bad yarn. Give me the package after it has been wound.'	English	5
13.00 *End of observation*			

ANALYSIS

	Description	Frequency	Contact with Asians
1*	Social contact on work site	3	4
2	Social contact away from the work site, e.g. smoking box	3	2
3	Workmate(s) needed him	4	2
4	He needed to speak to his workmate	3	0 (his workmates were Polish)
5	He needed the supervisor	2	0
6	The supervisor needed him	2	0
TOTAL		17	8

OBSERVATIONS

On the job, a backwinder had very little need to speak at all. On average he spoke once every three minutes, but each time merely one or two sentences or brief remarks. There were four contacts with his supervisor during this period.

An Asian worker is in contact with other workmates in social and work situations nearly four times more often than with his supervisor. Whereas his contact with other Asians was more voluntary and spontaneous, it was often restricted with the English workers to cases of specific need, such as 'Can you pick up my clips?' or 'You dropped your knotting machine.'

TRAINING MATERIAL 4:1 CHANGING THE CYCLE OF
COMMUNICATION [Hugh Pidgeon Warwickshire ILT, 1982]

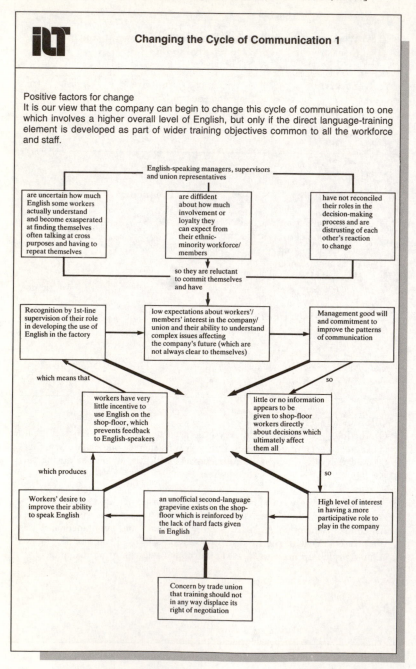

Changing the Cycle of Communication 1

Positive factors for change
It is our view that the company can begin to change this cycle of communication to one
which involves a higher overall level of English, but only if the direct language-training
element is developed as part of wider training objectives common to all the workforce
and staff.

English-speaking managers, supervisors
and union representatives

are uncertain how much
English some workers
actually understand
and become exasperated
at finding themselves
often talking at cross
purposes and having to
repeat themselves

are diffident
about how much
involvement or
loyalty they
can expect from
their ethnic-
minority workforce/
members

have not reconciled
their roles in the
decision-making
process and are
distrusting of each
other's reaction
to change

so they are reluctant
to commit themselves
and have

Recognition by 1st-line
supervision of their role
in developing the use of
English in the factory

low expectations about workers'/
members' interest in the company/
union and their ability to understand
complex issues affecting
the company's future (which are
not always clear to themselves)

Management good will
and commitment to
improve the patterns
of communication

which means that

so

workers have very
little incentive to
use English on the
shop-floor, which
prevents feedback
to English-speakers

little or no information
appears to be
given to shop-floor
workers directly
about decisions which
ultimately affect
them all

which produces

so

Workers' desire to
improve their ability
to speak English

an unofficial second-language
grapevine exists on the shop-
floor which is reinforced by
the lack of hard facts given
in English

High level of interest
in having a more
participative role to
play in the company

Concern by trade union
that training should not
in any way displace its
right of negotiation

TRAINING MATERIAL 4:1 CHANGING THE CYCLE OF
COMMUNICATION [Hugh Pidgeon Warwickshire ILT, 1982]

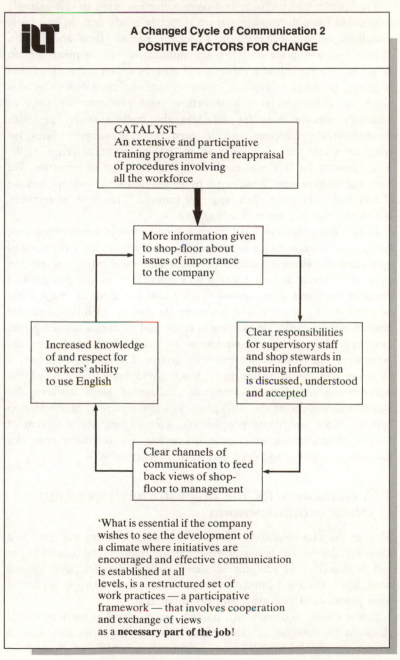

ilt

A Changed Cycle of Communication 2
POSITIVE FACTORS FOR CHANGE

CATALYST
An extensive and participative
training programme and reappraisal
of procedures involving
all the workforce

More information given
to shop-floor about
issues of importance
to the company

Increased knowledge
of and respect for
workers' ability
to use English

Clear responsibilities
for supervisory staff
and shop stewards in
ensuring information
is discussed, understood
and accepted

Clear channels of
communication to feed
back views of shop-
floor to management

'What is essential if the company
wishes to see the development of
a climate where initiatives are
encouraged and effective communication
is established at all
levels, is a restructured set of
work practices — a participative
framework — that involves cooperation
and exchange of views
as a **necessary part of the job**!

participative practices that involve cooperation and an exchange of views as a necessary part of the job.

The approach to language and communication given in this example is a considerable development from the early needs analysis and basic functional courses described in *Industrial English* (Jupp and Hodlin 1974). The workplace and the communicative environment are no longer simply providing a context and authentic data for work-related language training. Instead, a more systems-orientated approach is taken in which changes in structures and practices are seen as necessary preconditions for affecting the communicative practices throughout the company and in turn providing opportunities for communication and so motivation to develop communication skills. The difficulty for ILT was establishing the limits of its expertise. We were not management consultants by inclination or knowledge but we clearly had to be more than language trainers. This issue of territory is a debate that has never been resolved.

In this discussion we have taken a broad view of communications, looking at communicative practices and their impact on attitudes and opportunities. However, these practices and their outcomes are the cumulative result of individual interactions. It is in the fine-grained detail of good and poor communication that the seeds of cooperation or suspicion are sown, and it is during the process of interaction that evaluations are made, decisions are taken and positions taken up that can have long-term consequences for individuals and for the perception and treatment of minority groups. For the ILT service, it therefore became of major importance to examine the relationship between the general socio-economic position of black workers, the social environment of the workplace and the processes of interaction between black and white people. We were looking for a system of analysis of interaction which would examine how linguistic processes fed into judgements and decisions made in interaction.

4   A framework for the linguistic analysis of inter-ethnic communication

Most of the data collected in early ethnographic surveys was used as a basis for developing language-teaching approaches and materials, as will be described in Chapter 5. Some detailed linguistic analysis was done, but it remained limited in scope and depth and largely separated from processes of evaluation and discrimination.

It was clearly necessary to establish and to develop more technical skills for the analysis of inter-ethnic communication so that general statements about workplace communication could be rooted in properly analysed data. For us, as specialists in language, it was important to try to show the relationship between the way conversations were accomplished (or not) and the wider context of workplace decision-making. The analytical framework described below was developed by a group of ILT teachers concerned to collect together a much wider data base of naturally-occurring inter-ethnic communication and to improve their skills in the analysis of such data.

The analysis was also done with training goals in mind, both cross-cultural training and language training. So we were concerned with how both sides might interpret each other from the evidence of the data. In other words, we were attempting a kind of slow-motion replay of communicative events to try to account for why the interactions went the way they did and for their outcomes.

Such analysis begins with an overall view of an interaction and its context in order to form one initial view with regard to the overall schema of each participant. The schemata in turn are dependent upon perceptions and assumptions, speaker perspectives and interpersonal relationships. In seeking an initial overall view of the interaction, there is less concentration on the fine-grained detail of linguistic analysis, other than the use of linguistic features as clues to the formulation of an initial hypothesis. Data 4.7 demonstrates how a hypothesis can be formed in this way.

DATA 4.7 THE HOUSE IN BANGLADESH. (see page 203.)
[Material collected by Cathy Ballard, Leeds ILT, and analysed by Peter Sayers, Bradford ILT, and Celia Roberts, NCILT]

DATA 4.7 CONTEXT
This tape was produced as a training aid for Citizens Advice Bureau workers. To avoid problems of confidentiality the tape was a simulation by the two participants of an earlier interview and they deliberately went over subject matter already familiar to them. The participants are an unemployed Bangladeshi worker and an English advice-centre worker. The Bangladeshi, B, is restating a problem he knows the English advice worker has already heard before. He is deliberately performing for the tape and enjoying doing so – there is little tension or anxiety in his delivery of the problem. He is not, therefore, as concerned to be understood as he might be in a 'live' interview.

An earlier interview between the Bangladeshi worker and another adviser, an Asian woman, had also been recorded. In this previous interview, B's financial and domestic problems emerged and were understood. This information helped in the analysis of the interview with the English adviser.

The English advice worker, A, is also aware of the 'training' purpose behind the tape and therefore endeavouring to keep the interview on a predetermined course, and on occasions her replies attempt to redefine the direction of the interview, rather than respond to the previous utterance of the Bangladeshi worker. There are, clearly, difficulties with recording and analysing simulated data. The English advice worker, who was quite well known to ILT, was perceived as exaggerating her natural style of communication for the purposes of the recording. Her turns were longer and more explicit than she would routinely use, and comments such as 'I know you're not lazy' replaced her more usual back-channel signals such as 'uh huh' and 'mmm'. Such modifications suggest that she was playing to the tape-recorder and, implicitly, telling the world that she knew and had a good relationship with the Bangladeshi worker. The effect of these modifications is to convey a patronising attitude. Despite these changes, her overall style in this interaction, including her questioning and prompting strategies, remains typical of her communicative style in counselling interviews (Ballard, personal communication).

Introduced in this extract is the subject of a house in Bangladesh which B owns, but which is lived in by his brother. His brother has recently come under pressure from a local landlord in Bangladesh who is attempting to intimidate him, and thereby B in England, into giving up the property. One of B's sons, Akkas, has recently returned to Bangladesh to get divorced and marry again.

DATA 4.7 AGENDA
The Bangladeshi worker's aims in the interview are:
(a) to get advice on what to do next;
(b) to get the Citizens Advice Bureau to intercede on his behalf with the authorities in Dhaka.
To do this he has to persuade the advice worker to take an interest in the house in Bangladesh and write letters on his behalf and offer constructive advice.

The advice worker, on the other hand, does not want to get involved in problems abroad, of which she has little direct knowledge at a time when, in her opinion, B has enough problems to sort out in this country. It is, however, her job to listen patiently to him.

The formulation of a preliminary hypothesis as to what is going on in the interaction is the first step in a framework for analysis developed by a group of ILT trainers concerned to broaden the data base of naturally-occurring inter-ethnic communication and to work together systematically on an analytical approach. This framework is based upon the 'expanded view of language' outlined for the reader in

DATA 4:7 THE HOUSE IN BANGLADESH – TRANSCRIPT

1 B: ... one year's no working, you see.

2 A: Yeah.

3 B: Me no lazy, me.

4 A: Oh i know.

5 B: Work is very good.

6 A: Yes I know you're not lazy.

7 B: <cough> Is no money is my country too much yesterday is a my brother is a letter is somebody your nother house is er I don't know English name.

8 A: You know quite a lot.

9 B: Yeah – eh.

10 A: What about Akkas have you heard, another letter?

11 B: No letter.

12 A: Mmmm.

13 B: Akkas no letter.

14 A: Mmmm.

15 B: Akkas no letter is my brother is letter is Akkas give me money go to very soon is go to England.

16 A: Yeah.

17 B: Me telling where is my money now.

18 A: You know i don't think he's going to be able to bring his wife if he comes back he'll have to leave her and then apply again for her.

19 B: No with me Akkas wife?

20 A: No? what is it Habibur? what's her name Hajinder no Habibur.

21 B: Er no Hamida Rehman.

22 A: Hamida mmm she won't be able to come with him she'll have to come afterwards if he comes back soon.

23 B: Very soon.

24 A: Mmmm.

25 B: Erm after.

26 A: She can come after, yes.

DATA 4:7 TRANSCRIPT *continued*

27   B: Ah

28   A: But if he comes back soon she'll have to stay there

29   B: Where is your letter is er Dhaka you?

30   A: I sent a letter to Dhaka yes

31   B: No

32   A: But I haven't had

33   B: Oh

34   A: One back yet mmmm

35   B: Is 'm somebody's my <cough> three house is 'm my five boy
       two girl my country three house

DATA 4.7 COMMENTARY

1. Overall Schema
Perhaps much more than in typical Advice Bureau interviews, the
goals of this interview are not clear from the outset and there are
attempts to negotiate them in a series of apparently sudden shifts in
topic and mood. Both sides seem to be working very hard on the
'positive face' and this is even more apparent when neither side knows
which way the conversation is going (Lines 3–6). B's negative face
wants become more obvious after more detailed analysis:

> <cough> Is no money is my country too much yesterday is a my
> brother is a letter is somebody your nother house is er I don't
> know English name   (line 7)

introduces a topic which is only returned to on later in the interview,
on both occasions preceded by a clearing of the throat:

> Is 'm somebody's my <cough> three house is 'm my five boy
> two girl my country three houses   (line 35)

The topic of the house in Bangladesh is what B wants to talk about,
although it is not at all clear what his expectations are from A. A on
the other hand, is pursuing clear ideational and inter-personal goals
once the interview is under way, viz.: *get the latest progress on certain
family matters, show concern and comment generally on the information
M gives her, show solidarity and give some general information.*

DATA 4.7 COMMENTARY *continued*

---

2. Perceptions and Assumptions

Since there is a lack of shared knowledge and assumptions about the goals of the whole interaction, we would expect a high level of misinterpretation or 'overriding' of speaker intent. This seems to be the case, e.g. B says 'I don't know English name'. A may interpret this as a general statement about not knowing enough English. Or she may choose to combine in her statement 'You know quite a lot' both a general reassurance, which she sees in keeping with her role, with a message to the tape recorder and so to the wider world, that she knows B and his problems well. Certainly, the general reassurance does not help B with his specific lexical search and would sound patronising to most people.

3. Speaker Perspectives

In the whole interaction A's high level of commenting is in contrast to the earlier interview with the Asian advisor. A hypothesis would be that throughout the interaction B does not understand A's intent when she gives a general comment.

The blurring between comment and advice, between ideational and interpersonal, positive-face, goals may be a major cause of lack of success of the interaction.

4. Interpersonal relationships

The speakers' roles seem very clear. B only initiates to introduce the topic about the house, and possibly to raise the question of the letter to Dhaka. Otherwise A initiates with questions or advice/comment. However, the disconcerting topic-switching which occurs throughout the interaction seems to contrast with the clear role demarcation. Combined with B's elliptical language is the uncertainty on both sides of where the conversation is going.

The *hypothesis* is a schema mismatch, viz.:

B: I am talking to A because she called me in and I want to talk about the problem I have with my house in Bangladesh. I expect specific information and advice on any item discussed.

A: I am talking to B because he seemed to want to talk to me. I want to show concern, and I can, at the same time, do a progress check and warn him about possible difficulties over his new daughter-in-law.

So they seem to 'guess and grasp' in an attempt to maintain thematic cohesion.

Chapter 1 (section 3). In particular, the framework draws upon the concept of meaning in interaction arising in the dynamic relationship between schema, frame and language use and form. The background to the concepts has been more fully explained in Chapter 2. The framework consists of five steps:

FRAMEWORK FOR LINGUISTIC ANALYSIS

[Devised by Margaret Simonot, Walsall ILT, and Sian Dodderidge, Kirklees ILT]

1. Forming a preliminary hypothesis
2. Preliminary prosodic analysis
3. Rewrite: modifying and elaborating the working hypothesis
4. Prosody, syntax and lexis
5. Synthesis

This framework was used for the analysis of a small part of Data 2.4 in Chapter Two. It forms the basis of the chapter 'Understanding, misunderstanding and breakdown in second language acquisition by adult immigrants' in Perdue's *Second Language Acquisition by Adult Immigrants* (1984), the field manual for the European Science Foundation project on the untutored second-language acquisition of ethnic-minority workers in five European countries. The framework appears as an appendix to the manual.

Step 1 Forming a preliminary hypothesis

In forming a preliminary hypothesis it is necessary to take into account the wider social and cultural contexts in which ethnic-minority workers are expected to acquire English. We have discussed in Chapter 1 how low communicative power is one component in a negative cycle of disadvantage and discrimination. And we have discussed the problems faced by ethnic-minority workers in having to communicate in order to learn, and learn in order to communicate.

We have also demonstrated in earlier chapters of this book how when the participants in an interaction have differing cultural backgrounds and are, as a result, working on differing assumptions, the greater the difference between the assumptions, the greater the amount of language needed to establish common ground and achieve satisfactory negotiation of meaning.

Analysis begins, therefore, with an examination of interactive discourse in terms of its schematic implications. We can then use the further analysis of syntax and prosody as a reality check for our initial hypothesis.

Speech triggers expectations and assumptions about what is going on, and it is only when some aspect jars on our perception that we look at the lower level of syntax and prosody to give us clues for reinterpretation of our hypothesised schema about the interaction.

In forming hypotheses, and in seeking to check these out through the close linguistic analysis, we suggest that the following variables should be borne in mind since they will influence the negotiation of meaning between participants. These variables concern cultural assumptions and their signalling through language. The success of the interaction will depend on the ability of the participants to establish or negotiate these variables in such a way that they are mutually compatible.

(a) *Ethnic identity.* By this we mean the degree of ethnicity, ethnocentricity and racism present in the individual interactants, and the degree to which language is used to establish or maintain a self/group identity. The degree to which ethnicity, ethnocentricity or racism affects the participants' view of each other may or may not affect the topics or goals of an interaction. We suggest that ethnicity should not prove a barrier to the successful negotiation of meaning, except in so far as it might impede the recognition of other views of reality, appropriacy and signalling conventions. Ethnocentricity, with its high correlation to characteristics such as difficulty in coping with ambiguity, will result in increased difficulty in negotiation. Racism will increase this difficulty further.

(b) *Co-membership.* By this we mean the degree to which co-membership is present or negotiable in the course of the interaction. Erickson and Shultz (1982) have demonstrated the importance of establishing co-membership in gatekeeping encounters. By co-membership, they mean particularistic attributes of status shared by interactants such as ethnicity, the 'old school' network, interest in a particular hobby and so on. In analysing the data, it is of interest to discover the extent of co-membership and the weight this is given in shaping the attitudes of the participants to one another in the interaction. For example, a participant expressing a strongly ethnocentric identity may not in fact be moved by the evidence of a particularistic co-membership with the other participants. Equally, the same co-membership factor may carry different weights in different contexts. For example, having a workplace in common is likely to be more significant in situations where a 'team' identity is fostered, as in the public-transport industry, than in situations where people are much on their own, as in most noisy factory environments.

(c) *Role, status, power.* Most interactive data will be in gatekeeping situations where one speaker holds power and is evaluating the other in order to grant, or not to grant, access or privilege. How this situation is perceived by either side, and whether the modes of signalling relative status, etc., are recognised, will play a part in the success or otherwise of the interaction.

(d) *Ascribed attitudes and emotions.* By this we mean the way in which attitude and emotion are signalled by verbal and non-verbal means and the extent to which these are mutually interpretable. These may be **displayed** involuntarily (e.g. blushing), **indicated** through verbal behaviour (e.g. accent, pitch or loudness) or **signalled** in speech (e.g. statements about emotional state) (cf. Allwood 1978). An interactant interpreting another's behaviour through their own norms and expectations may ascribe attitudes and emotions that are not in fact present in the other. Equally, they may fail to interpret emotions that *are* present.

The analyst having formed a hypothesis (taking account of the above variables) about context, purpose, speaker perspectives and schemata in the interaction, the rest of the analysis has as its aim to investigate the 'text' in depth as a check on the hypothesis made, and to modify/change the hypothesis in the light of the findings.

For example, one's overall hypothesis about role, status and power in the interaction can be checked by looking at features such as prosodic patterns, turn-taking, directness/indirectness, the structuring of the argument. Alternatively, one might observe a feature like recurrent hesitation in the text, hypothesise that this indicates that the speaker perceives himself to have low status, and then check against other evidence in the data. Or recurrent hesitation might simply indicate lack of fluency in the language. We can expect that the more that is shared in the way of cultural assumptions and their linguistic signalling, the less language will be required to reach understanding; and conversely, the smaller the congruity of shared assumptions, the greater the amount of language required to negotiate meaning.

Step 2 Preliminary prosodic analysis
Prosodic features have ideational and interpersonal functions and will therefore signal both ideational and interpersonal schemata. As we have suggested in Chapter 2, prosodic features are more important in inter-ethnic communication than has generally been acknowledged. The difference in use of prosody may influence the extent to which speakers from different ethnic backgrounds will be able to communicate smoothly. At all levels of fluency in a second language, a speaker may be making grave misjudgements about what is meant and in their own production of language giving their partners an incorrect impression of what they are meaning.

All European languages share to some extent the use of prosodic features to express mood, attitude of the speaker and to focus attention within the text on issues of importance or to differentiate between new and given information. One of the properties of pitch and stress is to provide cohesion (see Chapter 2, section 3.4). Although the way pitch and stress are used may vary in degree from one European language to another, they still retain this common function. Within our own experience, North Indian languages and, we would suppose, other pan-ethnic groups of languages, use other devices for signalling cohesion, or use pitch and stress too, but in a different way and for different purposes. They may not be identical for any two given languages, but they are related and may be inherently different from those used in European languages. Inter-ethnic communication will not necessarily break down because of this, but where there are schema differences and little or no co-membership, differences in the uses of prosody are more likely to lead to loss of information or misinterpretation of attitude.

Discrepancies in the management of these features may cause **breakdown of interaction**. Unshared knowledge and assumptions and different schemata may cause **breakdown of understanding**. By examining discourse where breakdown of interaction does not overtly occur but where there is breakdown of understanding, and by analysing the discourse process and how speakers pursue an argument, we may be able to distinguish between these kinds of breakdown.

For language to be processed in ongoing interaction it has to be presented in units that are both manageable and meaningful. The unit that best fits the purpose is the information (or sense) unit. In English, the information unit may be regarded as primarily syntactic, but it is coterminous with, and only takes on its full meaning through, its prosodic expression, the tone group. However, when examining the prosodic and syntactic structure of some South-Asian English speech, we found that prosodic features are frequently substituted for syntax rather than supplementing it as in what we have called Anglo – English (AE). It emerged that in attempting to correlate the AE tone-group system with South-Asian English, we were distorting our perceptual experience to fit our preconceptions and indeed overlooking patterns that might have emerged if we had tried to derive them from the South Asian speaker's discourse itself.

As a guideline we assumed that patterns and rules of use of pitch and rhythm will emerge that have definite identifiable discourse functions in the South Asian language and the analyst can begin to suggest what those patterns and functions might be. For example, are particular pitch or rhythmic changes or patterns used to signal important or new information? Is pitch used within the clause to indicate focus? Does pitch have a referential function, binding different parts of the discourse together? We can also begin to determine whether these signals are being read by the other party to the interaction, and whether the South Asian speaker is picking up on the prosodic signals of the English speaker. This process is made possible by the insights and knowledge of bilingual trainers and informants.

Step 3 Modifying and elaborating the working hypothesis

Relating the prosodic analysis back to the initial working hypothesis about the whole interaction will give a first check on whether the data appear to confirm, deny or modify the initial perceptions. It will certainly provide a more detailed view of what is going on than the initial 'top-down' hypothesis process, and will also show points of interest or difficulty in the interaction, where the bilingual speaker's discourse may appear to a monolingual speaker to lack cohesion and coherence.

This process requires the analyst to **rewrite** the interaction. The purpose of rewriting is not to set a model for what 'should' have been said, but to alert the researcher to recurrent features of interest or difficulty, and the kinds of relationship that exist between the formal features of the language used and the whole communicative interaction. Rewriting will take place in order to provide such information as is understood or elided, but not verbalised. By rewriting, one is conjecturing what the speaker perspective may have been, and checking this for internal consistency. One may rewrite in different ways to give rise to different hypotheses. This may result in the generation of more hypotheses from which a final selection can be made, rather than narrowing down the range of choice. In this way one can finally select which of the alternatives has the greater probability of carrying the speaker's meaning. At the end of this process one should have a hypothesis of the interaction which is much more detailed than the initial one and which more accurately reflects the way in which meaning is being negotiated throughout the interaction. We have already given an example of this rewriting in Data 2.4 (Chapter 2).

Step 4 Prosody, syntax and lexis

In this step the analyst attempts to derive patterns from the syntactic and prosodic features that seem to have definite signalling functions for that speaker. As relationships between prosody, syntax and lexis emerge they either support or refute the hypothesis initially formulated in Step 1 or modified in Step 3. We are not, therefore, simply looking for and describing features that are different from native-speaker practice; we are looking for factors of two types:

(a) features different from those of English which are used systematically and meaningfully by the bilingual speaker;
(b) syntactic features similar to those used in English which may not actually have the same intended meaning.

Throughout this process of trying to correlate the formal features of the language used with their illocutionary intent, one is constantly cross-checking with the hypothesis and refining one's views of the detailed operation of the variables in the interaction. The process of relating prosody to syntactic and lexical features of the discourse involves an examination of the cohesive role they play at the clausal level, the interclausal level, and the discourse level (i.e. the whole interaction):

	Prosody	Syntax
Within the clause:	to signal focus;	to signal focus.
Interclausally:	to relativise/topicalise old/new, important/less important information;	to relativise and cohere: e.g. conjoining, embedding, repetition, structural parallelism.
At the discourse level, i.e. the whole interaction:	pitch and rhythm changes used to signal cohesion between one part of the interaction and another	deictic reference used to refer to something other than what a native speaker would expect; structural parallelism used to make connections between parts of the discourse which may be quite distant from each other.

This stage is illustrated by the following analysis of a small section of Data 2.4 (see page 212). There is a full discussion of Data 2.4 in Chapter 2.

A further example of this process is given in the detailed analysis within this framework of an extract from Data 4.7 (see pp. 203).

Step 5 Synthesis

With the insights gained into the ways in which the ethnic-minority speaker uses the second language, the researcher can now draw a much more detailed picture of what occurs in the interaction, and is able to look more meaningfully at features of the discourse management from two points of view:

(a) *Cooperation between speakers.* Here, the interactants' strategies for production and interpretation of the following features are examined:
  - Opening, closing, turn-taking; introduction of self, politeness formulae, phatics. [Such interactive features may be crucial to the development of attitudes on either side, particularly if the second-language speaker uses conventions different from those of the native speaker.]

DATA 2.4 STAFF DISCUSSION AT A BUS COMPANY [lines 3–9 of Data 2.4: analysed by Sian Dodderidge, Kirklees ILT]	
Transcript	**Prosody**
1 if you /	2 Main point conveyed through evenly spaced stress. To 'Anglo' English (AE)-speaker the main point is entailed and so may be lost.
2 ⌐early turns we'll `make 'up // er	
3 'you `do firˆst bit & `second 'bit	3 Stress not used to mark contrast between 'first' and 'second'. Leaves anaphoric 'that' without a clear referent.
4 we will ⌐cover thatˆ //	
5 and 'if you `middle turn /	Again, stress used here to mark self-correction but no stress on 'no' which AE-speaker would expect.
6 no 'if 'you late turn /	'Middle' and 'late' are contrasted by stress but only sub-stress on verb
7 we will `make 'up you know /	'make 'up' so that contrast may not be clear to AE-speaker.
8 `middle turnˆ //	
9 so / ⌐why they ˆhave	
10 `change change miˆnd	
	Discourse Management
	1 Exemplification (of release arrangement).
	3 Restatement of example with amplification.
Transcript	**Syntax and lexis**
1 if you /	1 'You' as if in direct speech, i.e. management said 'If you ...',
2 ⌐early turns we'll `make 'up // er	
3 'you `do first bit and `second 'bit /	2 No verb in 'if' clause. No anaphoric pronoun referring to 'early'

DATA 2.4 STAFF DISCUSSION AT A BUS COMPANY *continued*

Transcript	Structural Parallels	Commentary
4 we will ⌐cover that //		turn' in main clause. 'We' = management.
5 and 'if 'you mìddle turn /	5 Exemplification and self-correction.	4 Main verb at end of the clause.
6 no 'if 'you làte turn /		5 & 6 No verb in 'if' clause.
7 'we will 'make 'up you know /		7 'Make up' = 'cover', used here to parallel same lexical choice in 2 (above).
8 mìddle turn //		
9 so / ⌐why 'they 'have	9 Main point occurs at the end in the form of a rhetorical question.	9 No inversion of question. 'They' = management here, but see 1 above where 'you' used in direct speech to imply reported speech.
10 'change change mìnd		

Transcript	Structural Parallels	Modes of cohesion
1 if you / ⌐early turns 'we'll make 'up // er	**Structural Parallels**	**Modes of cohesion**
2 you 'do first bit and 'second 'bit /	2 parallels 7.	Detailed structural parallelism is a major way by which meaning is conveyed.
3		
4 'we will ⌐cover that //		
5 and 'if 'you mìddle turn /	5 & 6 are parallels.	'Make up' used as a superordinate to *contd.*

DATA 2.4 STAFF DISCUSSION AT A BUS COMPANY *continued*

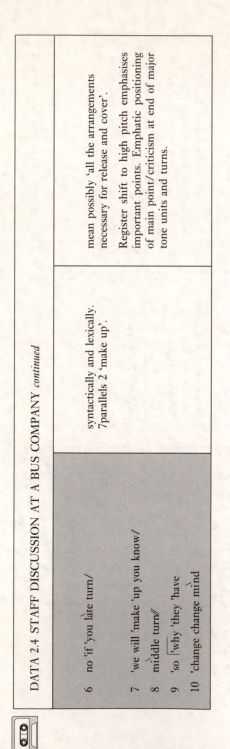

| | syntactically and lexically. 7parallels 2 'make up'. | mean possibly 'all the arrangements necessary for release and cover'. |
| | | Register shift to high pitch emphasises important points. Emphatic positioning of main point/criticism at end of major tone units and turns. |

6 no 'if 'you `late turn/

7 'we will 'make 'up you know/

8 `middle turn//

9 'so ⌐'why 'they `have

10 'change change `mind

- Feedback elicitation and giving: verbal/non-verbal back-channelling; self/other correction; maintenance/alteration of perspective.
- Recognition and repair of misunderstandings; acknowledgement; perlocutionary effect in relation to illocutionary intent; mitigation.
- Appropriacy: of content (sequencing); of register (status, role); of non-verbal gesture and body language; directness/indirectness in relation to respect for the other; agreeing/disagreeing.
- Meta-talk; confirmation, summary of own or other's meaning.

(b) *Illocutionary meaning*. This will involve an examination of how the second speaker achieves coherence in English through:
- Topicalisation; modes of focusing to distinguish important/less important, old/new information.
- Relativisation; demonstration of relationships between information units; deixis; reference to person, place and time; contrastiveness.
- Speaker perspective; signalling, display or indication of emotions and attitude; involvement in what speaker is saying.
- Structuring the argument, e.g. repetition or elaboration; sequencing of content; reference and correctives.
- signalling meaning through prosody, choice of lexis.

As a result of this examination we can make an informed choice between the hypotheses made at the rewriting stage.

We can also make an assessment of the success of the interaction in relation to the goals of the interactants. Success is likely to be influenced by the mutual compatibility of these goals. For example, the speaker's intention may be conveyed to the hearer, but the instrumental goals of one speaker may still not be achieved if they are incompatible with the goals of the other. Conversely, an attitudinal goal (such as wishing to show respect) may not be attained because the perlocutionary effect fails to match the illocutionary intent but, given good will and sympathy on the part of the native speaker, the bilingual speaker may still be successful in achieving such goals.

To illustrate Steps 2 – 5 we give an example of the detailed application of this framework to part of Data 4.7 (which was used to illustrate Step 1 – the formulation of a preliminary hypothesis).

DATA 4.7 THE HOUSE IN BANGLADESH [Extract from Data
4.7: material collected by Cathy Ballard; analysed by Peter
Sayers and Celia Roberts]

1　B: … one years no working you see.

2　A: yeah.

3　B: me no lazy me.

4　A: oh i know.

5　B: work is very good.

6　A: yes i know youre not lazy.

7　B: <cough> is ⌈no money ¦is my / country / too much/⌊yesterday
　　　/ is a / my brother / is a letter // ⌊is somebody / your nother
　　　house // is..er..I don't ¦know / english name //

8　A: you know ¦quite a lot //

9　B: yeah..eh //

10　A: what about akkas // have you heard / another letter //

11　B: no letter //

12　A: mmm //

13　B: ⌊akkas / no letter //

14　A: mmm //

15　B: akkas / ⌈no letter / is my brother / is letter / is / akkas / give me
　　　money / ⌊go to / very soon is / go to england //

16　A: yeah //

17　B: me telling / where / ⌈ is my money now //

18　A: you know / ..i ¦dont think / he's going to be able to bring his
　　　wife // if he ¦comes back / he'll have to leave her / and then
　　　apply a¦gain for her //

19　B: no / with me / akkas wife //

20　A: no / what is it / ..habibur / whats her name / ..hajinder // no..
　　　habibur //

21　B: er / no / hamida rehman //

22　A: hamida..mm / ..she wont be able to come / with him // she'll have
　　　to come / afterwards / if he comes back soon //

23　B: very soon //

24　A: mmm //

25　B: erm .. after //

DATA 4.7 THE HOUSE IN BANGLADESH *continued*

26 A: she can come after / yes //

27 B: ah //

28 A: but if he come 'back soon / she'll have to 'stay there //

29 B: where is your letter is / er / Dhaka / you //

30 A: i 'sent a letter to Dhaka / yes //

31 B: no //

32 A: but i 'haven't had //

33 B: oh //

34 A: ..a one back yet / mmm //

35 B: is 'm somebody's my <cough> three house is 'm my five boy
two girl my country three house ....

APPLICATION OF FRAMEWORK FOR LINGUISTIC ANALYSIS TO DATA 4.7

Step 2 Preliminary prosodic analysis

B's opening utterances, prefaced by what appears to be a significant
cough, highlight with raised pitch and a high level of chunking that
he is introducing an important topic. There is raised pitch on
'money', 'my', 'yesterday' and 'your'. The same rapid pitch changes
occur at line 15:

---

15 B: akkas / no letter / is my brother / is letter / is / akkas /
give me money / go to / very soon is / go to england //

16 A: yeah //

17 B: me telling / where / is my money now //

---

and again when he finally pulls round the conversation to the topic of
the house (again after a cough) in the utterances immediately
following the analysed extract. The high pitch of these utterances is a
typical phenomenon for speakers of North Indian languages and
signals the great importance the speaker attaches to what he is saying.

The second time this high pitch is used (line 15) there is also a marked increase in speed of delivery. This too is an indication of the importance to the speaker of this utterance. B's other utterances are not marked in the same way.

A's utterances are characterised by smoother contouring, and the care with which key syllables are stressed illustrates the 'advice mode' she is in. Although the conversation is not going the way B wants it to, he is readily able to pick up A's stressed syllables, and repeats key words:

22 A: h‾amida / mm / she 'won't be able to come / with him //
          she'll have to c‾ome / afterwards / if he comes back soon //

23 B: very s‾oon//

24 A: mmm//

25 B: erm .. áfter//

26 A: she can come àfter/y‾es//

27 B: ‾ah//

It is difficult in this data to analyse the role of B's prosody in signalling information flow and syntactic relations because there are so few performatives in his utterances. However, preliminary analysis in Step 2 seems to confirm the working hypothesis, with B's important new information ignored by A, and A introducing topics and questioning B on them while playing a reassuring/advising role.

Step 3 Rewrite
Attempts at rewrites serve to highlight the crucial role of bilingual researchers, and how important background information is. Without some initial discussion in Bengali about what B's concerns are, it is extremely difficult to guess at his complete meaning.

The stress pattern in line 1 follows the 'Anglo' English (AE) pattern for 'I have no money in my country' but the intonation pattern does not. The intonation pattern links the meaning in 'my country' back to 'no money' and forward to 'too much yesterday' which may mean 'I had or sent a lot previously' (i.e. 'too much' = a lot, and 'yesterday' = time past).

The lack of any substantial tone-group boundary after 'yesterday' also links it to the next phrase, indicating a past time reference for 'is a my brother is a letter' (i.e. 'I **have got** a letter from my brother' or 'my brother **sent** a letter').

The next phrase, 'is somebody your 'nother house', is direct speech and is about the contents of the letter, i.e. 'there is somebody in your other house', but this phrase is difficult to understand for a number of reasons:

(i) The use of direct speech with no separate intonation pattern to mark it. In AE a lack of distinctive intonation usually indicates indirect speech. There is no indirect speech in the grammars of the North Indian languages.

(ii) The pronoun 'your' where AE–speakers would expect 'my' if it is the speaker's house.

(iii) The stress on 'nother' (AE 'another') which seems to suggest this is either new information from his brother (i.e. 'there's somebody in another house – in addition to the one you already know about') or information inserted for the English listener (i.e. 'my brother's letter told me there's somebody in my house – I've another house in Bangladesh'). The lack of preposition 'in' (if indeed that is what is meant) seems trivial compared with the above.

The lack of interjection or phatics from A suggests that she is having difficulty understanding lines 1 and 2, but by the end of line 2 the pitch is low (or normal) again while B searches for words. The phrase 'I don't know English name' is given an intonation pattern similar to AE – it is almost as if B has borrowed the phrase wholesale from English – it is, in a sense, not part of his Bangladeshi English.

This 'borrowed' phrase is easy for A to understand and gives her the chance to come in again. It relieves, for her, the tension created through listening to the previous part of the utterance and gives her something to respond to, but not enough for her to maintain the subject. Line 4 is another of A's patronising comments which also functions as enabling her to take the initiative and change topic.

The stress pattern of line 15 offers the AE listener some idea on how to 'fill the gaps'; i.e. 'Akkas no letter' can be interpreted as 'Akkas hasn't sent a letter' and 'my brother is letter' as 'my brother has sent a letter'.

The function of 'is' (the /z/ morpheme) is more difficult to interpret. It seems to have two functions:

(i) as a general verb – there are very few other verbs in B's speech;

(ii) as a phrase-linker or -introducer: 'Akkas no letter' is linked contrastively to 'my brother is letter' by an 'is' where AE would use 'but'; i.e. 'Akkas hasn't sent a letter, but my brother has'.

The next two phrases, 'Akkas give me money' and 'go to very soon is go to England', are direct speech (but, again, like 'somebody your 'nother house' (line 7), have the same intonation as the previous phrases which in AE convention would indicate indirect speech).

The phrase 'Akkas give me money' could be interpreted as 'my brother's letter said Akkas gave him the brother some money' if it were not for line 17, 'me telling where is my money now?', which makes the issue of who is giving or demanding money to or of whom problematic. Is this part of the report of the brother's letter? If so, 'Akkas give me money' (line 15) is more difficult to interpret. Perhaps the situation is: 'My brother had asked Akkas to give him money but he hadn't and is now asking me (B) where his money is'.

This interpretation is very possible as it is normal for money to be transferred from family in England to family in Bangladesh and it is reasonable for the brother to expect money via Akkas, not knowing B's current financial difficulties in England. But if this is the case it doesn't explain why 'go to very soon is go to England' comes in between, unless it is A's 'yeah' which leads him to pursue the money issue. A's 'yeah' in fact signals her wish to change the subject to Akkas's wife.

If this interpretation of line 15 is correct, then line 1 can probably be interpreted as 'I haven't been able to send any money to my country', and 'too much yesterday' as 'I managed to send a lot before'. This interpretation is probable given the difficulties B is having meeting bills and other demands on his income.

In this exchange, both the subject and content of A's reply to his question take B by surprise:
The intonation of line 17 shows surprise and, in a way, detracts from the rather odd use of 'me'. It doesn't refer back to the speaker, but to

> 17 B: me telling / where / is my money now //
>
> 18 A: you know / ..i dont think / he's going to be able to bring his wife
>   // if he comes back / he'll have to leave her / and then apply
>   again for her //
>
> 19 B: no / with me / akkas wife //

Akkas – it is almost as if B is speaking Akkas's lines instead of his own. 'With me' is taken as one component similar to 'give me' (in 'Akkas give me money' above). The pronouns used are from the perspective of the person most affected, not from the perspective of the speaker.

B has little to say on the subject of Akkas's wife. He is waiting for a chance to come back to his topic – the house in Bangladesh – which is what the question (line 29) 'Where is your letter is er Dhaka you?' refers to. The meaning here is something like 'What happened about the letter you sent to Dhaka?' The first word sounds as if it could be 'what', rather than 'where'.

Step 4   Prosody, syntax and lexis

Line 7, up to 'nother house'. Prosodically, the utterance appears very staccato, with many short feet marked. But the shifts in pitch register, which are even more marked, appear to group certain parts of the utterance together: e.g. / too much / yesterday / . The supposition that // is no money is my country too much / is merely an introduction to / yesterday .../ etc. does not seem to hold up given that / too much/yesterday is all on a low tone. The question of money is tied in prosodically with 'brother' and 'letter' and 'your'. The pitch drops on 'house', but perceptually is clearly stressed. The drop in pitch seems to suggest that a post-modifier will follow (but he does not know the English word). The smooth contour and rather apologetic lower tone of // I don't know/English name // is in marked contrast to the accented quality of the rest of the utterance. It is similar to // akkas / no / letter // in line 11 which, again, contrasts with the same words in line 12.

Line 10. Here B returns to the topic of his brother and uses the high pitch of lines 1 and 2. In the first part of the utterance B stresses the first syllables in 'akkas', 'letter' and 'brother', then there is a change. / is letter/is akkas / give me money/. The stress on the second syllable of 'letter' and the low tone and speeded-up /give me/ suggest that this part of the utterance hangs together. B is probably trying to signal the contrast between a letter from Akkas and a letter from his brother. He may be trying to set the topic of Akkas on one side, and raise the question of money, or he may be trying to integrate the topic of Akkas (raised by A) into the brother– letter–money–house theme.

Line 19. This is very ambiguous. It is possible B misinterprets A's 'leave' as 'line' or says 'with me' when he means 'with him'. The lengthened, quite high-pitched syllable 'no' might show disagreement but there is so little pause between 'no' and 'with one' that B seems to be simply questioning whether Akkas's wife will or will not be with him.

In the rest of B's utterances there is none of the marked, accented language of the brother–house topic. He appears to be just picking up on A's comments to maintain the conversation, waiting for a suitable moment to return to this topic. The question of the letter to Dhaka seems to be part of this conversational maintenance, linking in some way with the Akkas theme.

With a few exceptions B's utterances consist of noun phrases and adverbial phrases modifying verbs which are not verbalised. There is very little explicit conjoining or relativisation, and this, combined with the ambiguity of pronoun references, means that it is very difficult to disentangle agent from object. So in the two key utterances of lines 7 and 15, A is unable to develop his theme with him and instead takes control of the conversation by introducing the topic of Akkas's wife.

It is hard to decide whether B's lexical repetitions are, in fact, a form of thematic cohesion. The 'letter' repetition is confused by A's introduction of the idea of a letter from Akkas. In the first fourteen lines, 'money' is introduced three times, but again it is not clear whether B is referring to the same money each time. Clearly, though, this is an important issue which A fails to respond to since she wants to pursue the question of Akkas's wife – B's echoing of A, e.g. 'very soon' and 'after', suggest:

(i)   that he is simply maintaining her topic (see above); and/or
(ii) he has not understood her conditional remark 'If he comes back soon'.

Step 5 Synthesis

What is interesting about the interaction in this extract is that, despite a clear desire for conversational cooperation and presentation of positive face, there is not a single instance when the two speakers actually cooperate in developing a mutually agreed line of argument. On the two occasions when one of the speakers asks a direct question and gets an answer, the topic is not central to the listener; i.e. Akkas's letter is not what B wants to talk about, and the letter from Dhaka is not what A wants to talk about since there has been no progress on it. On the other occasions when B picks up a lexical item from A's conversation, apparently to check the meaning, there is no indication that he wants to pursue this topic.

A introduces the Akkas theme and then develops it in relation to his wife, overriding B's major concern. Again she stalls B's topic at the beginning by her in-role reassurance about his knowledge of English. They are quite clearly in different schemata here, and in the chunk analysed do not find a way of matching/sharing schemata. The fact that they are both trying to do different things is compounded by L1/L2 misinterpretations, or assumptions about misinterpretations;

e.g. A thinks B is not clear about who she is talking about and so launches into a set of questions about the name of Akkas's wife.

At lines 7, 10, 18 and 29 a new topic is introduced after something of a hiatus, as if both sides wanted to maintain the conversation. A does this to maintain and display her role as friendly, helpful adviser and B because he has a problem which needs sorting out and he therefore wants to keep A's continued involvement in his concerns.

The fact that, despite so little real conversational cooperation, the interaction appears to progress smoothly without hitches or too many interruptions, silences or expressions of irritation or frustration is a reflection of the good will and familiarity of the interactants.

This analysis also provides evidence about the level of second-language acquisition by the bilingual interactant.

Clearly, the most problematic areas for B are:

(i) A's inability to pick up on the important topic of brother–letter–money–house – although its importance seems to be clearly signalled prosodically.

(ii) His own difficulties in making references clear, both proper nouns and pronominals. This is particularly acute when he is using indirect speech to talk about what is in the letter(s).

(iii) Confusion over noun and pronoun references makes it hard to establish both what the topic is and what the speaker perspective is, e.g. //me telling where is my money now//. Is he anxious about lost money? Or simply stating a fact about his or his brother's money?

This piece of data demonstrates the linguistic complexity and linguistic demands of giving a personal narrative account, typical of the routine interactions which occur on a daily basis in advice centres and social security and housing offices. South Asian workers, long resident in Britain but with little encouragement or opportunity to develop English, are faced with having to present themselves and their cases in English. B's experience here would have been very different if the advice worker had been a Bengali-speaker or there had been an interpreter.

The data also shows how two people can apparently interact together with no overt breakdowns in communication but with no evidence that either side has understood the purpose of or the information given in the interaction. There are enormous dangers in interactants assuming that they have been understood and assuming that they understand. Time is wasted, frustration grows, ethnic-minority workers feel – and in reality often are – discriminated against, and white people have their prejudices reinforced.

5　Ethnographic and linguistic analysis applied: a case study

The collection and analysis of data is an example of our concern, working as educationists in industrial and public-service contexts, to develop an understanding and pedagogy for the long term which can contribute to the improvement of inter-ethnic relations and to a more empowering approach to the teaching of English. The day-to-day short-term reality is the need to react positively to the immediate perceived needs of the particular situations of individual 'clients'.

The illustrative case study which concludes this chapter is an example of responding to a particular situation in a way that was informed by linguistic and ethnographic analysis. It was an attempt to combine linguistic and ethnographic insights in a study which had important implications for race relations in employment.

ILT contribution to a formal investigation at an engineering company by the Commission For Racial Equality (CRE 1984)

The UK Commission for Racial Equality (CRE) is empowered by the 1976 Race Relations Act to undertake formal investigations of alleged discriminatory practice by companies and other organisations (see Appendix 3). Between 1977 and 79 the Commission made preliminary enquiries at the company in response to complaints under the Act. The plant under investigation was part of a large multinational engineering company. This plant made rubber components for the motor industry.

In the course of these enquiries, the company informed the CRE that in 1979, although 45 per cent of the operators were Asian, only three out of sixty-two foremen were Asian. The reason given for this disparity was that there had been few foreman vacancies over the last ten years, and in a number of cases Asian applicants had failed because of 'a lack of ability' to communicate in English.

The CRE was concerned that the promotion procedures, particularly the heavy reliance on the interview, demanded language skills which were not necessary for the satisfactory performance of the job. If this was found to be the case, then the company might be indirectly discriminating against bilingual speakers with English as a second language, and contravening Sections 1, 4 and 28 of the 1976 Act (again, see Appendix 3).

The CRE asked ILT staff to assess the communication skills needed to go through the company's established foreman-selection procedures. It was recognised that these procedures were typical of UK job and promotion interviews and that the findings of the ILT assessment would therefore be relevant to many other organisations.

The task was to compare the language skills necessary for the foreman-selection procedures with the skills needed to do the job of a foreman on the shop-floor and to see if the former were different and more complex. ILT was also asked to assess the level of English of Asian workers who had failed in their application for the job of foreman and who were still employed at the company. The remit sounded straightforward and relatively easy to accomplish; but once the context of the company in 1982 was taken into account, the task emerged as considerably more difficult and sensitive than had been conceived. To this extent, it is a good example of working in a complex human environment in which issues of language are generally seen as peripheral to the problems in hand.

Context
The company was suffering the effects of recession and the foremen, who were crucial to the investigation, were affected by redundancies. The foremen's union was in dispute with the company and this created a delicate situation in terms of industrial relations. Existing foremen, therefore, refused to be evaluated on their communication skills. In addition, the period of alleged discrimination was long past; many of those involved had left the company, and the company was not willing for an actual interview to be observed or for there to be any interviewing of shop-floor workers directly. The context was made more difficult by the fact that since 1977 the CRE had already carried out a number of enquiries at the company. All these factors made the task sensitive and difficult and were likely to affect and constrain the methodology in terms of informants, collection of data and ways of proceeding (see Training Material 4.2 page 226).

Task 1 Communication skills needed to be a foreman
As well as substituting simulations for real job interviews and recorded shop-floor talk, the entire assessment had to be carried out with great caution and sensitivity. Each step had to be explicitly negotiated and the data-collection procedures had to be fine-tuned to ensure that they were acceptable and provided the maximum amount of useful data with the minimum disruption. To this end, great reliance was placed upon the techniques of ethnographic interviewing (Spradley 1979; Agar 1980), and informed by these techniques a code of conduct was drawn up and agreed with the foremen and the foremen's union representatives (Training Material 4.3).

The three assessors drew up written notes on the method to be adopted for their own guidance, and the managers and foremen were also presented with an outline of what the interviews would consist of (Training Material 4.4 – 4.5).

TRAINING MATERIAL 4.2 SURVEY PROCEDURE [Assessors: Clarice Brierley, Sardul Dhesi, Birmingham ILT and Valerie Yates NCILT]

ilt

SURVEY PROCEDURES

Task	Informants	Data	Method
Find out communication skills needed to be a foreman.	Foreman promoted/ appointed during the allegation period.	Description of communication skills required.	Ethnographic interviews tape-recorded or full notes taken.
		Observation of communication skills required.	Shopfloor observation at key points in the day, e.g. changing shift.
Find out communication skills required for promotion interview.	Panel interviewers, i.e. Production Managers from different departments	Criteria used in job interviews.	Documents on formal procedures.
		Typical job interviews and expected answers.	Interview.
	Written information supplied by company.	Job descriptions, notes on interviewees etc.	Supplied by company.
Compare communication skill of 'failed' white & Asian applicants.	'Failed' white & Asian applicants.	Communication skills of white & Asian applicants in job interviews.	Simulated job interview (based on data collected).
		Communication skills of white & Asian applicants as 'foremen' on shopfloor.	Simulated shop floor talk with 'foremen' (based on data collected).
			Ethnographic interviews of white & Asian applicants.

TRAINING MATERIAL 4.3 CODE OF CONDUCT [Clarice Brierley, Sardul Dhesi, Birmingham ILT, and Valerie Yates, NCILT]

CODE OF CONDUCT AND TRAINING SURVEY INTERVIEWS

The principles of operation for conducting interviews in an ILT survey can be summarised as follows:
1. Consider interviewee in a survey first.
2. Safeguard interviewees' rights, interests and sensitivities.
3. Communicate survey and interview objectives.
4. Make reports available to interviewees.

These principles are expanded in the following way:

1. Safeguard interviewees' interests
Every effort should be made to cooperate with representatives of the company and individual members of the groups to be interviewed in the planning and execution of the survey.

All interviews must include inquiries to discover the interests and concerns of the interviewee.

2. Interviewees' rights
Interviewees have a right to remain anonymous. This right should be respected in all circumstances. This applies to the collection of data by means of tape recorders, cameras and other data collected in face-to-face interviews or in participant observation.

Those being observed or interviewed should understand why such devices are being used and be free to reject them if they wish. If they accept them, the results obtained should respect the interviewees' right to welfare dignity and privacy.

3. Communicate survey and interview objectives
Interviewees have a right to know the interviewer's aims. Communicating the aims of an interview should extend where necessary to communicating the aims of individual questions.

4. Make reports available to interviewees
No reports should be provided to sponsors that are not also available where practical, to the groups and individuals interviewed.

The ethnographic interviews were complemented by observation and recorded simulated shop-floor interactions and formal interviews.

TRAINING MATERIAL 4.4 INTERVIEW METHOD [Clarice Brierley, Sardul Dhesi, Birmingham ILT, and Valerie Yates, NCILT]

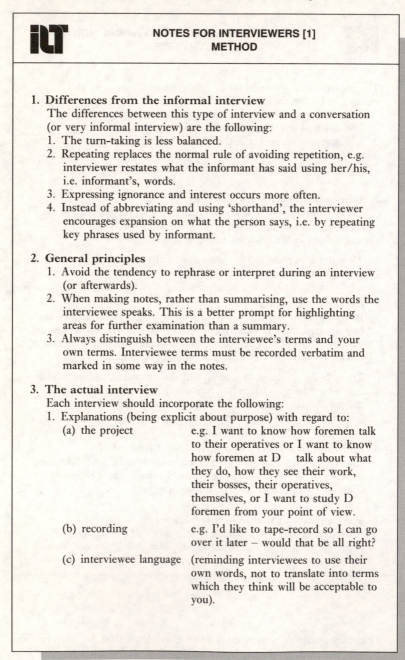

ILT

NOTES FOR INTERVIEWERS [1]
METHOD

1. Differences from the informal interview
The differences between this type of interview and a conversation (or very informal interview) are the following:
1. The turn-taking is less balanced.
2. Repeating replaces the normal rule of avoiding repetition, e.g. interviewer restates what the informant has said using her/his, i.e. informant's, words.
3. Expressing ignorance and interest occurs more often.
4. Instead of abbreviating and using 'shorthand', the interviewer encourages expansion on what the person says, i.e. by repeating key phrases used by informant.

2. General principles
1. Avoid the tendency to rephrase or interpret during an interview (or afterwards).
2. When making notes, rather than summarising, use the words the interviewee speaks. This is a better prompt for highlighting areas for further examination than a summary.
3. Always distinguish between the interviewee's terms and your own terms. Interviewee terms must be recorded verbatim and marked in some way in the notes.

3. The actual interview
Each interview should incorporate the following:
1. Explanations (being explicit about purpose) with regard to:

   (a) the project   e.g. I want to know how foremen talk to their operatives or I want to know how foremen at D   talk about what they do, how they see their work, their bosses, their operatives, themselves, or I want to study D foremen from your point of view.

   (b) recording   e.g. I'd like to tape-record so I can go over it later – would that be all right?

   (c) interviewee language   (reminding interviewees to use their own words, not to translate into terms which they think will be acceptable to you).

TRAINING MATERIAL 4:4 INTERVIEW METHOD *continued*

	e.g. If you were talking to an operative, what would you say, using your words?
(d) different stages of the interview	(when you move from one stage of the interview to the next) e.g. Now, I'd like to ask you some different kinds of questions.
(e) types of questions	(giving a reason why you are asking a particular type of question) e.g. These questions are meant to get you thinking about an average day at work.
2. Ethnographic questions	There are three main kinds.
(a) descriptive	e.g. Could you tell me what you do in the office?
(b) structural	(to tell the interviewer how interviewees structure their knowledge) e.g. What are all the stages of the XX procedure? Can you think of any others?
(c) contrast	e.g. What's the difference between an 'x' and a 'y'?

Presentation to management

One of the most difficult tasks for language specialists working with non-specialists is to present insights into language and its relationship to other aspects of social life in a way that is clear and relatively easy to remember and pass on to others without reducing its complexity to trite folk knowledge. For this project a working definition of communication was developed which took account of language as resource (i.e. the individual makes choices in using it), and language as rule-governed and constrained by sociolinguistic factors. The definition of communication is under three broad headings:

1. *Intentions* — taking into account the key factors of frequency, relative importance and complexity

2. *Context factors* — type and method of communication: face-to-face, one-to-one etc.
   — degree of control speaker has
   — people – personality, status
   — roles
   — relationships
   — conventions

TRAINING MATERIAL 4:5 INTERVIEW FRAMEWORK [Clarice Brierley, Sardul Dhesi, Birmingham ILT, and Valerie Yates, NCILT]

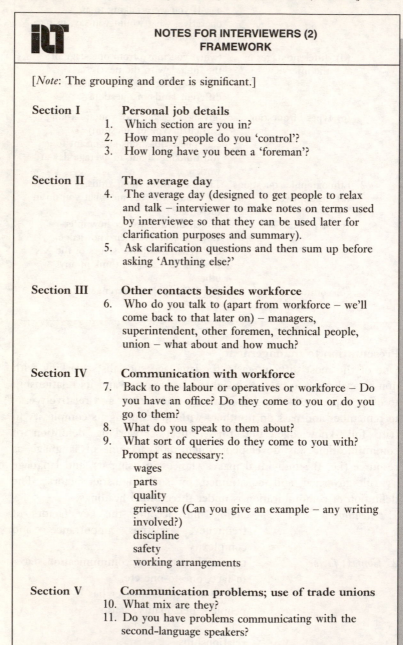

ILT

**NOTES FOR INTERVIEWERS (2)
FRAMEWORK**

[*Note*: The grouping and order is significant.]

Section I   **Personal job details**
1. Which section are you in?
2. How many people do you 'control'?
3. How long have you been a 'foreman'?

Section II   **The average day**
4. The average day (designed to get people to relax and talk – interviewer to make notes on terms used by interviewee so that they can be used later for clarification purposes and summary).
5. Ask clarification questions and then sum up before asking 'Anything else?'

Section III   **Other contacts besides workforce**
6. Who do you talk to (apart from workforce – we'll come back to that later on) – managers, superintendent, other foremen, technical people, union – what about and how much?

Section IV   **Communication with workforce**
7. Back to the labour or operatives or workforce – Do you have an office? Do they come to you or do you go to them?
8. What do you speak to them about?
9. What sort of queries do they come to you with? Prompt as necessary:
     wages
     parts
     quality
     grievance (Can you give an example – any writing involved?)
     discipline
     safety
     working arrangements

Section V   **Communication problems; use of trade unions**
10. What mix are they?
11. Do you have problems communicating with the second-language speakers?

TRAINING MATERIAL 4:5 *continued*

---

12. Do you use interpreters? (Check if TU reps used as interpreters.)
13. How often do you use TU reps to communicate with the workforce?

Section VI   **Paperwork (reading and telephone)**
14. How much paperwork is on the job? (Specify)
15. How does information come to you? (Reading)
16. What about the telephone?

Section VII   **Systems and procedures**
17. How did you learn them?
18. How did you learn to become a foreman?
19. What made you decide to become a foreman?

Section VIII   **Management style/job satisfaction**
If it hasn't emerged already or if they haven't elaborated on it enough:
20. (Refer to notes) You say 'you've got to (e.g.) know how to approach people' – what do you mean?
21. If you were to describe someone you think is a good foreman what would he be like?
22. If a younger bloke wanted to be a foreman what advice would you give him?
23. When you get to the end of a week and look back and say 'that was a good week', what has made you feel that way?
24. What do you dread most when you come in on a Monday morning?

---

3. *Means of expression*   – combination of skills and knowledge from which a person selects the means to communicate;
   – ability to hear and use the sounds of the language and its common intonation patterns
   – adequate passive and active vocabulary;
   – awareness of and ability to use grammatical patterns of the language;
   – awareness of paralinguistic features of language, e.g. loudness of tone, body language, facial expressions and gestures.

Each aspect of communication in this working definition was used to detail findings with regard to both Task 1 (the communication skills needed of a foreman) and to Task 2 (the communication skills needed for the foreman-selection procedures).

Task 2 Communication skills required by promotion procedures

Candidates for the post of foreman were required to produce two pieces of writing – a letter of application and a case-study exercise.

In the *letter of application* the conventions of formal letter-writing (layout and wording) applied. The applicant addressed the recruitment officer, whom he perhaps did not know at all. Even if he did, he was addressing her/him in the role of company representative and the tone therefore had to be distant and formal. The letter of application was to an individual, but to the individual as the company's representative, and whether or not the applicant knew the recruitment officer was irrelevant.

In the *case study* the applicant was required to write as foreman to his own manager, whom he would clearly know well. In terms of conventions the case-study report was a straightforward piece of prose written in the first person and in informal style.

In the *interview* the applicant's relationship with one of the panel members was likely to have been a long-term if perhaps slightly distant one, i.e. the superintendent and/or departmental manager responsible for his area. If selected, the applicant would continue to have long-term and fairly close contact with this person. The other panel members were likely to be more remote and the applicant may never have spoken to them. He may or may not know their jobs and names. If selected, he may still not have much contact with them in the future.

The interview at the company was in the tradition of British job interviewing, where a major decision for the applicant is dependent to a considerable extent on what happens in the space of half an hour. The situation is formal, at least at first. The applicant waits for the panel to start the interview by asking questions. However, apart from the question/response framework the interview structure can be loose and each interview goes in a different direction depending on which topics are selected and explored. The applicant will probably not know where the next question is coming from, nor will he be able to predict what it will be. The onus is on the applicant to indicate that he has the right qualities for the job. The proceedings are characterised by *indirectness*, particularly in the questioning, and by an understanding that panel and applicant alike preserve appearances. Thus 'boasting' is probably acceptable if introduced by the right sort of deprecatory remarks and substantiated by evidence to back it up. Criticism of company practices is acceptable if it stops short of naming names. Both the applicant and the panel 'agree' to ignore unpleasant facts. When the panel asks 'Do you think a foreman's job is easy?', it is unacceptable to say that it is. The applicant needs to know these conventions in order to communicate 'appropriately'.

It is in the area of interview conventions (unless they are made explicit) that the greatest difficulties for ethnic-minority candidates are likely to arise in establishing shared schemata and frames. The shared perceptions which are so necessary for a successful interview often elude ethnic-minority candidates. They do not have access in the same way to the conventions of the traditional interview. It is interesting to note that in the case of the engineering company, South Asian applicants were more likely to discuss the interview beforehand with other South Asians than with someone from the white majority group who had been through a successful interview and might know better what the conventions would be.

In the Indian subcontinent and East Africa the conventions which operate in interviews are very different. First, paper qualifications are very important and are used to back up statements like 'Yes, I can do the job'. Second, recommendations from a third party carry more weight than actual performance in the interview. It is this advocate's responsibility to describe the applicant's qualities and abilities. Finally, the intention of interviewers is to find out general weaknesses of character rather than to create an opportunity for candidates to 'sell themselves' in relation to a particular job. This often results in general questions unrelated to the job. In this convention the candidates' main intentions in answering are to appear compliant and unassertive. It is therefore reasonable to assume that some South Asian speakers from the Indian subcontinent and East Africa might not realise fully what their role in a British interview should be and miss the opportunity being offered to them.

The ILT assessors took each aspect of communication as defined in the working definition on pp. 229 – 231 above and compared the skills needed (i) to be a foreman and (ii) to go through the company selection procedures to become a foreman. Using an analysis of the simulated shop-floor and interview interactions, a summary of findings was made:

1. Intentions
On the shop-floor, communicative intentions which a foreman needed to express in his job were instrumental and related very closely to his work activities. These covered requests for information, giving instructions, social chat, seeking cooperation, detailed explanations, getting things done and achieving a smooth working relationship on the shop-floor. They were characterised by direct, explicit, informal language.

In the selection interview, candidates needed to have a full range of intentions at their disposal, including ones which they would use infrequently on the shopfloor such as giving opinions and hypothesising on imagined or general situations, i.e. describing actions on what might happen. The conventions expected were characterised by abstraction, the need to demonstrate required qualities and the use of formal and indirect language.

2. Context

On the shop-floor, exchanges were mostly short, to the point, and concrete. The atmosphere was informal and familiar. Communication was one-to-one and the person spoken to known and in a long-term relationship with the foreman, with roles and status clearly defined. Control of the interaction and the direction it took often lay with the foreman. The conventions of his own group (mostly local, English, white) were familiar to him and he had learned to adjust to the conventions of other groups on the shop-floor.

The interview, on the other hand, took place in an unfamiliar setting which was more formal and where longer, more abstract exchanges occurred. Communication was one to a panel of four or five, all white, and some of whom may only be known by sight or name. Control of topic and time lay with the panel, although candidates were expected to take the initiative at 'appropriate' moments. The conventions of the interview were probably unfamiliar, although the degree to which panel members were known and belonged to the same cultural group were important factors in helping candidates to pick up and respond to conventions.

3. Means of expression

On the shop-floor, the ability to be direct and explicit was highly valued. Conveying meaning more subtly through tone of voice and stress on words was not so important. Body language, facial expression and gestures used on the shop-floor to convey meaning were just as likely to be interpreted according to their intended meaning as not. Since many people on the shop-floor were second-language speakers the use of simpler grammatical structures and vocabulary might often be an advantage, as long as the meaning, particularly in relation to time and probability, was clear. Pronunciation and accent were important only if they impeded understanding. The literacy skills needed related to the ability to use forms such as requisitions, and to write short 3–4-line reports of past events.

In the interview it was important to be indirect, e.g. when 'criticising' existing foremen, and even more important to understand indirectness in the interview questions. It was necessary to use tone of voice, loudness or softness, pausing and stress on words, and appropriate body language to convey the impression that you were assertive but not aggressive, modest and reflective but confident. Since interpretation of these qualities lay solely with one cultural group (local English panel members) candidates from another group could be at a disadvantage and their intended meaning misinterpreted.

Accuracy of grammatical structures and vocabulary, and cohesion and clarity in line of argument, came under much more scrutiny in the interview. The ability to use structures and vocabulary which were not often used on the shop-floor, e.g. to hypothesise (say 'what you would do if you were...'), were very important. Pronunciation which was different from that of the panel members, and even slightly incorrect use of grammatical structures, could affect the panel's judgement of a candidate. Good will could be needed to make allowances for any differences if these were, in fact, insignificant and did not impede understanding. This also applied to the writing skills which were required as part of the selection procedure. These included the content and layout of a letter of application and the ability to write continuous prose about past or hypothetical events.

The general finding was that the communication skills required for a promotion interview were both different from and more complex than the skills required to do a foreman's job. This meant that applicants who had the communication skills to be foremen might be failed by the promotion procedure. This possibility was confirmed by data from the results of the simulated job interviews and simulated shop-floor talk with foremen. The bilingual speakers all performed better in shop-floor simulations than in interviews, whereas there was no significant difference in the performance of the native English-speakers between the interviews and shop-floor simulations. Similarly, whereas only one (out of six) of the bilingual speakers performed significantly differently from the native English-speakers in the shop-floor simulations, there were differences in self-presentation among all six bilingual speakers in the interview simulations.

Task 3 Comparison of the communication skills of white and Asian candidates

Simulated interviews were conducted for seven white and seven Asian applicants for foreman posts.

First, a content analysis was undertaken of the simulated interviews. No systematic differences between the two sets of speakers were found in this analysis. However, in terms of self-presentation at interviews there were both similarities and differences. The differences were significant enough to be identified as a likely reason for rejecting bilingual applicants.

Then a sample of nine recorded interviews (five native speakers and four bilinguals) were compared with regard to the response to each of the interview panel's set questions.

There were some similarities in the way white-majority and South Asian speakers presented themselves. There were also some differences, and these were significant enough for us to identify them as possible reasons why these South Asian applicants might have been assessed less favourably than other, white-majority applicants.

Similarities

The range of styles of speaking was wide among the applicants, both white-majority and South Asian. For example, some speakers gave long, narrative responses; others gave very brief responses. Some speakers questioned the interviewers about what was meant by a question; others did no questioning. All applicants tended to answer closed questions, i.e. questions which could be answered with a simple 'Yes' or 'No', very briefly.

Differences

There were, however, differences in overall self-presentation and the clarity of line of argument pursued in individual responses. These differences related to the subtle choices of language which have to be made in order to conform to the unwritten conventions of the interview. They were:

– Degree of directness or indirectness;
– Degree of immediate relevance;
– Clarity of line of argument.

In order to be able to evaluate these differences it is important to make the following points. They emerged only in the interviews and were not a factor in the shop-floor simulations. There were evidenced in most, but not all, the South Asian speakers. They were realised through several linguistic features, any single one of which might be significant in the way a candidate is evaluated. It might be the interplay of a number of these features or the cumulative effect of one or more of them which becomes significant in the evaluation process. Evidence of these differences is given below in extracts from the tape-recordings of the simulated interviews.

Degree of directness or indirectness

In the working definition of communication this relates to choice of intentions in the context of interviewing. Since interviews are all about self-presentation, the way in which the applicant presents his views is crucial. There appear to be very subtle distinctions in the recorded interviews between being firm, categorical and direct and being either too indirect and so not 'coming across well' or being over-emphatic, over-critical and possibly boastful. In the native-speaker interviews there is evidence of certain preferences for how direct to be which are likely to be shared by the panel interviewers (see Data 4.8).

Degree of immediate relevance
Relevance is more difficult to gauge in an interview than in a shop-floor conversation. The South Asian speakers might appear less relevant, partly because they do not share the same assumptions about how direct or indirect to be and partly because of non-native ways of speaking. The 'interviewers' in the recordings did check back from time to time with white-majority speakers to see how their comments tied in with the question but they did this more frequently when they were talking to South Asian speakers, the effect of which was to make their interviews more 'probing' than those of the white-majority applicants. An example is the response to the question about the failings of foremen (Data 4.9 p. 240).

Clarity of line of argument
In the interview situation there was both a greater demand placed on the applicants' linguistic ability, and a greater likelihood of some measure of misinterpretation or inability to process the information on the part of the native-speaker interviewers.

In interviews, where there is no practical context, there is less certainty about how direct to be and how long to talk for. All this puts greater demands on communication skills, particularly when referring to people, place and time. Therefore, the speaker is more likely to self-correct, make false starts and reformulate. In addition, many questions are couched in hypothetical terms, requiring answers using complex conditional forms of the verb. Linguistically, this means using modal auxiliaries such as 'would', 'might', 'would have' etc. and connectives such as 'if' and 'since'. In addition, meaning is conveyed as much through intonations as through grammar and words. It plays a crucial role in helping the listener to decide what is important, less important, new or old information and how the speaker ties in what he has just said with what he is going to say and whether he has made a false start and wants to correct or reformulate. In the type of extended responses required under the pressure of an

DATA 4.8 DEGREE OF DIRECTNESS [Clarice Brierley, Sardul Dhesi, Birmingham ILT and Valerie Yates, NCILT]

Question	Expected Convention	Native speaker	Bilingual speaker	Comment
Job satisfaction *What satisfaction will you get from being a foreman?*	Be positive and relate your qualities and skills to the challenge of the job.	Well, I think I'm capable of doing the job and I think I'd get more of a challenge you know …	If I'm if I'm knew that I am capable of doing that job as a foreman I would be quite satisfied if,…er,…the day to day operations went the way how I wanted them to be do it … If I was I wouldn't have applied for a foreman's job, I would have… it would have given me satisfaction that this is how my ability has been put into the (line).	AE appears firm IE appears indirect — the better quality of his answer may be lost because he appears to be unclear about the Panel's intention and has to reformulate.
Qualities for the job *Why do you feel you could do a foreman's job?*	Be direct and back up your claims with examples.	Erm. Number one, I am able to communicate, er, with all levels of people within the company, which is essential to that	Because since I've just started working in the firm, I think I would like to go even further in the management side…	AE appears firm, clear, gives specific examples.

AE = Anglo English

IE = English influenced by North Indian Languages *(Indian English)*

DATA 4.8 DEGREE OF DIRECTNESS *continued*

	position erm also certain forms of experience that I have with the present, with my present function. If I can give you an example, erm, I know the products, I know the materials, erm I know the requirements.		IE = Indirect with no examples.
Evaluation of current situation *What do you think are the common failings of foremen today?*			
Show you could effect change but don't be too critical of the status quo.	Erm. Yeah. Well it is a ... I don't know but I come across it quite a bit, you know, where they do, they lose their temper quite quickly.	Foremen haven't got the slightest ability or knowledge.	AE = Direct, but softens criticism. IE = Direct, but condemnatory and invites probing.

DATA 4.9 DEGREE OF RELEVANCE [Clarice Brierley, Sardul Dhesi, Birmingham ILT and Valarie Yates NCILT]

Transcript	Commentary
IE: Sometimes the foremans whether it is ( ), we should never underestimate some of the workers. If there is a suggestion .. if a worker is giving .. they should always try to concentrate on it and think about it. Probe: And you think some of them don't? IE: Yes, Sometimes it is a good suggestion .. Even it happens with the X Department. Now yesterday they just brought me a job, you know. And they said to me .. that I just had a complaint from the management side that it was heavy on ( ) but they said to me .. now when I just came round on the floor and find it out, what had gone wrong with that we found that the job has gone all right every way and still there was heavy on the( ). So we just found it out that only about .. through the extruder when it's going through .. only about ten or fifteen foot has gone through which was heavy on ( ) and that caused the problem you know. And they sent whole lot back, you know.	Here the applicant gives a very sound response – that foremen should listen more to the good suggestions that workers make. His response is gradual and indirect and the Panel push for an example. The candidate gives a good example about quality but does not tie it to the question explicitly through words or implicitly through intonation.

interview, it is more likely that there will be examples of non-native-speaker intonation. In some cases, this raises expectations in the listener which are not then realised, giving rise to the judgement that the speaker is somehow less coherent.

Take the following example from a South Asian speaker, in response to the question 'Is the job of the foreman easy?'

> Er, job of a foreman is not easy. But my experience on handling the people is THAT much I don't find, or I not find that job hard or difficult.

The speaker uses slightly unusual wording. A native English-speaker is likely to say either 'But my experience of handling people is so extensive that I don't find the job difficult' or 'I have so much experience of handling people that ...' From the South Asian speaker's words, the white-majority speaker would expect him to continue like this: 'My experience of handling people is that much of the time ...', where 'that' is a relating adverb. But the South Asian speaker uses 'that' as an emphatic adverb to modify 'much', used here as an adjective.

The expectations of the white-majority speaker are not met as he processes the stream of talk he hears. He may decide he cannot follow the South Asian speaker and judge his response to be unclear or not to the point. By contrast, although some white-majority applicants could be said to 'ramble on', their use of intonation makes it easy for the listener to process the information: Data 4.10 (see page 242) is an example of a South Asian speaker (A) responding to a question about job satisfaction. In this example, it is not quite clear whether A is reformulating after his first utterance, 'if I'm knew that I am capable of doing that job as a foreman', when he says 'I would be quite satisfied'. This utterance might refer to his opening words or to the words that immediately follow – 'if the day to day operations went the way how I wanted them to be do it'. Again, searching for the main topic is more difficult.

An even more subtle point is that he uses the past conditional 'if I'm knew' and follows it with the present tense 'I am capable', followed by a past-tense modal 'would' – 'I would be quite satisfied'. Since it is not clear whether 'I would be quite satisfied' is a main or subordinate clause, it could be taken as a main clause. In this case A is using what is called a hypothetical condition, which usually conveys the expectation that the condition will not be fulfilled. In other words, his opening words could be construed as suggesting that he is doubtful whether he has the capabilities for being a foreman. Clearly, he does not mean this, as he then says, quite explicitly, that he would not have applied if he did not think he could do the job.

The contrast with his recorded shop–floor simulation is interesting. In the transcript of a shop–floor interaction (Data 4.11 p. 243) he is 'A'. The interviewer is one of the assessors.

It was clear from this assessment for the CRE that the promotion interview failed to relate closely to the job of foreman in terms of the

DATA 4.10 LINE OF ARGUMENT [Clarice Brierley, Sardul Dhesi, Birmingham ILT and Valarie Yates NCILT]

Transcript	Re-write
A: If I'm if I'm knew that I am capable of doing that job as a foreman I would be quite satisfied if ....er... the day to day operations went the way how I wanted them to be do it... If I was I wouldn't have applied for a foreman's job I would have...it would have given me satisfaction that this is how my ability has been put into the (line).	[I would be satisfied] ... if I felt capable and if the day to day operations went the way I wanted them to go. I wouldn't have applied for the foreman job if I didn't have the ability to do it or think I could do it. It would give me satisfaction to put my ability in this way into the production line.

communicative abilities necessary. This might be expected. However, more importantly, it was also clear that Asian applicants who could communicate clearly and with considerable subtlety in simulated shop-floor talk were put at a disadvantage by the linguistic demands and unwritten conventions and criteria of the job and promotion interview.

The assessors reported that the inevitable outcome from these findings, unless procedures were changed, was that successful applicants for foreman jobs would be those who knew the white interview game and could communicate with managers. The people most likely to continue to be selected were those from the same linguistic cultural community as the white management who comprised selection panels. The people least likely to be selected were those from the same linguistic cultural community as a large proportion of the shop-floor workers. The enormous bonus of sharing the same first language and perspective as these workers (as well as being able to communicate and work well with management) was never considered as part of the promotion criteria, although it would have been within the spirit and letter of the Race Relations Act to do so.

Language training alone in this context would address symptoms, not the cause, of discrimination and could only serve to reinforce the existing and erroneous deficit view of some of the bilinguals' potential and abilities as communicators and managers. There were, however, clear indicators of the kind of promotion-related language training which could support the introduction of equal-opportunities policies

DATA 4.11 SHOP-FLOOR TALK TRANSCRIPT [Clarice Brierley, Sardul Dhesi, Birmingham ILT]

Int: What about your section Mr A. How are things going there, on the production side?

A: There is a slight problem. Actually, you see, I'm on the Maintenance.

Int: OK. Fine.

A: So there is a problem on one particular section on the 1.ET's, the problem being that the valve which we sent it for repair a couple of weeks ago... They haven't kept the promise to deliver it on time. Without that valve we can't =

Int: = And they haven't delivered it yet?

A: The reason they haven't delivered it is there is a price .. repair of the prices they quoted suddenly have gone up by £60.

Int: Really?

A: And nobody has yet agreed on   (   ).

Int: Well can you... Can you write a little report about that?

A: *Yeah.*

Int: To get the facts down. Then I can chase it up. OK? Um, all right, any absenteeism in the section?

A: We have got a couple of blokes. They haven't turned up yet but they're supposed to turn up later on.

Int: I see. OK. so we'll hope that they're going to turn up. Well in general about this problem of absenteeism. Well, what do you think we ought to do about it? Have you any ideas?

Int: ...I don't know. It's the same ones every week really ... seem to be off a lot. What do you think?

A: Well, as regards when they're sick I personally think we ought to have them examined by our works doctor.

Int: Yeah. Do you think the union would put up with that?

A: Well that's something you know, that I'd like you to think about.

Int: Yeah, I could have a word with the union about it... Seems a bit drastic doesn't it, really?

A: But there again, you know if a person complaints that I've got a bad back and all that, we can't do anything. We've just got to take their word. All the time ( ) We're a man down and that crew is (..) a problem.

DATA 4.11 SHOP-FLOOR TALK *continued*

Int: Well I certainly think it's worth trying. I think that's the right idea. Um, all right. Well, let's leave it at that for the time being shall we?

DATA 4.11 COMMENTARY

Intentions
Firm and detailed when reporting problems.

Uses polite suggestions to make his case about absenteeism.

Means of expression
Topic clearly introduced and the reason for the delay clearly explained. Accurately uses tense aspect and mood, plus modals and subordinating conjunctions.

Outcome
Suggestion accepted.

and procedures at the company. The 'failed' foreman applicants learned a lot from the simulations and the debriefing with the assessors. The assessors reinforced their view of the importance of an approach to language teaching which is related to skills and job progression, and of the impact of simulated role-play as part of the methodology used. These issues are discussed further in the next chapter.

Further reading

The surveys of racial discrimination in employment have already been referred to in the Further Reading section of Chapter 1. The perceptions and experiences of black people in employment are well described in Wallman's anthology *Ethnicity at Work* (1979), in the work of social anthropologists such as Saifullah Khan in *Minority Families in Britain* (1979) and in the collection edited by Westwood and Bhachu, *Enterprising Women* (1988).

Hammersley and Atkinson's *Ethnography: Principles in Practice* (1983) is a good introduction to ethnographic research. A more informal introduction to ethnography is Agar's *Speaking of Ethnography* (1985). Whyte's *Street Corner Society* (1981) is a classic introduction to participant observation. Three books that describe ethnographic research methods are: Burgess, R (ed) 1984 *Field Research: A Sourcebook & Field Manual*, Ellen, R (ed) 1984 *Ethnographic Research* and Whyte, W. *Learning from the Field* 1984.

Two useful books on ethnographic interviewing are Agar's *The Professional Stranger* (1980) and Spradley's *The Ethnographic Interview* (1979), and a recent book by Brigg, *Learning How to Ask* (1987), discusses interviewing from a sociolinguistic perspective.

The reading which informed the linguistic analysis in the second part of the chapter has been referenced at the end of Chapter 2.

5 Language teaching and learning

1 Introduction

This chapter describes in more detail the third aspect of ILT work: language teaching and learning. We have already described the other two major aspects of ILT: the work in cross-cultural training (Chapter 3) and the surveys and analysis of workplace communications and perceptions (Chapter 4). In Chapter 1, we briefly outlined the general framework for language education which has emerged from our work. We would emphasise that our approach to language teaching was continuously modified and redesigned as a result of the ethnographic work and other forms of data collection and linguistic analysis which we have already described. For many years, direct language teaching was the largest volume of work carried out within the ILT scheme. It was necessarily immensely varied in type and methodology. It ranged from very elementary language teaching for students without any literacy skills in their own languages to very advanced work with mixed groups of first-and second-language speakers. The variety and scale of language training would in itself be difficult to generalise about, but, in addition, our language-teaching work was inevitably rooted in the wider pedagogies of English-language teaching and was influenced by the radical rethinking about language and communication-skills teaching generally which was taking place during this period. This chapter, therefore, starts with a section outlining in general terms the wider context which influenced the development of our language pedagogy. The bulk of the chapter then provides a description and analysis of four examples of language training. These four examples represent some of the more significant and specific characteristics of ILT language teaching, particularly in terms of the underlying analysis of language and interaction which informed curriculum design, the roles given to students' own language and experience and the endeavours to relate language teaching to the wider aspirations of students and to their socio-economic needs.

The four types of language-teaching programme reveal an evolution from an analytic focus on language at the post-elementary level in the first project to a more ethnographic and experiential focus on learner autonomy at a more elementary language level in the second. The third project, which was for unemployed workers, demonstrates some movement back again to an analytic focus, but includes cross-cultural learning of vocational skills, and retains the experiential/ethnographic focus in relation to individual learners. Finally, the fourth set of programmes illustrates how earlier language-training projects were combined with our experiences from cross-cultural training to provide courses in inter-ethnic communication for bilingual speakers. These four projects reflect an evolution of thinking and practice in language teaching over the period, and an attempt to link this firmly with social objectives with regard to ethnic-minority workers. This chapter, therefore, represents facets of the continual critique of our initial language-teaching solutions to which we refer in Chapter 1.

Our initial ILT language courses were aimed at an elementary level of English learner and provided workers with basic communication tools in English, particularly in relation to their immediate jobs, social contact, and solving personal problems (Jupp and Hodlin 1974; Laird 1975). The emphasis was upon studying the workplace in order to equip workers with the language to establish communicative relationships with English-speaking workers and to operate more effectively within the workplace. The participant observation and data collection required for these courses resulted in the collection of material such as Data 2.1 and 2.2 in Chapter 2 and the analysis of workplaces described in the first part of Chapter 4. This data, while highlighting the communicative resources and difficulties of some workers, also highlighted the oppression experienced by such workers from white fellow-workers, supervisors and shop stewards. This oppression was often exercised through stereotyping the language, communication and culture not only of ethnic-minority workers who lacked English, but also of those with relative fluency in English. Examples of the type of gross stereotyping routinely made by white people have been given in Chapter 4. We give another example below. The interaction was recorded in a textile mill. The supervisor's pervading stereotype of Asian workers allowed him to ignore the reality of the actual interaction. An Asian applicant had been speaking English fluently throughout a job interview when the supervisor, needing to complete a routine question on a form about knowledge of English, asked him:

Supervisor:	Can you speak English?
Applicant:	No (ironically)
Supervisor:	(addressing observer) Oh, you see, he can't speak English.
Applicant:	If I can't speak English, what am I speaking to you now?

(Etherton 1975)

Such experiences raised ideological, professional and practical issues which the four language-teaching projects described in this chapter represent attempts to resolve. The projects were informed by several years' study of multi-racial industrial workplaces and by the conscious exploitation of ideas and research which we considered relevant to developing curriculum and pedagogy.

The first project for post-elementary learners sought not to create but to change communicative relationships. As such, it was complemented by the further development of cross-cultural communication training as described in Chapter 3. The objective was to breach the established pattern of attitude and behaviour in interaction in a particular workplace (Wilson 1981). The approach was rooted in analysis based on social and interactional models of language and in behavioural objectives. It was argued that, in the end, it is behaviour and not attitude which matters and that change in behaviour will modify attitude, rather than vice versa. The focus, therefore, was on language as a social activity and on helping to create a positive social identity for the workers in relation to white management and workers. Such projects often improved the communication skills of participants; but as an overall language-learning model, this approach can encourage a deficit approach to the existing bilingual language skills of ethnic-minority learners, can encourage teachers to overlook learners' much wider opportunities to learn and use English outside the workplace, and can result in teachers insufficiently recognising both the cognitive dimension and the individual and group psycho-social dimensions of second-language acquisition.

The second project sought to counterbalance these tendencies by increasing learner autonomy. It also aimed to encourage the growth of a pedagogy which was better informed by the students' own perceptions of needs, built directly on their existing knowledge and skills, particularly with regard to language, and empowered them to take control of their own learning.

The third project moved away from a primary emphasis on language and communication. Building on experience gained from the two earlier projects and from the work on cross-cultural training, the project addressed wider issues of learning for education, training and employment, including the acquisition of technical knowledge and skills. These had not previously ever been in the forefront of ILT work. At the same time, the project recognised that success in technical fields was dependent on social interaction and power relationships with fellow students and technical instructors.

The fourth project was designed for bilingual speakers, already fluent in English. A range of diverse programmes was aimed at people whose work and responsibilities involved them in frequent, varied and often stressful communications, both oral and written. They were in white-collar jobs in the Civil Service and in public services such as health and transport, or had responsibilities, as supervisors or trade-union shop stewards, which required a high level of communication skills. This project drew on *Crosstalk* and cross-cultural training programmes and student ethnography.

There is an interesting parallel in these projects with development which were taking place over the same period (1975 to 1985) in general communicative language teaching.

2 Developments in language pedagogy

The concerns with equal opportunity, discrimination and racism explored in this book are firmly rooted in the systematic observations in workplaces and public services described in Chapter 4, and these, in turn, are confirmed by many other independent studies published over the last twenty years (Smith 1981; Brown 1984). Our endeavour to analyse and understand cross-cultural communication in these settings was informed by this observation and by the ideas and research of linguists and ethnographers outlined in Chapter 2. Language teaching and curriculum design were less consciously related to observation or theory. Teaching and learning methodology, rather like language itself, can be an invisible process because it is taken for granted by teachers to a point where it becomes largely unconscious, but at the same time incorporates particular values, experience and assumptions.

The pedagogy teachers use is grounded in the educational experience, training and professional experience of the teachers themselves. Early ILT staff were largely drawn from a background of teaching English, usually overseas, and with a specialist postgraduate teaching qualification or further study in applied linguistics. The scope of the professional background of staff was, however, to broaden fairly rapidly to include people with experience in industrial training, management training and adult basic education. More emphasis came to be put on experience and broader skills when recruiting staff, and on the experience and skills brought by staff who were themselves from ethnic-minority and bilingual backgrounds. From the beginning of the establishment of a national ILT scheme, there was a substantial in-service training programme and plenty of opportunity for staff to participate (see Laird 1977; Hoadley-Maidment 1981). However, pedagogy changes very slowly, and the development of learning and teaching methodology lagged behind ideas and analysis throughout the period of the materials presented in this chapter.

A consideration of how our view of language-teaching developed has to be placed in the wider context of foreign- and second-language teaching in general. Since the mid-1950s there has been a great upsurge in foreign-language teaching, reflecting a growing utilitarian demand for foreign languages as a tool of communication in work, leisure and education. As a result, the traditional academic approach to the study of foreign languages has been recognised as inappropriate. For example, in European schools there has been a demand for foreign-language learning for every pupil regardless of academic level; many university courses throughout the world require a knowledge of a second language; and an increasing number of jobs require a working knowledge of an international language. This book arises from the fact that millions of workers have settled in industrial countries with little or no knowledge of the local language, thus creating another area of language-learning demand with regard to people who would not previously or in other circumstances ever have been in a language-learning classroom.

No language has benefited more from all this upsurge of demand than English. The great expansion in English-language teaching has come about as a result of the needs of people with a broader spectrum of reasons for learning the language, ones which, particularly for adults, are central to their motivation and their response to the learning situation.

This upsurge was accompanied by the introduction of new methods and materials in the classroom, particularly during the 1960s. These changes were often radical and could be called a language-teaching revolution. But this revolution took little account of the varied contexts or motivation of the learners; it was about *how* people in general learn and *what* aspects of the language they need to learn. Most of the early innovation in the 1960s was based on Skinnerian learning theory (Skinner 1957) and descriptions and theories of language from structural linguistics. Consideration of *why* people learn a second language or evaluation of the results of teaching was more or less missing except in the type of situation which would be popularly referred to as bilingual – for example, Lambert's work on learners' attitudes and motivation (1972). Another feature of these changes has been the strong emphasis upon the differences between English as a Foreign Language, English as a Second Language, and bilingual education. For teaching purposes, these differences were categorised as situations which had little to learn from each other, and as a result there was little consideration of these concepts in terms of individual learners and their situations.

In the early 1970s, ILT contributed to and drew from the debate on language-teaching methodology surrounding the communicative language-teaching movement. Communicative language teaching has been concerned with an analysis and understanding of the role of language in communication and initially drew on early discourse-analysis and speech-act theory – for example, aspects of the work of Searle, Austin, and Sinclair and Coulthard described in Chapter 2. However, there was also from the beginning a strong methodological commitment to learning through communication, to respect for the autonomy of learners and to more control and choice for the learner. ILT originally developed in collaboration with the Pathway Centre (Davies and Hadi 1973) and Ealing College (Abbs 1975). Other important points of contact and exchange of ideas were with the University of Lancaster (Candlin, Leather and Bruton 1974), and with the developments in English for Special Purposes (Widdowson 1978). There was a lot of shared interest in analysis of context and of communication within it. The Council of Europe Modern Languages Project (Trim 1978; Van Ek 1975) provided practitioners with a sense of confidence and support for the view that language teaching was moving in a communicative direction. The stream of papers from the Council of Europe project in the mid 1970s was read with great interest in the context of training for ILT staff. However, while this work on communicative language teaching stimulated ideas and creativity on methodology and materials, the Council of Europe project appeared at that time to have two major limitations: a lack of analysis of language above the level of the sentence and a lack of recognition of the complexity and unpredictability of context and meaning, particularly in inter-ethnic communication; the culture was middle-class European and the context largely tourism or business. Later, the project was to address language acquisition by linguistic minorities and migrant workers (Jupp 1982), and the project's work on needs analysis and on student autonomy was a major source of ideas for the second project on student autonomy described in this chapter.

The communicative language-teaching movement radically changed foreign-language teaching in the 1970s and 1980s in three major ways:

1. by extending teachers' understanding of how language works interactionally and what is involved in becoming a successful communicator in another language;
2. by focusing on the autonomy and skills of the learner and consequently how power relationships can be changed in the classroom;
3. by linking language learning much more strongly to broader educational issues of content, cognitive development and learning skills.

In addition, in the socio-political context of a multi-ethnic society, it helped practitioners to see a way of empowering socially and linguistically disadvantaged language learners both within and through the language classroom. Communicative language teaching has been trivialised by some critics as no more than a pedagogic fashion. Such critics have suggested that communicative language teaching denied any place for grammar. This has never been the case, but because communicative language teaching questioned the centrality of structural linguistics to language teaching, its critics have often dismissed it as not being scientific (Swan 1985). Over the period which this book covers, communicative language teaching has met this challenge by developing and broadening its scope substantially. Pedagogic thinking first focused on an analytic approach in terms of behavioural objectives and skills, and later in terms of cognition and awareness. Subsequently, it also focused on an experiential or holistic approach which stressed the subjectivity of perception and learning and the value of process rather than product in developing skilled and self-programming learners. This third element can, although it seldom does in practice, accommodate the notion of a non-ethnocentric pedagogy. These two centres of focus – the **analytic** and the **experiential** – are sometimes presented as a polarity; they are more usefully seen as a continuum or as a mutually-informing circle. The language-learning work outlined in this chapter in a number of respects has followed a similar pattern of evolution and expansion to the communicative language-teaching movement generally. The following framework summarises the two major approaches which coexist in communicative language teaching and provides a point of reference for readers against which to analyse and evaluate the four descriptions of curriculum development which follow in this chapter.

The analytic focus	*The experiential / ethnographic focus*
The analysis of authentic texts and the definition of objectives on this basis.	Learner-centred, recognising that each person already has cultural identity and communicative competence.
An emphasis on performance 'skills' loosely defined, anything	An emphasis not on analysis and particular skills, but on experi-

from micro-skills (e.g.'scanning') to macro-skills (e.g. 'understanding a book').

encing and learning from the integrated and authentic whole. From this, the development of learner strategies for communication using a problem-solving approach.

A defined view of knowledge and of meaning.

A view of knowledge and of meaning relative to perception and interpretation.

An emphasis on evaluating performance.

An emphasis on the value of process.

A deficit view of the learner, i.e. lacks skills and knowledge.

A view of the learner as competent, i.e. needs to learn how to apply existing skills and knowledge

This provides a framework for analysing and evaluating examples of language-learning curriculum. For example, the following set of questions was developed for analysing and evaluating language-teaching courses for unemployed adults. Does the curriculum:

(i)   give learners enough opportunity to guess and take risks as they learn, to make mistakes and to learn from them?

(ii) give learners enough opportunities to get their message across in any way that they can?

(iii) give learners the opportunity to use a lot of language, both in the classroom and outside; and, through the *use* of language, learn the patterns and relationships in the *forms* of language?

(iv) give learners the encouragement to practise and to negotiate opportunities for themselves to practise?

(v)   give learners help and support in monitoring their own use of language and in making public and validating individuals' experience?

(vi) direct learners explicitly towards all the variables of purpose, setting, role etc. which help to create and determine meaning?

(vii) enable tutors to listen to their learners?

(viii) make clear to learners the short-term objective of an activity or exercise and how it relates to their long-term learning goals?

3 Project One: language and communication skills for post-elementary learners

3.1 *The context*

This project was concerned with short courses (about sixty hours) of training in paid work-release time and based on the 'needs' of the workplace. They aimed specifically to develop language and interactional skills in non-routine situations.

The project was planned and organised nationally through a coordinator of a network of teachers who attended periodic workshops, and through the publication of working papers and materials, including audio-visual materials. From the outset, the project aimed to build the curriculum on an analysis of context and of authentic data of the types described in Chapter 4, to relate consciously the development of practice to relevant and useful theoretical work of the types described in Chapter 2, to complement cross-cultural training and to pool the teaching experience of the teachers involved, so that the ideas, experience and materials from a large number of post-elementary courses could be drawn upon and collated centrally.

The project encompassed a large number of experienced shop-floor workers who had usually worked for a considerable time in the UK. They had few prospects in their work except the opportunity for relatively high earnings while overtime and shift work was available, and had a growing sense of alienation caused by their lack of control over their working lives, particularly in terms of supervisory, trade-union and management systems. There was often resistance from such students to criticism of their English (they were already using a range of linguistic skills and communicative strategies in English) and to suggestions that they needed to modify their approach to communication if they wanted to achieve their aims (they had already built up a set of experiences and perceptions of behaviour at work with English people). On the one hand, this was a real opportunity to pursue in depth the development of language and communication skills as a social activity and to discard narrow ideas about the study of linguistic systems which would be inappropriate for students at this level. On the other hand, there were several constraints in terms of expectations and outcomes. If employers were to count this work as training, they wanted in-company courses to address their agendas, particularly as supervisory and management staff were expected to contribute actively to meeting these objectives. Management thinking in such cases seemed to be either very clear and instrumental ('We want X to communicate about Y with Z') or very vague. In some cases, companies were willing to establish language training because they felt a sense of being 'cut off' and there was a deteriorating situation of industrial strife and racial polarisation and tension. Management may have seen language training as 'something to do' which was relatively neutral without analysing the existence or non-existence of causation between communication difficulties and their perceived managerial difficulties (which in turn they had not analysed).

Post-elementary courses very clearly posed the question of how far it was fair to the learners and misleading to others (including management) to expect an overall improvement in the situation when the only action being taken was language training.

The need for wider action was reflected in the often vague objectives of the company and the uncertainty or even hostility of some learners and sometimes of other South Asians in the factory. Significantly, these doubts and difficulties did not arise to such an extent when the course was for more senior people (e.g. supervisors) or when it was clearly tied to a particular objective (e.g. opportunity for promotion). The pressure of these doubts and difficulties led to the development of cross-cultural training at the same time as this project.

3.2 Data collection and needs analysis

This followed the pattern outlined in Chapter 4. Three main types of data were collected for, and as part of, the project:

(i) observation and ethnography;
(ii) audio tape-recordings;
(iii) data provided by students themselves.

(i) General observation and understanding of a range of workplaces

The aim was to understand how the workplace was organised, the communication networks and the variety and types of context, situation and issue for which mutually shared communication was really important. Two distinct groups of context and issue were analysed and characterised as follows:

Type A   *Issues on which there is a built-in clash of interest and a lack of shared perception of the problem by workers and management*
For example: Holidays and extended leave
The operation of bonus schemes
A discipline situation
The mode of trade-union organisation
These are contexts in which there are significant economic and cultural clashes. In each, there is a lack of shared concepts and interests. There is, therefore, an underlying problem which workers may not perceive; and, given lack

of shared communication, there is no way of making the underlying problem clear.

TYPE B   *Issues on which both sides fail to communicate, not because of a real clash of interest, but because of misinterpretation of one another's conversational strategies*
For example   A payslip query
Asking for the day off
Arriving at work late
Being unable to come to work because of sickness
These are contexts in which everyone agrees the common rights. It is therefore, in the interests of both parties to agree amicably.

Evidence from the project confirmed that these were key contexts in the following ways:

– When these subjects were raised they all evoked a ready response from both sides.
– These were the subjects which were most frequently raised with the trainers by managers although usually perceived as matters of attitude and behaviour (for example, being aggressive, withdrawn, unreasonable) rather than differences and difficulties in communication.
– In the training courses these were the subjects which provided interest, motivation and involvement for students and which lent themselves to meaningful role-plays and other communicative activities.

The two different types of context could be used to focus upon different types of skills for language-teaching purposes.

In type A context, where there are real clashes of interest and no shared perception, skills of argumentation are essential, i.e. careful presentation of facts and their relationships and implications, and avoidance of ambiguity. These skills are particularly dependent upon handling the linguistic forms which provide reference, such as time markers and logical connectives.

In type B contexts, on the other hand, skills of persuasion may be sufficient because there is no real clash of interest but just the need to show sensitivity, i.e. recognising the other person's point of view, responding, reassuring.

(ii) Audio tape recordings
The second type of data collected by the project was audio tape of people talking, often in the types of 'key' situation described above.

DATA 5.1:   A DAY OFF – TRANSCRIPT [Celia Roberts NCILT]

Op: Hallo, Fred. Can I see you for a minute?

Sup: Oh, well, not at the moment Tom, I'm very busy.

Op: It won't take long.

Sup: It won't take long I know but I'm very busy. I'm really tied up now.

Op: Could I see you this afternoon then?

Sup: Er ... say five o'clock then.

Op: Er ... little bit earlier ... four?

Sup: No, I'm afraid not Tom, five o'clock's got to be the time, I'm very busy, I'm =

Op: = five o'clock, all right, thank you.

Sup: OK

        [*five o'clock*] <sound of knocking>

Sup: Come in ... Come in.

Op: Hallo Fred. It's five o'clock, you said you'd see me at five.

Sup: Yes. What was it you wanted Tom?

Op: I'd like the day off tomorrow if it's possible, please

Sup: Tomorrow?

Op: Yes please.

Sup: What did you want the day off for?

Op: I've got to collect the pass my passport tomorrow. I've got this letter ...

Sup: You you've got to collect your passport tomorrow?

Op: Yes. I got this letter on Saturday telling me to ... collect the passport tomorrow.

Sup: Yeah, but ... you see ... you know my cleaning day's tomorrow don't you? I'm going to be short of men.

Op: I appreciate that and I'm ... I'm sorry but =

Sup: = Yeah, but let's have a look at this letter. Right, see, you could go on Thursday why don't you go on Thursday? I've got nothing on on Thursday, you could ... I could ... I could let you go on Thursday.

DATA 5.1   A DAY OFF – TRANSCRIPT   *continued*

Op: I'm sorry but it states here to go, states on that letter to go, tomorrow.

Sup: Yeah, but it's very difficult for tomorrow isn't it? You know I've got my cleaning day, Tom

Op: Yes, I appreciate that and I'm sorry.

Sup: Yeah, but what am I going to do if everybody wants to go on to tomorrow you know. I ... you ... I'm one man short already ... I'm about five men short already previously you know and one make six. I've only got two men left.

Op: (   ) Difficult and I appreciate the the problem you've got.

Sup: You've got to go tomorrow. Well, this says you must go tomorrow. Well, it looks as if I'm going to have to let you go doesn't it?

Op: I'm =

Sup: = I'm not very happy about it I might tell you.

Op: I'm sorry.

Sup: Well, OK Tom, you go.

Op: Thanks very much.

Sup: Please don't pull this one again on me, let me know beforehand.

Op: I couldn't let you know sooner, I'm sorry.

Sup: All right then, Tom.

Op: Thank you.

Sup: OK

Some of this talk was between two white English workers and some between white English workers and black bilingual workers. An extension of this type of data was to ask people to role-play typical encounters of this type for which we wanted good-quality recordings which could be used (often with a slide sequence) for presentational purposes in the classroom. Data 5.1 is a typical example of role-play data of this type between a white supervisor and a white operative, relating to a type B transaction to do with solving a personal problem. In this example, two supervisors agreed to role-play typical transactions, one of them taking the role of a worker and the other being himself. The worker wants the following day off to collect his new passport.

DATA 5.2 CLUTCH TROUBLE – TRANSCRIPT
[David Bonamy, Pathway]

104 was broke down first. Clutch trouble. We take it out, clutch and everything, right? And we didn't get clutch, was waiting. 107 broke down, bring it back here, for a gearbox. Now we take it out gearbox. Now what they say, take it out this one, 107 gearbox, put it in 104 because this gearbox no good. Take it out 104 gearbox, put it in this one, and let this vehicle going. Wait for this one new. To come out other gearbox from this engine. Now why we going to lose these all jobs, for say about 30 hours job altogether, when we spent on that one 60 hours?

(iii) Data provided by students themselves

The third type of data was provided by the students themselves in the form of discussion, narratives and role-plays of these types of key situation. This data reflected the need both to work with and build up the students' existing communication skills and strategies in English and to avoid imposing a white-English norm for 'successful' communication in such contexts. The example in Data 5.2 arises from a discussion – on a language-training course – of the bonus scheme for maintenance engineers in a local-authority garage. A maintenance engineer is describing an incident when two vehicles (referred to by number) broke down. He describes to his supervisor, who is visiting the class, the incident and the fact that he lost money under the existing bonus scheme. The data relates to a type-A situation.

This is the kind of data that can be used for two purposes: first, for cross-cultural training, to indicate the way in which different linguistic features and discourse styles can miscue native speakers of English; second, for language training. This is illustrated in section 3.3 below.

Discussion between teachers and students during courses elicited views of communication which were much more perceptive than those of management (Data 5.3).

Collecting, listening to and analysing the kind of data illustrated in Chapters 2 and 4 made an enormous impact on the normative traditions of the teachers involved which this project did much to break down. Language teachers were coming from a tradition of linguistically-defined tasks, of the teacher and the textbook as the

DATA 5.3 LEARNER PERCEPTIONS–TRANSCRIPT
[Moira Winsor, Brent ILT]

Do you think you have difficulty in Britain?

Student A: There is a fair amount of change that is having to take place. I think we are making an effort but it's a question of both sides – how much one is willing to understand each other.

In this company?
This company is rather a big elephant, the tail end may be nice, the trunk may not be nice.

Management does not understand some of the things which we mean – you can tell something, it means no harm, but the way you say it, it's completely different from someone from a different culture. It's the way you put the phrases down ...

An example?
I was talking to one of our storemen ... OK we take mickeys out of each other sometimes – I said to him 'Why don't you use your thick head?' That was just a joke but he took it very seriously. I didn't mean any harm to him. I can understand when they are joking but they don't understand me.'

Student B: It's the way of talking. My wife always tells me I'm rude, the way I talk sounds to her, I don't mean I want to be rude but the way I've been talking since childhood... it's all there unconscious, sometimes it sounds that way. [Student B had an English wife.]

main sources of access to the language, and of the teacher as defining the language and tasks on which students would perform and be tested.

The availability of authentic inter-ethnic material and the emphasis on communicative tasks which related to students' immediate and perceived needs revolutionised teachers' views of what and how they were teaching in three significant ways:

(i) They appreciated the complexity of communication beyond its linguistic encoding.

(ii) They recognised the existing language and communicative resources of students as something which had to be understood and built upon rather than regarded as 'incorrect'.

(iii) They recognised what a normative view they took of their objectives – linguistically normative (e.g. 'He needs to get his tenses right') and behaviourally normative (e.g. 'You can't hope to communicate if you do not behave properly'). As a result they began to recognise that such normative attitudes, transposed into a multi-ethnic classroom, can quickly become racist in their impact.

Although there was much contact and discussion between teachers and students during courses, it is notable that there was no structured pattern of data collection and analysis of students' own perception of communication and of their own needs and aspirations. This was something that the later student-autonomy project described in section 4 below deliberately set out to correct.

At the outset, it was evident that access to such rich contexts and data demanded new analytic tools. ILT elementary courses operated within a broad sociolinguistic framework of analysis, which exploited three main sources: Hymes' notion of the ethnography of speaking, with particular emphasis upon role, locale and context; pragmatics, particularly in terms of speech-act theory; and the work of Sinclair and Coulthard on classroom discourse (see Chapter 2). However, none of these sources contributed significantly to the issues of inter-ethnic communication and its paradoxes, which increasingly dominated project teachers' perceptions. Although linguistic accuracy and appropriacy were clearly important, they did not enable people to 'work out what was going on' in a conversation; speakers, both white and bilingual, however much inter-ethnic contact they had, often appeared to remain locked into their own styles of speaking and to misunderstand each other systematically, particularly in terms of attitude and intention, or to pick up and emphasise just the *wrong* piece of information. Teachers' attention was being directed increasingly to misunderstandings. There was a danger here that, while misunderstandings may be most susceptible to analysis and hypothesis – understanding is inevitably more invisible – they direct attention away from positive achievement towards a negative evaluation.

Earlier ILT work had recognised that both social knowledge and linguistic code were essential to communication, but had found difficulty in relating the two directly and, particularly, in understanding and valuing the consistent but non-standard linguistic code and communication strategies of South Asian speakers. The work of Halliday and Gumperz (see sections 3.3 and 3.6 in Chapter 2) suggested ideas which were both a stimulus and a support in structuring the project's ethnographic observations and analysing its data: both share a view of meaning that is linguistically and culturally relative. Early work in pragmatics, speech-act theory and discourse analysis, while recognising a gap between intention and understanding (illocutionary and perlocutionary force), neither assumed nor explored the impact of this on lack of shared meaning, and, while recognising that meaning depended on context, appeared to assume there was a 'correct' meaning of the text. Thus the popular idea of 'language functions', while a useful complement to structural analysis in the early communicative language movement, was unlocated in either cultural or linguistic systems, let alone in the relationship between the two. In other words, functions were an abstraction from real communication, were derived from middle-class and normative systems and took no account of an interactive and cooperative view of discourse which depends upon shared or at least understood cultural and social knowledge.

Gumperz's concept of contextualisation cues (see Chapter 2, section 3.6) provided a tool for understanding how people's cultural agendas and linguistic interpretation and use are linked and the crucial role of prosodic systems, particularly with reference to South Asian languages and English. He showed how a first-language system of prosody can be used with a second-language system of syntax and lexis, and how in this and other ways non-standard language varieties are not errors, but cohesive and coherent systems to which particular sorts of awareness and response strategies should be brought. In addition, Gumperz was able to confirm our powerful intuition/observation that prejudice and discrimination are built and reinforced through experience of interaction. This has subsequently been confirmed in work in critical discourse analysis (see Chapter 2, Section 3.4).

3.3 Curriculum design and methodology

Content

Authentic material, audio-visual role-plays and analysis were developed covering the following topics:

1. Solving a personal problem, e.g. asking for the day off.
2. Your job, e.g. negotiating for the fitter's time.
3. Trade unions, e.g. taking a grievance to your shop steward.
4. Use of the telephone, e.g. telephoning in when sick.
5. Interviews, e.g. seeing the manager for promotion.
6. Safety at work, e.g. explaining a safety hazard.
7. Dealing with people outside work, e.g. seeing your child's teacher.
8. Dealing with the public in your work, e.g. giving information at the enquiry desk.
9. Communicating as a supervisor, e.g. reporting to management.

On any particular course, only about three of these topic areas were likely to be covered. They would be selected on the basis of local needs analysis and student motivation and preference.

Skills

Learning and teaching with regard to the topics listed was focused on three major areas, with equal attention given to listening and productive skills. These areas were:

- transactional skills: dealing with stressful and difficult communication;
- discourse skills: the clear presentation of arguments and facts;
- information: filling gaps in information and understanding of workplace procedures, custom and practice.

These three categories were recognised at the time as arbitrary distinctions in some respects, but they were used as the key working concepts for teachers in analysing student needs, planning work for the classroom, and focusing classroom activity. They can be illustrated by relating them to the role-play transcript (Data 5.1, 'A Day Off') on p. 257 above. The situation here covers Topic 1 of the syllabus.

The **transactional language skills** required in that interaction relate to appropriate language and strategies which recognise the position of the listener, while retaining some control in the interaction for the speaker. In this case, the speaker needs to negotiate on time to speak, show he recognises the supervisor's difficulties and persist with his request despite opposition.

The **discourse skills** required are much more limited. They are more usefully developed where a long explanation needs to be given to solve the type of personal problem involved in topics 3, 5, 6, 8 or 9. In this role-play, the discourse skills are to do with the organisation of the discourse; i.e. ask for the day off, explain why and back up the explanation with the letter.

In terms of **workplace information**, the transactional skills require knowledge that asking for the day off at short notice is difficult and needs to be negotiated. In this case, knowing about the cleaning day and its significance also helps the worker to respond in a way which is likely to get his request granted.

Methodology

Methods were evolved for recording and working from an early stage with the students' own language strategies for the selected topics. Linguistic work – grammatical, prosodic and lexical – was then firmly based on identified student need with regard to the three categories of transactional skills, discourse skills and information.

In practice, the approach would work like this:

(a) As a result of observation in the workplace and initial contact with students, the teacher chooses a topic area.

(b) Selects a particular context to work on from the topic.

(c) Analyses material, e.g. 'A Day Off' (see Data 5.1) in terms of information, transactional skills and discourse skills.

(d) Selects role-plays and other communicative exercises which will be suitable to use.

(e) Checks availability of back-up linguistic exercises which may be needed.

(f) Introduces the context to the students (a variety of possible methods to choose).

(g) Builds up student performance on the basis of (d).

(h) Establishes student strengths and weaknesses. Builds up specific work on (g), (c), and (d). Selects and uses linguistic exercises (e) arising from identification of language use which results in communication breakdowns in (g). Builds up understanding of student preoccupations and motivation in this situation.

(i) Chooses further situations from the topic, dealing with them in the same way but more quickly, to develop and consolidate the work undertaken.

Methodology for transactional skills

Earlier ILT work, particularly at the elementary level, had tended to build up teaching methods around the *predictability* of sequences of language functions in relatively stereotyped transactions, which was the approach being developed in EFL communicative language teaching at the time. The work of some sociolinguists was suggesting that transactions were often predictable (Ervin-Tripp 1972; Halliday 1973) and language teachers were coming up with 'scripts' of 'functions' that could be realised in a limited number of ways.

ILT observation, on the other hand, suggested that the key difficulty in many inter-ethnic conversations was quite the opposite: the *unpredictability* for the South Asian worker of many transactions, particularly important ones. In addition, both speakers seemed to experience great difficulty in using repair and retrieval strategies when they misunderstood each other.

Gumperz's research and analysis on some ILT data raised questions about the concept of fixed language functions or fixed meanings in the context of the unpredictable nature of many transactions for South Asians who brought a different culture and communicative style, with little access to the specific social knowledge required in difficult workplace interactions and with limited linguistic fluency in English. An early project working paper outlined the new perception: 'The starting point of the discussion of language teaching methods contained here is the view that communication is a process of negotiation between speakers and hearers whose intentions and attitudes are subject both to constant modification in the course of interaction and also to their backgrounds and beliefs. Therefore, no meaning or function can be assigned to a particular piece of language without reference to the overall transaction in which it has occurred and to the particular speakers and hearers' (NCILT 1978a). This critique, which arose from ILT work, was confirmed by similar critiques concerned with the negotiation of meaning (Widdowson 1978; Candlin 1976) published at about the same time.

'Transactional skills' was in essence a pedagogical concept for focusing on those interpersonal communication skills which enable speakers to be sensitive to intention and attitude, to emphasise their key points clearly and appropriately, and to respond sensitively to others' intentions, attitudes and key points. One major difficulty in seeking to 'teach' such skills is that they are largely indefinable by their very nature. (This is not a problem that has gone away. For example, there is an ongoing debate in the late 1980s about whether learner strategies can be taught or whether they should be identified and built upon.) Only standard phatic and feedback language can be taught, together with set phrases to signal politeness, willingness to repair, persuasion and topicalisation. Limited though it is, such an approach may well have a certain practical value in contexts of inter-ethnic communication.

The crucial difficulty about practising transactional skills in a classroom is that intention, attitude and emphasis are largely signalled in areas of the linguistic system which are unconscious for the speaker and, therefore, applied and interpreted automatically, i.e. the prosodic system and certain syntactic devices above the sentence level. What was needed, therefore, was a classroom methodology for producing awareness of the fact that two speakers may misinterpret each other's systems. John Gumperz, in seeking to study misunderstanding in inter-ethnic negotiation and its impact on discrimination, had decided that it was in contexts of negotiation in which the goals of each side were conscious and identifiable that the meaning and interpretation of the participants could most easily be retrieved.

In response to this, Denise Gubbay and other colleagues from Pathway ILT started to evolve a methodology for classroom role-play, which she later developed into a comprehensive language-teaching methodology (Gubbay 1978). An early working paper which she contributed to the project summarised role-play in relation to transactional skills in the following terms:

> A situation is set up in which the teacher plays one party in the exchange and the student plays herself. The teacher directs the interplay in order to develop in the student:
>
> a) the ability to assess whether she's in a strong or weak position. This determines her attitude and helps her to understand the attitude of the other party. It is important that students are helped to go beyond their feeling of being at a disadvantage linguistically and assess their true 'negotiating' strength;
>
> b) the ability to listen carefully to what is said and to relate their response to it;
>
> c) the ability to response relevantly according to the point reached in the exchange, to move the exchange one step nearer resolution;
>
> d) the ability to be sensitive to the tone and implication of what is said; This requires the student to form some opinion of what the other person is thinking and feeling;
>
> e) the ability to deal with the consequences of an incorrect assessment at any point and to try to recover the lost ground;
>
> f) the ability to continue the exchange until a satisfactory resolution has been agreed by both parties;
>
> (Gubbay 1978)

In this method of role-play, it was critical that the students should, as far as they felt able in a classroom context, be themselves and it was also important to use familiar and stressful contexts and transactions. In these ways, it was intended that the student should become fully involved – often actually beginning to recreate a past experience – and consequently use language and negotiate meaning in the unconscious ways they did in reality. This would provide a role-play which represented an authentic use of language and could be recorded and used as a starting point for both awareness and for developing communication strategies and language skills in relation to the transaction. Analysis of tape-recordings of such role-plays confirmed that students used the same linguistic system and that the same misunderstanding arose as in data collected outside the classroom.

Pedagogic development arose from the application of the expanding view of language and new focus for analysis to a re-examination of teaching techniques already available and familiar – in this case teacher-constructed functional role-play dialogues. It is characteristic of these that learners are not often themselves and are in a comfortable but unreal world where communicative transactions have predictable outcomes. The objective was to replace these with inter-ethnic interaction models, generated by the students themselves, practised by the students as themselves, in situations which from their own perspective and experience were unpredictable, uncomfortable and stressful. In practice, the change in the level of stress put on the learners was generally welcomed by them as a more realistic mirror of their actual language-learning experience, graphically described by one student as 'the supermarket effect'. By this she meant the way in which there is an abrupt change from a cocooned, leisurely, solitary, self-directed process selecting groceries accompanied by Muzak, to the pressure of the check-out with money transactions, the focus of eyes, and the trolley pressure from behind.

The role-play approach begins with the presentation of the basic structure of a routine exchange in a familiar situation, such as tele-phoning for a plumber. For example, students are given the following telephone dialogue

Teacher:	Westwide Plumbing.
Student:	I need a plumber. My tap is leaking.
Teacher:	Name please
Student:	(supplies)
Teacher:	Address?
Student:	(supplies)
Teacher:	OK. I'll come this afternoon.
Student:	What time?
Teacher:	Between twelve and five. I can't be exact.
Student:	That's alright. Thanks.

[Material devised by Sheila Cogill and Denise Gubbay, Pathway ILT]:

After students have practised this successfully, the teacher suddenly starts giving a series of unpredicted and unwanted responses to 'My tap is leaking', such as:

wrong number:	'No plumber here. This is a private house.'
plumber ill:	'We're not taking orders. Mr. Jones is ill.'
plumber busy:	'We can't do anything for a week.'
request for direction:	'Where will I find you?'

At this stage, the teacher does not supply language but recognises and accepts the language strategies students offer and individualises it. This is done by encouraging all the language options offered and refining them by discussion and consent. In particular, discussion focuses on speakers' intentions and how each is reacted to, received and understood.

Students are then asked to begin the process of generating their own 'material' based on their experience. The contexts suggested by students from this experience identify the conditions in which ethnic differences in language style manifest themselves as interactions involving: authority v. inferiority; persuasion; accounting for actions; accounts of events; lengthy instructions involving listing, sequencing, alternatives; sudden shifts in narrative perspective; discipline.

In the class analysis of their tape-recorded role-plays, the focus is on the identification of functional, linguistic and rhetorical features where students can, as a matter of their own choice, mark their discourse to help English-speaking people to listen and respond to them. With the South Asian students involved, the areas of difference confirmed by the role-plays are: picking up and interpreting signals; differentiating between new and assumed information; distinguishing between contrastive, non-contrastive and 'bracketed' information; quoting the views or words of others; formulaic speech with uncompleted prompts; sequencing events; conveying own reactions.

The whole process involves students in explicit discussion of speaker intention, expectation and reception, and of the issues involved in language behaviour modification and assertiveness in a cross-cultural context. At this stage, it is necessary and desirable to involve white people, such as supervisors, in the discussion and analysis.

Gubbay's methodology focuses on relationships rather than language and aims to help students to do in English what they do in their first languages – that is, look beyond words to meaning and gauge the effect of their language use on others. The methodology depends, absolutely, on the teacher's ability to respond realistically to the students' utterances and at the same time be able to stand back from the exchange and analyse with the students what is going on. It is a methodology which in the right hands puts challenge and problem-solving at the centre, concentrating on the unpredictable and the stressful, and which recognises and develops the language resources learners already have. Although normative in its goals, this methodology proved to be an engaging and powerful tool with positive outcomes, especially when white interlocutors from the workplace were involved in the teaching process.

Methodology for discourse skills

Where the methodology for transactional skills was primarily analytical in terms of *relationships* within interactions, the discourse-skills component was essentially analytical in terms of *language use*. Transactional skills are those which help speakers/listeners to be sensitive to intention and attitude, whereas discourse skills are more concerned with how information or intent is conveyed in longer turns at talk.

Productive and receptive discourse skills were distinguished and schematised for pedagogic purposes in an attempt to make them teachable. More recent work in conversation analysis in particular has highlighted the joint structuring of speaker and listener activities, and such a division now seems arbitrary and does not reflect how interactions are accomplished. The use of the term 'discourse skills' is perhaps confusing. But we were looking for a shorthand way of describing both information-structuring and discourse cohesion (Halliday and Hasan 1976). In contrast to the 'transactional' or 'interpersonal' skills, 'discourse' at least has associations of lengthier chunks of narrative and of logic and argumentation. It was these associations that we were drawing on to develop the productive discourse skills required by the student in situations such as explaining personal circumstances to a supervisor, describing an accident or an incident accurately, explaining what has gone wrong with a machine or representing workmates' point of view in a meeting.

The aim of teaching discourse skills was to focus specifically on how information is organised and structured within a speaker turn. At the time of writing, we were not aware of any pedagogic analysis or materials which focused on oral discourse competence (in the sense used by Canale (1983); although more recently, for example in Brown and Yule (1983), this area has been tackled). We wanted to produce a rough taxonomy of the skills required both to produce turns at talk above the level of sentence and to help students to listen to explanations, reports and talks.

In the teaching of both productive and receptive discourse skills, teachers were advised to concentrate on the particular difficulties faced by South Asian learners of English as indicated by the analysis of naturally-occurring data. This target group had already gained a great deal of experience of English, often in a hostile environment, so the aim was to provide a supportive atmosphere in which they could work on their communicative effectiveness. The methodology assumed a continuing diagnostic process. Through diagnosing specific student difficulties and identifying where information loss occurred, either at the level of overall organisation or at the level of code, it was hoped that the courses and materials could be specifically geared to this group of students.

The *productive skills* which such students appeared to require were:

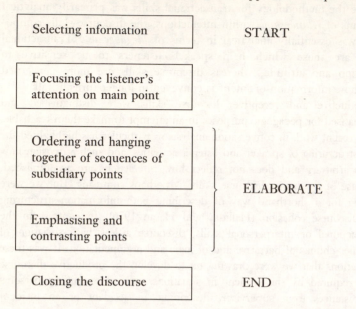

'Skills' were used as something of a catch-all term. It was intended to include both micro-skills such as the ability to use specific items of the linguistic code (lexical items, sentence connectives, prosodic features), and also macro-skills in selecting, organising and structuring.

The following is an example of 'over-lexicalisation' by a post-elementary learner:

> Yesterday my – plates and pots is the cupboard very upstairs and when we are bring the – up on the chair and get the back but upset-spoon is upstairs and I don't know that spoon is up with plates. When I tooked the plate and the spoon is come inside and they come out, my eyes and I can – eye, inside the spoon touch it and my eyes is all red.

The essential information which the student wanted to convey here was: 'I was getting a plate from a high cupboard and a spoon, which was up with the plates, fell into my eye.'

The *receptive skills* identified were those required when students have to listen to instructions or explanations given by a supervisor or when they have to listen to short talks by a supervisor or union representatives giving information about decisions that have been taken, the reasons for such decisions, and the action required now.

For post-elementary students to process what they are listening to and interpret it successfully they have to become active listeners and break habits of allowing language to wash over them, picking out key words which offer clues to the nature of the content. To achieve this they need skills in:

Recognising linguistic markers Recognising the structure of the discourse Sorting out more important/ less important points	1. Dealing with the linguistic features of the discourse (e.g. connectives, time markers, examples)
Anticipating	2. Dealing with the information content (e.g. background knowledge, narrative, instruction, description)
Establishing a rapport with the speaker Check-back skills	3. Responding to the speaker (e.g. signalling understanding, seeking clarification)

These discourse skills were taught by focusing on those which arose from the contexts provided by the nine course topics on p. 262 above.

In the teaching of discourse skills, the first aim recommended was to raise awareness for students of the nature and need for these skills. The method suggested for doing this was to contrast tapes of 'successful' and 'unsuccessful' use of discourse skills. Students decide what the differences are and these are written up as a checklist. Students can then go on to practise a similar situation using the checklist they have built up. An alternative approach was to work through an 'unsuccessful' piece of discourse, reworking the original into a new version agreed by the teacher and students. The following example uses Data 5.2 from p. 259.

TRAINING MATERIAL 5.1 BUSES 104 AND 107   [Developed by David Bonamy, Pathway ILT]

TRAINING MATERIAL 5.1 CONTEXT
The course was held in a bus company depot. The speaker is a maintenance engineer who is describing an incident to his supervisor

TRAINING MATERIAL 5.1 : BUSES 104 AND 107 (David Bonamy Pathway ILT)

ilt

DISCOURSE SKILLS
BUSES 104 & 107

Transcript
104 was broke down first. Clutch trouble. We take it out, clutch and everything, right? And we didn't get clutch, was waiting. 107 broke down, bring it back here, for a gearbox. Now we take it out gearbox. Now what they say, take it out this one, 107 gearbox, put it in 104 because this gearbox no good. Take it out 104 gearbox, put it in this one, and let this vehicle going. Wait for this one new. To come out other gearbox from this engine. Now why we going to lose these all jobs, for say about 30 hours job altogether, when we spent on that one 60 hours?

Transcript breakdown	*Re-write version*
A. 104 was broke down first. Clutch trouble.	*First*[h] of all, 104 broke down. Clutch trouble.
B. We take it out, clutch and everything, right? And we didn't get clutch, was waiting.	We took it out, clutch and everything, right? *But*[e] we couldn't get a clutch *to replace it*[b] [*or, another*[b] *clutch*], *so*[f], the job *had to*[g] wait.
	Then[h], 107 broke down, and was brought back here for a gearbox.
C. 107 broke down, bring it back here, for a gearbox.	*So*[f], we took out *the faulty one*[c] [*or, the old one*].[c]
D. Now we take it out gearbox.	Now the *chargehand/supervisor*[j] said, 'Take the gearbox out of 107 and put it in 104, because it's no good'.
E. Now what they say, take it out this one, 107 gearbox, put in in 104 because this gearbox no good.	
F. Take it out 104 gearbox, put it in this one, and let this vehicle going.	*and*[e] take the *good*[c] gearbox out of 104, and put it in *107*[a], and let *107*[a] go.' [Leave the garage]
G. Wait for this one new.	*So*[f] now we *have to*[g] wait for a *new gearbox*[d] *as well as*[e] a clutch for 104.
H. To come out other gearbox from this engine.	We have to take the *bad*[c] gearbox out *again, this time*[k] from *104*[a].
I. Now why we going to lose these all jobs, for say about 30 hours job altogether, when we spent on that one 60 hours?	*So*[f] why *should we*[g] waste [cf. 'lose'] time on all these jobs, and be *credited about 30 hours, when we spent 60 hours on *them*?[i] *vocab. point

TRAINING MATERIAL 5.1 BUSES 104 AND 107   *continued*

Commentary
(NB: the letters (a) to (k) correspond with letters used in the *Re-write version*.)

The speaker fails to:
- distinguish clearly between
  - (i)   104 and 107 (a)
  - (ii) 104 clutch and the replacement clutch (b)
  - (iii) 107 gearbox (a bad one) and 104 gear box (a good one) (c)
  - (iv) 104 gearbox and a gearbox from a new vehicle, or a new one (d).
- express clearly and distinguish between additions (*and, as well as*) and contrasts (*but*) (e)
- express consequence (*so, therefore*) (f)
- express and distinguish between actions, obligation and ability, i.e. modals: (*couldn't, have to, should we*) (g)
- express clearly the sequence of events (*first, then, next, now*) (h)
- use weak forms when no contrast is required (*that one*, instead of *them*) (i)
- make clear reference (*they* for *chargehand* – this is not of course confined to learners of English(j)
- make clear that there is a repetition of an earlier statement, with one item changed (*this engine* instead of *this time from 104*, which would make a meaningful contrast with the 107 gearbox. 'So we took out the faulty one') (k)

The method
1. Play the transcript and establish that it is confusing
   - to the Anglo-English listener who is unfamiliar with the bonus scheme context (e.g. the teacher)
   - to the Anglo-English listener who *is* familiar with context (e.g. the visiting supervisor who clearly fails to understand the passage: his response on tape is 'aha, aha' and then he turns to another example.)
   - to the bi-lingual listeners (e.g. other students – test comprehension to establish this).
2. Pose question *Why?* and explain what you mean by
   - contrasts
   - reference
   - sequence
3. Put on blackboard by eliciting from class the major contrasts, e.g.

TRAINING MATERIAL 5.1 BUSES 104 AND 107   *continued*

4. Then by playing tape section by section, plot sequence semi-diagrammatically (if students find it easy to relate to this type of symbolisation).

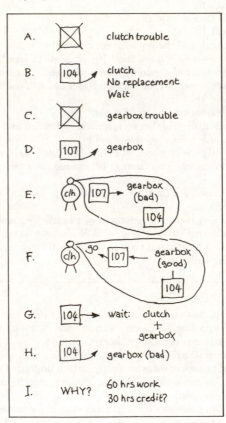

A.   clutch trouble

B.   104   clutch
           No replacement
           Wait

C.   gearbox trouble

D.   107   gearbox

E.   c/h 107 → gearbox
                  (bad)
                     104

F.   c/h go 107 ← gearbox
                    (good)
                        104

G.   104 → wait: clutch
                    +
                  gearbox

H.   104   gearbox (bad)

I.   WHY?   60 hrs work
               30 hrs credit?

5. Explain the value of clear sequencing. Go over the diagram in (4), getting them to say:
   – First X happened
   – Then ...
   – Then ...
   – Next ....
   – But now ...
   They should also use:
   – *So, and, but, as well as, also.*
   At this stage, ignore other mistakes, and concentrate on the above.

TRAINING MATERIAL 5.1 BUSES 104 AND 107   *continued*

6. Now concentrate on contrasts between
   – 104 *and* 107
   – 104 clutch *and* replacement
   – 104 gearbox (good) *and* 107 gearbox (bad)
   See (3) above.

   Ask 'How can we make these contrasts clear?' and again go over
   diagram (3), eliciting/teaching:
   – replacement
   – another clutch
   – the faulty one
   – the good one
   – a new gearbox, etc.
   See *Rewrite Version*, (a), (b), (c), (d). Intonation is vital to this
   section.

7. Now concentrate on item (g), modals, by playing relevant tape
   section and asking 'Is that exactly what he wanted to say?', e.g.
   'We didn't get clutch' could imply, 'we didn't bother'.

8. Tackle the individual points (i), (j), (k).

9. By again referring to diagram and tape, build up a version on
   blackboard or tape fairly close to the *Rewrite Version*. Tape the
   students for self-correction.

10. Cover other points (grammatical errors, but less vital to under-
    standing):
    – Past tenses: broke down
                     took out
                     brought back
                     said
    Some are in the present, some in the past.
    Explain the importance of consistency and get them to do it
    – in dramatic present throughout
    – in past throughout
    – Redundant 'it'.
    Exercises: e.g.
         A: We took out the gearbox
         B: Are you sure?
         C: Yes, we took it out all right.
    – Let + infinitive ⎱ These items of grammar can be tackled
                       ⎰ through exercises from existing published
    – Passive   ⎰ language materials.

who is visiting the language class to talk about the bonus scheme. He describes what happened when two buses (numbers 104 and 107) broke down, one with a faulty clutch and one with a faulty gearbox. He describes what went wrong, the waiting period involved, and the fact that this means they lose money under the existing system.

TRAINING MATERIAL 5.1 METHOD
Students listen to an unsuccessful example of discourse on a topic of personal interest to the group. They have to decide what they think the speaker is trying to communicate. This approach has the advantage that the students are trying to understand something and if they fail to do so the speaker's failure to communicate is evident. This type of work can also be developed on a topic which students do not already know about. The quality of the recording must be very good.

The teacher then focuses students on the analysis of their own discourse, particularly prosodic features, such as contrastive use of stress, and grammatical points.

Methodology for information skills
The third major area of the curriculum was information. For purposes of curriculum analysis and pedagogy, a distinction was made between the social knowledge required to organise interaction and present oneself effectively and the social knowledge acquired in the specific workplace in order to survive in it, make sense of it and gain benefits from it.

This latter type of social knowledge is defined as *workplace information*. Workplace information which may cause misunderstandings or is particularly motivating to students will include:
– Safety
– Quality – including how a job fits into the overall process
– Job flexibility
– Grievance and discipline procedures
– Trade unions – particularly frequent misconceptions about the
– function of unions and the role of stewards
– Wages
– Leave
– Background to the workplace

In addition, topics arise on more general issues of concern to the students:
– Educational system

– Legal matters, e.g. mortgage, rent tribunals, immigration restrictions
– Citizens' rights.

It was recognised that the amount and complexity of workplace information meant that only a small amount could be covered in a short training course and that, in any case, any one part of the information would have only limited general application. The major focus of a course was on transactional and discourse skills, so that the social knowledge for effective interaction could be acquired and most workplace information could then, it was hoped, be learned and negotiated through interaction. So the information unit represented a subsidiary, but nevertheless important, element. See Training Material 5.2.

TRAINING MATERIAL 5.2   WORKPLACE INFORMATION

---

ilt   **SELECTION, PRESENTATION AND**
                           USE OF INFORMATION

1. *Information as a part of language-skills teaching*

The need for students to have further information will arise from the topics and situations used for teaching transactional and discourse skills.

In topics to do with solving personal problems and safety, the types of information needs among students are seldom encompassed by a set of simple facts. It is the *implications* of the facts that students need to appreciate. For example, supplying facts about the required quality of a product (in a handbook or induction course) does not mean that workers have recognised or applied the implications to their own work. Similarly, unless workers have experienced using a particular procedure and have learned what they should or should not do, they will not actually know how the procedure works; despite whatever was said at their induction. In the course of a role-play exercise, or listening to an authentic tape, or planning a logical argument on topics like these, questions of implications, rigidity and custom in relation to particular facts and procedures will all crop up. This reality also shows the limitation of the distinction between social knowledge for interaction and social knowledge as workplace information (useful though it is in planning teaching materials) because it is *the significance of a set of rules within a British workplace culture* which has to be grasped by students. If there is a minor discipline problem, will the rule be invoked or will it be dealt with informally; when a shop steward negotiates, what is his concept of his power and position; when there is a human problem, how and how often can rules be bent?

TRAINING MATERIAL 5.2   WORKPLACE INFORMATION
continued second page

2. *The special need for information among ethnic minority workers*
The second reason for including some presentation of workplace information relates to the broader aims of a language training programme in
a multi-ethnic workplace. Lack of information and factual misunderstandings in themselves feed the general poor level of communication
and the negative attitudes on both sides. Where two people share language and culture, information about specific workplace procedures
and rules can be comparatively easily and rapidly acquired by one person
signalling to the other whether the other person has the correct information or not. We learn from our mistakes and store up the information for
a future occasion. In a cross-cultural situation, unless the information is
very explicitly conveyed and unless both sides have excellent transactional
skills, informal learning of vital information in this way does not happen.
In reality, workers are denied access to important information because
it is written in difficult English or because it is information available
on the English grapevine and has not filtered through to all the workers.
Workers themselves may often have an unrealistic view of how much
information they do have, and at the same time, they may find
management very arbitrary in the way that it interprets company rules.

3. *Information as a means of motivating and involving other workplace*
   personnel and students more fully in the training course
The third reason for including an information component in a language training course is to do with how people within the company
(including the students themselves) relate to and are motivated by the
course. Within the classroom, students' interest is obviously affected
by the subject matter – the content of the material. Other members of
company staff, both shop stewards and managers, will also at times
judge the course in terms of content.
It also provides an opportunity to give advice to management and
unions on the clear presentation of information.
The following is an example where the visiting manager fails to answer
the question and introduces irrelevant information, confusing the student.

Sick Pay

Student: I want to ask about my sick note pay, I sent to the
          social security office, but late, seven days late.

Manager: What we normally do with such pay which we like to
          try to explain to people here. We have a sick scheme
          here. We only want you to go sick if you are sick. We
          don't want you to go sick because you want a holiday.
          We don't want that. But you will get sick pay from
          the factory. This is the normal procedure that you get
          when you're sick. We don't want you to go to the ...
          er ... injuries part of the Department of Employment

TRAINING MATERIAL 5.2   WORKPLACE INFORMATION
continued third page

> ... er ... like you did one year. You had a little acci-
> dent and you put a claim in for Industrial Benefit – If
> you hurt your finger and you're away for four or five
> days, you don't go and get industrial benefit because
> that to me means you are sick because you've had an
> accident, and we will pay you sick pay, normal sick pay.

Faults: The manager
– fails to clarify the question, which must be based on some personal
  incident;
– fails to differentiate clearly between sickness and injury;
– does not make the reference to the Department of Employment clear;
– introduces, at the beginning, another point which is not relevant to
  the question.

This inclusion of an information element attempted to make explicit
those aspects of social knowledge which are acquired by white workers
whether through company information systems or through informal
contact with other workers, 'the grapevine'. Different assumptions
about what is fixed and what is discretionary, different notions about
where power resides – in the rule or in the individual, fears and suspi-
cions about rights and responsibilities are all part of the social
knowledge which enters into routine workplace communication and
cannot be ignored in any training to improve language and communications.

The enormous difficulties for students in acquiring this type of
workplace information are reflected in Data 5.4.

DATA 5.4 HOLIDAYS
[David Bonamy, Pathway ILT]

DATA 5.4 CONTEXT
This is an extract from a taped discussion between the teacher, two
managers and a union shop steward. The teacher has made notes on a
number of points of company procedure raised by students in class
discussion and is seeking clarification on procedures.

The assistant production manager is APM, the personnel manager
is PM, the union representative is SS, and the teacher is DB.

DATA 5.4 HOLIDAYS – TRANSCRIPT
[David Bonamy Pathway ILT]

APM: Mrs H ___ applied for long leave last year and got it. She had six weeks allowed. She took eight weeks, and came back saying that the air strike delayed her for a fortnight. She applied for it again this year, and I says no, you had it last year, and she wasn't very pleased. I gave her the minimum, which was a fortnight with pay and one week without

PM: I think it's only fair to say that the only reason she got her job back was that particular section was fairly slack.

APM: Yes, it if had been busy we would have replaced her.

DB: Why was she so upset that she wasn't going to get it this year when she must have known that the rule said she couldn't?

APM: She thinks she can bend them.

SS: No, the main reason is that she's entitled to three weeks over the year. At a time she can only take two weeks. She was not asking for six weeks extended leave, but four weeks. In her terms she was only asking one week extra.

APM: No, but she's not, because the rules states =

SS: = No, I'm saying in her terms.

APM: Oh, yeah, take a fortnight at once, three weeks at the discretion of the manager ... but I wasn't in a mood to be discretionary, because she'd had it last year and abused it ...

APM: And Mrs. B ___, she'd also had long leave last year, and also took a week extra. Now she had a bona fide medical certificate, so we couldn't say anything about that, I mean that was probably all above board, but she wanted it again this year, and we just couldn't let her. You create a precedent, you see. If people get long leave every year, people are going to say 'Ello, am I getting long leave every year?'

SS: The point about Mrs B ___ is that she could go home by car if she had the four weeks, but since it's reduced to three weeks she's got to fly home, which is much more expensive and not as exciting ... My point is this, at the moment the workers have not realised that they can take only two weeks at a time.

APM: Oh? Well, it's in the handbook.

PM: I think maybe a newsletter might clarify that situation.

DATA 5.4 HOLIDAYS – TRANSCRIPT   *continued*

> APM: No, we get three weeks and three days, but three of the days are company days, meaning they're given at the discretion of the company every year. The workers feel they want to take them when they want, but the company insists that they are company days and are given for the benefit of the company. But they want to take them ad lib.
>
> DB: And apart from that and the bank holiday, it's two weeks and a third week not less than six weeks either side =
>
> APM: = That's right
>
> DB: Is that strictly adhered to?
>
> PM: I wouldn't say so. We're fairly flexible ...

It is clear from this discussion that carrying out of company rules, however clearly stated, also depends on other factors such as the order books and how 'discretionary' the manager is prepared to be. This showed how important it was for students to be absolutely clear about the rules but also to be aware of what was discretionary.

The next example (Training Material 5.3) shows how such data might be used in the classroom. The teacher is identified as T.

TRAINING MATERIAL 5.3 HOLIDAYS [David Bonamy Pathway ILT]

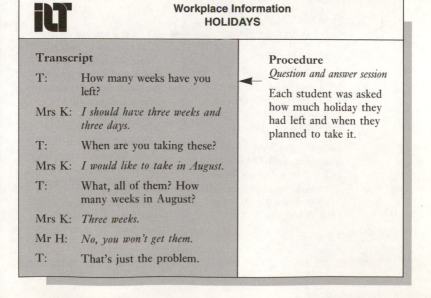

Workplace Information
HOLIDAYS

Transcript	Procedure
T: How many weeks have you left?	*Question and answer session*
Mrs K: *I should have three weeks and three days.*	Each student was asked how much holiday they had left and when they planned to take it.
T: When are you taking these?	
Mrs K: *I would like to take in August.*	
T: What, all of them? How many weeks in August?	
Mrs K: *Three weeks.*	
Mr H: *No, you won't get them.*	
T: That's just the problem.	

TRAINING MATERIAL 5.3 HOLIDAYS   *continued*

Mr A:	*I want to go oversea. I want to take six week.*
T:	How long have you been working in the company?
Mr A:	*Nearly one year.*
T:	Mrs B ____, could you explain to Mr A ____ what the rule is about this. Why will it be difficult for him?
Mrs B:	*Because this year it's changed. I don't know very well, because I try my holiday, and had little bit argument with my supervisor, and he told me this year it's a different rule. Last year I got three weeks holiday together, three weeks my own and one week unpaid leave, but not any more. I tried to fighting, why not get my holiday …?*
T:	When did you get this handbook?
Mrs B:	*Last year.*
T:	So this must be the new rule in here?
Mrs B:	*Yes.*
T:	How can he get overseas leave? What's the rule?
Mrs B:	*If you go to abroad, three weeks, no more, or lose the job.*
Mr H:	It depend head of department. Could be if he got enough staff to carry on work, he might be lucky, otherwise …
T:	Let's imagine that you've saved one week from last year, and you've got three weeks from this year, but you want to go to India for six weeks, what would you do then?

◄— Then the teacher turned to Mrs B ____, who has been working at the company for some years.

◄— Then the teacher spoke to the group in general. (Here the teacher is trying to elicit the rule that he can accumulate this year's and next year's leave, and take six weeks next year.) The teacher explained again the rule about accumulating, i.e. you've in effect got to give one year's notice of intent.

Students were then asked about unpaid overseas leave.

TRAINING MATERIAL 5.3 HOLIDAYS   *continued*

Mr S:	*We actually request the head of department, if it's possible to have another two weeks without pay. But if he refuses, we can't do anything, because we've taken our holiday.*	◄— The teacher explained the rule from the hand-book that if you haven't accumulated a full six weeks, you may take half the balance of the six weeks as unpaid leave. He put up various sums to illustrate what 'half the balance' means.

3.4 Evaluation

These post-elementary materials represent one end of the analytic/ experiential spectrum outlined at the beginning of this section. In terms of both language and working relationships, they are the most analytic materials produced within ILT and the materials most lacking in an experiential/ethnographic base. The over-emphasis on analysis and the lack of the experiential and ethnographic, although not defi-ned as such at the time, created doubts about this overall approach. However, our critique also indicated the major strengths of these courses, which were:

- an organising framework which is motivating in terms of content but develops transferable skills;
- an analysis of discourse not limited to either functions or a narrow and teachable view of grammar;
- an approach which helps to make social knowledge explicit;
- reliance on students' own data and on data collected by company staff in authentic situations;
- provision of specific help and guidance when misunderstanding and tensions arise;
- a methodology which builds unpredictability into transactions;
- content areas which require the involvement of company staff and so may expose them to possibilities of improving their own com-munication.

As we have suggested, there are also clear limitations to the materials which can be pinpointed by a series of evaluative questions:

- What are the limitations of materials based primarily on a needs analysis of workplace language?
- What are the dangers of emphasising performance and evaluation of performance by the teacher?

- What is limiting and damaging about taking a normative view of language in which students' performance is evaluated by criteria decided by the teacher?
- How can the unpredictability of interaction be handled without the class becoming teacher-centred and teacher-controlled?
- Who decides what should be taught and what is correct or appropriate? What are the dangers of focusing too much on the notion of appropriacy?
- At what point does establishing communicative differences and difficulties become, unwittingly, a racist strategy?
- How often does a genuine clash of interest between black workers and others get side-tracked into an issue of poor communications?
- How can the tension be resolved between running short work-time courses focusing on improved work relationships and courses which meet the self-identified needs of students?
- What opportunities did this project offer to students to develop their own learning strategies?

In terms of both curriculum and pedagogy, materials for the post-elementary learner appeared narrow in focus and teacher-controlled. Ideologically, they seemed uncomfortably normative and focused on a deficit view of the learners.

The need teachers felt for some liberation and release from these constraints led to the next project to be described, which focused on the development of student autonomy.

4 Project Two: Increasing student autonomy in ILT

4.1 The context

This two-year programme aimed to develop a more student-centred approach in ILT than had previously been used (for example in Project One), by understanding better students' own aspirations and perceptions as language learners, by cultivating awareness of and utilising their existing knowledge and experience of language and of communication, and by developing independent learning skills for use during and after courses. The project was also seeking to break out of the severe constraints of time and content imposed by short courses based on a workplace context.

There were two aspects to the overall project:

(i)   to increase understanding of, and methods for, finding out about how students perceive their own learning needs, especially through the use of ethnographic interviews in the mother tongue;

(ii) to produce a range of self-study materials to be used by students outside the classroom both as back-up to their ILT course and as a basis for continuing study after the course.

Two national working parties were established, each with support from a coordinator, to cover these two major aspects of the programme. The coordinators visited teachers, convened working groups, and disseminated working papers and a range of learning materials prepared by the respective working parties. This work constituted the UK contribution to the Council of Europe Modern Languages Project (CDCC Project No.4), a pilot study on 'The teaching of the national language of the host country to adult immigrants' which was also carried out in France, Germany and Sweden (CDCC (81) 38: Jupp 1982).

Three factors contributed particularly to the setting up of the student-autonomy project. First, during 1978/79, a survey was undertaken of methodology used on elementary courses. It was found that the functional behavioural model dominated to an extent which made the introduction of new methods difficult, and that certain skills were largely neglected on the courses – for example, listening and literacy. (Survey conducted by Elisabeth Hoadley-Maidment, NCILT, and Alison Slade, Yorkshire ILT.)

Second, although there remained a high commitment in ILT to the value of building a bridge from research to methods and materials, there was also a conviction that, as with education generally, there was not enough investment in classroom practice and the insights and expertise of teachers. These doubts were complemented and reinforced by a growing feeling, particularly among recently appointed staff who were black themselves, that ILT was over-committed to linguistically related theory, analysis and expertise, but underrepresented by a black perspective in its work, in terms of both students and teachers.

The third factor was contact with, and the opportunity to participate in, the pilot study of adult immigrants with the Council of Europe Modern Languages Project. The project, which started in 1971, sought to work in the following seven areas:

(i) *Needs analysis:* Methods and systems for the identification and assessment of the needs, motivation, characteristics and resources of different groups of learners.

(ii) *Specification of objectives:* Methods and systems for the specification of communicative language objectives for these different groups of learners.

(iii) *Methods and materials:* The devising of communicative language teaching methods and language learning materials which reflect work carried out under (i) and (ii). For example, a series of multi-media courses for adult foreign language learners of English.

(iv) *Evaluation and testing* of these language learning objectives with particular emphasis upon self-assessment.

(v)   *Student autonomy:* Principles and methods for learners to progress from a condition of dependence on the teacher to a condition of autonomy in which they take charge of their own linguistic development and can continue to develop language learning after formal teaching stops or as they move on to further education and training.

(vi) *Teacher-training:* The development of methods and materials for teacher-training based upon the approach of (i) – (v).

(vii) *Networks:* The development of professional networks of contact and co-operation throughout Europe.

CDCC (81) 38: Jupp 1982

These areas of work have a breadth and comprehensiveness which provided another very useful yardstick for evaluating broader development priorities within ILT. It also meant that we were able to take advantage of the expertise of colleagues in France, Germany and Sweden and share our ideas and experience with them.

Thus it was that internal preoccupations and external stimulus resulted in a project with two major and overlapping areas of work:

1. An analysis of student learning needs. This was to focus on the way in which the students themselves perceived their language-learning needs, abilities, motivations and expectations of the learning experience. The information obtained would form a valuable addition to the analyses already carried out before courses began: a communication survey of the company encompassing analysis of communication networks and patterns and language-testing of potential students.

2. A project aimed at the production of language-teaching materials with emphasis on the development of materials for use by students working on their own, i.e. self-study materials. The objective of this part of the project was to motivate the students to take responsibility for their own learning and to encourage them to continue their studies after the industrial language course had finished, as well as supplementing classroom instruction. We hoped to produce a student workbook as part of this project.

Unlike the earlier post-elementary language-learning project, this project did not seek to lay down specifications of learning objectives or curriculum design for courses, but to influence the thinking and resources available to teachers and to provide them with new processes and learning materials.

As with previous projects, contributions from theory and practice were taken in an eclectic way. First of all there was the influence of creative thinkers on pedagogy, notably Freire (1972) and other radical writers on education such as Head (1974) and Postman (1971). Freire's liberating thoughts on basic adult literacy forced the trainers to think again about the role of literacy on ILT courses, the respective roles of teachers and learners in its acquisition, and the importance of what happens in regard to conscious learning outside the classroom rather than within it. Freire's view of the dangers of paternalistic and control aspects of education fitted well with the need for teachers to redefine functions as those which, in the students' own terms, are fundamental in establishing, rather than negotiating, the right to be heard and to take control of their own life chances.

Taking on board more explicitly than before the idea that students' learning around and after the course could represent much greater opportunities for learning than the short workplace course itself, naturally led to looking beyond work-based materials to materials and readers used more generally in ESL and adult-literacy courses and materials for study skills such as Gubbay (1980), Wilson (1978) and the BBC adult-literacy handbooks (1975, 1979).

A final set of influences came from social psychology and the work in Europe on student autonomy and self-directed learning. We reread the work by Lambert (1972) and Taylor, Meynard and Rheault (1977) on student motivation and awareness, and also became more aware of Giles's work on language and ethnicity (1977). A number of recent publications by the Council of Europe, notably Holec (1981) and Richterich (1979), were complemented by work on language learning and awareness (Allwright 1976; Long 1976; Brumfit 1976) and a set of ELT documents on individualisation in language learning (British Council 1978).

4.2 Principles and planning

Certain working premises underpinned the project from which was derived a conceptual framework of interrelated topics, as described in Training Material 5.4 (extracts from a working party's project paper).

TRAINING MATERIAL 5.4 STUDENT AUTONOMY
(from Hedge 1980)

ILT   **Student Autonomy**
                    PRINCIPLES AND FRAMEWORK

1.0   Some working premises
We found that in considering both a conceptual framework and practical application, we kept returning to certain principles which had to be applied and interpreted at every level of the project.

1.1   Our approach to student autonomy presupposes that students will attend ILT courses, will receive help and support during the course in developing independent learning (including self-study), and will continue to receive support through a range of relationships (e.g. workmates, supervisors and shop stewards, occasional teacher visits, etc.) after a course formally finishes.

1.2   Our general goal is to help people to believe in themselves, to understand their own value and importance as human beings and as workers, and to realise the extent of their own knowledge and potential. Our learners need to modify their existing concept of both themselves and the contexts in which they communicate in order to learn and apply their new communication skills.

This goal has been articulated and demonstrated in the work of Paulo Freire and in aspects of recent work with adults on local working-class history, literacy skills, and some ESL work.

1.3   The learner's experience is central to the learning process. Learners should not see themselves only as passive receivers from the teacher whom they consequently perceive as at the real centre of the learning process. Such an approach must include valuing and recognising the learners' wider experience of life here and in their countries of origin. We must recognise in particular that many of our students have shown very considerable independence and self-direction in their lives generally (e.g. settling in Britain, adopting an entirely new working life, setting up community organisations, etc.).

It is important that we also find ways of recognising the learners' experience as members of ethnic minorities who need to use English in cross-cultural settings and who are often personally threatened by racism.

1.4   Student autonomy involves the acquisition of learning aims and skills by learners from the very beginning in order for them to practise independence and see themselves as central to the learning process. Thus we should be aiming from the very outset of an ILT course to enable students to acquire ways of learning

TRAINING MATERIAL 5.4 STUDENT AUTONOMY
(from Hedge 1980) *continued*

without a teacher (but not without relationships and support from other people). This is necessary both to develop learning autonomy and because our formal courses are so short. By adopting this aim at the very beginning of a course, we recognise that autonomy for a language learner and user is a *process* which must be developed from the outset and cannot be regarded as a *product* to be presented to a student or suddenly recognised by a student at the *end* of the language learning process.

1.5 Autonomy is a process which needs to develop with all *levels* of language learner. We recognise the practical difficulties for beginner level, but we feel the concept is as important for them as for any group – indeed more so because people who have already acquired some English already have some level of language learning strategy.

1.6 The large body of experience built up by ILT teachers over the years represents an enormous fund of knowledge of student motivation, learning strategies, personal successes and failures which must be fully analysed and used in every aspect of this project.

1.7 We recognise that there are particular difficulties in developing autonomy for *second-language* learning and self-study (i.e. second-language learning is a peculiarly non-autonomous activity), and that we have to reinterpret ideas developed in relation to mother tongue education for the disadvantaged and self-directed learning for academically fairly advanced work. We also recognise that we should guard against adopting goals for individuals in terms of self-identity which cannot possibly be acquired only through second-language learning.

1.8 The acquisition of learning skills is particularly difficult on an ILT course because the main learning/study skill for any learning is language itself. We are faced with the paradox of our learners not possessing at the outset a main resource (a shared language with the teacher and others) which they need for language learning. So we face the task of simultaneously teaching language skills and linguistic systems for use as a learning tool and for use beyond the learning context.

1.9 The use of the students' first languages has an essential role to play in this project and in the acquisition of learner autonomy.

1.10 The teacher's skills and experience are also crucial to the learning process. The teacher has skills to interpret the students' perception of needs as well as to analyse and define student needs from a perspective of language communication skills. For example, students might have difficulties in perceiving or articulating needs divorced from situations and contexts or from traditional goals like literacy, accent, etc.

TRAINING MATERIAL 5.4 STUDENT AUTONOMY
(from Hedge 1980)   *continued*

1.11 The aim of learner autonomy and self-study has important implications for the format and organisation of ILT courses generally
and is likely to lead to gradual changes in emphasis in terms of
methodology and classroom techniques as well as to experiments
with forms of organisation other than the conventional 60-hour,
12-14 week course.

The conceptual framework has been divided into six areas (see
Section 2) and we have tried to apply these working premises in
each one.

2.0 Topics For The Conceptual Framework
In order to plan a conceptual framework, we had to define a
number of topics. They require separate description, but they are
not independent, and practical applications of the framework will
probably always draw form several topics.

2.1 *Student-centred perception of needs*

This topic relates closely to the needs analysis side of the project
and includes motivation, awareness, attitudes, achievement
(successes and failures), knowledge of what makes people talk in
classes, etc. It also includes students' own observations of when,
why and with whom they need English, and in what respects they
lack independence because they lack language skill. These factors
are never static so their description can only be in relation to a
particular moment. Such factors can be expected to change rapidly during a course, particularly if mother tongue interviews and/
or language counselling are part of the course, and if students are
articulating their own changing needs.

2.2 *Student learning*
This includes:
   (a) the learning strategies students have before a course and
        how they change and develop;
   (b) the study skills, tools and techniques which learners need to
        develop and acquire in relation to language learning;
   (c) the relationships with people which learners need to develop
        and/or acquire during a course.

2.3 *Teacher methodology*
This includes:
   (a) ways of enabling students to verbalise course aims and objec-
        tives (at some level);
   (b) ways of enabling students to describe the function and
        significance of the language they are learning;

TRAINING MATERIAL 5.4 STUDENT AUTONOMY
(from Hedge 1980) *continued*

    (c) the teacher's strategies for language teaching;
    (d) the teacher's strategies for dealing with student anxiety.

2.4   *The language and communication skills syllabus*
    This includes:
    (a) the strategies and skills for language use which the course/-
        self-study materials aim to give the students (spoken and
        written)
    (b) the functional realisations of those strategies and skills
    (c) the linguistic realisations combined and added to in order to
        provide a 'core grammar'. This syllabus has to exist at two or
        possibly three levels (beginner, elementary, post-elementary).

This framework had important implications for the existing ILT approach in relation to pre-course surveys, objectives of courses and course methodology and organisation.

Workplace observation and surveys needed to take much more account of students' perception of needs.

Training objectives needed to be more explicit in order to dispel anxieties, explain the role of ILT, give learners an opportunity to think about teaching methods and their own learning methods and explain about the course. Students could be helped to draw up 'performance contracts' with the teacher, to accept study skills and self-study materials as part of the programme.

Teaching and learning implications were far-reaching, as outlined in this further extract from the working paper:

Implications for learning and course methodology
There will be at least three distinctly different kinds of learner in terms of learning how to study language and of any self-study materials.

Type 1. Learners (usually elementary) who are illiterate in their own language as well as in English. Such people will have little if any experience of formal education.

They may need special introduction to a language course, counselling in their own language, study techniques and self-study materials which are not dependent on literacy.

Type 2. Learners who are literate in their own language. They will probably have high motivation for literacy in English and will want self-study materials which include a transfer-of-literacy-skills element.

Type 3. Learners who are literate in English. They can follow a much more sophisticated type of study skills/techniques course leading to more conventional self-study materials.

Teachers need, as always, to be aware of possible learning difficulties, e.g.:
 - feeling there has not been enough practice;
 - feeling uncertain as to whether they have learned what is expected of them, feeling uncertain as to what the learning goal is;
 - anxiety over being able to remember what they have learned;
 - difficulties with literacy.

As yet we do not know what sort of methodology would accommodate the factors listed below, but we are sure they will need to be taken into account. Students need to:
1. Examine their previous experience of language learning and acquisition–first, second language and/or English.
2. Value and be aware of their existing stock of English. Could this be done with a communications network like those used often to demonstrate workplace contacts? Many students have a disproportionately large vocabulary to build on, and possibly a sight vocabulary.
3. Become aware of the resources they have for learning.
    (i)   their experiences of second-language learning (e.g. Urdu/Hindi);
    (ii)   other people (communications network again);
    (iii) their existing learning techniques.

(Hedge 1980)

Finally, *course organisation* needed to be rethought. For example, an introductory module to help make the objectives explicit was introduced in some courses. More importantly, systems were set up to help with the continuation of learning after the course, including study groups, links with other forms of local adult-education provision, links with informal 'teachers' such as workmates, friends or relatives.

Since both aspects of the project, the needs analysis and the materials, were to run simultaneously, some decisions on materials development had to be made before the full needs analysis was completed. Priorities for materials development were decided, therefore, about six months into the project. They were:

– listening – using the media;
– literacy;
– using students' personal resources

These were chosen to reflect the specific objectives of the project in relation to student autonomy. Literacy development would both help to give students more control over their lives and develop the skill needed for continued learning through self-study. 'Using the media' to develop listening skills was chosen to encourage students to use the natural and available language around them in a systematic way. Finally 'Using students' personal resources' aimed to assist students to chart and develop their existing communication networks and their access to and knowledge of services and people in the community and to assess their own success.

4.3 Establishing student requirements

The objective of this aspect of the project was to find out as much as possible about how students perceived their own learning needs. This elicitation of student perception of need completed the triangle of workplace needs-analysis surveys:

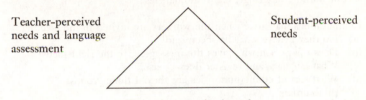

Teacher-perceived needs and language assessment

Student-perceived needs

Company-perceived needs

Although the ethnographic work described in Chapter 4 had gone some way to eliciting workers' perceptions of the workplace and their communication needs, this had not been done systematically or in enough depth.

ILT staff had little experience of the in-depth, semi-structured interview which it was decided was the only effective tool for encouraging students to talk about themselves and their learning in their terms. In this respect, interest in ethnographic interviewing for identifying appropriate language training was being developed alongside ethnographic interviewing to elicit more general experiences and perceptions as described in Chapter 4. Those involved in this aspect of the project put themselves through some training. One of their Asian colleagues wrote up his experience of conducting interviews in his and the workers' first language (cf. Training Material 5.5). The strong emphasis on encouraging motivation and being extremely sensitive to students' assumptions and anxieties is in contrast to earlier perfunctory questioning and language-testing (as in the assessment-interview model in *Industrial English*, Jupp and Hodlin 1974).

TRAINING MATERIAL 5.5 MOTHER TONGUE INTERVIEWS
[Charan Singh Bamhrah, Lancashire ILT]

---

iLT   **Student Autonomy**
                    MOTHER-TONGUE INTERVIEWS

A. **Use of mother-tongue before the survey**
Mother-tongue interviewers can play a very useful part by explaining
the nature of a survey to small groups of ethnic minority workers, .
either on the shopfloor or in the canteen, during breaks. This is, in
effect, selling to potential students. Management and the ILTU make
the practical arrangements, and workers are informed of the meeting
by their supervisor. Their first reaction is likely to be anxiety. Why
have this meeting? Who are they going to see? This has never
happened before – something must have gone wrong! Maybe it is some
sort of warning of change, e.g. redundancies.

Complications may arise when the workers are invited to the meeting:
(a)   Do they believe what has been said?
(b)   Does the person who gives the message, give the right focus?
(c)   What language and register does he use?
(d)   What sort of ethnic minorities are they? Ethnic groups:
       rural/urban?
(e)   What is their concept of such an occasion? (being told to see
       someone in a group but not a union meeting)?

The mother tongue interviewer/speaker has to check:
1.   What language to use; if Panjabi, what accent/dialect – Jhelum? –
      Mirpuri? – Amritsari?

2.   Age group: (i)   40+
                  (ii) 25 to 35?
                  (iii) 18 to 25
If majority 40+:   Be very careful in choosing words – appreciating
their work and interest (sparing the time to talk to you), when introducing language classes – make clear precisely the style of teaching,
how easy, how useful etc.
If 25 to 35:   Same as above but focus on the advantages of learning
the language, how easy it becomes to create harmonious relations on
the shopfloor, how easy it would be to talk and express your problems
to the management.
If 18 to 25:   Use amusing language – one or two anecdotes make them
laugh at first to ease their fears/doubts/anxieties; focus on the possibility of promotion after further training as an advantage of learning
English.

3.   If Muslims are in the majority, 'Allah' or 'Inshah Allah' should be
      used appropriately.

TRAINING MATERIAL 5.5 MOTHER TONGUE INTERVIEWS
[Charan Singh Bamhrah, Lancashire ILT]   *continued*

4. If a mixed group of Muslims and Hindus, use a mixture of both styles in language with a very diplomatic approach.

5. If it is 'Ramadan', one should speak more carefully, but keep in mind that the listeners could sit and be relaxed (check if that day is a religious day of any kind).

6. Suggest to them how interesting it would be to sit down in the factory/mill for an hour to learn, to relax and learn in classes according to their level of English.

7. At the end of the talk, a little exaggeration is called for in thanking them for listening to you. Wish them success, peace and happiness in the future. Also, a sort of assurance that ILT would do its best, if classes begin, to see that they learn what they need.

B. Use of Mother-Tongue Interviews in Survey
Before the interview, operatives should be welcomed, and the purpose of the interview explained precisely. This is to help ILTU (1) to understand your difficulties; (2) to organise classes according to your levels of English. NOTE: This has nothing to do with redundancy. Politely, and in passing, ask if they would agree to its being recorded. Tell them that we can't remember everything that is said, and it helps us to discuss together as I (mother tongue interviewer) can't listen to all of them at one time.

Who should be interviewed in the mother tongue
If possible all ethnic minorities except those who cannot speak the language of their ethnic group. (It is, however, interesting to find out why they can't speak it.)

   Older workers are likely to have spent more time in the mill. They often have interesting comments to make on their working experiences and the problems they have faced. They may also speak out on their attitudes towards their employers.

   Group leaders/South Asian supervisors. These workers need a sympathetic approach with extended friendly conversation. It is important to let them see that you realise they are important and have valuable information to contribute to the survey.

Points to remember when interviewing
1. The mother tongue interview can be used to expand on problem areas revealed in earlier interviews in English.

2. South Asians often think what they did in their country (or East Africa) is irrelevant. Their background, past experiences and skills should be emphasised.

TRAINING MATERIAL 5.5 MOTHER TONGUE INTERVIEWS
[Charan Singh Bamhrah, Lancashire ILT]   *continued*

---

3. Personal problems are expressed emotionally. It is very important to know where to stop? When? How?

4. Always listen attentively. Even if it is not interesting, don't interrupt abruptly (in the way an English person might).

5. How to change topics/move the interview forward. Pick up a very small incident described before and be apologetic in asking a question about that; the answer will either be a short one or there will be a pause. Use this opportunity to put other questions on the next topic.

6. Avoid listening too much to their grudges against a particular employee/supervisor/foreman. This always creates situations which are difficult to control, and the interviews will not be so useful. (Because you only have one side of the complaints.)

7. Be prepared for people to want to contact you at home or in the office with queries, but watch out, they might only be thinking of getting help in solving personal problems at work, or even in the family. It depends on you how far you want to commit yourself, but there is always a limit.

This was the first time that ILT had undertaken extensive interviewing in students' first language or attempted to elicit student perceptions in a systematic way. There had also been very little published giving the autobiographical experiences of ethnic-minority workers (with notable exceptions: Sharma 1971; Wilson 1978).

During this phase of the project, students on training courses were interviewed. The majority of them were interviewed before, during and after the course in order to chart their perceptions and any changes as a result of the course.

Data 5.5 is an extract from the report of an interview with a Punjabi worker who was on an elementary language course. HR had come to Britain in 1979 from the Punjab, where he had worked on his family's farm and then run a shop. He came to Britain to marry a Punjabi woman who had been educated in this country. For several months he either stayed at home or asked his wife to accompany him everywhere since he had no experience of English. But, as will be apparent from this data, his needs and aspirations go beyond instrumental language for survival; they rest on the need for power over the direction of his own life. To achieve this he needs to believe in himself as a learner and to use the course as a kick-start to seize the initiative for his own continued learning of English.

DATA 5.5 INTERVIEW DATA   [Walsall ILT]

His father-in-law and a few family friends tried to find some work for
H.Raj but only in places where other Panjabis were working. He
thought that because of his language problem he would never be able
to find a job.

After a few weeks of depression and frustration he managed to get
out of the house but would not dare go to employment agencies such
as the Job Centre. However, three months after his arrival he heard
from one of his Panjabi acquaintances that there was a job vacant in
the bakery and that if he were interested he must approach one of the
Asian foremen at the bakery.

The following morning H.Raj went to the bakery and asked (in
Panjabi) for the Panjabi-speaking foreman and when he told the
foreman about the vacancy the foreman took him to the production
manager and did most of the talking. H.Raj just stood there without
speaking a word. As the bakery wanted somebody urgently the foreman explained to H.Raj in Panjabi about the production line and
H.Raj's work and asked him to start work on the afternoon shifts of
the same day. He did not receive any training and received simple
instruction in Panjabi from the foreman. He was very happy as in that
job he did not have to do any talking and the work, he thought was
simple. 'There was nothing technical about this job, I learnt it automatically by watching other people do it.'

Gradually H.Raj came to know other Panjabi-speaking Asians in the
bakery, which gave him some comfort as he could communicate with
other people in Punjabi and did not have to face English-speaking people. At this stage H.Raj's ambition to learn English faded away as he
thought he did not need it at work or at home.

When we were to start the course at the bakery H.Raj was not clear
about his needs and our role. He thought he could manage without it
but when we explained in Panjabi, that he might be able to benefit
from the course he became a little bit interested. In the beginning he
found it extremely difficult but at the same time we gave him some
work on literacy. Within a few weeks he showed great enthusiasm and
improvement in his written work. With his writing he obtained help
and full support from his wife but was still confused by spoken
English and the difference in the sound system of Panjabi and English.

He tried hard to communicate in English and gained some self-
confidence, which had been shaken by his inability to explain under
stress on one occasion. At work he was accused by the manager of
throwing two large loaves in the rubbish bin, a deed which he had not
done. Despite repeating 'me no cleaner', he could not explain that it
was the cleaner who threw bread in the bin thinking it was scrap
(normal cleaning procedure at the bakery if the loaves are on the
floor). Eventually one of the Panjabi chargehands intervened and

DATA 5.5 INTERVIEW DATA *continued*

explained the whole incident to the manager, leaving H.Raj somehow annoyed and frustrated. 'I tried to explain to him but could not speak more than a few words, later on I realised that at least I could have said **"cleaner put bread in bin no me".**'

As a result of these experiences, his attitude towards his own needs had changed radically from when he first arrived in the UK. He now felt that both for home and work he needed to be able to communicate if he was to participate in the activities surrounding him.

His perception of language was also changing as the course progressed. Initially he had seen English as something static you either acquired or didn't acquire. It was not pure jesting on his part to ask if there was no injection for learning English. After some weeks he was more aware of the fact that acquiring a language is a dynamic process and that the two languages in question did not have equivalents on a one-to-one basis.

By the end of the course he was getting a lot of help from his wife in learning English, though she herself found it difficult to give satisfactory answers to his questions. It was not only evident to the tutors as a need, but he himself explicitly asked for further tuition.

Data 5.6 is a case study of another student, written up from three in-depth interviews in his native Panjabi and in English, and illustrates the restrictions and frustrations he has faced.

4.4 Materials development

As we have said, three areas had been selected for materials development to reflect the specific objectives of the project:
– listening – including using the media;
– literacy;
– using students' personal resources.

Listening skills

The objective of the listening materials was to activate the receptive skills students already have and use these to assist students in using the English they could hear around them to develop their oral language. Literacy was not a prerequisite. The focus was on helping people to develop their listening so that they could learn wherever they were.

DATA 5.6 THE COST OF JOB–SEEKING [Lancashire ILT]

Personal Background
He comes from India.
He is 29 years old, married with two children.
He came to England in 1977.

Education
He went to school in India for eight years, and during the last four years he learned some formal English. He also attended an in-company industrial language training course, which improved his spoken English. He himself commented on now being able to choose between different ways of saying things, according to the circumstances.

Previous employment
He had worked for three years as a winder at a textile mill, before being made redundant in June 1980.

Job-seeking
Initially he had had high hopes. He went to every possible factory for miles around in search of jobs, focussing primarily on textile and paper mills, and carpet factories. He calculated that he had visited forty factories. He not only asked about vacancies, but also tried to see the personnel officer, and left his address in case of any future vacancy arising.

He went to the local Jobcentre once a week, and subsequently fortnightly. He was under the impression that in order to have his name put forward for a job, a person had to be registered at that particular Jobcentre, so he registered at eight different ones in the area.

However, one incident caused him to doubt the usefulness of Jobcentres. He saw a vacancy advertised in the Jobcentre, and travelled straight to the factory, only to be told that there was no vacancy. He went back to the Jobcentre, saw the job card still on the board, and explained what had happened. The Jobcentre clerk merely replied: 'Sorry, maybe they have already appointed someone'. He was very depressed about this, and asked the interviewer; 'Do you think that in the space of ten minutes that vacancy had been filled?'

The Cost of Job-Seeking
He had a car which he used almost exclusively for job-seeking. He had travelled to virtually every town in Lancashire and Greater Manchester. All these efforts, combined with the rising cost of petrol, had been a considerable drain on his resources, with the result that he was having difficulties paying bills and his mortgage.

Finally, his wife became annoyed at the amount of money he was spending on travel, since she needed more to feed the children. At

DATA 5.6 THE COST OF JOB–SEEKING [Lancashire ILT]
continued

the same time he was worried how he could convince the DHSS [Department of Health and Social Security] that he needed money while he still ran a car. He argued that he used the car exclusively for trying to find work, and was upset when they visited his house to check on his circumstances. [His wife understood that such visits were normal, but she also wondered why the DHSS were not happy with the information they had provided.]

Seeking Work Abroad
He also contacted friends in a European country by letter about the possibilities of finding work there. He was told that there were jobs, but that accommodation was the big problem. One friend offered to help him for a month, but absolutely no longer. (Later he got information that jobs were not so easily available, and that there was sometimes a considerable waiting time, during which he would be unable to claim benefit.) He was also concerned – and unable to ascertain – if his wife would be able to claim benefit during his absence. She was not very happy about the prospect of him going there, but they would both have accepted the separation if it had been possible financially. In the absence of clear information, they decided that it was not feasible to maintain two households.

Training
He had also asked for an interview about training opportunities, but this had not been a success. He would have accepted any training available, and listed no less than six very different trades as being of special interest to him. However, he was simply told that there were long waiting lists, and advised to look at the job cards. He felt that their questions were irrelevant and was annoyed by them. This in turn caused him to doubt again to what extent the Jobcentre was prepared to help him.

Family Pressures
Because his relatives knew that he was out of work, they tended to come at any time and stay longer, thus actually becoming a serious financial burden. This caused friction between him and his wife, since each blamed the other for the lack of consideration shown by their respective relatives. Their sense of family duty however prevented them from saying anything to their relatives.

Recommendations for Improving the System
Like many other interviewees, he felt that Jobcentres would serve unemployed Asians more effectively if they employed an Asian who spoke different languages, and could explain not only the facts about jobs and training courses, but also the concepts behind them. For example, he

DATA 5.6 THE COST OF JOB–SEEKING [Lancashire ILT]
continued

himself had seen a job vacancy card for a driver which stipulated that building experience was required, but he was unable to find out why.

He also commented on English people's apparent urge for efficiency, and cited as an example the extent of work study carried out in the textile mills. He then queried whether any work study took place within the DHSS, and suggested as a suitable area of study the time involved in conducting interviews with Asians through friends acting as interpreters.

Overall comment
Having been unsuccessful in so many attempts at getting a job, he has begun to feel frustrated. He feels that if there ever are jobs, white un-employed people will get priority, possibly because employers feel more confident in their ability to manage them.

We concentrated on directing students towards using:

(a) *The media.* This really means television, as even very basic students appear to spend a lot of time watching a great variety of programmes.

(b) *The family.* Many students have members of their family, especially children, who are native or near-native speakers of English. A spin-off may well be an increased and constructive involvement of the family in the learner's efforts to acquire English.

(c) *Native speakers in the workplace.* Again, these could become a continuing resource for the student when the teacher has left.

(d) *The tape-recorder.* Many students have tape-recorders but have never viewed them as a language-learning resource except in the hands of the teacher.

The obvious problems in learning from the English spoken in the environment by native speakers are the speed and complexity of the language. The approach of the project was therefore to ask students to listen for specific elements or aspects of language at any one time. The listening materials focused on the following elements:

(i) Isolated features:
  – lexical, e.g. use of names;
  – structural;
  – tone and stress.
(ii) Broader features:
  – the meaning and significance of feedback;
  – functional topics, e.g. making requests.

As the first topics for developing this approach, we chose the use of names as an example of listening for lexis, and 'introductions' as an example of a functional topic. Two sets of materials were developed around these topics. Each set included materials to be used in the class and suggestions for independent activities. The materials also included background notes for teachers so that they could help students to develop cross-linguistic and cross-cultural awareness. These background notes were written for teachers who were not from a South Asian background but were teaching students who were. Training Material 5.6 is an example from the beginning of an elementary course.

Using the media, particularly well-known television programmes, became the most widely used independent activity. For example, in listening for appropriacy, the soap opera *Crossroads* was used, and students were given worksheets to identify how and why the central characters addressed each other in the way they did. Several exercises were set around the function of introducing self and others since in most cases in the Indian subcontinent, people find out indirectly who a new person is. Another method used to help students make cross-linguistic comparisons was to make literal translations of English tapes. Such strategies are illustrated in Training Material 5.7.

Literacy

The survey of elementary courses referred to in the introduction to this chapter had indicated clearly that little or no work was done on developing literacy because short in-company courses seemed to provide little opportunity for such development. In the context of the student-autonomy project, it was important that literacy was focused upon in such a way that students could be enabled to identify learning strategies comfortable to them and that students achieved some quick results which would develop confidence and motivation to continue after the course.

TRAINING MATERIAL 5.6 WHAT'S IN A NAME?
[Birmingham ILT]

ILT

STUDENT AUTONOMY
– LISTENING FOR LEXIS
NAMING

Procedure

Aim: (a) To enable students to discriminate words at the very simplest level.
(b) To introduce students to listening to a tape recorder.

Suggestions for Presentations
1. Video clip from *Speak For Yourself*. Program 2. The section on filing systems to establish the importance attached to names in this society.
2. Photographs of characters from TV series that students know or public figures known to the students.
   – ask for first/fore/Christian/other names. Surnames etc.
3. Photographs of factory personnel
   – ask for information on names and nicknames.

Suggestions for Activities
1. Tapes of 15–20 names including students' name
   – students required to bang the table or stop the tape when they hear their own name.
2. Discussion of nicknames – have some examples from English and mother tongue (see background notes 1).
3. Form filling – games, flash cards, etc of students' names.

Suggestions for Independent Activities
1. Ask students to find out the names of their children's teachers. Report back to the class.
2. Ask students to find out surname/first name/other (middle) names of an English person they work with or a neighbour. Report back to class.
3. Listen to the news on TV/Radio and tick the worksheet in the columns provided for first name, surname, title etc. of the people featured in the news. The worksheets can be prepared very quickly when the teacher knows which personalities are likely to be featured. The headings could be varied according to the literacy level of the students. Students literate in their own language could add other names they heard in the relevant columns.

TRAINING MATERIAL 5.6 WHAT'S IN A NAME? [Brigid Bird, Birmingham ILT] *continued*

> If this was the first exercise students were asked to carry out at home it would be necessary for the teacher to bring a video or tape recording of the news into the classroom and get the students to complete the worksheets with the teacher's help.
>
> **Background Notes**
> *First names* are not used as freely as in Britain. They are used to address only:
> (i)   a person either younger or of lower status;
> (ii)   a woman by a man unless she is higher status;
> (iii) close friends.
> (People living in England are beginning to use first names more in the British system.)
> Other ways to address people:
> *Titles expressing a family relationship*
> Uncles and Aunts have very specific titles in Panjabi.
> *Father's family*
> (i)   Father's older brothers Taia ji and their wives Taii ji (might distinguish between old Taia and young Taia and middle Taia if there are several – when talking about them).
> (ii)   Father's younger brothers Chacha ji – wives Chachi ji
> (iii) Father's sisters' husbands Fufurd ji and wives Bhua ji (Also, Father's sisters' husbands' brothers and their wives.)
> *Mother's family*
> (iv)   Mother's brothers Mama ji – wives Mani ji (again might distinguish between 'old', 'middle', 'young'.)
> (v)   Mother's sisters' husbands Masur ji – wives Masi ji (also Mother's sisters' husbands' brothers.)
> All these titles are also likely to be used to people of similar age who are the same villages.
> (iv)   'Uncle' and 'Aunt' are also used to older people who are unrelated or from connected villages.
>
> *Brothers and sisters*
> (i)   Usually only use names if they are younger otherwise Bhaji (brother), Behenji (sister). When talking about them might distinguish between vedda (older Bhaji) and chote (young) Bhaji.
> (ii)   The words for brother and sister are also used to address people who are strangers or not well known, although 'Bira' may be used for brother by Panjabis.
>
> *Other Relationships*
> People may be addressed or described in terms of their children or other relationships. A wife is especially likely to address her husband as 'Shindo's father' as it is traditionally inappropriate for a wife to use her husband's name at all.

TRAINING MATERIAL 5.6 WHAT'S IN A NAME? [Brigid Bird,
Birmingham ILT] *continued*

Other relationships might be used in this way, e.g. someone who
addresses his wife as 'Surinder's sister-in-law' – Surinder being his
own younger brother.

People may also be addressed by their professional titles with the
addition of Ji or Sahib, e.g. Master Ji (teacher) High Commissioner
ji etc.

Surnames

Surnames are used as in English to people of higher status or who are
almost unknown, with either Ji or Sahib after or Sardar before.
(Though some people use their surnames among friends all the time as
though it were a first name.)

It is always the case that ji or some other word of respect is added to
a name unless speaking to a child. It is very coarse to leave it out –
hence people looking for an equivalent and using Mr. with a first name
to a supervisor.

Literacy materials:
Example

Person	Title	First Name	Surname
Prime Minister	Mrs	Margaret	Thatcher

Person	Title	First Name	Surname
the wages clerk	Mrs		Jones
your supervisor			York
a friend			
your doctor	Dr		
your uncle			
your child's teacher			
your personnel manager	Mr	Harold	

TRAINING MATERIAL 5.7 INTRODUCTIONS (Birmingham ILT)

---

ilt

STUDENT AUTONOMY
LISTENING FOR FUNCTIONS
INTRODUCTIONS

Procedure
Aim: To enable students to recognise introductions.

Suggestions for presentation
1. Tape. (See Tape 5.)
   Discussion
2. Tape from an answering machine.

Suggestion for activities
1. Tape of good and bad introductions (students say which are good/bad and say why).
2. Tape of English and Panjabi introductions. (See Tape 8.)

Suggestions for independent activities
1. TV Soap Opera – *Crossroads*. Listen for people introducing. Worksheet on naming and structures used. (See Worksheet 6.)
2. Ask students to listen to any members of their family who phone in English. Tick off names and structures in logs – or write in mother tongue – or record them.
3. They might be able to record a supervisor or record themselves doing this at work?

Background notes
Introduction
Introducing yourself or other people is not a commonly used function in Panjabi

Introducing yourself
1. In a formal situation you would wait to be asked your name – would not offer it.
2. If alone with a stranger (e.g. getting/giving a lift) would ask which village in Panjab a man was from and who his father was – would offer same information about self – but not name.
3. With a new colleague – would not introduce self, would make indirect enquiries about new person – they would do the same.

Introducing others
This is very rarely done. Would not be done in these situations where it would be essential in British culture.
1. With friend A you meet friend B – you would not introduce them to each other.
2. At the home of an acquaintance whose family is unknown to you – you would not be introduced.
3. At a friend's house where there are other visitors there would be no introductions.
4. Even if you take a friend to a house where she/he was a stranger – there would be no introductions even if you stayed for a few days!

TRAINING MATERIAL 5.7 INTRODUCTIONS   *continued*

---

5. Taking a friend to start in a factory you would not introduce him to fellow workers.

In most cases, people would find out indirectly who a new person is. It is, therefore, important to establish how crucial introducing people is in British culture.

Materials

Tape 5   Listening for appropriacy: Introducing self.

Use this tape to notice

(a) the difference structures based on the telephone, i.e. This is ..., It's ... here;

(b) the information given, e.g. address, place of work, family details;

(c) what name is used to describe self.

A: Handsworth Jobcentre.

B: Good morning. My name's Bird, Brigid Bird. I signed on at your centre last week.

A: 554 3207

B: Hello Mr. Hamood? My name is Brigid. I believe you are an old friend of my husband Abbas Ridha – I think you were at school together, is that right?

A: Clifford Covering.

B: Good morning, my name is Mrs. Bird, I'm phoning on behalf of Sardul Dhesi. He works in your Dipping Section.

A: Hello Housing Department.

B: Hello. My name is Bird and I live in a council flat in Swindon Road, Harborne.

A: Transport and General Union.

B: Hello, this is Joanna Brown – shop steward at Thornton Engineering.

A: 4231097.

B: Hello Anne. It's Brigid here.

WORKSHEET 6		Introducing	
Tick when you hear a name ☑			
Full Name	First Name	Surname	Title

TRAINING MATERIAL 5.7 INTRODUCTIONS *continued – third page*

Tape 8
Tape of introductions showing abbreviated forms of the verb. (To be translated word for word into Panjabi.)

1. Hello Clarice, this is my father.
   Dad, this is Clarice she's a colleague.

2. Hello Barbara. This is Bill – he's a friend of mine. Barbara's our secretary.

3. Hello Sardul. This is Mrs.Brown, we're neighbours. Sardul's a colleague of mine.

4. Oh hello Joan. This is my daughter, Hester. This is Mrs.Elson our new secretary.

5. Good morning, Mr. Hollyhock. This is Bill Sandhu, he's from the Coventry office. Mr. Hollyhock's the Principal of the College.

6. Good morning, Mr. Jones. How are you?
   This is Theresa McKenna, she's just joined us in the department. She's still finding her way round.

7. Hello Annie. This is Peter and Susan, they're old friends of mine. Annie is a colleague from London.

Literal Translation into Panjabi of Tape 8
This tape can be used to:
(a) Demonstrate English word order which is very rigid compared with Panjabi. It especially shows how pronoun and verb come next to each other, hence shortened form.
(b) Because it will sound so odd in Panjabi it may help a listener to register more clearly and therefore remember the points being made about introductions and the information given and the way names are used.

1. Hello Clarice, eh heh mere pitta ji
   Papa ji eh heh Clarice.

2. Hello Barbara. Eh heh Bill. Eh heh ik dost da mera. Barbara heh sadi secretary.

3. Hello Sardul. Eh heh Sirimati Brown.

4. Oh hello Joan. Eh heh meri lurki Hester. Eh heh Sirimati Elson sadi nemi secretary.

5. Chungi sever Sardar Hollyhock ji. Eh heh Bill Sandhu. Eh heh ton Coventry dufter.
   Sardar Hollyhock ji heh Principal da College.

TRAINING MATERIAL 5.7 INTRODUCTIONS *continued – fourth* *page*

---

6. Chungi sever, Sirdar Jones. Kida hun tusin.
   Eh heh Theresa McKenna. Eh huni lugi ethe wich mehkmi. Eh heh hun tak lebdi apna rah gol dara. (Eh huli kam sukdui heh)

7. Hello Annie. Eh heh Peter te Susan. Eh hun purane dost de mere. Annie heh ik

Tick when you hear these words.

My Name Is	This is	It's ... Here

The first task was to raise awareness of the need to provide skills for students that lead to autonomous learning in literacy. It was recognised that many students on elementary courses had no literacy skills at all. Instead of attempting to teach basic word recognition with work-related material, it was decided to develop a general basic-literacy programme, using already well-tried methods in adult literacy. A phonic approach was adopted because it would support adult self-study. However, it provided a rigid checklist which was not orientated towards communication. This approach was complemented by Freire's method (Freire 1975), using a sight vocabulary of relevant key generative words to build up phonemic families and word fields. Finally, the language-experience method was used to generate written language and reading material from transcriptions of the students' own oral narratives and discussions.

In addition to very basic materials on sound / symbol relationships, handwriting and basic word-attack skills, the project developed two types of task-based materials. One type was to develop both reading and writing skills in obvious functional areas such as letter-writing and form-filling. The second task was to produce a series of reference materials, such as specialised context-specific dictionaries to develop access and reference skills. Training Material 5.8 gives examples.

TRAINING MATERIAL 5.8 LITERACY – FUNCTIONAL SKILLS

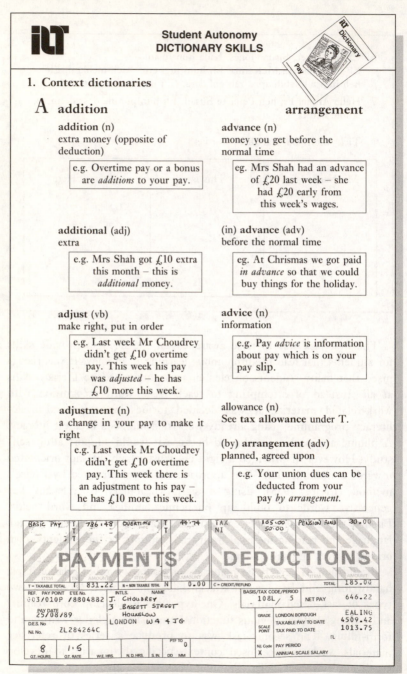

ilt

**Student Autonomy
DICTIONARY SKILLS**

1. Context dictionaries

A addition   arrangement

addition (n)
extra money (opposite of
deduction)

> e.g. Overtime pay or a bonus
> are *additions* to your pay.

advance (n)
money you get before the
normal time

> eg. Mrs Shah had an advance
> of £20 last week – she
> had £20 early from
> this week's wages.

additional (adj)
extra

> e.g. Mrs Shah got £10 extra
> this month – this is
> *additional* money.

(in) advance (adv)
before the normal time

> eg. At Chrismas we got paid
> *in advance* so that we could
> buy things for the holiday.

adjust (vb)
make right, put in order

> e.g. Last week Mr Choudrey
> didn't get £10 overtime
> pay. This week his pay
> was *adjusted* – he has
> £10 more this week.

advice (n)
information

> e.g. Pay *advice* is information
> about pay which is on your
> pay slip.

adjustment (n)
a change in your pay to make it
right

> e.g. Last week Mr Choudrey
> didn't get £10 overtime
> pay. This week there is
> an adjustment to his pay –
> he has £10 more this week.

allowance (n)
See **tax allowance** under T.

(by) arrangement (adv)
planned, agreed upon

> e.g. Your union dues can be
> deducted from your
> pay *by arrangement*.

| BASIC PAY | T | 786·48 | OVERTIME | T | 44·74 | TAX | 105·00 | PENSION FUND | 30·00 |
| | T | | | T | | NI | 50·00 | | |

PAYMENTS   **DEDUCTIONS**

| ITEMS | | AMOUNT | ITEMS | | AMOUNT | | AMOUNT | ITEMS | AMOUNT |

| T – TAXABLE TOTAL | T | 831.22 | N = NON TAXABLE TOTAL | N | 0·00 | C = CREDIT/REFUND | | TOTAL | 185.00 |

REF. PAY POINT	E'EE No.	INTLS.	NAME	BASIS/TAX CODE/PERIOD	
003/010P	18804882	J. CHOUDREY	108L / 5	NET PAY	646.22
		3 BASSETT STREET		
PAY DATE 25/08/89		HOUNSLOW		
		LONDON W4 4JG	GRADE	LONDON BOROUGH	EALING
D.E.S. No				TAXABLE PAY TO DATE	4509.42
N.I. No.	ZL284264C		SCALE POINT	TAX PAID TO DATE	1013.75
					rL

| 8 | 1·5 | | | PTF TO 0 | | N.I. Code | PAY PERIOD | |
| O.T. HOURS | O.T. RATE | W.E. HRS. | N.D. HRS. | S. IN. | DD MM | X | ANNUAL SCALE SALARY | |

TRAINING MATERIAL 5.8 LITERACY – FUNCTIONAL SKILLS
continued

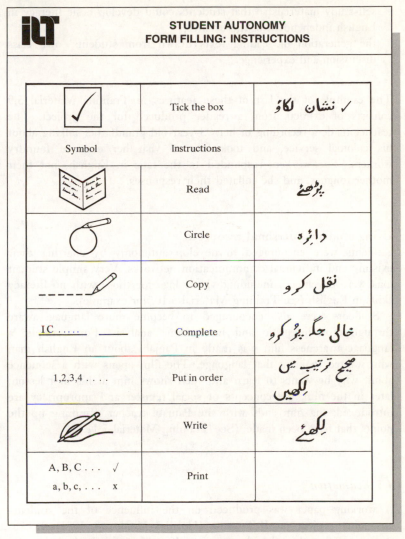

Symbol	Instructions	
✓	Tick the box	✓ نشان لگاؤ
	Read	پڑھئے
○	Circle	دائرہ
✏	Copy	نقل کرو
IC ..... ____	Complete	خالی جگہ پُر کرو
1,2,3,4	Put in order	صحیح ترتیب میں لکھیں
✍	Write	لکھئے
A, B, C . . . ✓ a, b, c, . . . x	Print	

The literacy materials were carefully graded, starting with very basic identification but using realia throughout.

Other features of these materials were:

- questionnaires about literacy use to encourage motivation;
- a focus on real material which included very few demands on literacy, e.g. greetings card;
- a focus on items requiring specific social knowledge, e.g. addresses

and how to address people (linked with the listening materials on names) (see Training Material 5.6, p. 303);
- self-study materials so that students could develop basic literacy in English independent of the teacher;
- the generation of reading texts drawn from students' own class discussion and experience.

The example of the last of these features in Training Material 5.9 consists of extracts from a reader produced for the project. The teacher made a recording of her 93-year-old grandfather talking about his colonial service, and took him to visit her class of foundry workers. The workers responded to the tape in English, not their mother tongues, and she collated their responses.

Using students' personal resources

Students were encouraged to develop autonomy by charting their existing and individual communication networks. Very simple student logs were developed, including visual logs for those with no literacy skills in English (see Training Material 5.10, for example).

Students were also encouraged to become more language-aware through cross-linguistic and inter-ethnic analysis. For example: a language-awareness film was made in Panjabi about an English man who wanted to learn that language. The film opens with a sequence about why he wants to learn and then shows him at his first lesson; later in the film, the concepts of social register and appropriacy are introduced; the film ends with the Panjabi teacher summing up the points that have been made. (See Training Material 5.11.)

4.5 Evaluation

A working paper was produced on the influence of the student-autonomy project on ILT units (Hoadley-Maidment 1981). It was recognised that there had been some difficulties with both the needs-analysis and materials-development aspects of the project. The ethnographic interviewing of students was limited both by the economic recession, which reduced the number of courses as factories closed or went on short time, and by some difficulties in finding and training enough interviewers who shared a first language with the students. The general conclusion from this aspect of the project was that needs analysis should be part of a continual dialogue with

TRAINING MATERIAL 5.9 ALL WE DOING IS DEFENDING
[Barbara Darling, Walsall ILT]

Student Autonomy
READING : ALL WE DOING IS DEFENDING

Teacher's Grandfather	*Students*

Those wonderful places

I had a lot to do with the British Empire. I served in the West Indies, I served in West Africa, and I served in China, in Singapore and Ceylon – all those wonderful places.
They learned all they knew from us. We took the trouble to teach them. We introduced our ways to all the different places.
The British Empire was a very good thing indeed.

All the same

They wanted to make themselves comfortable all over the world. Not to make other countries OK. They wanted to say to other countries, look, we are the greater. It might be that other people were without clothes, without money, without anything – and that is wrong.

Something for nothing

They come over here, they get dole, they get unemployment money – something for nothing.

We work

I completely disagree with it, that people come over here and are scroungers.
We work. We sweat for it. We come here to work hard. To be quiet. We don't get the money easily, we sweat for it. Believe me about this.
God makes people, and he promised all the people: all will be the same. All would be born after nine months. Some British people didn't understand. We don't blame them all.

These people come here

It's all very fine, these people to come here – they come to get their living of course – we know. And they take a living away from the native English. They're very well in their own way. One doesn't mind, one puts up with them.

The hard jobs

The coloured people come for the hard jobs.
– Not the easy jobs.
– For casting, for the foundries, for the hard jobs.
– On the heavy jobs.

What I say

If someone comes to me and says, 'You've got our jobs,' I say: 'Tell Thatcher!'

TRAINING MATERIAL 5.9 ALL WE DOING IS DEFENDING
continued

Brixton, 1981

If the police try to keep things decent, it isn't up to these people to go chucking petrol bombs at them and stones and God knows what: just because the police won't do what they want them to do.
They want to behave as though they were in Jamaica or Barbados – well, they're not in any of those places – they're in London!. Which is a bit different.
And it's up to them to adapt themselves to our ways, not us to conform to their ways! We are the majority. We provide the homes for them, their food, their outlook and everything else. And the police to look after them.

One day I was walking from Halesowen. I see some kids, they come up, they open the window of the car, and they are swearing – you know, I can't tell you what they are saying. You know, funny words. I said to them, OK, go home, it's no good for you to say that. And I know my colour. And I won't give you back an answer for what you say to me. Because I am not foolish like you. I feel sad. Moved by all this talking.

Thousands without work

Myself I've been here twenty five years. I never make no trouble, never fight no-one, I never steal from nobody, no, not at all. I've been working hard, I've been looking after my family, and I've been working for the company, the same company for twenty three years. I've never been heard them words, like I hear them now, on the TV and news and that. The problem. And this problem is from a few people, they don't understand. Now the problem is small. Maybe afterwards, the problem grows big. Same as Brixton, fighting, fifty six policemen, you know, have...accident. It's better for the government to stop this problem.
This problem is because no men work. They don't have work. Plenty of firms are closing. Thousands without work. All this problem started from the work. The man with children in the house. What can he do?

He's 93, an old man, he must be wise, know what's right. We're young, we must listen to him, to what he says.

TRAINING MATERIAL 5.10   ENGLISH CONTACT LOG

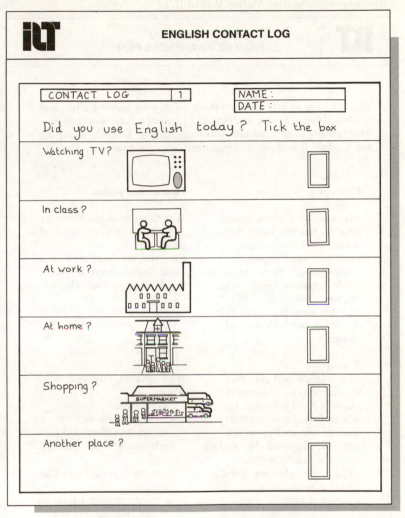

ENGLISH CONTACT LOG

CONTACT LOG   1   NAME :
                           DATE :

Did you use English today? Tick the box

Watching TV?

In class?

At work?

At home?

Shopping?

Another place?

students built into the course. So the major influence of the needs analysis was not to draw up any definitive list of students' language and literacy needs but to sensitise teachers to a much more student-centred view of the learning process, including syllabus negotiation.

Difficulties with materials development related to the challenge of developing autonomy among ethnic-minority workers with very little experience of English. First, it was difficult for students to accept concepts of using students' personal resources for self-direction when personal autonomy is eroded by discrimination and disadvantage. It

TRAINING MATERIAL 5.11 LANGUAGE AWARENESS FILM
[Ram Chandola and Alan Murray Walsall ILT]

ilt

Student Autonomy
LANGUAGE AWARENESS FILM

The film aims to help students think about what learning a language
involves. It aims to give students and teachers a basis to talk about
what is being taught and how it is being taught. The film is in Panjabi
and English. It is about an Englishman who wants to learn Panjabi.

Content

Scene 4

Alan goes for his first lesson.
Ram teaches him *words*. Some
are names of things: man,
hand, pen, skin, banana,
orange, mango. Some are verbs
(in the infinitive form): walk,
eat, sleep, fall, dance, fight.
Alan has some pronounciation
difficulties but both are well
pleased.

Scene 5

Alan is in the park. He sees
someone slip on a banana skin
and falls about laughing. He
sees an Indian man coming
along an and goes up to tell
him what happened. He tries to
use the words he learnt,
keeping to English word order.
The man is unable to
understand him.

Scene 6

Alan goes to see Ram again and
tries to tell him in Panjabi
what happened in the park.

Ram cannot understand at first
but then sorts out a meaningful
Punjabi sentence and gives
Alan the new version:-

Discussion points

Was this a good place to start?
What kinds of words are hard to
learn?
Can Alan use these words now?
What English words do students
find hard to say/hear clearly?

Why can't the man understand
Alan?
–   word order
–   verbs in infinitive;
–   no function words, to show
    relations between words; (of,
    on)
–   one word sounds very like
    another
–   a word can have 2 meanings
    in one language but not in
    another.

TRAINING MATERIAL 5.11 LANGUAGE AWARENESS FILM
continued – second page

(i) /chamṛi/ ਚਮੜੀ means *human skin* but not *fruit* skin.

(ii) /tərna/ ਤਰਨਾ means to swim,
/tʌrna/ ਤੁਰਨਾ means to walk.

(iii) 'banana' and 'skin' need a function word to link them /kele di chhɪl/ ਕੇਲੇ ਦੀ ਛਿਲ

(iv) the word order needs changing.

(v) /dɪgṇa/ ਡਿਗਣਾ (-fall) needs to be changed to /dɪg gɪa/ ਡਿੱਗ ਗਿਆ (fell).

Ram says, in Panjabi, that he has taught Alan some words but he needs to teach him how to put them together.

Scene 9
Alan and Ram are out together canvassing at various houses. Alan is keen to try out his Panjabi. He goes to the first house and a child answers the door. Alan greets him using a respectful title and a plural form of "you" and of the verb. The child giggles.

Why does the child laugh?

Alan turns to Ram for an explanation. He felt he made his question *sound* like a question. Ram explains that it is something else. He should have used different words.

What differences are there between talking to someone younger/older than you in Panjabi?

Alan tries at the next house. An old man comes to the door and Alan uses the forms appropriate to a child (as just taught by Ram).

/tū/ ਤੂੰ   /tʌsī/ ਤੁਸੀਂ

/rɛnde/ ਰਹਿੰਦੇ   /rɛnda/ ਰਹਿੰਦਾ

The young man standing behind the old man shouts at Alan that he has no respect for an older person.

Alan is very puzzled.

What differences can you make in English?

was difficult for students to assert themselves in choosing learning objectives, selecting methods, and transferring this assertiveness to other aspects of their everyday lives, when they feel under attack by a white society whose language they are expected to learn.

Second, the concept of autonomy, like that of identity, is itself a culture-bound notion. Its roots lie in Western and European notions of the self and the individual which have influenced recent practice in making the learner more independent and turning the teacher into a facilitator. The combination of cultural difference and language difficulties, when trying to introduce this concept, meant that some students found exercises in autonomous learning bewildering, irrelevant, and unfamiliar, given the strong tradition of learning through other methods which the majority had experienced. (It must be said that learner autonomy is often resisted by learners, whatever their ethnic and linguistic backgrounds.)

This mismatch between the ideological concept of autonomy and autonomy in practice also affected the quality of learning materials produced for the elementary level in some respects. It proved difficult to provide material and related activities which genuinely reflected the maturity and experience of learners who were at this level of acquisition, and who were back at the beginning whatever their age and status. Feedback from teachers and students indicated a need to rethink some of the logging activities suggested, and in particular to give attention to the learners' need to negotiate recognition of their student status within the family, especially with regard to women workers.

Lastly, most existing work on student autonomy had been developed with foreign-language students, often at higher-education levels. With such learners,

- choosing the learner objectives
- deciding the content
- assessing progress and performance
- selecting method and technique

(Holec 1979)

are all possible as part of a self-determining, critical-thinking culture. But for ethnic-minority workers with little oral English and no literacy skills either in their first language or in English, this approach often seemed irrelevant or was simply too difficult to convey.

Having acknowledged the difficulties, it was also important to identify in what ways the student-autonomy project was useful within a learner-centred approach. It changed and developed thinking and practice in a number of ways:

1. Both teachers and students understood better the objectives behind the course methods.

2. Students became more aware of language as a system and a resource and teachers helped them to develop a metalanguage in order to do this.
3. Teachers put much greater emphasis on listening skills, particularly in the way these could be developed through the media. These ideas were subsequently taken up by the BBC in their ESL series, *Switch on to English,* for which Clarice Brierley and Brigid Bird of Birmingham ILT were consultants.
4. Through log-books and diaries some students started to do their own needs analysis and to begin the process of self-assessment.
5. Students developed self-help in literacy skills.
6. There were organisational changes to courses partly influenced by the project and partly because redundancies and short-time working meant, in some areas, that students could attend longer courses. More follow-up sessions were organised to help students sustain their learning once the formal course was over, and students were counselled through links with local adult-education services.

The lasting positive benefits of the project, then, did not lie in a specific set of polished materials but rather in new ideas, methodology and a liberating sense that the traditional EFL/ESL approaches could be challenged. It introduced a more radical rhetoric into teaching methods and this rhetoric was at least in part matched by changed practice in broadening the curriculum. It encouraged use of first languages positively and systematically in the classroom to focus on student perception of need and to recognise and use the language knowledge and strengths of the students (most of whom already knew more than one language) to engage all students at whatever level of English in the analytic techniques developed for post-elementary students.

The project was about learning and second-language acquisition rather than syllabus and teaching. It represented a real departure from the analytic focus and a commitment to the experiential/ethnographic focus. ILT trainers no longer felt trapped in a type of programmed work in which data was collected and models of good practice introduced. There was a shift towards learning process rather than performance product and towards a relative view of language and culture. It took ethnography into the classroom and used the learners' experience and perceptions as teacher data and learner content.

All these effects were necessary and liberating. However, there was a danger of teachers reacting so strongly against analytic approaches that courses could become unstructured and essentially ephemeral as anything raised by students was admitted and a sense of goals and direction was lost.

The third development programme, therefore, which is described in the next section, represents a synthesis of the analytic and experiential. Part of this project was informed by the ethnographic interviewing of the student-autonomy project, and the curriculum design and methodology drew both on the communication skills based model described in section 1 of this chapter and on the increased attention to learning described in this section.

5 Project Three: Communication for opportunity and training

5.1 *The context*

During the late 1970s, ethnic-minority workers in traditional industry in the North and the Midlands were hit by mass unemployment. Many had worked for up to twenty years in unskilled jobs. ILT undertook a series of research and development projects to link language learning with access to vocational skills training and employment opportunities mostly for redundant workers. The programme described in this last section then had as its context the economic recession and the disproportionate impact of unemployment on ethnic minorities.

Even at this time of very high unemployment amongst the whole population, the ethnic minorities experience above average rates of unemployment. Within this disadvantaged group, Asians from the subcontinent are particularly badly affected. Groups of Indian subcontinent origin (but excluding East African Asians) make up over 50% of all the EMG unemployed and unemployment amongst these groups is growing faster than among any other ethnic groups.

	Nov 1979	Nov 1980	% increase
1. Total unemployed	1,292,284	2,071,188	+ 60.3%
2. Ethnic minority groups unemployed	48,420	82,541	+ 70.5%
3. Indian subcontinent unemployed	23,346	43,320	+ 85.6%

(Jupp 1981)

In response to the increasing numbers of redundant Asian textile workers in Lancashire (which was, until the late 1970s, the centre of the cotton textile industry in Britain), the CRE funded a research project which was carried out by Roger Munns, Charan Bamhrah and Peter Furnborough of the Lancashire ILT Unit, *In Search of Employment and Training* (Lancashire ILT Unit 1983). The research aimed to establish the training needs of redundant Asian workers. It aimed to do this by identifying the experiences and perceptions of these workers and their understanding of the agencies responsible for assisting them.

The methodology of the research was to use the ethnographic interviewing techniques, in the informants' first language, developed by ILT staff in the student-autonomy project. A hundred workers from three large mills who had recently been made redundant were interviewed three times over a period of a year. The profile of the workers that emerged from these findings showed:

59% were between 16 and 35 years of age and only 5% were over 55 years of age;
70% had lived in Britain more than 5 years;
90% had some secondary education, most of them in their country of origin;
15% had good levels of oral English;
14% could read and write well.

So there were large numbers of young men, well settled in Britain with a reasonable amount of education, but, for the great majority, not enough experience of written or oral English to gain employment again easily or to be accepted for existing retraining courses.

These findings were in stark contrast to the stereotyped assumptions of the Manpower Services Commission's employment and training services and company personnel officers which were elicited in informal discussions. The view of the world expressed by the informants challenged the stereotyped assumptions made by the agencies in a number of ways. Contradicting the prevailing stereotypes about them, redundant workers were not able to set up their own business because of lack of capital and business experience. They were not unwilling to work outside, for example in construction jobs, as the agencies thought. In fact, when asked, the great majority of workers said they would take any job. The final stereotype, that Asian workers were more mobile and would leave Britain to find jobs in Europe and elsewhere, again proved to be false.

The perspective on their situation which emerged was of a complex set of factors all working on each other to produce increased

Figure 5.1

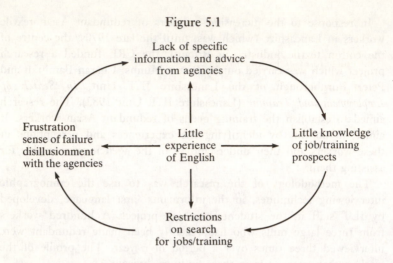

frustration, disillusionment and a sense of failure. (See Fig 5.1 above)
For those with little experience of English, the collapse of their
working lives was rationalised as a specific attack on the Asian
community. The decline of the textile industry was coupled with the
new discriminatory legislation on nationality and thus seen as part of a
deliberate policy to drive black people out of Britain.

The survey of redundant workers in Lancashire showed that 80 per
cent of the redundant workers were under 45. So most workers had
half or more of their working life ahead of them. They represented a
group for whom little experience of English had been no barrier to
employment in the past but who now found that they were not
seriously considered at all for employment or training unless they
could communicate well.

This cluster of disadvantages affecting Asian workers is devastating: race,
lack of skill, lack of varied work experience, lack of English. It is not
surprising that so many should be found on the bottom rung of the
unemployed despite the evidence that they are less selective than other
work seekers. Language enters into the process of indirect discrimination
and disadvantage, because the 'gateways' to employment and training
increasingly involve literacy and formal oral interviews. So people are
increasingly evaluated and judged on the basis of their ability to
communicate. In addition, an initial judgement is often made about
whether a person's English is good enough for them to be considered at all.
These judgements are almost invariably made on little evidence and by
people with little skill and no training in language assessment. The result is
that Asians often find themselves turned away before they are even
considered.

(Lancashire ILT Unit 1983).

For example, a tutor who took her English-language class for unemployed people to the local Jobcentre reported:

> An Indian male student then requested an interview about a bakery job in X. Before he went to the desk I explained the early hours to him. He came back without the job details. The girl who had interviewed him came up to me and all the group saying that the Indian did not know enough English. She said all of the group needed to speak English all the time and that it was no good just understanding their teacher. It was no good sending them for an interview unless it was an employer who took people like them. It was a waste of a £1 bus fare. At one point she looked at a student, who was looking at me for clarification, and said 'See, she doesn't understand *me*'.
> The students were rather disheartened after this but carried on looking around.
>
> (op. cit.)

In response, the Lancashire ILT Unit began to devise training programmes in which communication and basic education were linked to preparatory vocational training. While this initial work was being developed in Lancashire, NCILT carried out a research and development project on existing MSC-funded courses for both bilingual and white workers. Both programmes are described here.

These two projects were informed by two basic assumptions: the need to invest in research and development on learner experience and perceptions, as well as curriculum design, and the need to experiment with new types of provision which were both learner-centred and tackled the institutional barriers which discriminate against black people. The investment in research involved extensive interviewing of ethnic-minority workers and a programme of workshop and classroom observation so that the communicative styles and learning assumptions of both trade-skills instructors and trainees could be analysed.

These projects were also set within a wider context of redundancies and unemployment nationally. Course design and methodology had to take account of both the nature of future job opportunities and the quality of counselling and training provision currently available. Working primarily with redundant workers to enable them to retrain also provided a very different context from training employed workers. Redundant workers, typically, found themselves on a number of short courses with long gaps of unemployment between them and an increasing sense of frustration and loss of confidence. New types of provision, therefore, were needed which embedded formal training into longer periods of part-time training, self-study and support and counselling. The case was also repeatedly put for coordinated and stepped provision across the whole spectrum of education and training courses for adults.

The focus in all the projects was on learning rather than language. Language was not treated as a separate subject but was part of an integrated approach to the curriculum. Considerably more attention was paid to curriculum design from a learner-centred point of view and to the integration of basic education and vocational skills. So the conceptual framework was one which synthesised analytic and experiential/ethnographic approaches. The student-autonomy project had put learning at the centre and this, combined with our increased understanding of cross-cultural communication, made cross-cultural learning a much more explicit component of the curriculum.

The influences from both within and outside ILT on these projects stemmed partly from the theories of interaction (described in Chapter 2) but, more significantly, from research and documentation on racial discrimination and disadvantage in job-seeking and training (Jupp 1981; Smith 1982) and from observation and practice within ILT, including ethnographic interviewing of redundant workers, and observation and analysis at Jobcentres and training centres. Many of these insights were used in the cross-cultural training for government training and employment advisory officers, described in Chapter 3. In addition, writers on independent learning from outside the language field, for example Jourard (1972), influenced the Lancashire work on integrating independent learning into retraining courses.

In this section, we describe four specific projects which addressed this context of unemployment and discrimination. Each project provided a creative and subsequent critique of the previous project. The four projects are:

1. NCILT research and development on government-funded preparatory courses.
2. Lancashire ILT's communication for Employment and Training.
3. Lancashire ILT's Independent Learning Project.
4. Lancashire ILT's Training for Change programme.

5.2   College preparatory courses

This was a one-year research project (Roberts and Opienski 1985) to analyse and develop full-time courses (varying in length between three months and nine months), based in colleges of further education. The courses were designed both for bilingual adults who needed to develop their English skills further, and for fluent English-speaking adults (black and white). The project examined over forty such courses attended by 500–600 students. The major objective of the courses was to develop basic skills in literacy, oral communication and numeracy with the aim of enabling students to progress to full-time vocational training or into appropriate employment. The courses were government-funded by the Manpower Services Commission, which also funded the ILT service. The research project undertaken by ILT staff focused on courses for bilingual adults who needed to develop their English or on mixed courses which included at least 30 per cent of such adults.

There were several significant features of the research project from the point of view of the development of the perspectives for language education described in this book. All ILT education and training was 'green-site' provision in the sense that it was developed for the first time by ILT staff. This research project, however, required the modification of existing institution-based provision through the application of the new perspectives on inter-ethnic communication and language development with groups of very varied teachers who had not shared in ILT work. Another distinctive characteristic of preparatory courses was that the students were full-time, unemployed, and enormously diverse in terms of backgrounds, educational levels and work experience. The project, therefore, provided an opportunity to test whether and how ILT perspectives could be applied to established and institution-based provision of this sort as well as to widen the ILT perspective. The project contributed to broader thinking on an overall framework for language education and the notion of a contract which was also developing in the student-autonomy project and which is briefly summarised in Chapter 1 (sections 6.1 – 6.3). It was organised around three major themes: the trainees, in terms of the needs and aspirations both of those who came on the courses and of those who did not; the organisation of the courses in terms of the selection procedures and the evaluation of outcomes; and the course curriculum and methodologies.

The background to the students was built up in terms of recorded classroom discussions with many different course groups, through ethnographic interviews and on the basis of a factual survey questionnaire. The major finding was that the priority bilingual group for the courses – redundant Asian men – were least represented on the courses. The majority of participants were married women (who wanted to work for the first time) or recently arrived settlers who had not been able to find work. 'Part of the reason for this would appear to be that the courses are not seen as closely enough linked to practical work and skills training, and also that the complexity of the ESL speakers' problems in society and at work is not perceived. Language is seen simplistically as the only problem. It is important that a wider view of trainees' needs be taken and that the courses are seen to satisfy these needs' (Roberts and Opienski 1985). The analysis of the experience of trainees before they came on courses revealed a familiar picture of racial discrimination and language being used by white gatekeepers as part of a process of confirming their prejudices and reinforcing the low social power of black people:

> I tried to speak but sometimes people don't speak with me – sometimes ...
> I don't know why ... black and white different ... When I came from India
> I used to wear sari and when I changed my dress – most people speak with
> me.

> I applied for a laundry job – I was asked why I had come to Britain – Why
> Asians came – and after interview – she said 'Why don't you know
> English?' I replied 'I do know English I've been talking to you in English'.

> (op.cit.)

This study, together with the in-company needs analysis undertaken by ILT, contributed to the conclusion that the greatest single 'problem' for ethnic minorities in relation to language is the failure of native speakers of English to make sound judgements about them and their English. The study also contributed to our understanding of the gap between black people's expectations of the public training and employment services and how these services perceived their responsibilities.

> This gap between expectations and reality was confirmed by a wide-ranging
> survey on unemployment and racial minorities (Smith 1982): 'The public
> employment service and the special programmes administered by the MSC,
> if continued along present lines, will be about as effective in helping
> minorities as in helping whites who are out of work, and more effective in
> some cases; but without new provision they will largely fail to meet the
> special needs of Asians who have a poor command of English.'

> (op.cit.)

Our increased understanding of these issues based on talking to black people contributed to the development of cross-cultural training for employment services staff of the type described in Chapter 3.

Two-thirds of the bilingual students on courses were women. As we have explained above, this proportion did not reflect priority need; however, it did reflect very closely the proportion of adult men and women already participating in English as a second language courses within colleges and centres. It was thus an interesting example of how institutions and their gatekeeping process constantly recreate existing structural patterns even when they are intending to change them. It illustrates the nature of class and gender barriers as well as racial ones.

The analysis of the reasons for the proportion of women and men on preparatory courses is illustrative of the general point that intentions are not sufficient, but have to be matched by changed structures and values.

The second major focus of the project was assessment and evaluation. Assessment was a key factor to examine because, as with most education and training, it was the basic tool of selection, course modification and feedback, and of measuring final outcomes. There were three major contextual factors influencing all the processes of assessment:

(i)   Selection was primarily conceived in terms of lack of English, but final evaluation in terms of successful placement in further training or in jobs.

(ii) The courses (which carried training allowances for the trainees) were always substantially over-subscribed, so selectors were always looking for reasons *not* to accept applicants.

(iii) The funding agency was under pressure to use the preparatory course funding for other, more 'hard-nosed' training.

These factors pointed to the need to define the relationship between general social and learning skills and specific vocational skills. This key issue was explored in greater depth by the Lancashire ILT Unit, which developed new forms of training to resolve the difficulty (see section 5.3 of this chapter).

Initial selection for preparatory course was intended to be mainly through the public employment and training agencies, but these were neither an accessible nor a skilled selection route, so the majority of students found out about courses and presented themselves to the colleges through informal word-of-mouth routes. Whilst this was a more effective and flexible route, it restricted the range of students likely to apply. The research found that the single most important criterion for selection for a course was a certain level of English and this level of English had been constantly rising as places became scarcer and as vocational courses and employers raised the level of English they required. This illustrates a well-known paradox, that applicants must already have acquired the skills and resources which qualify them for the opportunities to acquire these skills and resources. There was a widespread recognition of other factors such as previous educational and employment experience, self-confidence and motivation towards training-but these very important matters were all assessed through a process of panel interviews. ILT staff, drawing on their wide experience of the gatekeeping interview (see Chapter 3), were concerned that the assessment of such crucial factors rested upon such a specialised culture–specific form of interaction. The project concluded that much more weight should be given to learning ability assessed through learnability tests because they assess potential and underlying skills on the candidates' own terms. The other factor highlighted was informed consideration of educational background.

The third focus of the project was course design and methodology. Many courses were found to be based upon a relatively limited model of language education, although there were notable exceptions. There was a clear tendency for English-learning to be located around the analytic end of the analytic–experiential continuum (see p. 252). In particular, there was an emphasis on language skills and on student deficits. The crucial issues of inter-ethnic communication and of cross-cultural learning were formally approached in terms of information-giving to students rather than through organised work on awareness of differences and negotiation of meaning. The strategy ILT staff adopted when responding to these findings was to consider how the expanded view of language and insights into inter-ethnic communication, which had been developed for workplace training, could be made available to preparatory-course teachers in ways which they could understand and develop on their own terms. The strategy adopted was to produce a sample syllabus and methodology for a defined course and range of students on it. This sample curriculum was built up around three key concepts:

– an expanded but non-academic analysis of language and communication, appropriate to examining the needs of second-language learners;
– the cross-cultural nature of learning on such courses for adult bilingual trainees;
– the need for all aspects of the courses – language, literacy, numeracy, introductions to vocational skills and work experience – to be 'integrated', and integrated with the work of fluent English-speakers.

The model curriculum started from this simple view of language and communication as based upon interaction and that interaction depends on two aspects: form and meaning. A language-learning syllabus was therefore presented in terms of these two elements, together with the need for students to develop awareness of appropriacy. The key aim of the syllabus was to develop for teachers a notion of language learning and teaching which was (i) multidimensional and cyclical, i.e. dealt with many different elements and on a recurring basis; (ii) could

TRAINING MATERIAL 5.12 PREPARATORY COURSE
CURRICULUM [Prepared by Jacek Opienski, Pathway ILT; and Celia
Roberts, NCILT]

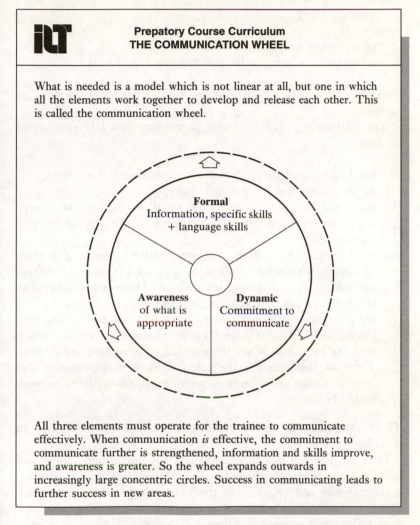

iLT

**Prepatory Course Curriculum
THE COMMUNICATION WHEEL**

What is needed is a model which is not linear at all, but one in which
all the elements work together to develop and release each other. This
is called the communication wheel.

Formal
Information, specific skills
+ language skills

Awareness
of what is
appropriate

Dynamic
Commitment to
communicate

All three elements must operate for the trainee to communicate
effectively. When communication *is* effective, the commitment to
communicate further is strengthened, information and skills improve,
and awareness is greater. So the wheel expands outwards in
increasingly large concentric circles. Success in communicating leads to
further success in new areas.

be used with white monolingual students as well as black bilingual
ones. (See Training Material 5.12.)

The cross-cultural learning component was given special attention
in the syllabus model. It was analysed in term of students' previous
learning experience, the particular aspects of language use required –
for example, for numeracy or clerical skills – and what implications
this had for the teachers of these areas.

The specimen curriculum was built up around five themes which were of direct relevance to all courses:
— seeking vocational training;
— working seeking;
— at work;
— making things work for yourself;
— making sense of living in Britain: at home and at work.

These themes could be developed for work on language, literacy and numeracy.

The methodology built into this curriculum aimed to ensure that teachers:

(i)   build on trainees' previous learning experience and strategies;
(ii)   do not assume that trainees lack concepts;
(iii) assess and are ready to teach the social and cultural knowledge and awareness necessary to make sense of the task of learning specific skills;
(iv)   avoid overloading trainees with information. Instead, give them opportunities to focus on the skills they need in social interaction and other skills for getting information. Trainees only assimilate information when they actually need to use it;
(v)   are sensitive in handling notions of correctness, particularly with literacy skills. Acknowledge trainees' expectations about correctness, but help them to see the significance of communicating first. They can then examine the effect of their communication and exercise choice as to how correct or standard their language should be.

These considerations are exemplified in the syllabus illustrated in Training Material 5.13.

How far was the guidance developed for curriculum design and methodology relevant and effective? Many teachers responded enthusiastically and critically to the ideas which were put forward. However, two factors prevented a long-term impact. Our expanded view of language outlined in Chapter 1 (Section 3), which is a major theme of the whole book, was not fully developed at the time of this study. The simple way we endeavoured to present ideas on language and communication was insufficiently rigorous to be useful for teachers. The second factor which reduced the impact was the pressures on preparatory-course teachers from the government-funding agency. The agency imposed simplistic notions of assessment and of evaluating outcomes and a requirement that courses be cut in

The Preparatory Course Curriculum
ILLUSTRATIVE SYLLABUS

Context	Trainee Needs	Communication	Analysis		
			Formal Language Element	Additional Language Work	Cross-Cultural Learning
A. Further Training	*Examples:* 1. Getting on to a course.	*Examples:* (i) Letter-writing. (ii) Telephoning. (iii) Face-to-face interviews. (iv) Travel outside the immediate environment.	*Examples:* Layout. Using a directory. Asking relevant questions etc.	*Examples:* Variety of language options. Giving unfamiliar names slowly etc.	*Examples:* Being aware of the interviewer's expectations. Knowing what is negotiable etc.
	2. Staying on a course.	(i) Studying. (ii) Socialising. (iii) Participating on a preparatory course.	Following written instructions. Appropriate greetings.	Coping with new language. Signposting intention.	Family involvement in what trainee is doing. Topics to talk about.

TRAINING MATERIAL 5.13 PREPARATORY COURSE ILLUSTRATIVE SYLLABUS *continued – second page*

Context	Trainee Needs	Communication	Analysis		
			Formal Language Element	Additional Language Work	Cross-Cultural Learning
B. Work-Seeking	*Examples:* 1. Finding out about jobs.	*Examples:* (i) Reading small ads. (ii) Reading job cards. (iii) Other methods of job search.	*Examples:* Significance of formal features of forms.	*Examples:* New job-description terminology.	*Examples:* Knowing what qualities are sought.
	2. Applying for jobs.	(i) In writing. (ii) By phoning. (iii) Interview.	Giving reasons for choosing the job.	Strategies for dealing with a poor line.	Knowing what information is relevant to application.
C. At work	*Examples:* 1. Socialising at work.	*Examples:* (i) Meal breaks.	*Examples:* Initiating.	*Examples:* Responding to a joke.	*Examples:* New notions of pace, timing, ways of negotiating.
	2. Taking responsibility for actions.	(ii) Timekeeping.	Leaving a message.	Getting listened to.	
	3. Being able to explain a problem.	(iii) Pay query or a grievance.	Acknowledging concessions.	Focussing on key issues.	

TRAINING MATERIAL 5.13 PREPARATORY COURSE ILLUSTRATIVE SYLLABUS *continued – third page*

Context	Trainee Needs	Communication	Analysis		
			Formal Lamguage Element	Additional Language Work	Cross-Cultural Learning
	3 Being able to explain a problem.	(i) Explaining a pay query or a grievance.	Formal features of extended discourse.	Sequencing and cohesion.	Knowing what is negotiable in the workplace.
D. Making Things Work for Yourself	*Examples:* 1 Being able to explain a situation.	*Examples:* (i) At the hospital. To the police. On the motorway.	*Examples:* Explaining the situation is urgent.	*Examples:* Making contrasts explicit.	*Examples:* Being able to ask the right questions to get the necessary information.
	2 Being able to negotiate.	(ii) Changing the date of an appointment.			
	3 Asking for information.	(iii) Talking about what subjects children should take at school.	Using reference material.	Alphabetical ordering.	

TRAINING MATERIAL 5.13 PREPARATORY COURSE ILLUSTRATIVE SYLLABUS *continued – fourth page*

Context	Trainee Needs	Communication	Analysis		
			Formal Language Element	Additional Language Work	Cross-Cultural Learning
E. Making sense of living in the UK.	*Examples:* 1 Access to resources already in home or place of work.	*Examples:* Making more sense of newspapers, TV, radio etc.	*Examples:* Identifying the topic in a programme.	*Examples:* Relating visual clues to written word.	*Examples:* Being more aware of how judgements of people are made on the basis of interactive norms.
In the community and at work.	2 Fuller participa-tion.	Being able to create opportunities to use English, with neighbours, at meetings etc.	Understanding and using turn-taking conventions in meetings.	Terminology of bureaucratic notices.	The culture of hierarchies in the workplace.

length to save money. These structural factors limited the overall development of the programmes and reduced the amount of language education and basic-skills work which the courses could provide. Overall, the agency was unhappy with the report because its recommendations and broad-curriculum approach did not accord with their narrower definition of what constitutes vocational training. Despite these increasing pressures to reduce the length and educational scope of preparatory courses, students still benefited from the courses and the commitment of their teachers. One of the most valuable findings to emerge from the project was the clear identification and analysis of the crucial gatekeeping roles and responsibilities of teachers themselves – both language teachers and teachers of other subjects and of vocational skills. The Lancashire project described in the next section illustrates a successful development form preparatory courses and an example of how language teachers and other teachers could develop programmes together.

5.3 Communication for employment and training

In 1980, as a response to the growing numbers of redundant Asian workers whose retraining needs were not being met, the Lancashire ILT Unit, directed by Roger Munns, developed a programme: Communication for Employment and Training. Subsequently, this programme was extended to other regions, and training for the unemployed became a coordinating priority for NCILT.

The courses were set up in further education colleges where there were well-established vocational departments. The key to the success of the courses was the extent to which the trade lecturers and communications lecturers shared goals and approaches.

The Communication for Employment and Training (CET) courses were designed to integrate training in the following areas:

(i)   Language and numeracy skills required for developing new trade skills.
(ii) Practice in specific basic trade skills and experience of the range of jobs available within those trades.
(iii) Skills necessary for gaining access to information about a particular industry and companies in the locality.
(iv) The whole range of skills required for job-seeking.

There were two main innovations in these courses. First, they were based upon research which elicited the experiences and perceptions of redundant Asian workers. Second, the syllabus was designed so that the communications and vocational skills were conceptually integrated. This was done in three ways:

- learning strategies for vocational skills were linked to communication strategies together with a suggested menu of linguistic features to be learned;
- the learning strategies for vocational skills were also, implicitly, learning strategies for communication;
- the cross-cultural awareness component linked into both vocational learning and language learning.

ILT trainers broke down typical vocational tasks, initially in engineering, into four main stages:

- planning;
- measuring;
- production processes;
- assessment.

Each of these stages had vocational skills associated with it which required the development of learning strategies. These, in turn, required communication strategies realised, in part, by linguistic skills. The syllabus was designed to link the vocational learning strategies (for example, planning how to make a tool box) with communication learning strategies (for example, planning how to present yourself for interview or how to take useful lecture notes). These relationships between cognitive strategies and language-learning strategies were presented to teachers in diagrams and examples of the type given in Training Material 5.14.

5.4 Development of independent learning

The Adult Literacy and Basic Skills Unit (ALBSU) offered the Lancashire unit funding to develop and integrate independent learning into their CET courses. This development was undertaken by Gurnam Heire and Peter Wilson and the findings were published as *Implementing Learner Autonomy* (Heire and Furnborough 1985). There were four interrelated objectives for this work:

(i)   to develop independent-learning materials as a bridge between CET courses and mainstream vocational training;
(ii) to develop a more self-directed style of learning on CET courses

TRAINING MATERIAL 5.14 : CET SYLLABUS [Lancashire ILT]

ilt   **COMMUNICATION FOR EDUCATION AND TRAINING SYLLABUS**

	Planning	Measuring and Marking	Production process	Assessment
Learning Strategies	visualizing end. product.	understanding relative to cost, speed quality.	recall using language.	setting objectives for self.
Communicative Strategies	reading drawings, diagrams.	understanding and explaining relative and comparative importance of various measurements.	perceiving a framework for the discourse (or imposing one by questioning).	stating own strengths and weaknesses.
Linguistic skills	symbols notations	modifiers comparatives	recognising discourse markers.	comparatives specific to technical language.

The syllabus grid has two other dimensions: cross cultural learning and awareness, which runs through everything; and the specific trade area(s) being used as a vehicle for the language training – eg fitting, centre lathe, milling, welding and fabrication.

TRAINING MATERIAL 5.14 CET SYLLABUS *continued*

Examples

1. *Link vocational and communicative strategies*

As students learn the communicative strategies they need to plan, measure, produce and assess an engineering task, they also learn that effective communication involves:

planning	– deciding what to say/write in a particular context.
measuring	– working out the details in terms of accuracy, register, etc..
production processes	– performing the communicative act.
assessment	– assessing the effectiveness of the communicative act, during and after.

Planning Understanding the target

2. *Link Learning strategies, Communicative strategies and Cross-cultural learning*

Learning strategies	*Communicative strategies*
Seeing end product	Reading/interpreting
Conceptualising end product	– technical drawing
	– rough sketch

Recognising the description of an object.

Notion of size, shape material

Cross-cultural learning

This requires the ability to conceptualise and visualise a finished three-dimensional object, the production of which involves a whole range of skills and information. These need to be combined in accordance with a coherent sequence; the first stage of this process often consists of interpreting diagrams.

Trainees are unlikely to be familiar with standard conventions for translating two-dimensional drawings into three-dimensional objects and their implications, e.g. at a simple level, the space in brickwork occupied by mortar is not shown on the drawings; at a more sophisticated level, conventional projections which reveal only part of the object.

In addition they may be unfamiliar with apparently 'normal' uses of symbolic notations, e.g. arrows to indicate variously locations, or directions of movement, double arrows to indicate length, and dotted lines show obscured sections of an object. In the same way, trade

TRAINING MATERIAL 5.14 CET SYLLABUS *continued*

> instructors cannot take it for granted that rough illustrative sketches
> will be understood.
> Initially, therefore, there are some advantages in relating the drawing
> and materials to an example or picture of the completed job before
> trainees start; equally, though, this practice should be discontinued at
> some point in order that trainees learn through problem solving
> rather than imitation.
>
> [Hedge 1980]

in order to equip trainees better for effective participation in mainstream vocational training;

(iii) to modify CET methodology in order to facilitate the
development of independent learning by students after finishing
the programme;

(iv) to survey existing part-time educational and training provision for
bilingual adults so that recommendations for improving learner
autonomy would fit coherently into a wider range of provision
than only CET courses.

One of the tasks of the project was to conceptualise the notion of
independent learning in terms of three dimensions critical to its
success:

1. *At an institutional level:* How trainees develop an overall
   perception of further education and training provision and of
   themselves as learners.
2. *At a course level:* How the organisation of a course can integrate
   independence into all trainees' activities.
3. *In terms of student self-study:* How periods of self-study, with
   tutor support but outside the formal structure of the course, can
   be provided.

To assess how an independent-learning component could be
integrated within the CET courses, an evaluation of existing teaching
and learning strategies on CET courses was made. Classroom and
workshop observation was carried out and over 250 people, both
former CET students and others, were interviewed in the process of

this evaluation. The findings (adapted from ALBSU Independent Learning Project: Heire and Wilson 1984) were as follows.

Conclusions from classroom observation
The following general conclusions were made:

(i) Much of the classroom work only related backwards to previous workshop sessions, so limiting the range of activities in the classroom and reducing the amount of responsibility trainees took for learning in the workshop.

(ii) Trade and communications skills tended to be linked at the level of content rather than methodology.

(iii) Several common problem areas for the trainees were observed. These included problems of *demonstrating* that learning had taken place (e.g. in explaining specific workshop activities); problems of perception (e.g. in translating two-dimensional drawings into three-dimensional objects and vice verse); problems of moving from concrete to abstract activities in certain unfamiliar areas (e.g. in discussing processes in electronics or relationships between planes in construction); and problems of locating the role of the learner in certain activities (e.g. group discussion of workshop practice).

Conclusions from workshop observation
(i) Trainees were firmly product-orientated (e.g. 'I'm trying to build a small wall') and so did not attend sufficiently to the intermediate steps which make up the process of producing something, for example planning or measuring. This led to errors being accepted which accumulated and it became increasingly difficult for students to recognise the source of their errors.

(ii) Trainees always relied on instructors for assessment and often thought implicit negative comments of the type 'It will have to do' were *positive* reactions. Completion of a piece of work rather than its quality was what gave them satisfaction. This emphasis on completion meant that they wanted to keep up with the others rather than spend more time on the quality of their own work.

(iii) Instructors assumed that all trainees were familiar with working with all sorts of tools when, in fact, some were not.

Conclusions from interviews with instructors and trainees at a government Skillcentre
It was difficult to establish a clear picture of what precise language

problems were occurring on the courses. Most trainees admitted they had occasional problems in understanding their instructor. Only two felt their technical vocabulary was insufficient – the others named speed of delivery, accent and other workshop noises as being problems.

Two of the instructors were able to pinpoint particular language difficulties – one trainee could not describe accurately what he had done without having the job laid out before him; another could not take dictated notes. Most of the trainees' problems on the courses were interpreted in attitudinal terms by the instructors. Taking the initiative, admitting mistakes and asking for assistance were the qualities the instructors believed were most lacking in their ESL trainees.

In almost every instance instructors and trainees had radically different conceptions about each other's role in the process of learning. In most cases this was a difference between the trainee-centered approach adopted by the instructor and the instructor-centered approach expected by the trainee.

These misconceptions were most noticeable during the initial assessment period of the course. Several trainees said it had taken them several weeks to adjust to this self-directed approach to learning. An interview with a trainee who had been removed from the course after three weeks confirmed that this lack of understanding about what was expected of him was the main reason for his failure.

Evidence of this independent approach to learning was gathered in different ways by the instructors. Several remarked that 'an independent attitude' (two used the phrase 'an aggressive attitude') to the course was needed. Examples of this included starting a new job from the manual when the instructor was absent, refusing to lend tools on request, and swearing at those who interfered with one's work! The independent nature of work in most of the trades in question was offered as the primary justification for this approach.

Most of the instructors interviewed had a clear perception of how the individual components of a course fitted into its overall aims. However, none of the trainees understood (or could remember) what these overall aims actually were.

Most of the trainees perceived the course as a series of concrete tasks to be performed or jobs to be done. Not one trainee offered the idea of the course as a process of understanding and acquiring skills that were transferable to tasks outside those on the course.

The way in which the courses were assessed also led to misconceptions by the trainees which related to this lack of shared perceptions. Some, having completed a task, perceived all questions about *how* they had completed it as implied criticisms: for them, completion in itself was evidence of their having reached their objective. Others were unsure how important speed was in completing a task. One trainee, who had failed part of the written assignment on his course, felt he was being assessed on his knowledge of English rather than his knowledge of the trade.

Conclusions from interviews with 250 actual and potential trainees (adapted from Heire and Furnborough 1985)

A composite profile of the group was constructed. Individuals were likely to:

- be between 19 and 45 years of age;
- have 5 to 10 years of education in their country of origin, largely non-technical in content;
- have nil to 20 years of work experience in one industry at an unskilled level, which they themselves regarded as irrelevant for the future;
- have a level of spoken English traditionally labelled between post-elementary and advanced, with rather lower reading and writing skills;
- lack the strategies and opportunities to promote themselves in new job markets;
- lack the information necessary to evaluate and successfully exploit existing training/educational opportunities;
- have 'inappropriate' learning strategies for success within the present training/educational provision.

Many had great faith in the power of the education system but little awareness of how it could help them in specific ways. The educational and training system had failed to provide systematic advice and information because there was little understanding within the system of the necessity for it.

Some had internalised their failure to get employment as personal failure and this sense of personal failure had been transferred to the educational system.

Trainees perceived craft skills as a set of 'visible' hand skills. They did not generally appreciate the 'mental events' such as planning and problem-solving which lay behind hand skills. So it was assumed that the approach to learning was 'look and learn'.

Trainees and instructors were working from quite different perspectives, and trainees found it difficult to appreciate the need for reading, drawing or maths skills, or the need to do any learning outside the workshop.

Trainees' concepts of themselves as learners were based almost exclusively on their ability to memorise. There were few indications that they used the following skills: selection, paraphrasing, imagery, reorganisation, summarising or categorisation, when dealing with new information.

Trainees vested complete and unquestioning authority in the teacher in all aspects of learning.

The important aspect of this evaluative project was that it put the approach to *learning* rather than *language* at the centre. At the same time it focused on possible cross-cultural issues relevant to the expanded view of language (described in Chapter 1) and linked this to the importance of awareness of underlying schemata (as illustrated in Chapter 3) by making explicit the differences in assumptions, experience and interpretation of the trainees and the instructors.

5.5 *Training for change*

The independent learning survey had started out as a project to enrich and extend the learning on CET courses. But the data collected on the project showed that the courses themselves needed changing if the insights gained from that exercise and the Learner Autonomy project were to be incorporated in them to resolve the identified difficulties encountered by instructors and trainees and forge a new relationship between independent learning and formal training.

In response, the Lancashire ILT piloted a new programme of training provision, *Training for Change* (1985).

It was decided that, for trainees to gain maximum benefit from the formal training funded by the government training agency for which training allowances were paid, the formal skills-acquisition phase would be sandwiched between two periods of orientation and development, like this:

Phase 1. Learner orientation	Part-time (10 weeks)	Self-study
Phase 2. Skills acquisition government	Full-time with in workshop and training allowance (18 weeks)	Learner autonomy classroom
Phase 3. Individual development	Part-time (6 weeks) average	Independent decisions about provision and institutions

Within this framework the existing CET curriculum was broadened in two ways:

(i)   To cover a range of basic education areas: basic technical education, visual information, problem-solving and technical drawing as well as communications. These provided essential and expected skills and concepts which workers with a limited or interrupted education had not necessarily acquired. Any lack was routinely interpreted by monocultural instructors as evidence of low intelligence.

(ii) A range of broad-based occupational-area modules from which trainees chose three:
      – electronic assembly;
      – fitting and assembly;
      – repair and maintenance;
      – scientific and technical services;
      – working with machines;
      – new technology.

This was in response to the economic climate in the UK, which was leading training agencies, notably the MSC, and industrialists to argue for an education and training system which gave people a broad educational background and transferable skills. It was becoming increasingly clear that the new industries and the influence of information technology on the established industries was likely to mean that workers needed cognitive and problem-solving skills as jobs were upgraded or as people found they had to change jobs.

Phase 1   Learner orientation

The aims of this component were:

(i)   to acclimatise learners gradually to the physical demands of learnings;

(ii)   to give trainees the opportunity to explore their own preferences in learning;

(iii) to make trainees aware of different types of learning, e.g. understanding, doing and memorising;

(iv)   to give trainees practice in different techniques for understanding, doing and memorising;

(v)   to make trainees aware of different methods of organising information.

It was clear from the survey findings that trainees needed not only to be made aware of alternative learning strategies from their own existing ones but actually trained in using them at this stage before the workshop phase of their training began.

Training Material 5.15 is an example of material which aims to create awareness and to provide practice in learning by problem solving. The example takes students through a series of steps which require them to analyse a process and then to problem-solve on the basis of their understanding of the process.

Phase 2   Skills acquisition

In this phase, all skills modules were optional, so trainees had to make decisions and select in terms of what was most in line with their long-term goals.

This second phase of the project was intended to develop broad-based transferable skills across three occupational-area modules. The classroom-based training, which took up one-third of the time, was focused on:

- listening and reading for specific information;
- reading technical drawings, and other visual information;
- measurements and calculations;
- technical understanding related to workshop tasks;
- planning and problem-solving;.
- self-assessment methods

The aims of the workshop-based preparation component were:

(i)   to make trainees aware of the whole range of skills and teaching methods employed in workshop training;

(ii)   to give trainees the opportunity to explore their own approaches to learning in the workshop;

(iii)   to make trainees aware of the roles of trainer and trainee in the workshop;

(iv)   to familiarise trainees with basic workshop procedures such as safety, obtaining tools and materials, and collaboration;

(v)   to focus trainees on the concept of standards, need to work to standards, and self-assessment;

(iv)   to focus trainees away from the end-product, and towards the concept of transferable skills and the learning processes which would be needed in order to develop these.

Previously, trainees had worked on their own within a tight set of procedures. This gave the impression of independence but, in reality, trainees could complete tasks without much understanding and were basically controlled by the instructor-devised procedures.

An alternative approach was to develop explicitly all the steps involved in solving a problem and completing a task. The starting point for this approach was to examine how problems are presented to all of us in real life, and what steps are involved in arriving at

TRAINING MATERIAL 5.15 CISTERN EXERCISE [Lancashire ILT]

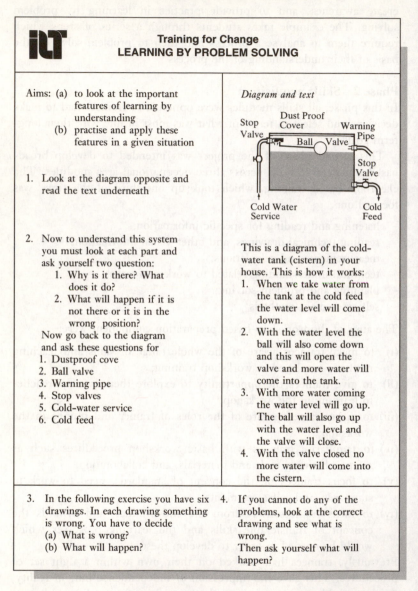

ILT

Training for Change
LEARNING BY PROBLEM SOLVING

Aims: (a) to look at the important
features of learning by
understanding
(b) practise and apply these
features in a given situation

1. Look at the diagram opposite and
read the text underneath

2. Now to understand this system
you must look at each part and
ask yourself two question:
1. Why is it there? What
does it do?
2. What will happen if it is
not there or it is in the
wrong position?
Now go back to the diagram
and ask these questions for
1. Dustproof cove
2. Ball valve
3. Warning pipe
4. Stop valves
5. Cold-water service
6. Cold feed

Diagram and text

Dust Proof
Stop   Cover   Warning
Valve   Pipe
Ball   Valve
Stop
Valve
Cold Water   Cold
Service   Feed

This is a diagram of the cold-
water tank (cistern) in your
house. This is how it works:
1. When we take water from
the tank at the cold feed
the water level will come
down.
2. With the water level the
ball will also come down
and this will open the
valve and more water will
come into the tank.
3. With more water coming
the water level will go up.
The ball will also go up
with the water level and
the valve will close.
4. With the valve closed no
more water will come into
the cistern.

3. In the following exercise you have six
drawings. In each drawing something
is wrong. You have to decide
(a) What is wrong?
(b) What will happen?

4. If you cannot do any of the
problems, look at the correct
drawing and see what is
wrong.
Then ask yourself what will
happen?

acceptable solutions. In real life we are normally presented with
'specifications' (i.e. the description of a problem, without any
procedure for solving it). We are at liberty to employ methods of our
own choice within certain limitations such as cost, availability of
resources and technical viability.

TRAINING MATERIAL 5.15 CISTERN EXERCISE *continued*

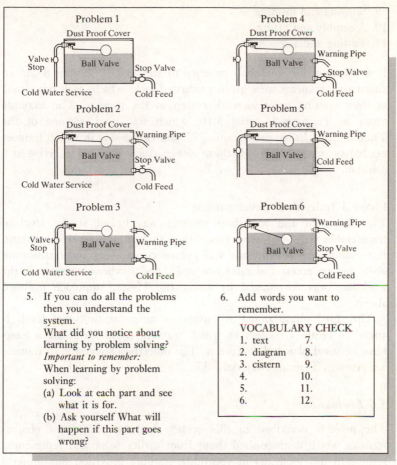

Problem 1

Dust Proof Cover
Valve Stop
Ball Valve
Stop Valve
Cold Water Service
Cold Feed

Problem 2

Dust Proof Cover
Warning Pipe
Ball Valve
Stop Valve
Cold Water Service
Cold Feed

Problem 3

Valve Stop
Ball Valve
Warning Pipe
Cold Water Service
Cold Feed

Problem 4

Dust Proof Cover
Warning Pipe
Ball Valve
Stop Valve
Cold Feed

Problem 5

Dust Proof Cover
Warning Pipe
Ball Valve
Cold Feed

Problem 6

Warning Pipe
Ball Valve
Stop Valve
Cold Feed

5. If you can do all the problems then you understand the system.
   What did you notice about learning by problem solving?
   Important to remember:
   When learning by problem solving:
   (a) Look at each part and see what it is for.
   (b) Ask yourself What will happen if this part goes wrong?

6. Add words you want to remember.

   VOCABULARY CHECK
1. text	7.
2. diagram	8.
3. cistern	9.
4.	10.
5.	11.
6.	12.

ILT staff therefore analysed what would happen if trainees were presented with tasks in this realistic manner. They found that in order to work from the specifications of a task or problem through to the finished product or solution, the trainee has to progress through the following steps:

1. Identifying the central task and formulating outline solutions.
2. Gathering relevant data.
3. Making modifications to the selected solution.
4. Making final decisions about size, shape and materials.
5. Planning methods of construction.
6. Planning sequence of construction.
7. Gathering resources.

8. Marking and setting out.
9. Shaping and forming.
10. Assembly and fitting.
11. Testing and assessing.

It is common for workshop practice to start a task at step 8. As an alternative, students were given graduated tasks which, each time, took as their starting point an earlier step in the process. The example given in Training Material 5.16, which was used on one of the Training for Change programmes, illustrates the way in which trainees needed to progress through these eleven steps in order to arrive at a solution.

Phase 3 Individual development
The classroom and workshop training was linked at the level of transferable skills and strategies rather than at the level of content. For example, more emphasis was put on questioning and clarification skills and on access and reference skills, and further autonomy in the workshop was encouraged by using the 11-step approach outlined above.

The third phase aimed at autonomy at an institutional level. It aimed to create a context in which trainees could formulate a long-term personal plan and execute it. The objectives suggested to trainees are given in Training Material 5.17.

5.6 Evaluation

The projects described in this section had two important characteristics which distinguished them from earlier work and represented significant developments in vocational-training provision for bilingual workers. The first is an integrated curriculum geared to employment and training prospects and premised on genuinely shared objectives and approaches between trade and communications/basic-education teachers. The second is in making explicit to all concerned all aspects of the curriculum and the learning strategies that underpin it.

These developments were based on extensive research in the community and in observation of actual training. Programmes were devised which were both analytical in assessing and finding solutions for cross-cultural learning difficulties and experiential/ethnographic in helping students to set their own goals and find their best ways of learning, in other words to develop a 'heuristic self-assessment cycle'.

The integrated curriculum is at the heart of a programme which aimed to develop transferable vocational skills and develop basic skills,

TRAINING MATERIAL 5.16 TRAINING FOR CHANGE
[Lancashire ILT]

ILT	**Training for Change** **PROBLEM SOLVING**

TASK

> Design and build two things which will safely hold
> the back end of a car at different heights from the
> ground. [The car can be raised by a jack or a
> pulley system.]
> These supports can be kept in the boot of the car
> after use.

STEPS

1. Read the specifications and understand what is required.
   Roughly outline or sketch solutions.
   Consult tutor and agree on one of these solutions.

2. Measure the distance between the ground and the back axle.
   Estimate maximum height to which the car needs to be raised.
   Decide on intermediate heights.

3. In this case the main modification necessary
   was to improve the top:

From   To

[Not many trainees had thought of the car rolling off.]

4. Make all decisions about size of pipes, and
   thickness of plates.
   Produce detailed sketches of joints.
   Decide on types of materials.

5. Plan how to cut and join the various pieces
   (mostly hacksawing and welding).
   Decide how to join a thin chain to a pin, and
   then to the body of the support (in this
   case, by brazing).

6. Plan out which pieces to make first and
   which to leave till the end.

TRAINING MATERIAL 5.16 TRAINING FOR CHANGE
[Lancashire ILT] *continued*

> 7. Go to stores and get the necessary materials.
>   Locate machines, hand tools and place to work.
> 8. Mark out the materials.
> 9. Cut, drill, saw and file the various pieces.
> 10. Weld and braze.
> 11. Examine for finish.
>   Test supports under a car.

including, of course, language, within areas of occupational training. The realisation of such a curriculum depended crucially on trade instructors and communications/basic-education tutors working closely together. In particular, it meant for both instructors and tutors the development of new strategies for teaching. These included:

– encouraging small-group work in trainees' first language;
– much greater use of analogy to bridge the perceived gap between abstract and concrete (both analogies across trades and analogies between trade areas and communications);
– making assessment more relevant (it was found that learning was often tested in different ways from how it was taught; for example, copying of drawings was used to test rules of geometry).

The notion of explicitness, applied to setting objectives and all aspects of learning strategies, was a necessary dimension of training for redundant Asian workers. But is also proved a helpful dimension for white trainees who started to come on to the programme. As is so often the case, the presence of ethnic-minority people had created change which was then found to make sense to the white community. The significant difference between the *Training for Change* programme, which became ethnically mixed, and other training on which both black and white people are represented, such as many of the preparatory courses described, was that this programme was designed for black people but worked for whites too, while the majority of other programmes are designed for white people and it is assumed that black people will fit in. Once training is established which is genuinely helpful for both groups, then those trainees who still do not have enough experience of English benefit so greatly from the presence of native speakers of English that we would question any separation of language learning from direct access to knowledge and skills other than language, and to native-speaking peers with shared goals.

TRAINING MATERIAL 5.17 OBJECTIVES FOR LEARNER
AUTONOMY (from Heire and Furnborough 1985)

ILT   **Training for Change**
               OBJECTIVES FOR LEARNER AUTONOMY

---

1. *Understand Context In Which Trainees Operate*
   This involves discussion and analysis of changes relating to
   employment and training opportunities, both nationally and at
   a local level.
2. *Analyse Long-Term Individual Aims*
   This requires examination of intended employment (either
   directly or via further training) in terms of competition, skills
   level required, and potential for the future (in the light of 1
   above).
3. *Evaluate Oneself In Relation To Aims*
   This involves self-assessment in terms of skills, motivation,
   suitability, aptitude and personal resources (for example time
   or money).
4. *Re-Evaluate Aims*
   If the goals formulated in 2 prove to be unrealistic when
   matched against 3, trainees need to return to the second
   objective and explore alternatives.
5. *Explore Various Routes*
   This involves examining and evaluating present provision in
   terms of one's aims and rejecting anything that does not
   contribute to the achievement of one's long term aims.
6. *Select An Appropriate Route*
   This obviously follows from 5 above; the route may involve
   one specific programme, or the use of a range of resources in
   combination.
7. *Execute Formulated Plan*
   The skills and strategies required at this stage are as follows:
   – development of skills for creating a personal network of
     contacts;
   – strategies for entering totally unfamiliar situations;
   – interview skills training;
   – training in employment-seeking skills;
   – developing skills for coping with setbacks and maintaining
     motivation.

This training also represents a bridge between training for bilingual
speakers and cross-cultural training for white management, unions and
gatekeepers, who in this instance are skills instructors and training-
services officers. Both types of training share a preoccupation with the
assumptions and experiences which form the schemata and underwrite
the interpretive frames of any interaction – whether it is face-to-face

interviewing for a place on a training course, or the interaction between the trainee and a text, or task, or instructor. Both share a concern that barriers to access and opportunity in the form of differences in language, perception and education be dismantled through training, awareness, and change in those procedures and practices which do not work to the equal advantage of everyone.

6. Project Four: Advanced communication skills courses for bilingual staff

6.1 The context

A number of ILT units developed courses for bilingual staff in white-collar jobs and positions of responsibility. A major initiative was organised with the Civil Service in the early 1980s (Hooper and Yates 1981) and advanced communications courses were run for clerical staff, and staff in the service industries including nursing (Gray 1982) and passenger transport (Dodderidge 1983). Similar courses were also run for key groups, such as trade-union shop stewards.

Most trainees came on such courses either because they perceived they were not getting access to promotional or training opportunities or because either they or their managers were aware of frustrations or difficulties in communications in their job. Trainees were fluent in English and had acquired and could use most of the formal features of English, but felt, like the trainees on the course in inter-ethnic communication described in Chapter 3 (Section 4.1), that aspects of communication were still a problem for them or for their immediate managers.

Bilingual trainees on courses run for a number of Civil Service departments during this period were representative of many trainees on advanced communication courses. The majority were overqualified for their jobs as clerical assistants or officers; many had degrees, and some postgraduate degrees: 'A higher proportion of new entrant coloured [sic] Clerical Officers possessed educational qualifications above the minimum, 46% compared to 14% for white COs' (Tavistock Institute 1978). Most of them considered the lack of skill in communication, whether actual or perceived, was damaging what they thought should be good promotional prospects. There were high expectations for promotion among ethnic-minority applicants: 'More coloured officers than white officers mentioned the importance of opportunities for promotion as a reason for joining the civil service' (op. cit.). The Tavistock Report had also found that ethnic-minority staff in clerical posts had been rated lower in 'expression on paper and oral expression' than their white colleagues. This combination of negative evaluation by their immediate supervisors and a sense of frustration and/or lack of confidence in themselves were frequently factors which led to the setting up of an advanced communication course.

6.2 Curriculum and methodology

The objectives of such courses can be summed up as follows:

(i)   to raise awareness about factors which shape communication, and to encourage participants to observe their own communicative practices both inside and outside the training room;

(ii)   to build on the language the group and individuals already have, and do such remedial work as seems necessary for the particular group.

(Dodderidge 1984)

To achieve these objectives, courses were flexible and responsive and no two courses, even for very similar groups of trainees, were alike in terms of specific training materials and content. The hallmark of advanced communication courses was that they shared a common methodology and common processes for handling the complex issues of language behaviour and culture which bilingual people bring to the training room. The methods-based approach and the complexity of issues makes such courses difficult to illustrate. Trainers did not seek to produce sets of materials. Instead, trainers often wrote up and analysed the experiences of each session as the way of planning the next session. The examples given below may appear either somewhat underdeveloped or, in the case of follow-up language work, too narrowly focused and decontextualised. However, this is a weakness in the way in which these illustrative materials, decontextualised from the

COURSE DESIGN

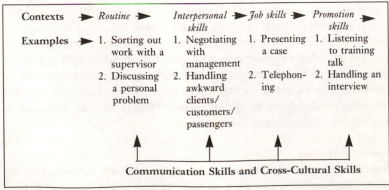

Contexts	Routine	Interpersonal skills	Job skills	Promotion skills
Examples	1. Sorting out work with a supervisor	1. Negotiating with management	1. Presenting a case	1. Listening to training talk
	2. Discussing a personal problem	2. Handling awkward clients/ customers/ passengers	2. Telephoning	2. Handling an interview

Communication Skills and Cross-Cultural Skills

classroom, are presented and not in the approach used by ILT trainers.

Advanced communication-skills courses combined the analytical and ethnographic approaches outlined at the beginning of this chapter. They did this by centring on student analysis of their own communicative behaviour and on the assumptions that underlay such behaviours. As well as dealing with oral and written skills development in familiar contexts, students were encouraged to make explicit and compare their assumptions and perceptions of role and status, attitudes to work and to work rules. The methodology for developing skills was broadly similar across a variety of courses but was developed through specific role-play exercises for each context (see Training Material 5.18).

Superficially, the skills components of advanced communications courses had much in common with the type of communication-skills training courses routinely run by companies for their employees, covering such matters as dealing with customers, being effective in meetings or report-writing. However, the emphasis was different and was placed upon the cross-cultural dimension and its implications for 'reading' linguistic and non-verbal cues; for example, a customer's attitude, the degree of certainty being conveyed about a decision or knowing whether you were winning the argument or not in a negotiation. In addition, students would bring to the training room misunderstandings, frustrations and requests of types which would rarely arise in the training of white staff.

In other words, there were schemata and frame differences which needed to be explicitly addressed. This was as important an issue in written communications as in oral communications (Cogill 1980). The focus on schemata and frame differences built on previous ILT work on cross-cultural training (see Chapter 3), with its focus on inter-ethnic communication, and many advanced communications courses included joint sessions involving white management and ethnic-minority trainees along the lines of the course described in Chapter 3 (section 3.1). The major developments from this earlier course were in the use of video role-play; a more explicit focus on analysing cultural differences and assumptions in role perceptions and status; and in integrating more extensive role-plays with specific language exercises in a further development of the post-elementary courses described in section 3.1 of this chapter.

Video role-play

Video role-plays were based on real and commonly experienced incidents, sufficiently open-ended so that trainees could incorporate their

TRAINING MATERIAL 5.18   PRESENTING A CASE   [Courses developed by Sian Dodderidge, Derek Hooper, Peter Wilson]

iLT   **Advanced Communication Skills**
            ROLE–PLAY: PRESENTING A CASE

Course	*Role-play*
Shop stewards' course	Management has put up a notice about a new packing line without consulting the trade unions. You have a meeting with management to state your view and find out how far you can negotiate with them.
Bus conductors' and drivers' course	There has been a complaint from a woman passenger that your bus braked suddenly, causing her to trip and injure her leg. You did not put in an accident report. The inspector has called you to talk about the complaint.
Course for clerical workers in a Civil Service department	You ask if you can 'jump the queue' for the May training course on office skills, as you are keen to apply for a new post coming up in the branch in July.

own experiences and views. These role-plays were graded in terms of interactional difficulty. The role-plays were enacted and video taped in the classroom and then immediately played back for analysis. Tension had to be maintained between a structured and systematic development of skills and a reactive and flexible dynamic in which student contributions were central to the learning. Data 5.19, an extract from a course write-up, outlines the methodology and some of the difficulties that have to be overcome.

One successful technique for making explicit similarities and contrasts in perceptions of task and role was to set up situations 'in reverse'. For example, a job interview was set up with a panel of bilingual staff interviewing a white applicant. As is so often the case for etnic-minority applicants, the white applicants routinely felt disorienteated by unexpected questions and were uncertain as to acceptable responses or what criteria were being used for their evaluation.

TRAINING MATERIAL 5.19 VIDEO ROLE-PLAYS [Sian
Dodderidge, Kirklees ILT]

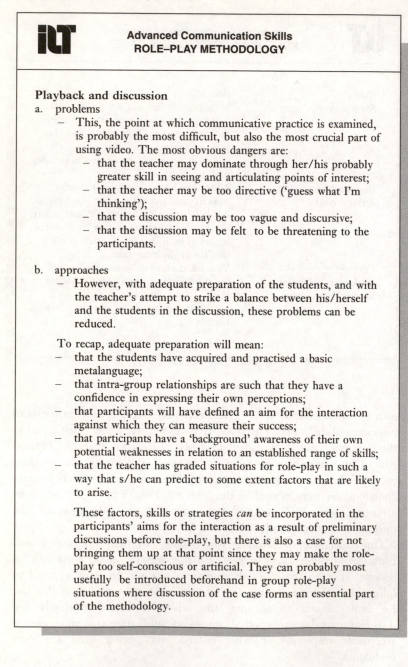

ilT   **Advanced Communication Skills**
              ROLE–PLAY METHODOLOGY

Playback and discussion
a. problems
    –   This, the point at which communicative practice is examined,
        is probably the most difficult, but also the most crucial part of
        using video. The most obvious dangers are:
        –   that the teacher may dominate through her/his probably
            greater skill in seeing and articulating points of interest;
        –   that the teacher may be too directive ('guess what I'm
            thinking');
        –   that the discussion may be too vague and discursive;
        –   that the discussion may be felt to be threatening to the
            participants.

b. approaches
    –   However, with adequate preparation of the students, and with
        the teacher's attempt to strike a balance between his/herself
        and the students in the discussion, these problems can be
        reduced.

    To recap, adequate preparation will mean:
    –   that the students have acquired and practised a basic
        metalanguage;
    –   that intra-group relationships are such that they have a
        confidence in expressing their own perceptions;
    –   that participants will have defined an aim for the interaction
        against which they can measure their success;
    –   that participants have a 'background' awareness of their own
        potential weaknesses in relation to an established range of skills;
    –   that the teacher has graded situations for role-play in such a
        way that s/he can predict to some extent factors that are likely
        to arise.

    These factors, skills or strategies *can* be incorporated in the
    participants' aims for the interaction as a result of preliminary
    discussions before role-play, but there is also a case for not
    bringing them up at that point since they may make the role-
    play too self-conscious or artificial. They can probably most
    usefully be introduced beforehand in group role-play
    situations where discussion of the case forms an essential part
    of the methodology.

TRAINING MATERIAL 5.19 VIDEO ROLE-PLAYS *continued*

c. a basic methodology
   – At the end of filming
      (i) ask participants to comment on how they felt in the situation: were they uncomfortable? did they succeed or not in their aims/in getting the message across? how do they think the other felt? etc.;
      (ii) ask the remainder of the group if they observed anything they wish to comment on:
         – that was good;
         – that could have been better;
      (iii) play the video-recording of the role-play, stopping it at various point, and asking the group to comment on specific factors or aspects, e.g.:
         – approach, manner, opening;
         – development of argument/sequencing of facts;
         – what is being done with the language (function or 'sentence-types');
         – whether participants are listening to each other
         – concluding/closing;
      (iv) *or*, alternatively, ask the students to look for one particular point in operation throughout a scene, and then replay the whole video-recording straight through; e.g.:
         – tone of voice;
         – appropriacy and role;
         – side-tracking/control;
         – body language/eye contact;
         – selection of facts;
         – whether participant A/B is listening to the other;
         – how turn-taking is signalled/carried out (interruption? mutual?).
      (v) Then perhaps replay at stages as at iii, focusing still on the one point for more detailed comments. This might be a point at which control of the video replay could be given to a participant or another student.
      (vi) Finally, add your own comments, and summarise what has been said, relating this to the key concepts already established.

Follow-up work
Use part of the next session to do follow-up work that arises directly from the needs of the students as they have emerged from the role-play. We tend to do three things:
a. Summarise the main points learned on a handout and use this for a recap.

TRAINING MATERIAL 5.19 VIDEO ROLE-PLAYS *continued*

> b. Pick up on factors which arise in role-plays but were not what
> we were focusing on, and use these as items to focus on in future
> role-plays.
> c. Do detailed language work or other exercises on any particualar
> aspects that caused problems, e.g.:
>   – a variety of exercises on giving explanations, such as:
>   – using transcriptions;
>   – exercises on selecting, ordering, presenting facts;
>   – report-writing, using one of the role-plays as the incident to
>   be reported;
>   – further role-play: explaining what happened in an incident to
>   a third party like an inspector on the buses, or a friend in the
>   canteen;
>   – other exercises devised from the needs of the group, such as:
>   concluding/closing;
>   intonation;
>   exercises in remedial grammar devised from needs of group,
>   such as the use of 'softeners'.

As in the post-elementary materials, advanced communications
courses were structured so that detailed language work arising from
the role-plays and their analysis was an integral part of the course.
Training Material 5.20 is an example of detailed language work from a
shop stewards' course.

6.3 Evaluation

Communication-skills courses for bilingual staff drew largely on the
philosophy of cross-cultural training, and in particular on *Crosstalk*,
and on those aspects of the post-elementary materials which used
student-elicited classroom data as the major input to the syllabus. The
experience of the student-autonomy project was also influential in the
systematic gathering of student perceptions and experiences. The
analytical and ethnographic approach was combined in an approach
which encouraged students to talk openly about perceived schemata
differences between themselves and their white peers and supervisors.
As we have suggested in Chapter 3 (section 4.1), students can develop
confidence and a new analytic language for talking about similarities
and differences in assumptions and language use with their line
managers, and joint sessions between bilingual trainees and their

TRAINING MATERIAL 5.20 WHAT CAN WE TALK ABOUT?
[Prepared by Peter Wilson, Pathway ILT]

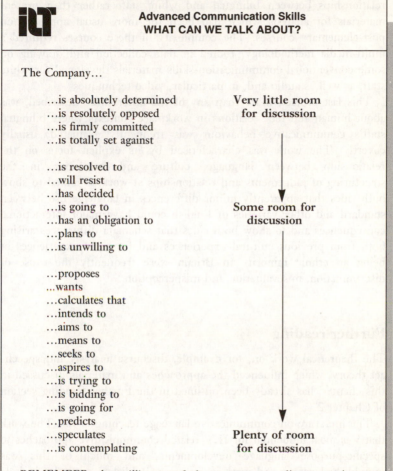

Advanced Communication Skills
WHAT CAN WE TALK ABOUT?

The Company...

...is absolutely determined   **Very little room**
...is resolutely opposed   **for discussion**
...is firmly committed
...is totally set against

...is resolved to
...will resist
...has decided
...is going to   **Some room for**
...has an obligation to   **discussion**
...plans to
...is unwilling to

...proposes
...wants
...calculates that
...intends to
...aims to
...means to
...seeks to
...aspires to
...is trying to
...is bidding to
...is going for
...predicts
...speculates   **Plenty of room**
...is contemplating   **for discussion**

REMEMBER: the *willingness* of the company to discuss an issue
must be balanced with the *importance* of the issue for the trade union.

supervisors were common practice on advanced communication
courses. Indeed, both sides often commented in post-course evaluations on their preferences for more joint sessions.

By their very nature, advanced communication courses are resistant
to any nationally coordinated curriculum and are difficult to present as

materials. The quality of students' existing awareness and therefore of their perceptions and experience was so high that the ILT trainers' role was to help structure these experiences and restructure the relationships between bilingual and white staff rather than present materials for analysis which had been the more usual approach on post-elementary courses. The complexity of these courses required a multi-media methodology, rooted in data collection and drawing on some conventional communication-skills materials developed for white staff, as well as audio and, in particular, video techniques.

This last project, more than any of the other three described, was about human and race relations in workplace contexts where bilingual staff's communicative behaviour was frequently evaluated, usually covertly. The work was characterised by its explicit focus on the relationship between language, culture and behaviour in the structuring of judgements and relationships at work. It aimed to show both sides that apparently minor differences in language use between standard and other varieties of English could have major interactional consequences and to show both sides that schemata differences arising both from previous cultural experiences and from the experiences of being an ethnic minority in Britain were frequently the cause of discrimination, misevaluation and misperception.

Further reading

The theoretical work on, for example, discourse analysis and speech-act theory, which influenced the approaches and materials discussed in this chapter, has already been outlined in the Further Reading section of Chapter 2.

The literature on communicative language teaching is vast. The work that was most influential for ILT related communicative approaches to specific-purpose language developments, and much of this was unpublished papers and work in progress. Published examples include 'English language skills for overseas doctors and medical staff' by Candlin, Leather and Bruton (1974), the series English in Focus edited by Allen and Widdowson, and Widdowson's *Learning Purpose and Language Use* (1983) and *Explorations in Applied Linguistics 2* (1984); see also Candlin's *The Communicative Teaching of English* (1981b). The Council of Europe Modern Languages Project provides useful background papers on language learning for adults, including the European Unit/Credit System (Wilkins 1976; Trim 1978, 1980; Council of Europe 1979) and *The Threshold Level* (van Ek 1975), and specifically on language acquisition by migrant workers (Jupp 1982).

The analytic focus in communicative language teaching is well illustrated in such publications as Yalden's *The Communicative Syllabus: Evolution, Design and Implementation* (1983), Munby's *Communicative Syllabus Design* (1978) (although this has received some criticism), and Johnson's *Communicative Syllabus Design and Methodology* (1982). In ESL materials, one of the best examples is *Building a Framework* by McAllister and Robson (1984).

The experiential/ethnographic focus has been developed in a number of ways in mainstream language teaching. Studies of the 'good language learner' such as Rubin's (1975) and Naiman *et al.*'s *The Good Language Learner* (1978) are complemented by observational studies on individual differences in the language learner, for example Wong Fillmore's 'The language learner as an individual' (1982).

A recent collection of papers, *Learner Strategies*, edited by Wenden and Rubin (1986), looks at learners from the point of view of how they introspect about their learning.

Other useful approaches derived from or influenced by ethnography are Curran's *Counselling – Learning: A Whole-Person Approach for Education* (1972), Loveday's *The Sociolinguistics of Learning and Using a Non-Native Language* (1982), Richards's *The Context of Language Teaching* (1985) and the collection edited by Rivera (1983), *An Ethnographic/Sociolinguistic Approach to Language Proficiency Assessment*.

The experiential/ethnographic focus has also been developed through process and procedural syllabuses. Breen describes the process syllabus in *ELT Documents 118* (1984) and this type of syllabus is also presented by Candlin (1987) in a collection edited by Candlin and Murphy. The procedural syllabus is described, at some length, in Prabhu's *Second Language Pedagogy: A Perspective* (1987). Finally, van Lier's book *The Classroom and the Language Learner* (1988) discusses the role of ethnography in classroom research and practice.

The approach which we called transactional skills is reflected in ESL materials such as *Use Your English* by Beech, Brierly and Moselle (1981); *A Study Guide for Topics and Skills in English*, by Barr and Fletcher (1983); and *At Home in Britain*, by Harding, Naish and Wilkins (1980).

Oral discourse skills have been given more prominence in a number of useful books not specifically designed for ESL contexts, such as: Brown and Yule's *Teaching the Spoken Language* (1983), Anderson and Lynch's *Listening* (1988), Ur's *Teaching Listening Comprehension* (1986), and *Speaking* by Bygate (1987). For adult ESL learners,

Lancashire ILT's *Listening for Information Study Materials* (1989) is useful.

On learner autonomy, the classic books by Friere *Cultural Action for Freedom* (1975) and *Education: The Practice of Freedom* (1974), and by radical thinkers such as Postman *et al.* in *Teaching as a Subversive Activity (*1971), give a background to the education philosophy and methods. Jourard's *The Psychology of Open Teaching and Learning* (1972) gives some useful definitions of independent learning. There are a number of publications by the Council of Europe, for example Richterich (1979), van Ek (1975) and Holec (1978), and other useful books and articles on independent language learning including Holec's *Autonomy and Foreign Language Learning* (1981), Dickinson's *Self-Instruction in Language Learning* (1987) and Nunan's *The Learner-Centred Curriculum* (1988). One of the few sets of published materials for independent language learning is *Help Yourself to English* by Leach, Knight and Johnson (1988).

Literacy materials for adult ESL learners include *A New Start* by Furnborough *et al.* (1980) and a series of workbooks produced by Birmingham ILT Unit including: *A to Z Writing Book; ABC; Write it Down;* and *In the News.* For more advanced students, Cogill's *Writing Business Letters and Memos* (1980) is useful. There are a number of readers specifically aimed at Asian women including *Asian Women Speak Out* by Wilson and Naish (1980) and *Breaking the Silence* by Mukherjee (1984).

More general adult literacy materials include the BBC *Adult Literacy Handbook* (1975) and the BBC *Writing and Spelling Handbook* (1979). The BBC's *Speak for Yourself* by Gubbay (1980) combines both literacy and oracy skills, as does *Signing Off* by Sayers *et al.* (1979), which is a handbook for unemployed job-seekers with little experience of English.

For language linked to skills, Lancashire ILT's publications include: *Communication for Employment and Training* (1982), *Independent Learning in Basic Education and Training: Implementing Learner Autonomy* (Heire and Furnborough 1985), *Training for Change: Evaluation Report on Pilot Programmes* (1985). A useful introduction to the principles of linking skills and language development is ILEA's *Linked Skills: A Handbook for Skills and ESL Tutors* (1983). A good example of a particular skills area is *English for Driving* by Barr and Fletcher (1984). Several recent publications in advanced communications skills by ILT staff or authors associated with ILT can be used with mixed groups of bilingual and monolingual participants: Gray's *Caring Communications* (1982), Bulloch and Cheetham's *Communication for*

Health (1987), Cheetham with Edwards's *Interview Skills: A Complete Resource for Tutors, Trainers and Others Working with Candidates* (1989). Finally, the Department of Employment's Training Agency has issued a materials guide for teaching communications and numeracy to bilingual speakers (1989).

6 Conclusion

1 Introduction

This book has explored issues about language and discrimination within multi-ethnic settings, based on research and training carried out by the ILT service. We have examined the linguistic dimension of disadvantage and discrimination as it has been illuminated by this provision of training in and about communication. The work described has been with people from ethnic minorities who are first-generation immigrants to the UK and reflects the experience of their interaction with the white majority in their workplaces and in seeking access to the public services – for example, housing and the National Health Service. These settings are strategic research sites and what happens in them affects the life chances of ethnic minorities in terms of their economic and social opportunities. ILT provided training opportunities for black and white people to improve their language and communication skills in their dealings with each other. The context, however, was firmly shaped by power relationships which reflect racism in Britain and associated attitudes to cultures and to community languages other than English. Although our insights into the relationship between language and discrimination are firmly rooted in this particular British context, our findings have important implications and conclusions for broader understanding of inter-ethnic communication and for further work in ethnography, linguistics and pedagogy.

ILT has been a success story in a number of respects. Thousands of people in hundreds of workplaces received training in a complex field. No other public service in the field of ethnic relations has a comparable record. The service began at a time when the UK was behind other countries, and no other service was involved practically in the race-relations aspects of industrial training. ILT has been unique in several other ways. It has been perhaps the only service to provide workplace training for unskilled and semi-skilled workers which is not narrowly related to, for example, health and safety or the introduction of new systems and technologies. It has been the only service to look systematically at the communicative environment in the workplace and train both white and ethnic-minority groups. This involvement in the workplace has entailed cooperation between shop-floor workers, trade unionists and management. Finally, ILT has also been an area of direct cooperation between educationalists, social policy makers and research linguists.

The work described in this book took place during a decade, the mid-1970s to mid-1980s, in which concepts of language, its teaching and the role of teachers were changing and deepening. In terms of the context of race relations, this was also a period of change. On the one hand, the decade saw the introduction into Britain of significant employment and race-relations legislation, and some strengthening of the black voice within the professions. But on the other, there was a rapid decline of many manufacturing industries which employed black people and an increase in overt racial violence and a fracturing and consequent decline in the power of the liberal consensus fighting for racial justice. This changing and increasingly polarised context was demanding for ILT trainers both professionally and politically. We found ourselves constantly needing to present rapid responses and suggestions for particular problems while acutely aware of underlying paradoxes and structural inequalities. In some cases, the conflicts for staff were difficult. For example, should they seek to persuade employers to provide training opportunities for redundant workers before they leave their jobs so they had some preliminary support for the difficult time ahead or would such training amount to little more than a public-relations exercise for the employer? An even more difficult issue was presented to staff by police interest in cross-cultural training immediately after the inner-city disturbances of 1981. The first priority seemed to ILT staff to be the recruitment of black people to the police and a fundamental change in police policy towards racially discriminatory behaviour within the force. ILT work was often far from adequate in its response to such difficult demands and opportunities, as we have demonstrated, but ILT was strengthened by a willingness to respond in practical ways to contexts as we found them and to make time to seek out the relationship between theory, practice and reality.

ILT practice was not always logical or linear, and, because to a large extent dependent on opportunities created by employers, its development was relatively unplanned. Because of the responsive and varied nature of the service, it was difficult to use the synergy of one development to inform another. For example, there could be simultaneous debates and developments on student autonomy, our response to the police's interest in human-awareness training, new initiatives from the MSC on youth training and methodological developments in training in advanced communications skills. There was an underlying philosophy informing all the work which, as we have shown, harnessed ethnography and analysis of data to practical outcomes relating to the linguistic dimension of discrimination. However, the difficulty lay in organising the detailed experiences of each project into a coherent, theoretical perspective which could inform all areas of work. In thinking about issues of theory and practice, one model is to act and then see if there is a theory which fits; another to learn about theory and then see if it can be proved; yet another is to concentrate upon either practice or theory to the exclusion of the other. In the event, we came with some theory, became immersed in practice which was only implicitly informed by theory, and sought out new theory at points where practice seemed stale, inappropriate or ineffective.

The findings of our work remain clearly relevant to developed and industrialised urban areas world-wide, and insights form ILT have been applied in Canada and the United States, in Australia and New Zealand, as well as in various parts of Europe. In recent years, there has been some shift of interest from language needs (often associated with the first generation of settlers) to an emphasis on culture within inter-ethnic communication. But our work shows that the separation of language and culture is a false one. Our use of the notion of the interrelationship between schema, frame and linguistic code enables people to understand that culture, language and social identity are constantly recreating and reconfirming each other. Addressing language issues does not of itself lead to improved opportunities for ethnic minorities, but is a means by which teachers and researchers can exercise their responsibility to challenge assumptions, to raise awareness and to empower language learners.

2 Issues about language as a hidden dimension within discrimination

There is, as we have illustrated in this book, a linguistic dimension to discrimination. But language continues to be one of the least visible, least measurable and least understood aspects of discrimination which can easily be squeezed out by a proper and understandable focus on structural and institutionalised racism. But language is a powerful instrument of control which can be, and has been, used globally to maintain power relationships, and more rarely to set people free, as in the Freirian tradition of literacy development or in countries of regions where speakers' first language has triumphed over an externally imposed language.

ILT, in different ways, always attempted to address the issues of language and power. In doing so, ILT staff found themselves involved in an ideological debate which was both moral and theoretical. The moral dilemma concerns the extent to which intervention at the level of face-to-face interaction can, in reality, change power relationships and the social positioning of most minority ethnic groups in a racist society. Or does such intervention either provide tools for individuals, consciously or unconsciously, to collude with the existing discourses of power or simply have little or no impact at all? The moral dilemma reflects the theoretical one. There is still relatively little theory on the relationship between wider social structures, institutional discourse and individual interaction. It is difficult to identify in precisely what ways the detail of interactions as unique encounters and as part of institutional discourse, both reflect unequal social structures and also actively structures this social inequality. The theoretical work on gatekeeping encounters and our own experience of such gatekeeping, both in the classroom and outside, strongly indicate that individual encounters, cumulatively, are actively structuring, as well as acting out structures. For example, both the behaviour of gatekeepers in interviews and their justifications for decisions after interviews feed into and help create social and economic inequality. The attempt in our work to draw upon and use theories which help us to understand the relationship between these issues has been vital, as has been the effort made in the practice described to make meaningful connections between these theories.

However, the underlying paradoxes involved make clarity and resolution elusive. The complexities and their message are for many difficult to grasp, and more difficult to accept. The message of the work is both pessimistic and challenging. It is that language will naturally contribute to prejudice and discrimination in a racist context, but even in a consciously liberal or anti-racist context real difficulties may arise if the truth and reality of language and cultural difference and its effects are not examined and understood. Often people from neither context will accept the message. Those working in a racist context and consciously or unconsciously colluding with it are frequently unwilling or unable to acknowledge difference or to discuss it as a white problem. Those wishing to challenge institutional racism often prefer, for political reasons, to ignore linguistic and cultural difference as a factor in discrimination. So although their motivation differs, both groups are reluctant to discuss the role of cultural and linguistic differences in discrimination. There is a further twist in the argument: focusing attention on difference, even in a liberal context, can itself encourage discriminatory decisions. As a result, many of the findings in this book have never been fashionable, and have often been misunderstood, avoided, attacked or, inevitably, seen as controversial.

There is no single theoretical model which will encompass the very many ways in which language reflects, reinforces and structures social relationships. We therefore list below in a rather bald form a number of statements, some of which are new and some of which are most certainly not, but all of which we have found demonstrated in our practical experience:

(i)   Language is used by people with power to sustain their power (consciously or unconsciously) and therefore plays a significant if invisible role in how discrimination operates.

(ii)   Language variation reflects and expresses social differences and so, as with class and gender, language reinforces existing social inequalities associated with ethnicity and with race.

(iii)   The greatest hurdle for ethnic minorities with regard to language is the failure of white-Anglo gatekeepers to make sound judgements about ethnic minority groups' knowledge of English and the tendency of such gatekeepers to draw incorrect conclusions from the way non-Anglos use English.

(iv)   Inter-ethnic communication therefore provides an unreliable context for applying systems of evaluative judgement developed within a single ethnic context.

(v)   Interaction between ethnic groups often confirms existing prejudices about each other and these prejudices are frequently justified by reference to aspects of language use and communicative style.

(vi)   Lack of knowledge and perception of how interrelated linguistic and cultural factors affect judgement amounts to a form of prejudice and has discriminatory outcomes.

(vii)   Good inter-ethnic communication is achieved only through a conscious effort of understanding based on an awareness of the real difficulties involved. Good policies, principles and intentions are not enough.

(viii) Action is required to expose to those concerned the ways in which individuals and institutions make judgements and control access through interactions which are based on unshared assumptions and expectations.

(ix)   Actions are required to demonstrate the link between individual interaction and institutional decision-making and discrimination, and to challenge the traditions of formalised interactions such as interviews, which inevitably discomfort, disadvantage and discriminate against ethnic minorities among others.

(x)   Changes in procedures and systems are potentially very helpful, but cannot in themselves guarantee 'fairness' because they do not necessarily affect the quality of face-to-face interaction which is the point at which decisions are made. So there have to be changes in interactive behaviour as well.

It is widely recognised that the major source of discrimination and racism is imbalance of socio-economic power and the way in which formal and informal systems can institutionalise and sustain this inequality. For this reason some people believe it to be dangerous to examine the detailed processes of discrimination which are based on differences of assumptions and expectations. These people believe that such an examination may provide excuses for discrimination and may also present its victims in a negative light. They do not see a focus on change in relationships and opportunities as a sufficiently direct attack on racism. Others regard all discrimination as a matter of fixed attitude and are suspicious of any approach which explains how some aspects of discrimination arise or are rationalised through the actual process of interaction. Our view is that, as language is frequently used as a factor in racial discrimination, every effort should be directed towards investigating what role language can play in combating disadvantage and discrimination. The view that language difference is a marginal consideration compared with the fundamental problems of racism and the need to tackle power relationships is an understandable one, but it can ignore the fact that communication is an aspect of power and that language and culture are major factors frequently mentioned or used implicitly in decision-making by white groups about minority groups.

This ideological debate has created problems for teachers in accepting or accommodating the necessary broadened base for their view of language and their pedagogy. The doubts, conflicts and dilemmas which characterise the work are constructive for some and debilitating for others. In Chapter 1 we suggested that there are some teachers who simply prefer to ignore the wider issues altogether. There are also numbers of teachers who more understandably prefer to avoid linking language difference and discrimination in case it provides an excuse for racism. They have withdrawn from teaching English in order to concentrate their energy on the training of white gatekeepers, or on a more direct challenge to racism through management training geared to change in institutional systems, or have turned to more direct ways of working to confront the system from a more overtly political position.

We would argue that adult learners of English from ethnic minority groups have a legitimate expectation and requirement for improved quality in their interaction with the white majority; for specific educational efforts to enhance their learning and vocational opportunities; and for greater awareness of communication and racism from society's gatekeepers. Without these, many people will continue to be failed by culture-bound tests and interviews and denied opportunities in their careers, rather than asserting control over their working lives, experiencing some measure of racial justice operating in the day-to-day decision-making processes of the workplace, and articulating and taking the lead in the need for structural change.

In addition to the pressure of uncertainty caused by lack of understanding and respect for the validity of their work in language, ILT trainers also faced difficulties in securing recognition for their professional expertise and in defining the boundaries of their work. These difficulties arose out of one of the central conclusions of ILT work, that the crucial factor in relations between different language groups is whether they meet as equals or not. Despite the name of the service, it was not possible to confine the work to language training. Both the context and the content of the work had to include issues of racism, inequality and cultural intolerance and so the power relations that existed outside the classrooms. Because the environment for language learning was not the classroom but the workplace, trainers acquired the responsibility to effect change in the practices, behaviour and attitudes of management. So ILT expertise had to be extended to include management training as well as language teaching. Both the opportunities and the responsibilities offered by the workplace setting were therefore greater for the ILT trainers than for many of their colleagues working in education, although both share a responsibility to define their role in promoting equal opportunities, to search for non-ethnocentric ways of presenting an analysis of language and to combat racism.

ILT trainers were sometimes unwillingly thrust into compromising situations which highlighted the boundaries of their work. For example, trainers were frequently approached by a company which had fundamental race-relations and management problems and saw language training as a relatively uncontroversial way of being seen 'to do something'. In such cases, the ILT service could be represented as tokenism or could be seen as having failed because the training provided had not solved the much more fundamental problems that existed. An equally difficult situation was where the boundaries for ILT work were drawn too narrowly. Trainers were asked to undertake language training but were excluded from consulting on and training in the wider field of equal opportunities. In other words, language was separated off from wider issues of rights and responsibilities, human relations and cultural differences in a way which is incompatible with effecting changes in communication and the human environment.

3 Topics for further development and research

3.1 Becoming hospitable to difference

At the heart of our examination of inter-ethnic communication and the focus on the analysis of individual interactions is the recognition that seeing difference as something positive is difficult. People sustain existing power relationships by misunderstanding each other's intent, talking past each other, opting out of the effort involved in listening to another perspective and accommodating it or being, simply, uncomfortable with difference without thinking through why they are. Those working in or associated with race relations and language learning are often more comfortable playing down or denying difference. Focusing on difference is perceived as focusing on deficit. Professionals often prefer to look for similarities in an assumed solidarity against racism and discrimination. However, such an undifferentiated view of racism denies the reality that people from black and ethnic-minority groups are regularly discriminated against because of differences in interactive behaviour.

Cultural difference plays a role in discrimination and it is therefore dangerous to deny the reality of cultural difference expressed through language, and it is important to continue to explore and understand it in the struggle to establish a climate in which such difference has validity. We are not discussing a narrow or static view of culture, but a view of culture defined as shared systems of meaning, derived from the experiences which people live through, which in turn influence the schemata which people bring to interactions and the interpretive frames they use in them. In this definition of culture, social, political and economic realities become part of people's culture. Some of the practice described in this book has explored ways of giving insight into such group conventions which enables better understanding between people and provides a basis for behaviour modification without loss of cultural identity for either side. It is important to continue to develop approaches to the analysis of inter-ethnic communication which do not patronise or problematise ethnic minorities but involve people in a process of examining differences together so that both sides see in a new light the ways in which they do the same things differently.

3.2 An inter-ethnic view of language and language learning

Our experience with the use of techniques of awareness and analysis of inter-ethnic communication in training has demonstrated that many bilingual people, and monolingual English-speakers who are not language teachers, do not have problems in relating to these concepts. They relate such analysis to their experience as language users and communicators, engage with the analysis enthusiastically, see further and broader, and have a better capacity for rhetorical analysis than language teachers from traditional backgrounds of language analysis who lack the confidence to move away from the functional analysis of language to the functional analysis of interaction. This has significant and positive implications for training as well as for language work much more widely in education – for example, with young people at school.

Another significant strand in our approach to language learning has been the way in which we have extended the role of the learner towards that of researcher. The researcher role moves people from a *functional* awareness of communication to a *strategic* one. We would define here functional as the ability to operate more successfully in certain situations, and strategic as being aware of and using language communication to negotiate as an individual. The significant factors in this teaching approach are, first, that the analysis of situation and language are made by the learner rather than by the teacher; and, second, the learners' own experience of inter-ethnic communication is used as the authentic data on which learning is based. Some examples of this approach have been illustrated in Chapter 5.

3.3 Ethnographic and linguistic analysis

Our experience has shown the need to undertake ethnographic analysis and to link it to linguistic analysis. An understanding of ethnography and practical experience underpins the expanded view of language developed in this book. Without ethnography, there is a danger of manipulating both people and language. A view of language and of language-learning needs is easy to impose upon learners; and without their perspective on the process, they are used, not using. In other words, learners can feel that the new language and the language-teaching process is constraining them and teaching them to accommodate, rather than feeling in control of and empowered by their use of the new language. Similarly, language divorced from its context—and this context can only be understood through ethnography—becomes language merely for linguistic manipulation.

Learners want to understand how their use of language creates a particular context and how this context fits into the wider social and political context of a multi-ethnic and racist society. Without this understanding, language becomes objectified as a formal system to be manipulated in order to achieve classroom linguistic goals. Ethnographic analysis, in any educational programme, puts learners at the centre of the process. Their perceptions and ways of looking at the world define learning objectives and learning outcomes.

Ethnography and sociolinguistic analysis combine participants' perspectives with a detailed account of language use in context. Educational anthropologists and sociologists in the USA have shown this combination working in theory-building and have also used it in a practical way. Schoolchildren in 'remedial' programmes, given some of the basic tools of ethnography, have analysed their own communication networks and uses of language and this experience has contributed to their long-term success in the educational system (Heath 1983).

In Britain, there has been a tradition of classroom ethnography based on action research programmes by teachers. ILT, from a different tradition, extended the concept of teacher as ethnographer to the workplace and created opportunities for learning out of a context relatively hostile to learning. ILT also took the concept of student as ethnographer to adult learners so, as we have suggested above, their experience became the data for language-learning programmes. There are some new research programmes developing. These link ILT experience and the work of classroom ethnography which has almost entirely been carried out in mono-ethnic settings, and aim to involve the teachers and students as researchers in action research projects on multi-ethnic classrooms. The classrooms selected are in the further-education sector where students are undergoing vocational or pre-vocational courses. The aim of this research is to identify good classroom practice which contributes to the success of young ethnic-minority people on such courses and to use the research findings to inform staff development (Further Education Unit 1989).

3.4 Pedagogy

Some of the work described in this book broke new ground in classroom methodology. A key concept, born out of the focus on the learners' actual communicative environment, was the use of contrasting native-speaker and non-native-speaker discourse as the content of materials. One important way in which this was done was to invite native English-speaking workers, trade unionists and supervisors into the language classrooms. This enables a process by which ethnic-minority people themselves make the majority white language group aware of how culture-specific rather than 'normal' are their assumptions and ways of interacting. The development of pedagogic processes for exposing and examining the ethnocentric notion of 'normal' needs taking much further in education and training generally. This is particularly true in the three areas of classroom interaction, learning style and understanding and sharing learning objectives between students and teachers. This need has been quite widely inspired by classroom ethnographers in the United States (Erickson 1986; Mehan 1979) and by curriculum developers in Britain – for example, in the recent work in the Technical and Vocational Education Initiative. However, this work does not include an understanding of language in the classroom in the sense of how it is used for evaluation of students, for imposing structures of meaning and for advantaging some and disadvantaging others. The skills-training work described in Chapter 5, carried out by Lancashire ILT Unit, has paid attention to learning styles and the communication of concepts by linking an understanding of language in the classroom with practical activities which demonstrate the learning strategies and key concepts. Such work often involves as much learning and awareness for teachers as for students.

The developments within ILT were certainly paralleled in language teaching in other areas of education. For example, there has been much excellent work on language support in subject classrooms in both schools and further education (Department of Education and Science 1986). It has been convincingly argued that separate educational provision for children who are learning English as a second language discriminates against their access to a proper educational curriculum (CRE 1987). On the other hand, language support within the mainstream curriculum is very demanding and needs much more work on collaborative teaching and on the development of a language syllabus for learners as they undertake other tasks. The principle of moving into the mainstream (Bourne 1989) is well established but practice tends to lag behind principle and language-support teachers can become no more than helpers and interpreters (see section 4 below).

3.5 Gatekeepers

Most of the issues and contexts described in this study apply to any predominantly English-speaking country which has relatively recently become a multilingual and multiracial society. Such societies will be subject to a struggle for change to achieve racial justice. As part of this process, education in language awareness with reference to inter-ethnic communication will be crucial to enabling gatekeepers and others in power to explore and make changes in their level of sensitivity and behaviour. Those in gatekeeping roles as defined in this book will need to be helped to develop skills in ethnography so that they can monitor and learn from their own interaction.

What is needed is a way of examining inter-ethnic communication in a non-ethnocentric way which relates actual instances of interaction to ethnically determined and differing conventions on the one hand, and on the other to the broad issue of negative evaluation, indirect discrimination and the perpetuation of systematised discrimination. ILT work seeks to identify and focus attention upon the role language plays so that the way difference is stereotyped and used against people can be meaningfully discussed in a way which extends people's understanding and empowers them to act by exploring acceptable ways of modifying unconscious behaviour in the interest of social justice. People who want to discriminate will of course always continue to do so, and this approach is not relevant to changing the committed racist.

A most useful and successful tool to emerge from ILT experience is the preparation of video material which requires managers to examine their own behaviour, analyse their interactions and develop skills relevant to the wider context of their company's equal-opportunities policies. There is an urgent need for a lot more video material which shows successful inter-ethnic interaction and positive evaluation and decision-making based upon it.

General management training in the UK completely ignores the inter-ethnic dimension and is thereby guilty of discrimination by omission. Training related to equal opportunities is primarily about implementing equal-opportunities policies and this usually involves issues such as monitoring and the consequent improvement of procedures. Equal-opportunities management training related to recruitment and selection is still dominated by the bureaucratic notion of 'fairness', and is concerned with standardising procedures and relating interview questions to person specifications. It is rarely about the detailed processes of evaluation based on what individuals say and yet this is the reality of how decisions are and always will be made. In reality, while well defined and sound procedures are necessary, the urgent challenge is implementing equal opportunities within these procedures rather than believing them to be sufficient. This is the point at which the process of interaction becomes all-important – whether in education, at work or in the public services. Much more work remains to be done. In particular, there is the need for more practical studies which examine how the same procedures can lead to different outcomes. For example, why does some equal-opportunities interviewing practice provide positive opportunities for ethnic-minority candidates to present themselves in a way which leads to successful outcomes for them while other similar practice does not? Communications training for managers which refers to multilingual and multi-ethnic workforces has also been narrowly defined. It has tended to stereotype on the basic of simple cultural differences or suggest simple tips for communication 'across the language barrier'.

3.6 Research

In the UK there has been no systematic study of inter-ethnic communication directed at analysing and preventing the abuse of unequal power. Ways need to be found of further involving practitioners in action research programmes with clearly defined goals. Research was important to ILT practitioners in that it confirmed some obvious but contentious observations and provided the broader insights and confidence for staff to further refine the tools of analysis and the quality of data. Work on language and discrimination in Britain has hardly started and practical work at present lacks the research which could provide it with a more systematic and more principled basis. At the same time, work in interactional socio-linguistics outstrips the availability of data and learning material, and of teachers and trainers with the capacity to act upon it and feed back into theory. This gap is linked to the pressing need to include the issues raised here in teacher training and curriculum development. This lack of research into inter-ethnic communication is a major failure of social responsibility on the part of leading members of the academic disciplines in Britain which could contribute. Like discrimination, it is systematic and structural: research proposals are not put up presumably because this is not seen as a 'sound' area for recognition and career development; in turn those who decide on research funding have little understanding of the issues and consequently are likely to turn down any such proposals. On the occasions when such research is carried out, there appears to be a lack of understanding of the type of significant data and strategic issues which should be examined. Whereas in America, from the 1960s onwards, there was perhaps an incautious eagerness for researchers from linguistics and anthropology to set up major research linked to ethnicity and discrimination, the opposite remains true in the UK, reflecting the extent to which issues of ethnic and race discrimination remain submerged for the majority of people in Britain and reflecting the still very traditional nature of British society in terms of both culture and class. A telling example of this is provided by the record of British universities in terms of admitting black and ethnic-minority students. While overseas students are welcomed at all levels, if they have finance, British black students secure a very small percentage of places. The record of polytechnics, it must be noted, is very different.

There are, however, signs of increasing research interest in language and power, which are beginning to feed into the debate about the national curriculum and, in particular, the teaching of English (Cameron and Bourne 1989; Fairclough and Ivanič, 1988). Those involved in this research argue that the teaching of English is presented as unproblematical in that there is insufficient analysis of language and its varieties with reference to the historical and political struggle between different groups and classes in society. Recent research on the place of language education in teacher-training courses reflects a rather half-hearted attempt to tackle language awareness and linguistic analysis as a central element in initial teacher training (Brumfit 1988). There is little research which combines ethnographic and linguistic analysis in the context of language and power, despite the considerable research devoted to language in education. Interestingly, there is now a view emerging from some teacher trainers concerned with foreign-language learning that a cultural-awareness programme would turn learners into ethnographers (Byram 1989).

4 Change in perception and practice in education

Inequality is not easily removed, as experience for example with class, with gender, and with black Americans demonstrates. The needs and legitimate demands of ethnic-minority language learners and the needs of white gatekeepers to help create a successful educational experience far outstrip the capacity of the education system to make appropriate provision, or of teachers to provide appropriate courses. This book has attempted to present a critical survey of the evolution and application of perspectives in second-language learning and cross-cultural training in a specific context, the workplace. In considering how this experience might be transmitted to the context of education in general, it may useful to consider how ILT developed its expertise.

Education has its own dynamic in which organisation can shift rapidly, but ideas travel and develop slowly. Policy in education has tended to be either *ad hoc*, incremental or ideological, and this is one of the reasons why policy often takes so long to be implemented or is resisted by the practitioners. Support for a centrally organised national service for language provision in industry came at one of those rare moments when educational anxieties, social realities and political will coalesced, albeit on a small scale and on a specific issue in relation to adults. Despite the inevitable shortcomings we have described, great strength was derived from the structure and organisation of a national service coordinated from a central resource base with close educational and community links (see Appendices 1 and 2). Such organisation allowed small specialist units to develop good local practice which could be rapidly drawn together and disseminated. It encouraged a coherent public image of the work, supported new initiatives and provided a national dimension to its promotion which gave the status and recognition that such work often lacks. Crucially, it was able to resource and develop its teachers and invest in their practice and insights in ways which supported and empowered them. ILT was exceptional in the resources available for a planned but evolving staff-development programme. Many of the projects outlined in this study highlight the important role of outside agencies – for example, individuals at the University of California (Berkeley) and at the University of Lancaster, the Council of Europe and the European Science Foundation – in providing the stimulus to act in a particular area and move forward in a concentrated way. Working with such agencies became a reality because ILT was a national organisation, known internationally. One of the most important lessons from the ILT experience was the great strength given to the work because it was nationally coordinated and locally organised.

The obverse of this undoubted strength was its inherent weakness once expertise was established. It is difficult from a specialist and marginalised position which is seen as focused on a specific disadvantage to transmit expertise and experience to mainstream institutions, services and individuals. Change in perception and practice takes a very long time, particularly in education, and it is difficult to achieve unless it is powered by matters of central importance such as nationally defined curriculum and examinations.

There also appears to be a typical cycle in educational innovation, wherever it is located, which stops short of achieving rapid dissemination. The cycle is one of expanding enthusiasm which draws in committed teachers, but at some point such groups often become self-critical and inward-looking. Energy is then directed at in-group debate, and the real task of spreading good practice takes a lower priority. Certainly, within the context of ILT, this pattern appeared to emerge after some years and to weaken very seriously the power of innovation and of dissemination of some local units. This meant that many of the ideas linking language, culture, and equality, developed within ILT, did not spread easily into institution-based provision. In particular, the process of redefinition of the meaning of language education developed separately in schools and colleges, where in most instances ILT had only an indirect influence.

Many of the ideas about how language encodes culture and how language maintains social identity have now been developed in schools and colleges as a response to the way linguistic diversity is developing in the UK. Many people now grow up in urban parts of Britain with knowledge of more than one language and so more than one set of norms and values. They possess a variety of language practices which both reflect and sustain cultural diversity. For example, many Londoners have available to them as models the standard variety of English, non-standard varieties such as London English or London Jamaican English, a range of creoles and local varieties of languages other than English such as Panjabi, Greek, Cantonese and Bengali.

Similarly, many of the ideas developed in ILT around the need to work with white and ethnic-minority trainees together, and to focus on raising awareness and changing the practice of the white majority, are also emerging in mainstream education. For example, in UK schools and colleges, specialist and separate language centres or classes are being abandoned on the grounds both of discrimination and what is known to be involved in second–language acquisition. But this change in educational practice is not reflected in government education and training initiatives, which continue to compartmentalise ESL, make no specific provision for the training of the white majority group, and provide support to ethnic-minority English learners through expensive teams of ESL 'support' teachers rather than make an investment in the language education of mainstream teachers. As with the integration into mainstream institutions of learners with special educational needs, the theoretical, social and educational thinking behind the pressure to do so frequently outstrips the knowledge and expertise of the institutions and teachers involved. They often lack both a confident theoretical base to provide an informed view of language and of the learning processes involved, and the training to draw together the intellectual, experiential and socio-political evidence which suggests what this view should be.

Despite the difficulties in making ideas travel, ILT has been able to influence mainstream practice in a number of ways. The research and development role of ILT made possible the publication of working papers, project reports and materials which found a readership beyond its specific field for whom little published material at that time was available. The student-autonomy project described in Chapter 5 in particular was seized upon because of its relevance to the ideological concerns of aware teachers, to developing notions of general learning practice and to an expanding view of what was involved in second-language acquisition. Local ILT units based in colleges of adult and further education or closely associated with them were able to feed into mainstream practice more directly. This has been particularly so with regard to the need for collaboration between subject and language teachers on integrated skills courses in further education. ILT trainers are also a source of training expertise relevant to the needs of educationists for culturally appropriate modification to classroom discourse and styles of interaction. Of particular importance to this is the capacity to provide training which affords concrete opportunity for the observation and analysis of cultural diversity and its effects on the learning process.

Many of the current developments in education are characterised by the search for an approach concerned not only with access to society but also with the right to be different within it. This has led to increased provision of courses which integrate the acquisition of English with meaningful content, activities and skills, and a greater acknowledgement and use of learners' preferred learning styles in self-access study-skills programmes. Of particular value to the development of an understanding of language in the context of inter-ethnic communication is the introduction of 'language awareness' work. This teaching may involve the exploration of language and of language diversity by all learners in a class, including the exploration by language learners of their own language history and experience as language learners and users (Heath 1983; Harris and Savitzky 1988). The acceptance of language-awareness topics as course work for recognised examinations has stimulated the publication of suitable teaching materials.

Our experience leads us to believe that increasingly issues of opportunity, equality and the quality of learning will centre on language and learning for all, with the onus on the communicative knowledge and flexibility of teachers and the focus on the opportunities for learning to be derived from the strengths of working in both multicultural and monocultural groups.

5 The future

The funding for a national Industrial Language Training service came to an end in 1989. The National Centre for ILT was closed in 1987. The decision to cease funding was in line with government policy to move from nationally organised, long-term-funded training to employer-led, financially competitive short-term contracts. This decision, no doubt, also reflected a lack of commitment to fund a service with a substantial research and development element, and one which aimed to tackle issues of racism and equal opportunities as well as language. Some ILT units are closed, others are being absorbed into wider further and adult education provision.

It is difficult to predict whether the characteristics and achievements of the work described in this book can be maintained. Roger Munns, Director of the former Lancashire ILT Unit, now renamed Equality At Work, offers this view of the future for such work in his area at the time of writing:

Ironically, interest in ILT type work from employers and training agencies is more apparent now than it was perhaps in the past. Demographic trends (the significant decrease in the number of young people 16–25) means that employers will have to employ people, such as ethnic minorities, who they have not considered before. They will also have to think about job progression for their existing workforce. This has already happened in the commercial sector, such as banking, and is beginning to happen in manufacturing industries. Industry and education have already come together to help young people on work experience, there will be more cooperation to help adult work-seekers soon. Unfortunately, there is now no national service to capitalise on industry's awareness that it will need to employ more ethnic minorities and offer better career prospects. Work with unemployed bilingual workers continues to be a high priority. But instead of being funded to develop programmes like Training for Change [see Chapter 5], we have to compete for short-term contracts from a number of different sources including the Department of Employment. This has a number of consequences. Firstly, we cannot engage in any mid-term or long-term planning and more extensive developmental programmes like Training for Change have to be fragmented, re-packaged and sold as short courses. Secondly, we have to work with an increasing number of training brokers, such as management consultants, which means there is less money for training providers. Thirdly, and perhaps most importantly, research and development activities are not built into the contracts. This development work which has been the hallmark of the ILT service now has to be proposed and funded as separate project activities.

More positively, the skills and experience developed by ILT have equipped staff to respond to the 'market place' challenge that many in education find threatening. We also have the autonomy and flexibility to change our own status and possibly become a limited company. This is an example of deregulated state education/training and a step nearer to a private operation.

We shall continue, as far as we can, to provide training and consultancy on equal opportunities for the private and public sectors, direct training for ethnic minority workers both at work and seeking work and trainer training. My hope for the future is government policy and resourcing which ensures *coherence* for this kind of work and a coordinated programme of access to and enhancement in employment. This has to be a programme which is not narrowly employer-led but includes a real educational element.

This book has ranged widely over a number of disciplines and areas of practical activity. Many working in these fields prefer to keep them separate for theoretical reasons. Others who are bounded by the 'syntax' and modes of discourse of their particular professional responsibilities do not make the connections we have suggested here. But we hope, since this book is fundamentally about how people understand and respect each other, that it will be consulted by a wide spectrum of people who wish to examine issues of race, language and social identity with regard to education and the management of people. Of particular importance are those with access to the training of teachers and the training of people other than the teachers – in all these groups the general level of language awareness remains very low. It is important that these concepts be understood by all those concerned with language education and with education generally in multi-ethnic communities, and by those involved in management and industrial-relations training especially in the fields of industrial psychology, communication and human-resource management. Finally, we hope that this book will inspire more research in Britain and elsewhere in the field of inter-ethnic communication and that, in keeping with the spirit of this book, it is research that will have practical outcomes for racial justice and equality.

Further reading

This concluding chapter has referred to the lack of research and materials which address issues raised in the book with regard to management and teacher training needs and to the independent learning requirements of bilinguals in work or vocational training. Useful and relevant recent publications include the BBC *Mosaic* series of which *Counselling and Advice across Cultures* (1990), *Crosstalk at Work* (1991) and *Recruitment Interviewing across Cultures* (1991) are examples. A recent major ESOL initiative funded by the Department of Employment has produced multi-media open learning materials for bilinguals from basic literacy to advanced communication skills for business. These are supported by staff development packages for training agencies and other gatekeepers [*Go to Work on Your English*, *Open For Training*, [NFER in press].

Appendix 1: Industrial Language Training: its origin, aims and objectives

The ILT service was first established as a national service in 1974 when government funds were made available to local authorities. A National Centre for ILT (NCILT) was also set up at this time (see Appendix 2).

The Department of Employment described the purpose of the proposed scheme in the following way:

> ...up to about 100,000 immigrant workers, the majority of whom were Asians, were unable to develop their skills and abilities because of language difficulties, and would benefit from training. Where language training had already been introduced it had improved communications and standards of safety, and increased productivity. Relations between immigrants and indigenous workers had also improved.
>
> Language training could also have important social consequences, enabling immigrants to participate more fully in the life of the Community...[1]

Over the fifteen years of ILT, in-company language training remained a primary focus of the services. But the broader issues of improved communications and relationships have become increasingly important. Discussions at policy-making level in the government have always placed language and communications in the broader context of its contribution to combating racial disadvantage and discrimination. When central government took over the funding of ILT nationally through the Manpower Services Commission, the rationale for so doing was stated as follows:

> These decisions reflect the importance the Government attached to the improvement of the Industrial Language Training Service, and its recognition of the contribution the service makes to racial equality policies....[2]

---

[1] *Report of Home Affairs Select Committee on Race Relations and Immigration, Session 1973-4, Vol. II: Memorandum of 11 July 1974 by Department of Employment, para. 2.*

[2] *Mr John Grant, Parliamentary Under-Secretary of State for Employment, in a written reply to a Parliamentary Question from Mr George Rodgers MP (Chorley).*

*The aims and objectives of Industrial Language Training in the workplace**

1.0 We consider better communications in multi-ethnic workplaces can contribute significantly to human relations, to opportunities for individuals, to participation and to overall industrial efficiency.

2.0 *Aims*
  (a) to help individuals learn the skills and acquire the self-confidence to communicate effectively in English in a multi-ethnic workplace;
  (b) to undertake this work in a way which contributes constructively to the needs of everyone in the workplace who supports the aims of ILT including the management and the trade unions;
  (c) as a result of ILT, to enable individuals to continue developing their communication skills in English and their self-confidence, and apply them in all aspects of their lives;
  (d) to work in the specific field of employment towards the building of a genuinely multi-racial society.

3.0 *Priorities*
  (a) to train people who speak English as a second language;
  (b) to train English-speaking people who work with these people;
  (c) to assist with organised procedures and practices which depend upon good communications (for example, induction, interviewing).

4.0 *Approach*

4.1 We have developed certain fundamentals in our approach:
  (a) We study and work on the whole process of interaction, which involves language, culture and psychological perception;
  (b) We work with everyone involved in the process of communication, native English-speaking people as well as speakers of English as a second language;
  (c) As well as helping individuals learn skills within the context of a set of communicative relationships, we seek to influence that context and the communicative relationships;
  (d) We study the workplace and establish specific aims and methods as a result. However, these aims relate to all aspects of communication at work, and ILT staff have to use their professional expertise to choose the best methods of teaching the necessary communication skills which may not be narrowlly job-related in terms of content;

---

* *From NCILT Information Sheet No. 29.*

(e) We recognise that learning to communicate effectively requires that people learn to speak for themselves and, as a result, to increase their control over their own environment. Our teaching methodology has, therefore, to respect and build upon our trainees' existing skills and experience in using English and has to encourage and develop self-directed learning.

4.2 In order to apply our approach and to meet our aims, we need access to the workplace, paid time for students, and flexible use of resources. Promotion and explanation of our work is a necessary precondition for these.

4.3 We cannot define permanently the type of training course we provide, or where and how it is provided. These things develop in response to changes in the employment context – particularly at the present time. The quality of our work has to be continually developed and strengthened in order for us to respond to these changing needs.

Aims and objectives of ILT: communication and awareness training*

Workplaces with a multi-ethnic clientele

1.0 This training is aimed at improving the services offered by professional/commercial/clerical staff who have dealings with ethnic minority clients and customers.

2.0 We consider the training for agencies offering these services can help minority groups to gain opportunity and get more control over their own lives. ILT can contribute towards the eradication of institutionalised racism both as it affects the service offered to minority groups and as it affects their employment opportunities within these agencies.

3.0 *Aims*
(These are broadly similar to the aims for ILT in the Workplace)
(a) To help individuals develop the awareness, commitment, skills and knowledge necessary to provide a fair and effective service to clients and members of the public from minority ethnic groups.
(b) In particular, to undertake the work in a way which will help individual staff develop the kind of client relationship with minority groups from which they can continue to improve the service offered.

---

* *From NCILT Information Sheet No. 29.*

(c) To help agencies make a real contibution to increasing minority groups' access to their organisations and, as employers of minority groups, to promoting equal opportunity within their organisations.

4.0 *Priorities*

This training must directly contribute to opportunities and access for minority groups. We undertake training:

4.1 As part of an intergrated programme of language/communications training:

- MSC Staff training linked to re-training for redundant workers;
- training for Local Authorities who employ minority group staff and who have a multi-ethnic clientele;
- minority and majority group nurses.

4.2 For services which:

- most people in the community have some level of contact with on a regular basis (e.g. NHS, Local Authority Services, DHSS);[1]
- may critically affect an individual's opportunities, rights or well-being (e.g. teachers or magistrates as opposed to shop assistants);
- offer some kind of personal service/contact which provides an opportunity for developing some form of communicative relationship however limited (e.g. Jobcentre staff, police).

4.3 For organisations which are willing to face up to their own institutionalised racism so that our training can be placed within the developing policy and activities of the organisation and is not simply a cosmetic exercise.

4.4 For organisations which have the capacity to develop new programmes which could provide employment/expertise for minority ethnic groups previously exluded.

- social workers now recruiting Asian foster parents.
- Local Authorities setting up a work experience scheme for young bilinguals.

5.0 *Fundamentals in our approach*

5.1 (i) We study and work on the whole process of interaction linking language, culture and perception to social values and social identity;

---

[1] *National Health Service, Department of Health & Social Security*

(ii) We study and work within the context in which interaction takes place. This means analysing all points of contact between the organisation and the individual client/member of the public, and examining the full range of services offered, i.e. how each service is presented, what access people have to it, how information is presented, written contact (forms, letters etc.), and all levels of face-to-face interaction;

(iii) In training individuals at the point of contact with minority group members of the public, we do not limit our objectives to teaching narrow task-orientated skills (e.g. specific panel interviewing skills) or giving information (e.g. substituting advice on one diet for another), but we do aim to develop awareness, commitment, skills and knowledge so that individuals in agencies can learn through interaction to adjust their service to the needs of their clients;

(iv) In helping individuals to reconsider the values on which their system are based and to adjust their practice, we should also be ready to address ourselves to issues of policy and provision. In this way we aim to affect the institution's policy and practice as an employer of minority ethnic groups;

(v) We work in cooperation with other organisations to achieve our aims and in close partnership with the institutions using our service;

(vi) We work in both formal and informal contexts and link training to actual experiences of inter-ethnic communication both inside and outside the classroom.

5.2 In order to meet our aims, we need a flexible model which tackles the training problem in a way which reflects the experience of disadvantage of minority groups. This disadvantage is a combination of racism, low social power and weak communicative power. Our training, therefore, needs to be a combination of awareness, specific communications skills and information.

5.3 For training to have a real impact on the environment of the organisation we need:

access to the organisation for needs analysis, data collection and post-course evaluation;

time commitment comparable to a language training course (one-off seminars can do no more than give information. They cannot develop skills or change behaviour);

support from senior management and unions for the training and changes as a result of the training.

Appendix 2: The role of the National Centre for Industrial Language Training (NCILT)*

1. The centre was established at the request of Local Education Authorities (LEAs) at the inception of the Industrial Language Scheme in 1974, during discussions between Local Authorities and Department of Education and Sciences (DES), Department of Employment (DE) and the Home Office. The Centre opened in 1975 and was fully funded by the Training Service Division (TSD) of the Manpower Services Commission (MSC) from the outset.

2. Treasury approval was given in July 1978 to extend the life of NCILT until 1987, to enlarge its role and increase its funding. This was seen as a necessary support to enlarged MSC funding for an expanded ILT service by LEAs.

3. The terms of reference of the Centre were:
   (a) The training of staff employed by any Education Authority in Great Britain, engaged in teaching the English Language to members of ethnic minorities with language difficulties in, or about to enter, employment or industrial training.
   (b) The development and dissemination of teaching material and other aids to this teaching together with advice and technical assistance to those engaged in this teaching.
   (c) The provision of an information service about Industrial Language Training.
   (d) Advice on the development of a national strategy for Industrial Language Training.
   (e) Such other functions as may be agreed by TSD.

The responsibility for the general oversight of the programmes designed to carry out these functions was vested in the Industrial Language Training Advisory Committee which included LEA officers representing regions where ILT was provided, representatives of government departments and other bodies, and members of the ethnic minority groups.

NCILT was set up, initially, to develop and, later, support ILT units throughout the country. By 1978, there were thirty units funded

---

* Based on NCILT Information Sheet No. 29.

by the MSC and based in LEAs. These units were part of the Local Education Authority's service to minority ethnic groups but the units were also part of a national service coordinated by NCILT. Although LEAs dealt directly with the MSC on matters of finance, NCILT was expected to provide advice on professional and technical matters and often became involved in advising on financial matters as well. NCILT was also the national focus for advising the MSC on matters of policy and development.

4. The programme of work of the Centre each year covered:
   (a) *In-service training of LEA staff employed on ILT*
       Particular importance was attached to systematic induction of new staff for this work and there was also the need for an ongoing programme of staff development. Finance and staff release needed to be planned by ILT units and LEAs.
   (b) *The development and dissemination of teaching materials*
       Much of the development of training materials was done at local level and NCILT's role was to advise on and disseminate major project materials. In addition, NCILT had a programme of a special projects and of reviewing major areas of training, and much of this work was planned on a joint basis with particular ILT units.
   (c) *Resources and information centre*
       There was a constant two-way flow of training materials, reports and information between NCILT and ILT units. The Centre also provided a number of publications and leaflets to units and required certain regular factual returns from them.
   (d) *Planning and policy for ILT nationally*
       The Centre's task was to:
       (a) liaise closely with LEAs on the needs and development of their ILT service;
       (b) contribute to the development of a national strategy for ILT work which reflected (a) and the views of industry and other users;
       (c) advise MSC on the development of the service and liaise with other appropriate national bodies;
   (e) *Liaison and services to ILT units and LEAs*
       Examples in addition to those mentioned above were:
       – Regular field visit to ILT units;
       – Convening of working parties on particular topics;
       – Providing advice on the appointment of staff at the invitation of LEAs and colleges.

(f) *Promotion and information work*
There was constant demand for information and advice from many sources including employers. There was also a programme of planned development work with identified key bodies such as certain industrial training boards, certain trade unions and various specialist bodies.

Appendix 3: Race Relations Act 1976*

The Race Relations Act 1976 makes it unlawful to discriminate against a person, directly or indirectly.

Direct racial discrimination arises where a person treats another person less favourably on racial grounds than he treats, or would treat, someone else. 'Racial grounds' means any of the following grounds: colour, race, nationality (including citizenship) or ethnic or national origins (s.1(1)(*a*)). Indirect racial discrimination consists of treatment which may be described as equal in a formal sense as between different racial groups but discriminatory in its *effect* on one particular racial group (s.1(1)(*b*)).

The Code of Practice (p.6) explains this further :

Indirect discrimination consists of applying a requirement or condition which, although applied equally to persons of all racial groups, is such that a considerably smaller proportion of a particular racial group can comply with it and it cannot be shown to be justifiable on other than racial grounds. Possible examples are:
- a rule about clothing or uniforms which disproportionately disadvantages a racial group and cannot be justified;
- an employer who requires higher language standards than are needed for safe and effective performance of the job.

Under the terms of the Act (s.56), if an employer or another is found to have acted unlawfully, they can be asked to take appropriate action to remedy the situation.

The Race Relations Act covers: all employers, trade unions, government and other training bodies, education, local authorities, the provision of goods, facilities and services and premises, advertisements and contracts. There are two main exceptions to the Act:

(i) where being of a particular racial group is a genuine occupational qualification (e.g. cook in a Chinese restaurant) (s.5(1));
(ii) where there are special needs of racial groups in regard to education, training or welfare (s.35).

---

* Based on *Racial Discrimination: A Guide to the Race Relations Act 1976 (Home Office)* and the Commission for Racial Equality's Code of Practice.

The Race Relations Act also established the Commission for Racial Equality to help enforce the legislation and to promote equality of opportunity and good relations between people of different racial groups generally.

For ILT the Act's sections on selections for recruitment, promotion, transfer, training and dismissal (s.4 and s.28) were particularly important. There have been a number of cases brought under the Act in relation to language and literacy in the recruitment and selection process. (The following account of some examples is based on NCILT Information Sheet No.18, 1981.)

(i) *Ullah et al.* v. *British Steel Corporation*

In this case, seven Bangladeshi applicants were employed for some years at BSC. After a period in Bangladesh they applied to BSC to be re-employed. They were refused re-employment because they had failed the specially devised language test which had been recently introduced as a precondition of recruitment. The case was taken by the Commission for Racial Equality to an industrial tribunal but a settlement was made between the parties without the tribunal giving judgement. BSC agreed to employ the seven applicants, make them an *ex gratia* payment, and employ a testing expert to review English language testing.

Several years later, ILT was again invited to comment on BSC's test (this time a newly devised one based on a video of authentic situations). Again, the test was considered to be discriminatory, although an improvement on the original test. However, the issue was never finally litigated for a number of reasons. First, there had been massive redundancies so that the issue of re-employment was no longer a consideration. Second, the law had changed so that the tribunal was no longer able to say the test was valid or not. The applicants, therefore, accepted the CRE's advice not to pursue the case any further.

(ii) *Isa and Rashid* v. *British Leyland Cars Ltd*

Isa and Rashid, two Pakistani applicants, enquired about re-employment at BL cars. Both were given an application form to complete in their own hand. Since they were unable to read or write English, they could not fill out the form and were told that they could not be considered for employment.

The industrial tribunal found that BL had discriminated against the applicants and BL agreed to ensure that in future the filling-out of an application form would not be used as a test of literacy in English.

(iii) *CRE Formal Investigation into Polymer plc*
This formal investigation sought to establish whether Dunlop had indirectly discriminated against Asian applicants for foremen's jobs in their Leicester plant. For further details, see Chapter 4, section 4.

Bibliography

Abbs, B, Ayton, A and Freebairn, I 1975 *Strategies*. Longman

Agar, M 1980 *The Professional Stranger: An Informal Introduction to Ethnography*. New York: Academic Press

Agar, M 1986 *Speaking of Ethnography*. Beverly Hills: Sage

Allen, J and Widdowson, H 1975 *English in Focus* Series. Oxford University Press

Allwood, J 1978 *On the Analysis of Communicative Action*. Papers in Theoretical Linguistics 38. University of Gothenburg

Allwright, R 1976 Language learning through communication practice. In ELT Documents 76/3. British Council

Anderson, A and Lynch, T 1988 *Listening*. Oxford University Press

Atkinson, M and Heritage, J 1984 *Structures of Social Action: Studies in Conversation Analysis*. Cambridge University Press

Austin, J 1962 *How to Do Things With Words*. Clarendon Press

Bamhrah, C 1980 Mother-tongue interviews. Unpublished paper. Lancashire ILT Unit

Barr, V and Fletcher, C 1983 *A Study Guide for Topics and Skills in English*. Hodder and Stoughton

Barr, V and Fletcher, C 1984 *English for Driving*. National Extension College

Bartlett, F 1932 *Remembering*. Cambridge University Press

Bateson, G 1972 *Steps to an Ecology of Mind*. New York: Ballantine

Bauman, R and Sherzer, J (eds) 1974 *Explorations in the Ethnography of Speaking*. Cambridge University Press

Baynham, M 1986 Talking to Halliday: An Interview with Michael Halliday. Language Issues 1. National Extension College

BBC 1975, 1979 *Adult Literacy Handbooks* BBC

BBC 1979, 1991 *Crosstalk, Crosstalk at Work* BBC

BBC 1990 *Counselling and advice across cultures* BBC

BBC 1991 *Recruitment interviewing across cultures* BBC

Beebe, L and Giles, H 1984 Speech accommodation theories: a discussion in terms of second language acquisition. *International Journal of the Sociology of Language* 46: 5–32

Beebe, L and Zvengler, J 1983 Accommodation theory: an explanation for style shifting in second language dialects. In Wolfson and Judd 1983

Beech, B, Brierley, C and Moselle, M 1981 *Use Your English*. Hodder and Stoughton

Berger, P and Luckmann, T 1967 *The Social Construction of Reality*. Penguin

Bhardwaj, M 1982 A summary of the interaction of accent, rhythm, tone and intonation in Panjabi. Unpublished paper. Walsall ILT Unit

Bhardwaj, M 1988 Longitudinal studies in target language English. In Bhardwaj, Dietrich and Noyau 1988

Bhardwaj, M, Dietrich, R and Noyau, C (eds) 1988 *Second language acquisition by adult immigrants: Temporality*. Unpublished final report to the European Science Foundation

Bird, B 1981 *What's in a Name? Developing Listening Skills for Independent Learning*. NCILT

Birmingham ILT Unit [n.d] *A to Z Reading Book*. Birmingham ILT Unit

Birmingham ILT Unit [n.d.] *A to Z Writing Book*. Birmingham ILT Unit

Birmingham ILT Unit [n.d.] *Write it Down*. Birmingham ILT Unit

Birmingham ILT Unit [n.d] *In the News*. Birmingham ILT Unit

Blanc, M and Hamers, J 1989 *Bilinguality and Bilingualism*. Cambridge University Press

Bloch, M (ed.) 1975 *Political Language and Oratory in Traditional Society*. New York: Academic Press

Bonamy, D 1975 *Participant Observation in a Hospital Catering Department*. Pathway Industrial Unit

Bourdieu, P 1977 *Outline of a Theory of Practice*. Cambridge University Press

Bourne, J 1989 *Moving into the Mainstream*. Nelson/NFER

Brazil, D, Coulthard, M and Johns, K 1980 *Discourse Intonation and Language Teaching*. Longman

Breen, M 1984 Process in syllabus design and classroom language learning. In ELT Documents 118. British Council

Brierley, C and Bird, B 1985 *Switch on to English: A Handbook for Developing Reading and Writing*. Adult Literacy and Basic Skills Unit/BBC

Brigg, C 1987 *Learning How to Ask*. Cambridge University Press

Bright, W (ed.) 1966 *Sociolinguistics*. The Hague: Mouton

British Council 1978 *Individualisation in Language Learning*. ELT Documents 103. British Council

Brooks, T and Roberts, C 1985 No five fingers are all alike. In Brumfit, Ellis and Levine 1985

Brown, C 1984 *Black and White Britain: The Third PSI Survey.* Heinemann

Brown, G and Yule, G 1983a *Discourse Analysis.* Cambridge University Press

Brown, G and Yule, G 1983b *Teaching the Spoken Language.* Cambridge University Press

Brown, P and Levinson, S 1978 Universals in language usage: Politeness phenomena. In Goody 1978

Brown, P and Levinson, S 1987 *Politeness: Some Universals in Language Usage.* Cambridge University Press

Brumfit, C 1976 Teaching pupils how to acquire language. In ELT Documents 76/3. British Council

Brumfit, C (ed.) 1988 *Language in Teacher Education.* National Council for Language in Education: Centre for Information on Language Teaching

Brumfit, C, Ellis, R and Levine, J (eds) 1985 *English as a Second Language in the United Kingdom.* ELT Documents 121. Pergamon Press

Bulloch, C and Cheetham, B 1987 *Communication for Health.* NCILT

Burgess, R (ed) 1984 *Field Research: A Sourcebook and Field Manual.* Allen and Unwin

Bygate, M 1987 *Speaking.* Oxford University Press

Byram, M 1988 *Cultural Studies in Foreign Language Education.* Multilingual Matters

Cameron, D and Bourne, J 1989 Grammar, nation and citizenship: Kingman in linguistic and historical perspective. Occasional Paper. Institute of Education, University of London

Canale, M 1983 From communicative competence to communicative language pedagogy. In Richards and Schmidt 1983

Canale, M and Swain, M 1980 Theoretical bases of communicative language teaching and testing. *Applied Linguistics* 1 (1): 1–47

Candlin, C 1976 Communicative language teaching and the debt to pragmatics. In Ramesh 1976

Candlin, C 1981a Discourse patterning and the equalising of interpretive opportunity. In L Smith 1981

Candlin, C (ed. and trans.) 1981b *The Communicative Teaching of English.* Longman

Candlin, C 1983 Syllabus Design as a critical process. In Brumfit 1983

Candlin, C 1987 Towards task-based language learning. In Candlin and Murphy 1987

Candlin, C, Leather, J and Bruton, C 1974 *English language skills for overseas doctors and medical staff: work in progress*. Reports 1–4. University of Lancaster

Candlin, C, Leather, J and Bruton, C 1976 Doctors in casualty: applying communicative competence to components of specialist course design. *International Review of Applied Linguistics* 14 (3): 245–72

Candlin, C and Murphy, D (eds) 1987 *Lancaster Practical Papers in English Language Teaching* Vol. 7. University of Lancaster

Carroll, J (ed.) 1957 *Language, Thought and Reality: Selected Writings of Benjamin Lee Whorf.* Cambridge, Mass.: MIT Press

Centre for Contemporary Cultural Studies 1982 *The Empire Strikes Back: Race and Racism in 70s Britain.* Hutchinson

Chafe, W (ed.) 1980 *The Pear Stories: Cognitive and Linguistic Aspects of Narrative Production.* Advances in Discourse Processes Vol. 3. Norwood, NJ: Ablex

Chandola, R and Murray, A 1981 *Language Awareness Video.* Walsall ILT

Cheetham, B 1989 *Interview Skills: A Complete Resource for Tutors, Trainers and Others Working with Candidates.* National Extension College

Cicourel, A 1968 *The Social Organization of Juvenile Justice.* New York: Wiley

Cicourel, A 1974 *Cognitive Sociology.* Penguin

Cicourel, A 1981 Language and medicine. In C Ferguson and S Heath (eds) *Language in the USA.* Cambridge University Press

Cicourel, A 1983 Language and the structure of belief in medical communication. In Fisher and Dundas Todd 1983

Clarke, M and Handscombe, J (eds) 1983 *On TESOL 82: Pacific Perspectives on Language Learning and Teaching.* Washington, DC: TESOL

Cogill, S 1980 *Writing Business Letters and Memos.* NCILT

Cole, P and Morgan, J (eds) 1975 *Syntax and Semantics 3: Speech Acts.* New York: Academic Press

Commission for Racial Equality 1983 *Implementing Equal Opportunities Policies.* CRE

Commission for Racial Equality 1984 *Polymer Engineering Division of Dunlop Ltd. Leicester: Report of a Formal Investigation.* CRE

Commission for Racial Equality 1987 CRE Investigation, Calderdale LEA.

Cook-Gumperz, J (ed.) 1986 *The Social Construction of Literacy.* Cambridge University Press

Coulthard, M and Montgomery, M 1981 *Studies in Discourse Analysis.* Routledge and Kegan Paul

Council of Europe 1979 *A European Unit/Credit System for Modern Language Learning by Adults.* Strasbourg: Council of Europe

Curran, C 1972 *Counselling Learning – A Whole-Person Approach for Education.* Illinois: Apple River Press

Darling, B 1982 *All We Doing Is Defending.* NCILT

Davies, E and Hadi, S 1973 *Ready for Work.* Scope Senior Course. Longman

Davies, E and Jupp, T 1974 *The Background and Employment of Asian Immigrants.* Runnymede Trust

Denzin, N 1970 *The Research Act.* Chicago: Aldine

Department of Education and Science 1986 *Education for All.* Report of the Select Committee, chaired by Lord Swann

Department of Employment 1974 *The Role of Immigrants in the Labour Market.* Department of Employment

Dickinson, L 1987 *Self-Instruction in Language Learning.* Cambridge University Press

Dodderidge, S 1981 Staff discussion at a bus company. Unpublished paper presented at seminar on Analysing Authentic Conversation, NCILT

Dodderidge, S (ed.) Using video role-plays. NCILT Working Paper 38. NCILT

Doeringer, P and Piore, M 1971 *Internal Labour Markets and Manpower Analysis.* Lexington: Heath

Drew, P and Wootton, A (eds) 1988 *Erving Goffman: Exploring the Interaction Order.* Polity Press

Ellen, R (ed) 1984 *Ethnographic Research.* Academic Press

Ensink, T, van Essen, A and van der Geest, T 1986 *Discourse Analysis and Public Life.* Foris Publications

Equality at Work 1989 *Listening for Information: Study Materials.* Equality at Work, Blackburn College, Lancashire

Erickson, F 1986 Qualitative research on teaching. In Wittrock 1986

Erickson, F and Mohatt, G 1982 Cultural organization of participation structures in two classrooms of Indian students. In Spindler 1982

Erickson, F and Shultz, J 1982 *The Counselor as Gatekeeper.* New York: Academic Press

Ervin-Tripp, S 1972 On sociolinguistic rules: alternation and co-occurrence. In Gumperz and Hymes 1972

Etherton, P 1975 The language of supervisors and operatives in a spinning mill. Unpublished MA dissertation. University of Lancaster

Fairclough, N 1985 Critical and descriptive goals in discourse analysis. *Journal of Pragmatics* 9: 739–63

Fairclough, N 1989 *Language and Power*. Longman

Fairclough, N and Ivanič, R 1988 Language education or language training? A critique of the Kingman model of the English language. Paper presented at BAAL Conference, Exeter, September 1988

Fisher, S and Dundas Todd, A (eds) 1983 *The Social Organization of Doctor–Patient Communication*. Washington, DC: Center for Applied Linguistics

Fishman, J (ed.) 1968 *Readings in the Sociology of Language*. The Hague: Mouton

Ford, W *et al.* 1976 *A study of human resources and industrial relations at the plant level in seven selected industries: A study commissioned by the Committee to Advise on Policies for the Manufacturing Industry*. Canberra, Australia: Australian Government Publishing Service

Foucault, M 1970 The order of discourse. In Shapiro 1984

Fowler, R, Hodge, K, Kress, G and Trew, T 1979 *Language and Control*. Routledge and Kegan Paul

Frake, C 1964 How to ask for a drink in Subanun. *American Anthropologist* 66(6/2): 127–32

Frake, C 1972 Struck by speech: the Yakan concept of litigation. In Gumperz and Hymes 1972

Freedle, R (ed.) 1977 *Discourse Production and Comprehension. Advances in Discourse Processes* Vol. 1. Norwood, NJ: Ablex

Freire, P 1972 *Pedagogy of the Oppressed*. Penguin

Freire, P 1974 *Education: The Practice of Freedom*. Writers and Readers

Freire, P 1975 *Cultural Action for Freedom*. Penguin

Furnborough, P, Cogill, S, Greaves, H and Sapin, K 1980 *A New Start*. Heinemann.

Furnborough, P, Jupp, T, Munns, R and Roberts, C 1982 Language, disadvantage and discrimination: breaking the cycle of majority-group perception. *Journal of Multilingual and Multicultural Development* 3 (3): 247–66

Further Education Unit 1989 *Staff Development for a Multi-Cultural Society (RP390) Book 4: Teaching and Learning Strategies*. Further Education Unit

Gardner, R and Lambert, W 1972 *Attitudes and Motivation in Second Language Learning*. Rowley, Mass.: Newbury House

Garfinkel, H 1967 *Studies in Ethnomethodology*. Englewood Cliffs, NJ: Prentice-Hall

Giles, H (ed.) 1977 *Language, Ethnicity and Intergroup Relations.* New York: Academic Press

Giles, H 1979 Ethnicity markers in speech. In Scherer and Giles 1979

Giles, H and Powesland, P 1975 *Speech Style and Social Evaluation.* New York: Academic Press

Giles, H and St Clair, R (eds) 1979 *Language and Social Psychology.* Basil Blackwell

Giles, H and St Clair, R (eds) 1985 *Recent Advances in Language. Communication and Social Psychology.* Lawrence Erlbaum

Gladwin, T and Sturtevant, W (eds) 1962 *Anthropology and Human Behavior.* Washington, DC: Anthropological Society of Washington

Glazer, N and Young, K 1983 *Ethnic Pluralism and Public Policy.* Heinemann

Goffman, E 1955 On face-work: an analysis of ritual elements in social interaction. *Psychiatry: Journal of Interpersonal Relations* 18: 213–31

Goffman, E 1959 *The Presentation of Self in Everyday Life.* Penguin

Goffman, E 1967 *Interaction Ritual: Essays on Face-to-Face Behavior* New York: Doubleday Anchor

Goffman, E 1974 *Frame Analysis.* Harper and Row

Goffman, E 1981 *Forms of Talk.* Basil Blackwell

Goffman, E 1983 The interaction order. *American Sociological Review* 48: 1–17

Goodenough, W 1964 *Explorations in Cultural Anthropology.* New York: McGraw-Hill

Goodenough, W 1981 *Culture, Language and Society.* 2nd edn. Menlo Park: Benjamins

Goody, E (ed.) 1978 *Questions and Politeness: Strategies in Social Interaction.* Cambridge University Press

Gray, J 1982 *Caring Communications.* Department of Health and Social Security

Grice, H 1975 Logic and Conversation. In Cole and Morgan 1975

Grice, H 1981 Presupposition and conversational implicature. In P Cole (ed.) 1981 *Radical Pragmatics.* New York: Academic Press

Gubbay, D 1978 *The Teaching of Communication Skills through the Use of Role-Play to Speakers of English as a Second Language.* NCILT

Gubbay, D 1980 *Speak for Yourself.* BBC

Gumperz, J (ed.) 1971 *Language and Social Groups.* Stanford: Stanford University Press

Gumperz, J 1977 Sociocultural Knowledge in conversational inference. In Saville-Troike 1977

Gumperz, J 1978 The conversational analysis of inter-ethnic communication. In Ross Lamar 1978

Gumperz, J 1982a *Discourse Strategies*. Cambridge University Press

Gumperz, J (ed.) 1982b *Language and Social Identity*. Cambridge University Press

Gumperz, J 1984 *Communicative Competence Revisited*. Berkeley Cognitive Science Report Series. Berkeley, Calif.: University of California

Gumperz, J 1986 Interactional sociolinguistics in the study of schooling. In Cook-Gumperz 1986

Gumperz, J, Aulakh, G and Kaltman, H 1982 Thematic structure and Progression in discourse. In Gumperz 1982b

Gumperz, J and Cook-Gumperz, J 1982 Introduction: Language and the communication of social identity. In Gumperz 1982b

Gumperz, J and Hymes, D (eds) 1972 (new edition 1986) *Directions in Sociolinguistics*. Basil Blackwell

Gumperz, J, Jupp, T and Roberts, C 1979 *Crosstalk*. National Centre for Industrial Language Training

Gumperz, J and Roberts, C 1980 *Developing Awareness Skills for Inter-Ethnic Communication*. Singapore: Seamo Regional Language Centre. Occasional Papers No. 12

Gumperz, J and Roberts, C 1991 Understanding in intercultural encounters. In *Proceedings of the 1987 Meeting of the International Pragmatics Association*, ed. J Verschueren and J Blommaert

Gumperz, J and Tannen, D 1979 Individual and social differences in language use. In Wang and Fillmore 1979

Gurnah, A 1983 *The Politics of Racism Awareness Training*. Sheffield City Polytechnic

Haberland, H and May, J 1977 Editorial: Linguistics and pragmatics. *Journal of Pragmatics* 1: 1–12

Habermas, J 1976 What is universal pragmatics? In Habermas 1979

Habermas, J 1979 *Communication and the Evolution of Society*. T McCarthy (trans). Heinemann Educational

Halliday, M 1967 *Intonation and Grammar in British English*. The Hague: Mouton

Halliday, M 1973 *Explorations in the Function of Language*. Edward Arnold

Halliday, M 1975 *Learning How to Mean: Explorations in the Development of Language*. Edward Arnold

Halliday, M 1976 System and function in language. In Kress 1976

Halliday, M 1978 *Language as Social Semiotic*. Edward Arnold

Halliday, M 1985 *An Introduction to Functional Grammar*. Edward Arnold

Halliday, M and Hasan, R 1976 *Cohesion in English*. Longman

Hammersley, M and Atkinson, P 1983 *Ethnography: Principles in Practice*. Tavistock Institute of Human Relations

Harding, K, Naish, J and Wilkins, M 1980 *At Home in Britain*. National Extension College

Harris, R and Savitzky, F 1988 *My Personal Language History*. New Beacon Books

Hawkins, E 1985 *Awareness of Language*. Cambridge University Press

Head, C 1974 *Free Way to Learning: Educational Alternatives in Action*. Penguin

Heath, C 1986 *Body Movement and Speech in Medical Interaction*. Cambridge University Press

Heath, S 1983 *Ways with Words*. Cambridge University Press

Hedge, A (ed.) 1980 Increasing student autonomy in industrial language training. NCILT Working Paper 14. NCILT

Hedge, A (ed.) 1984 Work with the unemployed. NCILT Working Paper 32. NCILT

Heire, G and Furnborough, P 1985 *Independent Learning in Basic Education and Training: Implementing Learner Autonomy*. Lancashire ILT Unit

Heire, G And Wilson, P 1984 *Adult Literacy and Basic Skills Unit Independent Learning Project*. Lancashire ILT Unit

Henley, A 1979 *Asian Patients in Hospital and at Home*. King's Fund and Pitman Medical

Henley, A 1983a *Asians in Britain*. National Extension College

Henley, A 1983b *Caring for Hindus and their Families: Religious Aspects of Care*. Health Education Council, DHSS, King Edward's Hospital Fund for London: National Extension College

Henley, A 1983c *Caring for Sikhs and their Families: Religious Aspects of Care*. Health Education Council, DHSS, King Edward's Hospital Fund for London: National Extension College

Hoadley-Maidment, E 1980 Training manual for teaching staff No. 5: Guidance for new staff on the first ILT project. NCILT

Hoadley-Maidment, E 1981 Introducing autonomous learning. NCILT Working Paper 23. NCILT

Hoadley-Maidment, E and Slade, A 1979 Methodology Surveys 1–3. NCILT

Hodlin, S 1970 Preliminary Survey in a Food Factory: Introductory Discussion, Personnel Records and Participant Observation. Pathway Industrial Unit

Holec, H 1981 *Autonomy and Foreign Language Learning*. Pergamon for the Council of Europe

Hooper, D 1980 Communications Skills Training for Bilinguals. Inner London Education Authority (South) ILT Unit

Hooper, D and Yates, V 1981 Communications Skills Training for Bilinguals: *A Case Study.* NCILT

Hymes, D 1962 The ethnography of speaking. In Gladwin and Sturtevant 1962

Hymes, D 1966 Two types of linguistic relativity. In Bright 1966

Hymes, D 1968 The ethnography of speaking. In Fishman 1968

Hymes, D 1974 *Foundations in Sociolinguistics: An Ethnographic Approach.* University of Pennsylvania Press

Inner London Education Authority 1983 *Linked Skills: A Handbook for Skills and ESL Tutors.* National Extension College

Jenkins, R 1986 *Racism and Recruitment.* Cambridge University Press

Jenkins, R and Solomos, J 1986 *Racism and Equal Opportunity Policies in the 1980s.* Cambridge University Press

Johnson, K 1982 *Communicative Syllabus Design and Methodology.* Pergamon Press

Jourard, S 1972 *Transparent Self.* Van Nostrand Reinhold

Jupp, T 1981 *Language, Disadvantage and Ethnic Minorities.* Evidence given to the House of Commons Home Affairs Committee, Race Relations and Immigration Sub-Committee Session 1980-81, 22 January 1981. HMSO

Jupp, T 1982 *The Teaching of the National Language of the Host Country to Adult Immigrants: Consolidated Report and Recommendations.* Strasbourg: Council of Europe: CDCC [Council for Cultural Cooperation] Project No. (81) 38

Jupp, T and Hodlin, S 1974 *Industrial English.* Heinemann Educational

Jupp, T, Roberts, C and Cook-Gumperz, J 1982 Language and disadvantage: the hidden process. In Gumperz 1982b

Katz, J 1978 *White Awareness: Handbook of Anti-Racism Training.* University of Oklahoma Press

Keenan, E 1975 A sliding sense of obligatoriness: the polistructure of Malagasy oratory. In Bloch 1975

Khan, S and Pearn, M 1976 *Worktalk: A Trainer's Manual.* Runnymede Trust/BBC

Knapp, K, Enninger, W and Knapp-Potthoff, A (eds) 1987 *Analyzing Intercultural Communication.* Berlin: Mouton de Gruyter

Knowles, L 1980 Student autonomy and literacy. NCILT Working Paper 19. NCILT

Kress, G (ed.) 1976 *Halliday: System and Function in Language.* Oxford University Press

Kress, G and Hodge, R 1979 *Language as Ideology.* Routledge and Kegan Paul

Labov, W 1969 Contraction deletion and inherent variability of the English copula. *Language* 45 (4): 715-62

Laird, E 1975 *English for Domestic Staff.* King's Fund Centre

Laird, E 1977 *Training manual for teaching staff No. 1: An introduction to functional language training in the workplace.* NCILT

Lakoff, R 1973 The logic of politeness: or minding your p's and q's. In *Papers from the Ninth Regional Meeting of the Chicago Linguistic Society*: 292–305. Chicago

Lakoff, R 1974 *What you can do with words: politeness, pragmatics* and *performatives. Berkeley Studies in Syntax and Semantics* 1: 1–55

Lambert, W 1972 *Language, Psychology and Culture.* Stanford: Stanford University Press

Lancashire ILT Unit 1982 *Communication for Employment and Training.* Lancashire ILT Unit

Lancashire ILT Unit 1983 *In Search of Employment and Training.* Commmission for Racial Equality

Lancashire ILT Unit 1985 *Training for Change.* Lancashire ILT Unit

Lancashire ILT Unit 1989 *Listening for Information Study Materials.* Equality at Work, Lancashire

Laubach, F 1961 *Thirty Years with the Silent Billion: Adventuring in Literacy.* Lutterworth

Leach, R Knight, E and Johnson, J 1988 *Help Yourself to English.* National Extension College

Leech, G 1983 *Principles of Pragmatics.* New York: Longman

Levinson, S 1983 *Pragmatics.* Cambridge University Press

Long, M 1976 Encouraging language acquisition by adults in a formal instructional setting. In ELT documents 76/3. British Council

Loveday, L 1982 *The Sociolinguistics of Learning and Using a Non–Native Language.* Pergamon Press

McAllister, J and Robson, M 1984 *Building a Framework: Developing Communication Skills with ESL Students.* National Extension College

McDermott, R 1976 Kids make sense: an ethnographic account of the interactional management of success and failure in one first-grade classroom. Unpublished dissertation. Stanford University

McIntosh, N and Smith, D 1974 *The Extent of Racial Discrimination.* Political and Economic Planning Report 547

Mayers, P, Henley, A and Baxter, C 1985 *Health Care in Multi-Racial Britain.* Health Education Council and National Extension College

Mehan, H 1979 *Learning Lessons: Social Organization in the Classroom.* Harvard University Press

Mukherjee, M 1984 *Breaking the Silence.* London Centreprise Publishing Project

Munby, J 1978 *Communicative Syllabus Design: A Sociolinguistic Model for Defining the Content of Purpose-Specific Language Programmes.* Cambridge University Press

Naiman, N, Frohlich, M, Stern, H and Todesco, A 1978 *The Good Language Learner.* Toronto: Modern Language Centre, Ontario Institute for Studies in Education

NCILT (National Centre for Industrial Language Training) 1976 Post-elementary language and communication skills in the workplace. Working Paper 1. NCILT

NCILT 1977 Annual Report. *1976.* NCILT

NCILT 1978a *Language and Communication skills in the Workplace for Post-Elementary Learners: Content, Analysis and Methodology for the Teaching of Discourse Skills.* NCILT

NCILT 1978b *Language and Communication skills in the Workplace for Post-Elementary Learners: Selection, Presentation and Use of Information.* NCILT

NCILT 1983 *Report of an assessment carried out by the ILT service for the Commission for Racial Equality in Dunlop Polymer Engineering Company.* NCILT

NFER (in press) *Go to Work on Your English* NEC

Nunan, D 1988 *The Learner-Centred Curriculum.* Cambridge University Press

Peppard, N 1983 Race relations training: the state of the art. *New Community* 11 (1/2): 150-9

Perdue, C (ed.) 1984 *Second Language Acquistion by Adults: A Field Manual.* Rowley, Mass.: Newbury House

Phillips, S 1983 *The Invisible Culture.* New York: Longman

Pidgeon, H 1984 Changing the cycle of communication. Unpublished paper presented to the Industrial Language Training Advisory Committee, 31 January 1984

Postman, N and Weingartner, C 1971 *Teaching as a Subversive Activity.* Penguin

Prabhu, N 1987 *Second Language Pedagogy: A Perspective.* Oxford University Press

Ramesh, C (ed.) 1976 *27th Round Table Monograph Series on Language and Linguistics.* Washington, DC: Georgetown University Press

Rex, J and Tomlinson, S 1979 *Colonial Immigrants in a British Society: A Class Analysis.* Routledge and Kegan Paul

Richards, J 1985 *The Context of Language Teaching.* Cambridge University Press

Richards, J and Schmidt, R (eds) 1983 *Language and Communication.* Longman

Richterich, R 1979 *Identifying Language Needs as a Means of Determining Educational Objectives with the Learners in a European Unit/Credit System for Modern Language Learning by Adults.* Strasbourg: Council of Europe

Richterich, R and Cancerel, J 1978 *Identifying the Needs of Adults Learning a Foreign Language.* Strasbourg: Council of Europe

Rivera, C 1983 *An Ethnographic/Sociolinguistic Approach to Language Proficiency Assessment.* Multilingual Matters

Roberts, C (ed.) 1983 Analysing authentic video. NCILT Working Paper 39. NCILT

Roberts, C 1985 *The Interview Game.* BBC

Roberts, C and Opienski, J 1985 *ESL: The Vocational Skill.* NCILT

Roberts, C and Sayers, P 1987 'Keeping the gate': how judgements are made in inter-ethnic communication. In Knapp *et al.* 1987

Ross Lamar, E (ed.) 1978 *Interethnic Communication.* Athens, Ga.: University of Georgia Press

Rubin, J 1975 What the 'good language learner' can teach us. *TESOL Quarterly* 9 (1): 41–51

Sacks, H 1971 Unpublished lecture notes. University of California

Sacks, H, Schegloff, E and Jefferson, G 1974 A simplest systematics for the organization of turn-taking for conversation. *Language* 50: 696-735

Saifullah Khan, V 1979 *Minority Families in Britain.* Macmillan

Saville-Troike, M (ed.) 1977 *28th Round Table Monograph Series on Language and Linguistics.* Washington, DC: Georgetown University Press

Saville-Troike, M 1982 *The Ethnography of Communication.* Basil Blackwell

Sayers, P 1983 Topic collaboration and interview skills. Unpublished MA dissertation. University of Lancaster

Sayers, P, George, T, Greenwood, S and Petersen, R 1979 *Signing Off.* NCILT

Sayers, P and Roberts, C 1981 The house in Bangladesh. Unpublished paper presented at seminar on Analysing Authentic Video, NCILT

Schank, R and Ableson, R 1977 *Scripts, Plans, Goals and Understanding*. Hillsdale, NJ: Lawrence Erlbaum

Schegloff, E, Jefferson, G and Sacks, H 1977 The preference for self-correction in the organization of repair in conversation. *Language* 53 (2): 361–83

Scherer, K and Giles, H (eds) 1979 *Social Markers in Speech*. Cambridge University Press

Schumann, J 1978 *The Pidginization Process: A Model for Second Language Acquisition*. Rowley, Mass.: Newbury House

Scollon, R and Scollon, S 1980 *Inter-Ethnic Communication*. Alaska: Alaska Native Language Center

Scollon, R and Scollon, S 1981 *Narrative, Literacy and Face in Inter-Ethnic Communication*. Norwood, NJ: Ablex

Scollon, R and Scollon, S 1983 Face in inter-ethnic communication. In Richards and Schmidt 1983

Searle, J 1969 *Speech Acts*. Cambridge University Press

Searle, J 1975 Indirect speech acts. In Cole and Morgan 1975

Shapiro, M (ed.) 1984 *Language and Politics*. Basil Blackwell

Sharma, V 1971 *Rampal and His Family*. Collins

Simonot, M and Allwood, J 1984 Understanding, misunderstanding and breakdown. In Perdue 1984

Simonot, M and Dodderidge, S 1981 A framework for linguistic analysis. In Perdue 1984

Sinclair, J and Coulthard, M 1975 *Towards an Analysis of Discourse*. Oxford University Press

Singh, R 1976 Language Teaching Needs of the Asian Employees of a Cotton Textile firm in Lancashire. Nelson and Colne College

Sivanandan, A 1985 RAT and the degradation of the black struggle. *Race and Class* 26(4): 1–33

Skinner, B 1957 *Verbal Behavior*. New York: Appleton-Century-Crofts

Smith, D 1977 *Racial Disadvantage in Britain: The PEP Report*. Penguin

Smith, D 1981 *Unemployment and Racial Minorities*. Policy Studies Institute No. 594

Smith, F 1982 *Writing and the Writer*. Heinemann Educational

Smith, L (ed.) 1981 *English for Cross-Cultural Communication* Macmillan

Smith, L (ed.) 1983 *Readings in English as an International Language*. Pergamon Press

Spindler, G (ed.) 1982 *Doing the Ethnography of Schooling*. New York: Holt, Rinehart and Winston

Spradley, J 1979 *The Ethnographic Interview*. New York: Holt, Rinehart and Winston

Stubbs, M 1981 Analysts and users: different models of language. Paper read to Applied Linguistics Colloquium, Berne, June 1981

Stubbs, M 1983 *Discourse Analysis*. Basil Blackwell

Swan, M 1985 A critical look at the communicative approach. *English Language Teaching Journal* 39(1): 2–12; 39(2): 76–87

Tannen, D 1981 New York Jewish conversational style. *International Journal of the Sociology of Language* 30: 133–49

Tannen, D 1982 *Spoken and Written Language: Exploring Orality and Literacy*. Advances in Discourse Processes Vol. 9. Norwood, NJ: Ablex

Tannen, D 1984a *Conversational Style: Analyzing Talk Among Friends*. Norwood, NJ: Ablex

Tannen, D (ed.) 1984b *Coherence in Spoken and Written Discourse*. Advances in Discourse Processes Vol. 12. Norwood, NJ: Ablex

Tannen, D and Wallett, C 1983 Doctor/mother/child communication: linguistic analysis of a pediatric interaction. In Fisher and Dundas Todd 1983

Tavistock Institute of Human Relations 1978 *Applications of the Race Relations Policy in the Civil Service*. HMSO

Taylor, D, Meynard, R and Rheault, E 1977 Threat to ethnic identity and second language learning. In Giles 1977

Taylor, T and Cameron, D 1987 *Analysing Conversation*. Pergamon Press

Thomas, J 1983 Cross-cultural pragmatic failure. *Applied Linguistics* 4(2): 91–112

Thorp, D 1983 Letting him down lightly. NCILT Working Paper 37. NCILT

Training Agency (Department of Employment) 1989 *English for Speakers of Other Languages: Materials Guide*. Careers and Occupational Information Centre, Sheffield

Trim, J 1978 *Some Possible Lines of Development of an Overall Structure for a European Unit/Credit Scheme for Foreign Language Learning by Adults*. Strasbourg: Council of Europe

Trim, J 1979 Paper presented at the Hasselby Colloquy, Sweden: quoted in Jupp 1982

Trim, J 1980 *Developing a Unit/Credit System of Adult Language Learning*. Pergamon Press

Ur, P 1986 *Teaching Listening Comprehension*. Cambridge University Press

van Dijk, T 1977 *Text and Context*. Longman

van Dijk, T (ed.) 1985 *Handbook of Discourse Analysis* Vols 1–4. Academic Press van Ek, J 1975 *The Threshold Level: Systems Development in Adult Language Learning in a European Unit/Credit System for Modern Language Learning by Adults.* Strasbourg: Council for Cultural Cooperation, Council of Europe

van Lier, L 1988 *The Classroom and the Language Learner.* Longman

Vohra, M and Vasudeva, P [n.d] *Impressive Interviews.* New Delhi: New Light Publications

Wainwright, D 1980 *Learning from Uncle Sam.* Runnymede Trust

Wallman, S (ed.) 1979 *Ethnicity at Work.* Macmillan

Walsall ILT Unit 1980a Interview data. Unpublished paper. Walsall ILT Unit

Walsall ILT Unit 1980b Unpublished report. Walsall

Wang, W and Fillmore, C (eds) 1979 *Individual Differences in Language Ability and Language Behavior.* New York: Academic Press

Wenden, A and Rubin, J (eds) 1986 *Learner Strategies.* Oxford: Pergamon Press

Westwood, S and Bhachu, P (eds) 1988 *Enterprising Women.* Routledge

Whyte, W 1981 *Street Corner Society.* Chicago: University of Chicago Press

Whyte, W 1984 Learning from the Field. Sage

Widdowson, H 1978 *Teaching Language as Communication.* Oxford University Press

Widdowson, H 1983 *Learning Purpose and Language Use.* Oxford University Press

Widdowson, H 1984 *Explorations in Applied Linguistics 2.* Oxford University Press

Wilkins, D 1976 *Notional Syllabuses.* Oxford University Press

Willis, P 1977 *Learning to Labour: How Working-Class Kids Get Working-Class Jobs.* Saxon House

Wilson, A 1978 *Finding a Voice.* London: Virago

Wilson, A and Naish, J 1980 *Asian Women Speak Out.* National Extension college

Wilson, P 1981a Changing communicative relationships. NCILT Working paper 27

Wilson, P 1981b *Evaluation of Shop Steward Training.* Pathway Industrial Unit

Winograd, T 1972 *Understanding Natural Language.* New York: Academic Press

Wittrock, M (ed.) 1986 *Handbook of Research on Teaching.* New York: Macmillan

Wolfson, N and Judd, E (eds) 1983 *Sociolinguistics and Language Acquisition.* Rowley, Mass.: Newbury House

Wong Fillmore, L 1982 The language learner as an individual: implications of research on individual differences for the ESL teacher. In Clarke and Handscombe 1983

Yalden, J 1983 *The Communicative Syllabus: Evolution, Design and Implementation.* Pergamon Press

Yates, V, Christmas, E and Wilson, P 1982 *Cross-Cultural Training: Developing Skills and Awareness in Communication. A Manual.* NCILT

Young, K and Connelly, N 1981 *Policy and Practice in the Multi-Racial City.* Policy Studies Institute

Index

Numerical Index of Training Material

Numerical index of data